Frequently Asked Questions
in
Anti-Bribery and Corruption

Frequently Asked Questions
in
Anti-Bribery and Corruption

David Lawler

A John Wiley & Sons, Ltd., Publication

This edition first published in 2012
Copyright ©2012 David Lawler

Registered office
John Wiley & Sons Ltd, The Atrium, Southern Gate, Chichester, West Sussex, PO19 8SQ, United
Kingdom

For details of our global editorial offices, for customer services and for information about how
to apply for permission to reuse the copyright material in this book please see our website at
www.wiley.com

Wiley publishes in a variety of print and electronic formats and by print-on-demand. Some
material included with standard print versions of this book may not be included in e-books or
in print-on-demand. If this book refers to media such as a CD or DVD that is not included in
the version you purchased, you may download this material at http://booksupport.wiley.com. For
more information about Wiley products, visit www.wiley.com.

Designations used by companies to distinguish their products are often claimed as trademarks.
All brand names and product names used in this book are trade names, service marks, trademarks or registered trademarks of their respective owners. The publisher is not associated with
any product or vendor mentioned in this book. This publication is designed to provide accurate
and authoritative information in regard to the subject matter covered. It is sold on the understanding that the publisher is not engaged in rendering professional services. If professional
advice or other expert assistance is required, the services of a competent professional should
be sought.

Library of Congress Cataloging-in-Publication Data is available

ISBN: 978-1-119-97197-9 (pbk)
ISBN: 978-1-119-96057-7 (ebk)
ISBN: 978-1-118-40105-7 (custom pbk)
ISBN: 978-1-118-35981-5 (ebk)
ISBN: 978-1-119-96058-4 (ebk)

A catalogue record for this book is available from the British Library.

Typeset in 9/10.5pt Cheltenham-Book by Laserwords Private Limited, Chennai, India
Printed in Great Britain by TJ International, Padstow, Cornwall

To Cathy and Harry
for putting up with this, and me.

Contents

Contents

Frequently Asked Questions

About the Author

David Lawler specializes in resolving complex and high risk financial and investigative problems. His clients range from individuals to multinational groups, many of whom are under investigation by regulators or prosecutors or are involved in disputes.

An expert in using database and visualization techniques to find needles in massive data haystacks, he has conducted bribery reviews in Asia, Africa, the Middle East, the Former Soviet Union and Europe. He has helped numerous companies design and test their anti-bribery compliance systems and negotiate the penalties when things have gone wrong. An experienced accountant, he has also been called on to provide expert evidence to courts and arbitration tribunals on questions of corporate governance, solvency, and profitability.

Dr Lawler gained his first degree at Durham University, and his PhD from the University of London. He is a Fellow of the Institute of Chartered Accountants in England and Wales, a Certified Fraud Examiner, a Member of the Academy of Experts and an accredited commercial mediator. He is currently based in London.

Acknowledgements

I am grateful to many people for help, both direct and indirect, during the evolution of this book.

I could not possibly name everyone who has contributed to my understanding of the subject, but I would particularly like to thank all my friends and colleagues at FRA. Their work helped extend my involvement in this fascinating field, and motivated me to write this book. Their own research, comments and questions have enlightened, supported and encouraged me. Particular thanks are also due to several corporate clients who, for obvious reasons, do not want their involvement with a bribery specialist to be made public.

In addition I would like to thank all those regularly writing about bribery and corruption who have shared their ideas over the years. I would be remiss if I did not mention at least Carolyn Lindsey and the rest of the team at Trace International who put together the Trace Compendium of cases (https://secure.traceinternational.org/Knowledge/ Compendium.html); Mary Jacoby (http://www.mainjustice .com/justanticorruption); Richard Cassin (http://www.fcpablog .com); Mike Koehler (http://www.fcpaprofessor.com); Barry Vitou (www.thebriberyact.com); Howard Sklar (http://openairblog.wordpress.com) and Tom Fox (http://tfoxlaw.wordpress.com).

The book would never have come together without the team of editors at John Wiley, in particular Jenny McCall who first approached me to write this, and Gemma Valler and Grace O'Byrne who saw the project through to completion. I'm grateful to Viv Croot for her comments on the draft manuscript, and to Rhory Robertson for his support and perceptive advice.

For indulging my long nights and weekends at the computer, when they thought I was playing rather than working, I'd like to thank Cathy and Harry.

Without doubt there will be errors, omissions and over-simplifications, for which I take absolute responsibility, while hoping that the rest of the material will be enough to stimulate some insights and above all, some action.

Bribery Acronyms and Terms, and a Quick Index

- **FCPA:** The US Foreign Corrupt Practices Act 1977. (See 'An essential summary of the FCPA', page 73.)
- **The Bribery Act:** The UK's Bribery Act 2010, which finally came into effect on 1 July 2011. (See 'An essential summary of the Bribery Act', page 81.)
- **The Bribery Act Guidance:** The Ministry of Justice publication *Guidance about Procedures which Relevant Commercial Organizations Can Put into Place to Prevent Persons Associated with Them from Bribing (Section 9 of the Bribery Act 2010)*, which was published to coincide with the Bribery Act coming into effect. (See 'An essential summary of the Bribery Act', page 81, and Question 8.)
- **The OECD Convention:** The Organization for Economic Cooperation and Development's Convention on Combating Bribery of Foreign Public Officials in International Business Transactions Convention, which came into effect in February 1999. (See 'An essential summary of the OECD Convention', page 93.)
- **The Sentencing Guidelines:** The US Federal Sentencing Guidelines set out a uniform sentencing policy for individuals and organizations convicted of felonies and serious misdemeanours (including bribery) in the US. (See Questions 20 and 22.)
- **DOJ:** The US Department of Justice, responsible for enforcing the anti-bribery provisions of the FCPA.

- **SEC:** The US Securities and Exchange Commission, responsible for overseeing the capital markets and enforcing the accounting provisions of the FCPA against companies listed on the US stock markets.
- **SFO:** The Serious Fraud Office, the lead agency in England, Wales and Northern Ireland for investigating and prosecuting cases of domestic and overseas corruption.
- **FSA:** The UK's Financial Services Authority, the independent body that regulates the financial services industry in the UK. (For more on all of these see Question 6.)
- **TI:** Transparency International, a global organization leading the fight against corruption. TI members in more than 90 countries include government, business and the media. They promote transparency in elections, public administration, procurement and business. The annual TI Corruption Perceptions Index (CPI) ranks countries in terms of perceived levels of corruption. (See 'Where is bribery most prevalent?', page 25.)
- **TRACE International:** A non-profit membership association that provides due diligence, compliance assistance and a great online Resource Centre with law and case summaries. For more information, go to http://bit.ly/raMXVw (https://secure.traceinternational.org/Knowledge/Compendium/Welcome.html).
- **DPA:** A US deferred prosecution agreement.
- **NPA:** A US non-prosecution agreement (see Question 25).
- **CRO:** A UK civil recovery order (see Question 27).
- **CCO:** A company's chief compliance officer (see 'Three essential prerequisites', page 352).
- **POCA:** The UK's Proceeds of Crime Act 2002.
- **SOCA:** The UK's Serious Organised Crime Agency (see Question 33).

Introduction

'Few men have virtue to withstand the highest bidder.'

George Washington

Bribes can vary tremendously in both their size, and their nature. Suitcases filled with notes and given to African presidents to secure a multi-million pound contract are invariably bribes, but bribes can also be backhanders to reward a friend for passing some business your way, or small denomination notes tucked into a passport at a makeshift checkpoint on a deserted central European road. All are technically bribes perhaps – but some bribes just *feel* more wrong than others.

So-called 'grand corruption' – money paid to win major deals, change government policy, and secure venues for sporting events – grabs the headlines and is seen as causing the greatest social harm. It's well correlated with stunted economic growth and higher levels of poverty, and it's rightly where prevention and deterrence are focused. Most people agree that grand corruption is wrong, and people who engage in it should be severely punished.

But small 'facilitation' or grease payments to obtain basic services from minor government functionaries are far more prevalent. These types of bribes are generally extorted: people don't pay them to get any special treatment, but pay them simply to get what they are entitled to. (Whether they subsequently admit it or properly report it is another matter.) Although business groups continue to take a pragmatic approach and argue that it is simply impossible to do business in lesser-developed countries without paying bribes, agreeing to make facilitation payments can be seen as the thin end of the wedge and surely fosters a culture of corruption among government officials. Is it, therefore, far from a victimless crime?

But even before we get onto these sorts of discussions, we need to consider what bribery and corruption really are, and just why they are so bad. Why is slipping a few pounds to a London restaurant manager to obtain a better table seen as acceptable (even admirable) behaviour, but slipping far less money to a customs official in Lagos likely to reward you with a lengthy spell in prison?

The regulatory environment and enforcement regime is getting ever stricter. US prosecutors are regularly fining both US and non-US companies hundreds of millions of dollars, and UK lawyers have talked themselves into a frenzy about the Bribery Act. But is the Bribery Act really stricter than the US Foreign Corrupt Practices Act (FCPA)? What does it say, and how will it be enforced? Working in a global company, exactly what am I allowed and not allowed to do?

There are two types of oil services companies: those that have already been investigated for bribery violations and those that are going to be investigated for bribery violations.

Most companies have already heard about how they should take notice of global bribery laws, and are starting to do so. Most of the multinationals that have already been caught out by the FCPA have now developed a decent compliance regime. Other companies may have some sort of an anti-bribery compliance policy, but for many it's there in name only. Several have stalled along the way and got bogged down in what can seem like a daunting and unrewarding compliance quagmire, and are paying vast amounts of money to the biggest and brightest legal and accounting firms to tell them what should be blindingly obvious. The UK's Ministry of

Justice has published guidance that is meant to tell business all they need to do to comply with the Bribery Act. But it doesn't.

In fact there is very little guidance available that tells business managers, in digestible, succinct, but above all *practical* terms, what the key bribery laws say, what happens (and what you should do) if someone accuses you of breaking them, and how you can have a great compliance system without spending a fortune.

This book is what I wish that I had been given when I was starting out helping companies address their bribery concerns. It tries to give direct answers to the above questions and many other difficult ones that I am frequently asked by corporate counsel, external lawyers, internal auditors, corporate accountants, compliance specialists, HR specialists, fellow forensic accountants and just normal business people who have heard about bribery, realize they need to address it and are asking the question 'But what should we actually *do*?'

This is not a law book (although by necessity it contains some law). Neither is it an FCPA or a Bribery Act book. I've tried instead to make it relevant to business people working internationally. As such, and although I deal with other key jurisdictions – notably China, and some African and European countries – I've focused on the laws and enforcement regimes that are most relevant to businesses operating globally in 2011, which are those of the US, the UK and the OECD. I also move beyond business and consider bribery in sport, politics and the media.

The mainstay of the book though is practical advice to help business people start, and improve their anti-bribery compliance. The main problem when faced with setting up or improving a compliance regime is knowing where to begin. In this book I set out some simple and common-sense steps that can take a company from having no compliance regime to being FCPA, Bribery Act and OECD compliant. (And if you're compliant with these, you can sleep easy at night wherever you may be based.)

Further reading

This book is not an academic work, designed to contain all you need to know about a topic. Quite the contrary. I hope it will provide an introduction for some and refresher for others of the things they need to know, and act as a jumping-off point for further research. For each topic I have therefore set out some suggested further reading, both in this book and externally. I have not referenced everything, or put references in standard academic format (it's just not that sort of book), but what I have done is provided links to some articles that I think are particularly relevant and interesting.

I have attached the URLs of many sources for further reading. I have also set out URLs as bitly web addresses. (Bitly is a URL-shortening service, which avoids you having to retype long website addresses.) Just direct your browser to http://bit.ly/xxxxx, where xxxxx is the permanent combination of four to six letters and numbers given in the text (they are case-sensitive), and you will be taken straight to the relevant website.

One final note: I am writing this from London, and so throughout the book I use UK spelling and terminology.

I hope that everyone who ever has to get to grips with how client entertaining needs to be 'proportionate' and 'reasonable' will appreciate this book.

David Lawler PhD, FCA, CFE
London, January 2012

Chapter 1
Timeline

Up to 1970: The Dark Ages for Commercial Bribery

Bribery is certainly not a recent phenomenon, and there are several reports of bribery among ancient Egyptian writings and in the books of The Old Testament. Leaving these historical accounts aside, though, bribery was first properly outlawed when the UK passed the Corrupt Practices Act of 1695, a law designed to prevent bribery during parliamentary elections. This forerunner of the modern bribery laws prevented prospective candidates or their associates from making any 'gift, reward or entertainment' in exchange for votes.

Although most lawmakers slowly reflected popular opinion by criminalizing political corruption, the prevailing wisdom was that bribery was a fact of life when doing business, particularly internationally, and so for the first 80% of the twentieth century there were almost no prosecutions for bribery outside the political arena anywhere in the world.

The UK was one of the first countries in the world to have explicit statutory provisions outlawing bribery. But although they sounded impressive, they were little used, and piecemeal reforms over the years had given rise to a myriad of overlapping offences contained in the common law, and in dated legislation.

1971: Lockheed

In 1971 the US government helped Lockheed Corporation, at the time the country's second largest defence contractor, to avoid bankruptcy by providing it with a $250m loan guarantee. Soon afterwards, regulators discovered that Lockheed had been paying numerous bribes to foreign governments over the course of many years, with multi-million dollar backhanders having been made to obtain contracts in Holland, Japan and Italy. These were not just payments to low and mid-ranking bureaucrats, but bribes to very senior figures. The scandal that resulted damaged relations both inside and outside the US.

Lockheed was reluctant to cooperate with subsequent governmental investigations and refused to stop making political payments, claiming that it was simply doing what was necessary to carry out business in certain parts of the world. Such payments, it said, were essential to maintaining sales and were 'consistent with practices engaged in by numerous other companies abroad'.

1972: Watergate

In June 1972, the US Democratic Party offices at the Watergate hotel complex were broken into. The subsequent FBI investigation revealed that the Watergate episode was just one part of a huge operation to spy on and sabotage the Democrats' election chances.

Republican candidate Richard Nixon was ultimately re-elected, and although he maintained that he knew nothing about the matter, when he refused to comply with an order of the Supreme Court to hand over tapes of conversations that took place inside the White House, he was impeached and charged with obstruction of justice.

Meanwhile, in 1973, during his fifth year as Nixon's Vice President, Spiro Agnew was under investigation by the US Attorney's office in Maryland on charges of extortion, tax fraud, bribery and conspiracy. Rather than face a bribery trial, he was allowed to plead 'no contest' to a charge of evading income tax, with the condition that he resign his office.

In August 1974, Nixon – facing increasing pressure over his role in the Watergate scandal – resigned, the first US president to do so. When Vice President Gerald Ford became president in his place, he later pardoned Nixon of all charges related to the Watergate case.

1976: Post-Watergate Repercussions

During his investigation of corporate payments to Nixon's election campaign, the Watergate special prosecutor found evidence of hidden 'slush funds' being set up by some of the US's largest companies, including such stalwarts as 3M, American Airlines and Goodyear Tire & Rubber. These payments had been used to make illegal payments to the Republican election campaign. Subsequent probes uncovered numerous cases of corporate money being illicitly passed to domestic politicians, foreign officials or often both.

Motivated more by an attempt to reduce share price volatility resulting from major contracts being obtained by bribery as any moral imperative to try to eliminate it, the US regulators proposed a programme of voluntary disclosure. The SEC encouraged any company to come forward and self-report a bribe or illicit payment, whereupon they would be informally assured that they would not face prosecution. In return, however, the company would have to conduct an independent investigation into the payments and disclose the results before putting right any problems uncovered.

Some companies complied, others partly complied; some resisted. The resulting 1976 SEC publication, *Report on Questionable and Illegal Corporate Payments and Practices*, analysed information obtained from 89 companies, many of which were part of the Fortune 500, which had self-reported bribes or other illicit payments made to foreign governmental officials. The SEC recommended establishing new and stricter accounting, record-keeping and management practices for large US companies.[1]

Mid-1970s: Easing of Tensions in the Cold War

The 1970s also represented a period of more cordial relations between NATO and the Warsaw Pact countries. Both sides were feeling that the financial cost of the nuclear arms race was becoming unsustainable, particularly in the US, where the economy was under pressure from having to pay for the Vietnam War at the same time as the welfare state was being expanded. Diplomats recognized there was no longer a pressing reason for the US government or its agents to support corrupt regimes around the world under the guise of national security, and became conscious that paying bribes tarnished the US image abroad and weakened its standing in global politics. To build and preserve alliances, the US government embarked on a post-Cold War agenda of transparency.

1977: Foreign Corrupt Practices Act Passed

Fuelled by scandals of Watergate, news of widespread international bribery and the easing of international political relations, US voters had grown wary of shady deals and questionable dealings by the country's political and business leaders, and started to demand a new accountability. Under US law, bribery of domestic politicians had for some time been illegal, however, even the most blatant bribery overseas was not an offence. Senator William Proxmire proposed new rules to extend existing anti-bribery legislation to payments to overseas officials.

After considerable debate, the Foreign Corrupt Practices Act 1977 was enacted by President Jimmy Carter on 19 December 1977. The legislation was designed not only to ensure more ethical conduct by US business by punishing those caught bribing, but also as a foreign policy tool to build economic and political goodwill by encouraging US businesses to invest in developing economies.

1978: First FCPA Settlement

The US-listed oil exploration company, Katy Industries, together with two of its directors, settled claims brought by the SEC under the new FCPA.[2] The company acknowledged that it had used an agent to pay bribes to government officials in Indonesia to obtain an oil exploration concession.

1988: Amendment of the FCPA

Despite the FCPA having been in place for nine years, small petty bribes were still occurring largely unabated. The legislation was reworded to refocus efforts on the 'grand bribery' schemes that caused the most economic harm. Under the legislative amendments, overseas 'facilitation payments' were exempted from the FCPA, meaning that businesses would not be prosecuted in the US for making certain small payments overseas to secure basic services.

1994: The 'Cash for Questions' Scandal

The tortuous history of legal reforms that eventually gave rise to the UK's Bribery Act has its roots in the 1994 'cash for questions' scandal. The revelation that two Conservative

Members of Parliament had accepted money for asking questions in the House of Commons led to the UK Prime Minister, John Major, setting up the Committee on Standards in Public Life to address concerns about unethical conduct amongst MPs. Former judge Lord Nolan chaired the Committee.[3]

1997: OECD Convention

The OECD Convention on Combating Bribery of Foreign Public Officials in International Transactions – which for obvious reasons I shorten in this book to simply 'the OECD Convention' – was signed in December 1997 after several years of private and not-so-private international diplomacy. The OECD Convention created a degree of parity between US businesses – which had felt themselves disadvantaged having been subject to the FCPA since 1977 – and businesses in the other OECD countries. US business concerns were not satisfied this time by relaxing the FCPA, but instead by strengthening the laws of other countries, and also by enforcing the FCPA in particular against non-US companies. The OECD Convention entered into force on 15 February 1999, once it had been ratified by the required number of member states.

The OECD Convention is the most effective international convention to date, with widespread support by governments and business organizations.

1998: Further Amendments to the FCPA

With the signing into law of the International Anti-Bribery and Fair Competition Act 1998, the FCPA was amended once again to comply with the US's obligation to enact the OECD

Convention. These amendments expanded the scope of the FCPA to include jurisdiction over some foreign nationals, as well as acts by US nationals overseas.[4]

1990s Onwards: Vigorous Prosecution of the FCPA

The DOJ and SEC made the FCPA a prosecution priority, targeting not only US firms for their overseas corruption, but also non-US overseas firms operating in the US. Most of these cases did not come to court, but instead settled under non-prosecution agreements or deferred prosecution agreements, with heavy fines and a period of supervised corporate probation.

1996–2010: Multi-Lateral Anti-Bribery Treaties

During this period, most of the major country groups enacted conventions and treaties against bribery, committing their members to enacting their own anti-bribery legislation. These include:

- Inter-American Convention Against Corruption (adopted 1996)[5]
- The European Union Convention on the Fight against Corruption involving Officials of the European Communities or Officials of Member States of the EU (1997)[6]
- Council of Europe Conventions (1998 and 1999)[7]
- The Asian Development Bank/OECD Action Plan (2001)[8]
- European Union Framework Decision on Combating Corruption in the Private Sector (2003)[9]
- African Union (2003)[10]

- United Nations Convention against Corruption (2003)[11]
- The G20 committed to adopt and enforce laws against transnational bribery, such as the OECD Anti-Bribery Convention (2009).[12]

2001: UK Enacts the OECD

In December 2001, the UK enacted aspects of the OECD Convention. It achieved this by including provisions within the Anti-Terrorism, Crime and Security Act 2001 that extended UK jurisdiction to bribery committed abroad by UK nationals, and widened the bribery laws to encompass foreign public officials.[13]

2003: Draft UK Corruption Bill

The Nolan Committee's first report in 1995 created waves in Parliament by recommending full disclosure of MPs' outside interests. More interestingly for present purposes, it also suggested that the Law Commission should consider a revision of the law on bribery. The subsequent report, *Raising Standards and Upholding Integrity: The Prevention of Corruption* was crafted into the UK's (first) Corruption Bill.[14]

The draft Bill did not however win the necessary Parliamentary backing; the Joint Committee that subjected the bill to scrutiny was critical of its vague nature. The fact that private sector bribery was reduced to the betrayal of trust placed in an agent by a principal meant that some corruption would not be covered by the proposed rules (for example, when principals bribe each other). A further government consultation paper, *Bribery: Reform of the Prevention of Corruption Acts and SFO Powers in Cases of Bribery of Foreign Officials*, was published in 2005 – but no clear consensus emerged on how this should be achieved and the project floundered.[15]

2003, 2005, 2007 and 2008: OECD Criticism of the UK

Meanwhile, the OECD produced a series of reports that continued to be critical of the UK's outdated and fragmented bribery laws and apparent reluctance to put in place an effective regime for corporate liability for bribery. It stated that there was:

> 'a lack of clarity among the different legislative and regulatory instruments in place. ... The current substantive law governing bribery in the UK is characterized by complexity and uncertainty.'[16]

In its October 2008 report the OECD expressed continued disappointment with the UK's lack of progress in fully implementing the OECD Convention, and requested that the UK government enact:

> 'modern bribery legislation and establish effective corporate liability for bribery as a matter of high priority.'[17]

2008: Balfour Beatty Settles Bribery Allegations in the UK

An important result for the Serious Fraud Office came when it obtained the UK's first civil recovery order against UK-based engineering company Balfour Beatty plc. The matter related to irregular payments made in connection with a huge Egyptian engineering project, the Bibliotheca Alexandrina. Balfour Beatty was not charged with a criminal offence; instead, the matter was dealt with using the SFO's new civil powers, allowing property obtained by illegal actions to be recovered without the need for a criminal prosecution.[18]

2008: Siemens Settlement

In December 2008 Siemens settled charges brought by US and German prosecutors, paying a record-breaking $1.6bn in penalties.[19]

2009: Second UK Bribery Bill

Following the failure of the first UK Bribery Bill, the Law Commission was asked to draft a law that was simpler and more appropriate to modern times. In its report *Reforming Bribery*, published in October 2008, it rejected the principal/agent, or the breach of trust approaches to defining bribery. Instead its new definition of bribery was based on offering or accepting *an advantage* in connection with the *improper performance* of the recipient's functions. The draft Bribery Bill was published by the Ministry of Justice in March 2009.[20]

2010: BAE Settlement

The DOJ and SEC continued to prosecute the FCPA very vigorously and successfully, and out-of-court settlements had become routine. In 2010, BAE Systems entered into a simultaneous plea agreement with the US and UK prosecutors to resolve bribery charges. While the US court had no problems approving a $400m fine against the company, the UK court had a number of criticisms and reservations. Eventually, however, it approved the agreed penalty of £500,000 plus £28.5m in reparations to be made to the people of Tanzania.[22]

2010: UK Bribery Act Passed, then Delayed

The Bribery Act 2010 received Royal Assent on 8 April 2010. It did not immediately though come into force. The most important changes to the legislative structure – the corporate offence of failing to prevent bribery carried out on its behalf – was a sweeping change to existing practice and the government stated that this would only became law once guidance on the 'adequate procedures' defence had been published by the Ministry of Justice. It was initially expected that these would be published in early 2011, and the Act would become fully effective in April 2011.

July 2011: UK Bribery Act Comes into Force

The Bribery Act Guidance was finalized on 30 March 2011; the Bribery Act fully came into effect on 1 July 2011.

September 2011: First Prosecution under the Bribery Act

A court clerk, Munir Patel, was the first person to be prosecuted under the Bribery Act. He admitted to taking £500 from a member of the public to avoid putting details of a traffic summons on the court database. The now former clerk was charged under Section 2 of the Act (as well as charges of misconduct in public office and perverting the course of justice, which related to other alleged misconduct during his employment) for allegedly requesting and receiving a bribe intending to improperly perform his functions. He was sentenced to six years' imprisonment.[21]

2012 Onwards

It remains to be seen what the impact of the Bribery Act will be. I set out some of my predictions in 'What Are My Predictions for 2012 and Beyond?' on page 455.

Further reading

Carr, I. and Outhwaite, O., The OECD anti-bribery convention ten years on, *Manchester Journal of International Economic Law*, **5**(1), 3–35, 2008. Available from: http://bit.ly/ogRaFP (http://epubs.surrey.ac.uk/578/1/fulltext.pdf).

Corruption in the crosshairs: a brief history of international anti-bribery legislation, Public Broadcasting Service, 7 April 2009. Available from: http://to.pbs.org/nXdjM7 (http://www.pbs.org/frontlineworld/stories/bribe/2009/04/timeline.html).

Lockheed's defiance: a right to bribe?, *Time*, 18 August 1975. Available from: http://ti.me/rnuzzo (http://www.time.com/time/magazine/article/0,9171,917751,00.html).

Martin, A.T., The development of international bribery law, *Natural Resources & Environment*, **14**(2), 1999. Available from:

http://bit.ly/rmYzlI (http://www.transparency.ca/Reports/Readings/SR-G02.pdf).

Posadas, A., Combating corruption under international law, *Duke Journal of Comparative & International Law*, **10**, 345–414, 2000. Available from: http://bit.ly/oe8QAT (https://www.law.duke.edu/journals/djcil/downloads/djcil10p345.pdf).

Chapter 2
Who Pays Bribes?

Bribery and corruption cover a wide variety of behaviours and a multitude of different actions that depend on circumstances for their criminality. Most people agree that passing suitcases full of money to officials to act in ways in which they should not act (for example, by wrongly awarding a contract to the bribing party) must be outlawed and vigorously prosecuted. (This is what people refer to as so-called 'grand bribery'.) But facilitation payments – payments made to simply get an official to do something that they should already be doing, and is not really motivated by dishonesty – cause far more varied reactions. In this section I look at the different types of bribes: I start with commercial bribery, but move on to other, often overlooked areas, where bribery is just as pernicious. Bribery and corruption is not just about oil contracts and infrastructure projects, although that is where recent enforcement activity has been focused. Bribery is also taking place regularly in sport, politics and the media, and I also consider them here...

Bribery in Business

The line between different types of commercial bribes is not a bright one, and the favours or benefits that are 'purchased' with bribes can vary tremendously in both size and scope. Some would argue (with some justification) that because all bribery is wrong it is meaningless to attempt to categorize bribes, and it can in fact be socially damaging and a retrograde step to treat 'big' bribes any differently from 'small' bribes. Although the sums involved are higher and the stories innately more interesting with major 'grand bribery' schemes, the aggregate costs of petty corruption and facilitation payments, in terms of social and economic effects, are far greater. It remains the case, however, that public attention is focused on 'grand bribery', and the international efforts to bring this under control, and so I retain the distinction in this book.

Grand bribery

Grand bribery tends to be associated with international business transactions and massive infrastructure or military supply contracts, often involving politicians as well as bureaucrats. These bribes are associated in popular culture with brown envelopes, used notes and smoke-filled rooms, but the bribes are more often nowadays proceed through the electronic transfers of large amounts of dollars through various front companies, fictitious consultants and dodgy subcontractors.

Bribes and kickbacks to get contracts

Some bribery schemes start out with the contractor or supplier having a pre-determined plan to identify the responsible officials and offer bribes to ensure that they win a particular contract. Once the contract is awarded and becomes cash-positive, it is possible to pay a kickback in cash (at anything between 1% and 15% of the contract price). Often agents are used to pass on these bribes and kickbacks, which are disguised as some sort of 'consulting fees'.

Other schemes are suggested first by the official responsible for the contract. The requests can take various forms, such as:

- suggesting that the project official would like to receive gifts, or indicating their preferences for lavish entertainment
- requesting paid travel or trips to visit overseas facilities (of course with their family, and amounting to a paid holiday)
- hinting that they are struggling to pay for the school and college fees for their children

- offering to rent property owned by the official to the contractor – the contractor pays money to the official to 'lease' office space but is actually making bribe payments; often the space is never occupied
- highlighting the charity they are patron of or the local area that would benefit from improved facilities. The greater the donations to this charity or area, the greater the kudos and political power flowing to the official.

All of these payment categories – gifts, entertaining, travel, school fees, property costs and charitable donations – are high risk areas, as they are the places where bribes are usually hidden. (This means that particular attention is warranted in these cost categories during the process to design and implement controls, and during compliance reviews.)

Front companies and inflated supply contracts

Sometimes one sees corrupt officials who have set up a contracting or subcontracting business that is employed by the client on the project. Sometimes they own a company selling equipment to the project. The business might be owned directly by them, or (more likely) the ownership is disguised using friends, relatives or professional advisors. Invariably, though, the surplus profits in the business are diverted back to the corrupt official.

Take for example a construction project that requires 100 computers to be used by the project team. The contractor would normally buy them from one of the international computer manufacturers at the going rate of say £1000 each. Corrupt officials though make it a condition of winning the work that the company uses their 'preferred' supplier. This supplier, a front company, buys the same computers for £1000, but sells them to the contractor for £1500. The profit of £50,000 made by the front company flows back to the corrupt official.

Bid rigging
Dodgy government officials would rather work with their preferred contractors, because they are the ones they know will pay the bribes and kickbacks. They find many ways to award supply contracts to their favourite contractors and give them the best chance of winning tenders and bids, including:

- splitting large contracts into several smaller contracts that are individually below the level needed to have to go out to competitive tender
- very narrow drafting of the contract or bid specifications to exclude other bidders
- secret promises by officials that they will approve later lucrative amendments to the contract so the contractor can bid low enough to win
- secret promises that some of the line items subject to the bid are not required, meaning that the preferred bidder can low-ball these items.

Contractor fraud
Often bribes or kickbacks are paid to officials by contractors to get their sub-standard or non-existent work signed off and paid without issue. Sometimes, extra charges are billed to projects to recover the cost of the kickbacks. Among the most common situations are:

- overcharging for goods and work
- billing for expenses never incurred, sometimes with elaborate counterfeit supporting documents
- false late payment and other fees and charges
- delivering used equipment in place of new, or counterfeit instead of genuine
- misrepresenting the contractor's or staff qualifications and experience.

Petty bribery and facilitation payments

At the other end of the bribery spectrum lie more petty bribes to more junior officials. These are paid to obtain services that are not normally provided without payment, or else are provided in a different form (usually slower and not as comprehensively). The bribes may be kept by the individual officials involved, or pooled and then shared with superiors and colleagues.

So-called 'facilitation' or 'facilitating' payments may be considered to be a type of petty bribery: the distinction being that bribery gives the person paying a bribe something they would not normally have received, whereas a facilitation payment simply gives access to a service that should otherwise be provided without payment. Facilitation payments might be permitted under the international bribery laws of some countries, including under the FCPA, but they are invariably illegal in the local jurisdiction where the payment is made.

Often these facilitation payments are demanded or extorted by the recipient, and so the paying company has an incentive to stop the practice. The most difficult petty bribery to detect, however, is that which occurs at the same time as theft by officials. Take for example the situation where a tax inspector accepts a bribe in return for levying a reduced tax payment. In this case the tax inspector may keep the entire bribe and the reduced tax for himself, and so is guilty of both accepting a bribe and theft. If the amount of the reduced tax and the bribe combined is less than the full amount of the tax that should have been paid, the company paying the bribe is also gaining financially and so has less incentive to refuse to engage in the bribery. In the situation of 'pure' facilitation payments, the bribers have an incentive to inform on the corrupt officials because the bribers will save money by not having to pay the bribe.

Even small bribes are still bribes, and allowing any payments to obtain an advantage sets a permissive tone. Thus facilitation payments are the thin end of a wedge and can lead to ever-increasing demands, ultimately poisoning the ethics of the paying corporation. The OECD and others are calling for more government action concerning facilitation payments.

Where is bribery most prevalent?

> 'No service without money, and poor service with little money.'
>
> Attributed to the Mayor of Shanghai[22]

Corruption is inherently difficult to measure, and does not fit well into simple socio-economic models. Owing to the scarcity of reliable objective corruption measures throughout the 1970s and '80s, most of the early country risk assessment models had to be based on the opinion polls of the 'perception' of corruption within each country. However, the relentless rise in enforcement, and with it the requirement for reliable country data to feed companies' compliance programmes, has generated a demand for better metrics.

The most usual approach to determining country risk today is to look to one of the new generation of more nuanced 'aggregate indicators' that rank the riskiness or corruptness of countries. These are constructed by combining several primary measures. Many are proprietary and differ in their details, but all consist of groups of company executives, researchers or other groups believed to have first-hand knowledge of corruption, who are asked to rate corruption within the particular country. Responses are then collated and normalized onto a numerical scale.

Problems with indicators
The complex statistical constructions of modern aggregate indicators can easily create an illusion of spurious accuracy that leads users to interpret them as measures of actual corruption – which is not the case. They are based on perceptions, because the availability of 'real' information is scarce, if not simply non-existent. This means that even the best perception-based metrics have a potentially very large margin of error, particularly when compared with real conditions on the ground. Nevertheless, while imperfect, it is widely accepted that there is a degree of correspondence between perceptions of corruption and reality, albeit one that is subject to numerous caveats and limitations.

Furthermore, the widespread use of perception data does cause concern about perceived bias. This means that there is a risk that being portrayed as being a corrupt country on one index can lead to this becoming a self-fulfilling prophesy that is difficult to shake off. Executives doing business in high-risk countries, for example, expect to and therefore do pay bribes in those countries, leading to a vicious circle developing where expectations fuel actual bribery.

Private risk-assessment firms produce their own indicators. One of the best known is the International Country Risk Guide, which attempts to capture the likelihood that senior government officials will demand 'special' payments. This is a paid-for service.[23] Three of the not-for-profit indices stand out because of their widespread use among anti-corruption professionals.

Transparency international's annual corruption perceptions index
TI's Corruption Perceptions Index (CPI) was launched in 1995 and is widely used. Despite a few academic detractors, the CPI is acknowledged to be an invaluable resource, and is accepted worldwide. It is built by aggregating and normalizing a set of components constructed from different

country experts (both resident and non-resident) and business leaders, who assess overall extent of corruption by perceptions and experiences of both frequency and size of bribes in the public and political sectors. Sources for the CPI include the World Economic Forum, the Institute for Management Development, PriceWaterhouseCoopers, Freedom House and Gallup International.

The 2011 survey ranks 183 countries by their perceived levels of corruption, ranking countries on a scale from 0 (perceived to be highly corrupt) to 10 (perceived to have low levels of corruption).

The world bank's worldwide governance indicators
The Worldwide Governance Indicators (WGI) project has combined the views of a large number of business, citizen and expert survey respondents for 213 economies since 1996. It considers six dimensions of governance:

- voice and accountability
- political stability and absence of violence
- government effectiveness
- regulatory quality
- rule of law
- control of corruption.

The global integrity index
Global Integrity is an international, independent non-profit organization. Its Index assesses the existence, effectiveness and citizen access to key anti-corruption mechanisms at the national level in a country. Since 2004, the Global Integrity Report has covered more than 90 countries around the world, rating countries by 'integrity' subcategories. The Index uses a methodology based on empirical on-the-ground research by experts who assess the existence and effectiveness of anti-corruption and good governance mechanisms. It does not measure corruption per se or perceptions of corruption.

So what countries are most risky for a business to operate in?

The 2011 CPI shows the following:

- Central and South America, south-east Asia, India and Africa are riskier than North America, Europe, Japan and Australasia.
- Nearly three-quarters of the 183 countries in the index score below 5, indicating a serious corruption problem.
- New Zealand is in first place with a score of 9.5, with Denmark, Finland, Sweden and Singapore all above 9.
- Unstable governments, often with a legacy of conflict, continue to dominate the bottom rungs of the CPI. Somalia and North Korea (included in the index for the first time) come in last with a score of 1.1, with Afghanistan and Myanmar close behind on 1.5.
- There was an improvement in position from 2010 to 2011 for Norway, the UAE, Rwanda, Cuba, Bangladesh, Eritrea and Iran.
- There was a decline for Ireland, Costa Rica, Oman, Tunisia, and Trinidad and Tobago.

Transparency International also reported in 2011 on the Progress on the Enforcement of the OECD Convention, concluding that it had not yet reached the point at which the prohibition of foreign bribery was being consistently enforced.[24] The clear worry is that if business organizations continue to be sceptical of anti-bribery enforcement and see it as a competitive obstacle, and there is lack of political will, then the Convention is at risk of stalling. TI concluded that only seven of the 36 countries evaluated were actively enforcing the OECD Convention to which they are a party. These countries – representing approximately 30% of world exports – comprise Denmark, Germany, Italy, Norway, Switzerland, the UK and the US. (Iceland was not included in the review). Denmark, Italy and the UK had recently advanced from moderate to active enforcement. There was moderate enforcement in nine other countries, being

Argentina (recently advanced to moderate enforcement), Belgium, Finland, France, Japan, South Korea, Netherlands, Spain and Sweden.

The 20 countries with little or no enforcement in the decade since they signed up to the Convention does call into question the real political commitment by some governments to eliminate bribery. These countries are Australia, Austria, Brazil, Bulgaria, Canada, Chile, Czech Republic, Estonia, Greece, Hungary, Ireland, Israel, Mexico, New Zealand, Poland, Portugal, Slovak Republic, Slovenia, South Africa and Turkey.

One-third of world exports come from countries that are still not party to the OECD Convention, including China, India and Russia.

The high-risk sectors

'Although many of these cases come to us through voluntary disclosures, which we certainly encourage and will appropriately reward, I want to be clear: the majority of our cases do not come from voluntary disclosures. They are the result of pro-active investigations, whistleblower tips, newspaper stories, referrals from our law enforcement counterparts in foreign countries, and our Embassy personnel abroad, among other sources.'

US Assistant Attorney General Lanny Breuer[25]

Sector-specific investigations
International prosecutors, led by the DOJ, are coordinating sector-wide investigations, as they have in the oil and gas, medical devices, and freight forwarding industries. Sector-specific investigations are attractive to the prosecutors, and we are likely to see more of them.

It works like this: first the prosecutors find a transgression whereby a company – perhaps an agent – is breaching the

FCPA. Particularly if the prosecutor is able to (through subpoena or cooperation agreement as part of a relatively lenient penalty) obtain the books and records of the agent, it can then see which other clients the agent is working for, and the extent to which they might have broken the law also. They can then identify other players in that industry (if not almost the entire industry) that are operating in similar ways. This strategy was first seen in 2007, during the investigation of Vetco, when the DOJ started looking proactively to expand this investigation. Vetco led the DOJ to Panalpina, the freight forwarder that it had used to pay bribes. Once it had subpoenaed Panalpina's records, the DOJ could see all of Panalpina's other customers, which were then investigated in turn. In its announcement of the Panalpina-related settlements in November 2010, the SEC also stated that '[t]his is the first sweep of a particular industrial sector in order to crack down on public companies and third parties who are paying bribes abroad'.[26]

There is also the temptation for companies involved in investigations to inform on their competitors, who may have corrupt schemes of their own. The DOJ will give credit for this, and so the investigation expands. Pharmaceutical company Johnson & Johnson saved at least $17m in its DPA by informing the DOJ of its suspicions involving its competitors.[27]

High-risk sectors
It will be noted from the list on page 434 that several of the top 10 bribery settlements relate to oil and gas industry, and several others including Willbros, Chevron and Baker Hughes are just below the top 10. The highest risk sectors at the moment are:

- oil and gas (still)
- extractive industries: mining and metals
- technology
- healthcare and life sciences
- defence and aviation

- transport and logistics
- telecommunications
- consumer products
- construction and infrastructure
- automotive
- asset management, and private equity
- banking and capital markets.

Further reading

'Panalpina and customs violations', page 440.

Questions 18 and 41.

Francisco, J.U., Assessing corruption – an analytical review of corruption measurement and its problems: perception, error and utility, Georgetown University, 2007. Available from: http://bit.ly/pQ4GMt (http://unpan1.un.org/intradoc/groups/public/documents/apcity/unpan028792.pdf).

Global Integrity Index: http://bit.ly/nDW4yH (http://report.globalintegrity.org/globalIndex.cfm).

Transparency International's Corruption Perceptions Index: http://bit.ly/oZerqK (http://www.transparency.org/policy_research/surveys_indices/cpi).

The Worldwide Governance Indicators (WGI) project: http://bit.ly/raXzTU (http://info.worldbank.org/governance/wgi/index.asp).

Bribery in Sport

'Olympism is a philosophy of life, exalting and combining in a balanced whole the qualities of body, will and mind. Blending

> sport with culture and education, Olympism seeks to create a
> way of life based on the joy of effort, the educational value of
> good example and respect for universal fundamental ethical
> principles.'
>
> The Olympic Charter[28]

> 'The two top officials of Salt Lake City's bid to hold the 2002
> Winter Olympics have been singled out by an inquiry into the
> biggest corruption scandal in Olympic history. The inquiry
> report, which runs to several hundred pages, says large sums
> of money were paid to members of the International Olympic
> Committee to secure the bid.'
>
> BBC News, February 1999[29]

Sport – in some shape or form – is a feature of most people's
lives. It is estimated that up to 1.2 billion people regularly
participate in it; many millions more volunteer; and there
are very few in the world who don't watch the occasional
professional event. Its scope ranges from the lone amateur
pursuit, such as a spot of fishing or a bike ride, to international football tournaments that are billion-pound issues for
the clubs and the locations hosting them. The London 2012
Olympics awarded £6bn worth of business through 1400 separate contracts, creating around 75,000 separate opportunities
for companies along the supply chain.[30]

The professional nature of modern sport allows it to develop,
build new facilities, be broadcast in high definition round the
world and provide coaching for youngsters. But with money
and commercialization comes the temptation to cheat. Doping
and the use of performance-enhancing drugs have been dealt
with over the last couple of decades, using experts, scientists and international coordination, with a degree of success.
Bribery and corruption has not yet been properly addressed,
however. Even just focusing on the financial effects, any loss
of confidence in sport's integrity is a major threat because
of the knock-on effects to attendance, television demand and
sponsorship. Although only a tiny part of sport will ever be

affected by it, the part that is involves the upper echelons of professional sport where the scandals are played out in the media. People have seen business clean up its act and now expect the same in sport.

It is almost impossible to get any numbers at all (let alone accurate ones) for estimating the magnitude of corruption in sport. Detected or reported corruption is always only the tip of the iceberg and is not conclusive as to where the problems might lie. But it's clear that corruption still flourishes because the risks for criminals are minimal and control systems are weak. Players are normally young and easier to influence: by bribing just one key player, the outcome of an inconsequential part of a game can be manipulated and generate huge revenues from betting. At first glance, bribery in sports appears to differ significantly from bribery in business; but once you scratch the surface, you see it is little different from the mainstream commercial bribery dealt with elsewhere in this book.

The role of betting

Betting and sport are inexorably linked. The laws of both cricket and golf were formalized in 1744 to allow a governing body to settle disputes using consistent rules – a development that was largely driven by the needs of gamblers to get a definite outcome to their wagers. Betting in sport has had scandals throughout history; today, a series of rigged events from horse racing, soccer, cricket and tennis prompts people to question whether the development of internet betting is a driver of increased match-fixing, and whether they are safe betting online at all.

Spread betting and betting exchanges
Sports betting is legal in the UK, with both betting shops and online gambling sites being regulated by the government. However, in the US, China, Japan, Hong Kong and India

online gambling is generally prohibited. The internet has revolutionized sports betting, with betting exchanges having grown massively since the late 1990s when the gambling industry was deregulated. A betting exchange matches people backing to win and those backing to lose, allowing customers to bet at odds set by themselves or by other customers rather than by bookmakers. The exchange takes a commission on the net winnings of a customer of 2–5%. Many professional gamblers use the exchanges because they can get better odds. Betfair, one of the market leaders, processes more than seven million transactions every day – more than all the European stock exchanges combined.[31]

Crucially though, on an exchange – unlike at a conventional betting shop – it is much easier to bet to lose. Gamblers can make money by finding a loser and 'laying' it to those wanting it to win. This is clearly especially attractive to those who know, rather than just hope, that a horse or human will not be winning. As markets become bigger and therefore more liquid, the ease of manipulating the market – and the potential pay-offs – are greater. In a small market a large bet can change the odds and the risk of detection is increased. Potentially the greatest absolute rewards to illicit activity are in the most liquid markets, which are typically football, cricket and tennis.

Match-fixing
The reasons for match-fixing may be numerous, but most are connected to betting. I set out here a couple of notable stories from snooker and horse racing.

John Higgins: Six-Month Ban from Snooker[32]
The world number one snooker player, John Higgins, was suspended in 2010 from the professional snooker tour for allegations he had agreed to deliberately lose frames in return for cash. Higgins was filmed by an undercover newspaper

reporter seemingly agreeing to accept €300,000 in return for throwing four frames.

Higgins' manager immediately resigned from the board of the World Professional Billiards and Snooker Association (WPBSA). At a disciplinary hearing, the WPBSA cleared Higgins of match-fixing, but found him guilty of 'giving the impression' he would breach betting rules, and of failing to report the approach made by the newspaper. Higgins received a six-month ban and was fined £75,000.

Kieren Fallon: Acquitted of Race-Fixing[33]

Kieren Fallon's acquittal for race-fixing has been one of the most notorious cases in flat racing. Fallon was British champion jockey six times between 1997 and 2003, but in September 2004, he was arrested for interfering with the running of horses to ensure they lost races. This was part of a police investigation into the alleged fixing of over 80 races. He was later charged along with seven other people for conspiring to defraud Betfair, together with money laundering.

At his trial he was accused of being involved in a conspiracy worth £2.2m masterminded by a professional gambler that included deliberately coming second in a race at Lingfield in March 2004. The judge dramatically dismissed the charges because the main prosecution witness, an Australian racing steward, seemed to have little direct knowledge about British racing rules.

(The Jockey Club, the regulator and enforcer of the Rules of Racing, had discontinued its investigation into the allegations back in 2004. The Horseracing Regulatory Authority took on the Jockey Club's role of policing the sport in April 2006.)

There is a grey area between fixing a match and exploiting inside information. Take, for example, a player who takes a tactical decision not to over-exert themselves to win: perhaps they are injured or focusing on the next tournament. This practice of underperformance – well known to the horse racing fraternity – existed long before online betting but was confined to the stable's direct connections. But now the player, and friends and associates in on the plan, can more easily use their knowledge and the internet to lay bets for their own gain.

Refereeing and judging
A famous example of judge's bias happened at the 2002 Winter Olympics.

Marie-Reine Le Gougne ('The French Judge'): Olympic Figure Skating[34]

Neither the pundits nor the crowd at the 2002 Winter Olympics in Salt Lake City could believe that the pairs figure skating gold medal had been awarded to the Russian team over the Canadians. The result was largely down to the scores given by the French judge, Marie-Reine Le Gougne.

Confronted by the chair of the International Skating Union's Technical Committee, Le Gougne reportedly broke down, admitting that she had been pressured to vote for the Russians as part of a vote-swapping deal with Russia to favour the French team in the forthcoming ice-dancing event. This she later denied.

After an International Olympic Committee investigation, the Canadian couple were awarded a gold medal, though the Russians were also allowed to keep theirs. After a hearing of the International Skating Union (ISU) council, Le Gougne was found guilty of misconduct and suspended from the sport for three years, with the president of French skating receiving the same punishment.

After the 2002 Winter Olympics scandal, the International Skating Union switched to a system of anonymous 'secret voting'. The rationale for this was to reduce the advantage to skaters of having a friendly judge on the panel (which can result from both home country bias and vote-trading), at the same time freeing judges from pressure from their federations. However, following the switch, the home judge advantage was found in fact to increase – most likely because secret voting prevented the public and media from being able to identify home country bias.

Spot or proposition bets
The range of available bets has increased in recent years to provide more interest for gamblers seeking higher rewards for higher risks. In many professional sports, the competing players or teams are usually fairly well matched and so the odds of winning or losing do not depart much from evens, or 50:50.

Bets like these are unlikely to be attractive to gamblers with a high-risk preference – those who are used to backing horses might be looking for a 10:1 or even a 100:1 shot. Such gamblers are catered for with bets including who scores the first goal, the number of free kicks or the time of the first throw-in because these provide a much wider range of odds. These proposition or 'spot' bets can be made throughout the game and can obviously be manipulated. Spot-fixing though differs from outright match-fixing in that the entire result is not manipulated: spot-fixing just relates to specific incidents within the game. As such, it can take just one member of a team to engineer a fix, making a conspiracy both harder to detect and more cost-effective.[35]

Matt Le Tissier: Football Throw-ins[36]

Former Southampton footballer Matt Le Tissier boasted in his book that he colluded with a team-mate to take advantage of spread betting markets by making money on the time of the first throw-in. Le Tissier 'bought' the under one minute time slot in a match between Southampton and Wimbledon in 1995, and stood to win £10,000 if successful.

'The plan was for us to kick the ball straight into touch at the start of the game and then collect 56 times our stake. Easy money...I couldn't see a problem with making a few quid on the first throw-in.'

As it happened, Le Tissier attempted to kick the ball out of play directly from the kick-off – but a team-mate who was unaware of the bet kept the pass in play.

The amount gambled on an important one-day international cricket match can approach £1bn – particularly on in the Indian sub-continent, where bookmakers, gamblers and even cricketers have not been discouraged, despite gambling being illegal. Cricket offers endless options for gambling on small incidents within the match, and there are markets on whether each particular delivery will be hit for a four or six, or whether it will be a no-ball, a wide or will produce a wicket. All of these events can be manipulated, with little effort required to produce 'errors' at the prescribed moment. One notorious example is the series of no-balls that Pakistan bowlers were accused of fixing during the August 2010 test matches.

Salman Butt: Cricket Spot Betting[37]

Former Pakistan captain Salman Butt and bowlers Mohammad Asif and Mohammad Amir were accused of 'spot-fixing' during the 2010 Test series against England. Amir and Asif were alleged to have deliberately bowled no-balls to the instructions of their agent, who received money from a third party, while Butt was said to be aware of the arrangement. The

International Cricket Council announced that the three were banned from playing the sport – Butt for 10 years with half of that suspended.

The UK's Crown Prosecution Service has also charged the cricketers and their agent with conspiracy to obtain and accept corrupt payments under the 1906 Corruption Act, and conspiracy to cheat under the 2005 Gambling Act. The charges carry maximum prison sentences of seven and two years respectively. In November 2011, the four defendants (including the agent involved) were jailed for between six and 32 months.

'It's not cricket was an adage. It is the insidious effect of your actions on professional cricket and the followers of it which make the offences so serious. The image and integrity of what was once a game, but is now a business is damaged in the eyes of all, including the many youngsters who regarded three of you as heroes and would have given their eye teeth to play at the levels and with the skill that you had.'[38]

> Mr Justice Cooke sentencing Butt, Asif,
> Amir and Majeed. November 2011

Corrupt sports organizations

International sport federations, with their often-enormous wealth and limited external oversight, are at an especially high risk of corruption. Many have had business-related scandals that do not really differ from any other variant of commercial bribery or corruption, involving:

- corrupt elections to committees and senior positions
- embezzlement or misuse of funds
- ticket touting
- corruption in hosting of events

- bribery in relation to media and sponsorship rights
- corruption in transfers of players.

Media organizations have been accused of paying bribes to rights holders to gain access to lucrative television rights. FIFA – international football's governing body – is one of the organizations that has attracted unwelcome media attention for several years. International Sports and Leisure's (ISL's) complex relationship with FIFA is still very much in the public spotlight, ever since ISL was alleged to have paid bribes to FIFA officials to secure the rights to international football.[39]

International Sport and Leisure (ISL)

International Sport and Leisure, the marketing agency that had worked with FIFA, the International Olympic and the International Association of Athletics Federations, collapsed in 2001 with debts of £153m. ISL held the media and marketing rights for events including the FIFA World Cup and the Olympics.

During the investigation into the ISL collapse initiated by FIFA, it emerged that between 1989 and 2001, ISL paid undocumented 'personal commissions' worth £100m to secure television and marketing rights to major sports events, paid through a complex web of companies in various countries. The former executives of ISL argued that commissions such as these were a reality of business in securing rights for sports events, but ISL received no receipts for the payments supposedly because of the recipients' sensitivity over publicly accepting such payments.

FIFA dropped its investigation, but it was alleged in late 2010 by the BBC that three senior FIFA officials were among those who had received the bribes that FIFA had failed to investigate. The allegations were made three days before the trio took part in FIFA's vote on the venue for the hosting for the 2018 and 2022 World Cups, which England dramatically lost.[40]

In June 2011 it came to light that the International Olympic Committee had started inquiry proceedings against FIFA's honorary president Joao Havelange – who was FIFA President from 1974 until 1998 and an IOC member for 48 years – into claims that he accepted a $1m bribe in 1997 from ISL.

However, in November 2011 Havelange resigned, citing health reasons. This meant that the IOC dropped the investigation, and any suspension or expulsion was avoided. At the same time, though, the president of international athletics, Lamine Diack, and the head of African football, Issa Hayatou, were both disciplined by the IOC over their parts in the alleged bribery scandal.[41]

Corruption in order to host games and win franchises

It is common practice for countries or cities to 'bid' against each other with state-of-the-art stadiums, tax benefits and licensing deals to secure or keep professional sports competitions. Bribes are inevitably occasionally offered and FIFA again made headlines in 2011 with its voting on the venues for the 2018 and 2022 World Cup.

The FIFA Football World Cups in 2018 and 2022

FIFA is headquartered in Zurich. With 208 member associations it is responsible for the organization of football's major international tournaments, including the World Cup. FIFA's vote in December 2011 to award the 2018 World Cup to Russia and the 2022 World Cup to Qatar, was widely criticized, at least by the English-speaking media. England was bitterly disappointed to lose the 2018 bid, particularly as their bid seem to have the best infrastructure, stadiums, transport, and facilities. But *The Daily Telegraph* summed it up as follows:[42]

'The FIFA source I spoke to yesterday insisted that, for some members of the committee, the attractiveness of the Russian bid was obvious: the kickbacks given to the voting committee – sometimes cash, sometimes payment-in-kind, such as an expensive month's holiday for two.'

In May 2011, a British parliamentary inquiry heard from a whistleblower that two African members of FIFA's 24-man executive committee were paid $1.5m by Qatar. These allegations have been denied. Two other members of FIFA's executive committee had already been banned from all football-related activity in November 2010 for allegedly offering to sell their votes to undercover newspaper reporters.

Although no formal investigation has been opened, FIFA president Sepp Blatter has said that the organization's newly created Good Governance Committee would have the authority to review the awarding of the 2018 and 2022 tournaments.[43]

Trading of players and 'bungs'

Sporting scandals often arise in the transfer market. In Australia, rugby league club Melbourne Storm were at the centre of a scandal in 2011. The team had won three premierships since its formation in 1998 and was doing exceptionally well, seeing that it was some way out of rugby league's traditional heartlands of New South Wales and Queensland. Australian club rugby operates a salary cap to ensure that the talent is spread among the different clubs rather than being concentrated in the richest, but the board of Melbourne Storm arranged for illicit payments of A$1.7m outside of its declared and audited payroll. The payments were made via third parties to its best players to keep them loyal while avoiding the salary cap. When it came to light, the club was stripped of its premiership trophies, fined A$500,000 and made to pay back A$1.1m in prize money.[44]

In the UK, people have always used bribery to try to circumvent the strict rules regarding payments to lure and sign players. Football transfers require agents, and both players and clubs retain them. But an agent is not permitted to 'approach a player who is under contract with a club with the aim of persuading him to terminate their contract prematurely or to flout the rights and duties stipulated in the contract' – this is known as 'tapping up' or 'tampering'. But unscrupulous agents might pay a club official a slice of their commission (a 'bung') for recommending that a club buys one of 'their' players and helping a transfer go through.

Investigating and prosecuting

Judging by the reported number of convictions, sport initially seems to be of relatively low risk with regard to corruption, if not squeaky clean. Prosecution data is not a good indicator for this, however – mainly because except for the most egregious cases, corruption in sport is not often prosecuted. One obstacle is the widely held perception that sport is a purely private leisure activity, and state resources should not be spent on it. This goes hand in hand with the closed, family-like nature of international sport federations. Getting tangible evidence from internal sources is difficult, because many sports federations pay only lip service to democracy and whistle-blowers are rare in the 'family'.

Spotting match-fixing via the betting markets

> 'Furthermore, while professional tennis is not institutionally or systematically corrupt, it is potentially at a crossroads.'
>
> Professional Tennis Associations, Environmental Review of Integrity in Professional Tennis[45]

Match-fixing is also extremely hard to spot and difficult to prosecute. A key investigative tool is found in the betting market, however. At first glance, the betting exchanges appear to have little direct financial interest in investigating and prosecuting cheating; they receive their commission regardless of who wins and who loses. They do become motivated if their clients think that the market is not a fair one and is dominated by dishonest punters, though. All online gambling leaves an audit trail, so any suspicious betting patterns – when, for example, a favourite's price mysteriously increases – is reported to the sport's governing body.

The Association of Tennis Professionals was recently forced to tighten its betting rules after unusual betting patterns were seen during matches, most notably one involving the Russian star Nikolay Davydenko with an outsider in a Polish tournament. Nine people based in Russia had bet US$1.5m against Davydenko during the match, even after he had won the first set 6–2. Davydenko withdrew from the match during the third set with a foot injury. (There was ultimately no finding against Davydenko.[46]) After these events, an independent panel was established and concluded in May 2008 that 45 professional tennis matches out of the 73 examined required further review because of 'suspicious betting patterns'.[47]

Stopping it
Sports federations have rules preventing bribery and corruption. Take for example FIFA's Code of Ethics, which was last published in 2009, and applies to all FIFA officials.[48] It provides that:

> 'Officials may not accept bribes; in other words, any gifts or other advantages that are offered, promised or sent to them to incite breach of duty or dishonest conduct for the benefit of a third party shall be refused.

> 'Officials are forbidden from bribing third parties or from urging or inciting others to do so in order to gain an advantage for themselves or third parties.'

The Code is seriously lacking when compared with the legislation faced by other commercial organizations: notably, it fails to define 'bribe' and 'bribing', and there is no standalone clause to prevent members seeking an advantage. In addition to the Code, FIFA published additional rules regarding bids for the 2018 and 2022 World Cups. This document ran to two whole pages (!) and, while there are obligations on the bidding countries, there are none on FIFA members.

Sport is lagging behind business in achieving transparency. While ethical responsibility is more than a paper programme with many corporates, this is still not the case with the sports federations. Sports federations are notoriously slow to take any meaningful action, and the criminal justice system has been reluctant to get involved.

As a first step, the federations should clearly state their disapproval of and intention to fight criminal manipulation. Such a move would send out a signal to potential crooks and encourage people to speak up. To be taken seriously, though, federations then need to go through the same compliance procedures as set out in this book. Unless they are pressured to do so by criminal prosecutors who actively bring sports into their remit, the media, sponsors and fans, they are unlikely to do so willingly.

Further reading

Forrest, D., McHale, I. and McAuley, K., Risks to the integrity of sport from betting corruption – a report for the central council for physical recreation, The Centre for the Study of Gambling, University of Salford, 2008. Available from: http://bit.ly/nOwUMB (http://www.epma-conference .net/Download/22012009/SalfordREPORT_Feb08.pdf).

Transparency International, Corruption in sport. Available from: http://bit.ly/sR48VB (http://www.transparency.org.uk/ anti-corruption-resources/71-corruption-in-sport).

Bribery in Politics

'You can buy now and then a Senator or a Representative; but they do not know it is wrong, and so they are not ashamed of it.'

Mark Twain and Charles Dudley Warner,
The Gilded Age: A Tale of Today

In the lobby

Lobbying is seeking to influence decisions made by members of government or public office holders. Lobbying – named after the discussions and gatherings in the hallways or lobbies of the Houses of Parliament – can involve a wide variety of activities and motivations, influencing decisions ranging from the specific (such as the content of legislation) or the general (such as the direction of policy).

All citizens should have the ability to lobby their elected representatives, who in turn should want to canvass facts and opinions from their constituents. As well as individuals who may lobby their elected representatives, organizations and pressure groups regularly make representations to politicians and civil servants. The right to be consulted when legislation is drafted is a courtesy generally extended to important organizations, as well as the public. Lobbying in its purest form is therefore an essential and positive feature of any democracy – certainly not unethical or shady.

Some organizations lobby directly; others employ multi-client lobbying firms to seek to influence on their behalf. Although lobbying takes place in all democracies, the extent to which lobbyists can use money to influence depends on the extent to which politicians require campaign finance. This is particularly relevant in the US – where, as well as the usual personal meetings and schmoozing, lobbyists also funnel donations and campaign finance to politicians. In these situations, and when money is directly involved, the difference between legitimate lobbying and bribery is rarely a sharp one.

Lobbying in the US

The US party system is much weaker than that of the UK and many other countries, and with direct primary elections, members are not dependent on the party for renomination. This means that election campaigns are candidate-centred affairs, leaving more room for pressure groups to persuade candidates to support their cause on their election agendas and manifestos. Pressure groups also have the advantage of a federal system that has got plenty of access points to politicians as well as the First Amendment, which safeguards rights of speech, expression and association.

Whereas UK Members of Parliament are reportedly contacted by lobbyists 100 times a week, in the US, lobbying is a major Washington industry; there are 17,000 federal lobbyists based there, many on 'K Street', and $3.27bn was estimated to have been spent on US federal lobbying in 2011.

▼ LOBBYING, 1997 – 2010 $30,417,000 SPENT ❶

LOBBYING ON BEHALF OF BAE SYSTEMS

FIRM HIRED	AMOUNT
Northpoint Strategies	$4,280,000
Baker, Donelson et al	$1,980,000
Robison International	$1,220,000
Hvisk & Fix	$1,070,000
American Defense International	$1,050,000
King & Spalding	$970,000
Podesta Group	$880,000
Martin Fisher Thomoson	$860,000

Names of Lobbyists: Janet L Powell, Robert Fitch, Randall L West, Steven M Hvisk, Herbert Lee Dixson, Frank C Collins III, James Fraser, Michael Herson, Donald J Fix, Heather Gagne.

Most Frequently Disclosed Lobbying Issues: Defense, Fed Budget & Appropriations, Energy & Nuclear Power, Transportation, Trade, Government Issues, Homeland Security, Taxes, Aerospace, Law Enforcement & Crime

Force campaign contributions to be made on an anonymous basis, and see how quickly they dry up.

The Honest Leadership and Open Government Act of 2007 requires lobbyists to file a semi-annual report of donations and contributions, along with a certification that the filer understands the gift and travel rules of both the House and the Senate.[49] The website Influence Explorer collates lobbying spend.[50] (As an example, the $30.4m spent by BAE on US lobbying firms between 1997 and 2010 can be seen in the screenshot above.)

Because candidates need cash to campaign effectively, lobbyists can seek to influence/buy votes (depending on your point of view on this) by making campaign donations. Much of the lobbying activity that takes place in the US would probably be prosecuted under the FCPA if it took place overseas, and would also fall foul of the Bribery Act. Nevertheless, lobbying thrives in the US and, because the legislators are the recipients of lobbying largesse, it is unlikely to change any time soon.

Jack Abramoff[51]

Jack Abramoff was a Republican lobbyist based in Washington DC, and was widely regarded as one of the most influential 'super-lobbyists'. Made famous by Kevin Spacey in the 2010 film *Casino Jack*, his name is now is now inexorably linked with political corruption. One of Abramoff's key interests was lobbying for casinos on some Native American reservations. The Choctaw and other tribes complained that they had been paying millions of dollars to Abramoff but were getting little in return. The resulting FBI investigation of Abramoff's lobbying business 'Operation Rainmaker,' uncovered donations worth $1.7m to more than 200 members of Congress on behalf of a number of commercial interests.

Two of the Republican Party's most powerful figures, Bob Ney and Tom DeLay, were at the centre of the investigation for their close financial ties to Abramoff. With Ney, for example, the FBI uncovered evidence that he received substantial campaign contributions from Abramoff's clients, lavish trips, meals and drinks, and tickets to sporting events and concerts. In exchange, Ney agreed to support and oppose legislation at Abramoff's request, and influence decisions of people in Executive Branch agencies.

In January 2006, Abramoff pleaded guilty to fraud, tax evasion and conspiracy to bribe public officials, as part of a deal for his role in an earlier fraud involving the purchase of the 'cruise to nowhere' SunCruz Casinos operation, but Abramoff initially remained free 'so that he [could] continue to aid in the investigations that swirl around him and his former lobbying practice'. He began his sentence in 2006. In September 2008, he was sentenced to a further four years in prison for these corruption offences.

Ney entered into a plea agreement in September 2006, admitting to conspiracy to violate the federal laws governing mail and wire fraud, making false statements and post-employment restrictions for former Congressional staff members. He was sentenced to five years in prison, and agreed to cooperate in an investigation into his dealings with members of Congress. There are still people to be charged with public corruption as a result of Operation Rainmaker.

The lobbying conflict of interest was first addressed by Congress in 1907, when it enacted the Tillman Act. This made it 'unlawful for any national bank, or any corporation organized by authority of any laws of Congress, to make money contribution in connection with any election to any political office'. Much has happened since 1907, with numerous court challenges, more rules and more loopholes. Currently the Bipartisan Campaign Reform Act 2002 (known as the McCain–Feingold Act) regulates lobbying activity.[52] This allows campaign donations, but with limitations – unregulated contributions to national political parties are banned, for example – although its impact is being eaten away with various legal challenges trying to have it ruled unconstitutional.

Lobbyists would argue that giving money to political groups in exchange for hoped-for favourable legislative or political decisions is entirely legitimate, and contributions by lobbyists and individuals define and shape the priorities of officials. It is the absence of a specific and definite quid pro quo – a vote in exchange for a specific amount of money – that prevents lobbying moving into the realm of bribery.

'Bundling' campaign contributions

The McCain–Feingold law sets a cap of $2000 from an individual to a single candidate in a single election. However, switched-on lobbyists use money 'bundling' to great effect when they funnel multiple contributions to campaigns without running foul of the campaign rules. (George W. Bush made especially effective use this during his presidential races, with those who contributed $100,000 being deemed 'Bush Pioneers', and those who contributed $200,000 'Bush Rangers'.[53]) But whatever amount the bundlers deliver, the fundraising buys them access and power, and they want and expect something in return – this might just be a photo opportunity they can show off at the golf club, or it might be a more tangible quid pro quo.

The law and bribery

In the US, statute 18 USC § 201 governs the offence of bribery of public officials and witnesses. It is similar to the Bribery Act in that it covers both active and passive bribery, shown in square brackets below. The section makes it an offence to:

'offer, promise or give [or demand, seek, receive or accept] a thing of value to [by] a public official or one who has been selected to be a public official with corrupt intent, or intent to influence [or be influenced] an official act, or fraud on the United States, or an act in violation of an official's lawful duty.'[54]

(A public official can include anyone who occupies a position of public trust with official federal responsibilities.)

Illegal gratuity

The very next section of the code sets out the elements for another type of bribery, commonly referred to as 'illegal gratuity'. An illegal gratuity is a less serious offence than bribery, although it also applies to *former*, as well as present and future public officials. While bribery requires a specific intent to give or receive something in exchange for a specific official act (the quid pro quo), an illegal gratuity only requires that the gratuity be given *for or because of* an official act.

Europe and the UK

'The powerful will always beat a path to politicians' doors. A crime is committed only when they are flung open in exchange for money. That is where lobbying ends and corruption begins.'

The Guardian, March 2010[55]

In some countries, political parties are run solely from subscriptions and membership fees; others, such as France, ban the corporate funding of political parties. (Instead, the government funds parties according to their success in elections and allows funding of political 'campaigns' only up to certain limits.)

In the UK, lobbyists' contact with ministers and MPs is currently regulated through a number of non-statutory codes of conduct. Election campaigns and policies are party affairs, and politicians are reliant on party support for renomination. Money is therefore less of a factor in London and Brussels than in the US. Furthermore, strong party discipline means that the party persuades an MP, not pressure groups, since MPs only have a free vote on 'matters of conscience'. Lobbyists clearly do have some influence: they can persuade MPs to question ministers, or to table a motion or bill calling for change that will help gauge the level of parliamentary support – although again, more on matters where there is no distinct party line.

Lobbying crossed the line in the 'cash for questions' scandal, where MPs agreed to take money in return for tabling parliamentary questions. This led, via the Nolan Committee, to the reform of UK bribery legislation (see pages 11 and 13).

Pressure groups also find it difficult to exert influence in the judiciary, because the doctrine of parliamentary sovereignty puts strict limits on the power of the courts. Any law passed is by definition constitutional – the UK courts can declare ministers to have acted beyond the powers bestowed upon them, but there is no equivalent of the US judicial review of legislation.

The 'revolving door'

> 'Strange as it may seem, the British system allows current members of parliament to be paid consultants to business interests and they are free to act as advocates for their employers, often doubling or tripling their income. Behaviour that would be classed as corruption in Africa or Asia or Latin America somehow passes as legal lobbying when it happens in the West.'
>
> *The New Internationalist*[56]

In most jurisdictions, including the US and the UK, former MPs can act as lobbyists, and can move between positions in government and industry, and back again, through the so-called 'revolving door': sometimes seemingly being on both side of the door at once.

In March 2010, five former UK Labour Party cabinet ministers were filmed by an undercover reporter posing as a representative of a lobbying firm. They were discussing the terms of their services for consulting and sitting on an advisory boards. One described himself as 'a bit like a cab for hire – at up to £5000 a day' and claimed to have access to a lot of confidential information 'because of his links to No. 10'. Another was reported as saying that they could 'help a client who needs a particular regulation removed' but later denied it. All three former MPs were stripped of their parliamentary passes and reprimanded for 'breaching rules preventing ex-politicians from cashing in on their privileged access to parliament to make money as lobbyists'.[57]

Despite the industry's attempts to self-regulate through voluntary codes of conduct, some lobbyists still use tactics that many find unacceptable. The coalition agreement published by the Conservative–Liberal Democrat government in May 2010 said that the government would introduce a statutory register that would require people to register as lobbyists and to register the identity of the clients they were acting on behalf of. Legislation is expected in 2012. Many reformers would also like to see the introduction of an extended cooling-off period before elected politicians and senior officials can work as lobbyists, which should go some way to preventing privileged access to decision makers. The US rules were modified in this direction by Barack Obama when he took office. It is still too early to assess how effective these measures have been in stemming corruption – but, needless to say, the lobbying industry still thrives!

The 'cash for influence' scandal in 2009, involving politicians from the UK's House of Lords, shows a rather more lenient treatment: parliamentary privileges were taken away for a whole six months.

The House of Lords' 'Cash for Influence' Scandal[58]

The House of Lords is the upper chamber in the UK parliamentary system, where non-elected peers review and advise on proposed legislation. Two of the fundamental principles in the Code of Conduct for peers are that members 'must never accept any financial inducement as an incentive or reward for exercising parliamentary influence' and 'must not vote on any bill or motion, or ask any question in the House or a committee, or promote any matter, in return for payment or any other material benefit (the 'no paid advocacy' rule).'

Two peers, Lord Taylor and Lord Truscott, were found guilty of misconduct in 2009 after telling an undercover reporter that they would take money for helping to alter legislation. Lord Taylor was recorded saying that 'some companies that I work with would pay me £100,000 a year...That's cheap for what I do for them.' Neither actually received any money.

They had their membership of the House of Lords withdrawn for six months (which is the first time that this has happened since Oliver Cromwell threw out supporters of King Charles I in 1643). They will not face criminal charges as the police have already dropped their investigation.

Further reading

Alliance for Lobbying Transparency: http://bit.ly/qIdl7j (http://www.lobbyingtransparency.org/).

Collora, M.A. and Ryan, J.M., Sentencing in political corruption cases, Dwyer & Collora LLP. Available from: http://bit.ly/olqTcf (http://www.collorallp.com/law-articles/business/political-corruption-sentencing.aspx).

House of Commons Public Administration Select Committee, *Lobbying: Access and Influence in Whitehall*, first report of session 2008–09, 9 December 2008. Available from:

http://bit.ly/nGc1Rg (http://www.publications.parliament.uk/pa/cm200809/cmselect/cmpubadm/36/36i.pdf).

Maer, L., Lobbying, House of Commons Library Note, 27 January 2011. Available from: http://bit.ly/nY3J4W (http://www.parliament.uk/documents/commons/lib/research/briefings/snpc-04633.pdf).

Yost, Jr., M.A., The history of campaign finance reform, Towson University, 1 December 1999. Available from: http://bit.ly/reTtmT (http://www.juntosociety.com/government/campaignfinance.htm).

Bribery in the Media

> 'Eighty per cent of my wardrobe was free; I haven't really bought clothes, unless they've been heavily discounted, for the past 15 years. I have eaten in some of the world's best restaurants (£300 a head), been on regular holidays that include first-class flights (a whole package could hit the £15,000 mark), get my hair cut by celebrity stylists (£250 every six weeks), and I've never once had to worry about the bill afterwards.'
>
> Unnamed fashion journalist, reported
> by *The Times*, August 2011

Transparency needs to reign supreme whether in business, sport, politics or the media. Fortunately, the overt bribing of journalists to buy stories is a practice that has all but died out in the modern press, at least in the more economically developed countries. In the last couple of years, though, the activities of the media have once again come under intense scrutiny as journalists have been seen to cross the line of acceptable conduct. The law-breaking has involved both active bribery (paying for information to go into stories) and passive bribery (receiving money or favours to influence the direction that articles will take).

Freebies and junkets – the journalists' little secret

Any kind of review piece, where a journalist needs to sample or use a product and give their opinion on them, makes any journalist's integrity vulnerable. Fashion is one of the most susceptible areas for manipulation, but any reviewer of books, travel, wine, cars, music, technology and consumer goods is likely to face continual temptation. Gifts or loans of products are a fundamental part of the review cycle. Virtually every major publication has received review items for years and without them, the vast majority of review-centric publications and columns could not take place.

But the journalist's opinions are highly influential. Public relations agencies exist to try to influence these opinions with 'goodie bags' of free items at product launches. Most journalists are above reproach, but the symbiotic relationship with PRs pushing the freebies can be difficult to resist.

Reciprocity, started by 'gifts' of review items from a retailer, makes a writer more likely to write positively about a product than they would otherwise. Such freebies can be subtly corrupting, undermining a reporter's detachment and objectivity.

> '"When we sign a new label, usually the first thing we do is organise a send-out to our favourite celebrities," a prominent fashion PR told me. "Top of the list in the UK is obviously Alexa, followed by Kate Middleton, Jade Williams and Karen Gillan. If you get a product on any of those girls, the label is basically an instant success and the celeb keeps the clothes. Job done."'
>
> Unnamed fashion journalist, reported by *The Times*, August 2011

An absolute prohibition on freebies is still not common practice throughout the UK print industry; some journalists, such as the fashion journalist above, supplement their wages with thousands of pounds' worth of free goods that they see as the perks their jobs. Fortunately, the trend seems to be towards increased transparency. An increasing number of print publications now have strict return policies and return or give away review items or freebies. Similarly, travel journalists invariably disclose that a trip has been paid for, or else the newspaper picks up the tab.

Journalist codes
Readers are increasingly savvy and cynical. They expect to be told whether writers have a financial interest in the company that they are talking about, or whether they have received free products, so that they can, if necessary, take the reviews with a pinch of salt. Indeed, such disclosure, in meaningful form, is essential to safeguard the trustworthiness of the media.

Journalists are taught the importance of remaining unbiased and ethical: the National Union of Journalists' Code of Conduct sets out the main principles of British and Irish journalism. The 2007 code states that a journalist:[59]

'Does not by way of statement, voice or appearance endorse by advertisement any commercial product or service save for the promotion of her/his own work or of the medium by which she/he is employed.'

Another issue faced by fashion journalists is the 'no plug, no interview' dilemma, where they are effectively forced by PR agents to promote products in order to secure interviews. In effect, they are told that they can get an interview with a fashion A-lister as long as they mention that celebrity's latest perfume, handbag, fashion collection or whatever.

The new (August 2011) editorial code at *The Guardian* aims to stop this, stating that:

'Journalists should not agree to promote through copy, photographs or footnotes the financial interests of prospective interviewees or contributors, or their sponsors, as a means of securing access to them.'[60]

Bloggers and journalists

The internet has spawned the amateur journalist. Some bloggers are highly successful professional journalists, included by President Obama at White House press conferences; most, however, are without journalism training and have not been imbued with the ethical background that anyone with a journalism degree should have. The 'old style' print media employs journalists who are answerable to editors of major corporate institutions. Most bloggers are entirely independent, even though they are trusted sources of unbiased recommendations for many people. Many bloggers believe that they deserve a chance to profit from their writing just like the professionals do, and have become very mercenary – demanding cash, paid travel to conferences or free samples in return for posts or links. (Or, more recently and more worryingly, threatening bad reviews if the vendors refuse.)

In December 2009, the US Federal Trade Commission (FTC) updated its 'Guide Concerning the Use of Endorsements and Testimonials in Advertising' to take into account internet endorsements by bloggers. Under the new rules, 'cash or in-kind payment to review a product' is considered an endorsement, and any endorsements must be clearly disclosed. Failing to disclose endorsements can now attract a fine of up to $11,000 per incidence or post. This applies to blogs, Twitter, Facebook and other forms of new media promotion, as well as celebrity endorsements. So if celebrities endorse a product and make false or unsubstantiated claims, or don't disclose 'material connections' between themselves and the advertisers in ads and outside the context of the ads (talk shows, social media, etc.), these celebrities can be held liable under the FTC rules.

Anntaylor.com: Relationships with Bloggers[61]

The women's fashion retailer Ann Taylor invited fashion bloggers to preview a summer 2010 collection, promising that those writing about the event would be entered into a 'mystery gift card drawing' where they could win between $50 and $500. The invitation explained that bloggers must submit their posts to the company within 24 hours in order to find out the value of their gift.

The FTC made public its investigation into Ann Taylor and wrote to its management, although it declined to take any action. The FTC was particularly concerned about marketing campaigns that appear to be 'grassroots' but are actually carefully choreographed and bloggers fail to disclose that they received gifts for posting blog content about that event.

Many bloggers and journalists though are moving also towards full disclosure:

> 'I don't accept any money, free products or anything else of value from the companies whose products I cover, or from their public relations or advertising agencies. I also don't accept trips, speaking fees or product discounts from companies whose products I cover, or from their public relations or advertising agencies. I don't serve as a consultant to any companies, or serve on any corporate boards or advisory boards.
>
> I do occasionally take a free T-shirt from these companies, but my wife hates it when I wear them, as she considers them ugly.'

> Walt Mossberg, author of the 'Personal Technology' column in *The Wall Street Journal*, whose ethics and openness are unfortunately not shared by all his journalist colleagues[62]

Financial journalism

Financial journalists write about company transactions that may be just about to happen, and may be highly price-sensitive. This means that there is a clear opportunity to trade on inside information, or manipulate the price of shares (in a 'pump-and-dump scheme') for their own gain. Because information in the City is worth real money, the Financial Services Authority (FSA) exists to ensure that such information is not abused and that insider trading does not go unpunished.[63]

The *Daily Mirror*'s 'City Slickers'[64]

Anil Bhoyrul and James Hipwell were journalists on the *Daily Mirror*'s 'City Slickers' share-tipping column in the 1990s and into early 2000. In 2000, Bhoyrul and Hipwell bought shares in Viglen Technology, an electronics firm owned by Sir Alan Sugar, the day before they tipped the company in their column. They sold out at a profit once the share price had risen. In effect, they were stealing from their own readers.

They were subsequently prosecuted and found guilty under the Financial Services Act of 'conspiring to profit by creating a misleading impression as to the value of a company'. Their defence had revolved around a claim that 'everyone was at it'.

The *Daily Mirror*'s editor at the time, Piers Morgan, also admitted to buying Viglen shares at the same time. Although criticized by the Press Complaints Commission, he was cleared by a DTI inquiry of any wrongdoing.

Payola

US Federal law requires that broadcasters must disclose commercial sponsorship, specifying that:[65]

'All matter broadcast by any radio station for which money, service or other valuable consideration is directly or indirectly paid, or promised to or charged or accepted by, the station so broadcasting, from any person, shall, at the time the same is so broadcast, be announced as paid for or furnished, as the case may be, by such person.'

Payola is the practice of record companies paying radio stations to play a specific song. The practice is permitted, but it must be disclosed on the air as being sponsored airtime rather than appearing as being part of the normal day's broadcast. Penalties for payola violations can be as high as $250,000 and can threaten a station's licence.

Use of agents
Payola has existed since the advent of pop music, and was rife in the 1970s and '80s. Radio stations and record promoters thought that they could get around the payola problem by paying 'independent promoters' to give the radio stations 'promotion payments'; but as recently as 2005, former New York Attorney General Eliot Spitzer indicted companies engaging in pay-for-play practices and settled out of court for a total of $30m with Sony BMG Music Entertainment, Warner Music Group, Universal Music Group and EMI. The move was welcomed by independent record labels, who thought that this would allow them more access to airtime.

Sony BMG: Avoiding Payola Rules[66]

In 2005, Sony BMG Music Entertainment, one of the world's leading record companies and owner of a number of major record labels, agreed to stop making payments and providing expensive gifts to radio stations and their employees in return for airplay for the company's songs.

The inducements or 'payola,' took several forms:

- outright bribes to radio programmers, including expensive holidays, electronics and other valuable items

- contest giveaways for stations' audiences
- payments to radio stations to cover operational expenses
- retention of middlemen, known as independent promoters, as conduits for illegal payments
- payments for 'spin programs', or airplay under the guise of advertising.

To disguise a pay-off to a radio programmer at KHTS, for example, Epic Records (part of Sony BMG) called a flat-screen television a 'contest giveaway.'

Another Epic employee who was trying to promote the group Audioslave to a Clear Channel programmer asked in an email: 'WHAT DO I HAVE TO DO TO GET AUDIOSLAVE ON WKSS THIS WEEK?!!? Whatever you can dream up, I can make it happen.'

The company paid a penalty of $10m to settle the investigation, acknowledging the improper conduct and pledging to abide by a higher standard. The penalty was distributed to not-for-profit entities funding programmes aimed at music education and appreciation.

Product placement

> 'What we are doing is really immersing products into programmes...so that they really feel like it is part of the show.'
>
> Guy Sousa, Executive Vice-President for advertising sales at Fox Cable Sports[67]

American Idol judges drink out of Coca-Cola branded cups in a clearly paid-for placement, but without notification.

The law is clear on the point that stations must identify content sponsors so that audiences can distinguish a sponsored message from the surrounding programming. There are, however, major exemptions, and there has been little action to date on product placement on television. I predict that this is set for tightening up in the next few years.

Paying for information

The 2011 scandal over journalists illegally obtaining information led to the closure of the UK's largest circulation newspaper and questions being asked about media ownership, the police, relationships between politicians and journalists, as well as, of course, bribery.

Newspapers have always used undercover means to obtain certain stories. Acting more like private detectives than traditional journalists, they have followed people, eavesdropped on conversations or pretended to be someone they are not. And when they have been unable or unwilling to put into practice the 'dark arts' themselves, they have paid professional investigators to do it. (Which, to the extent that a crime has been committed, scarcely insulates them, as they would likely be liable anyway as a co-conspirator.)

Unlawfully obtained information
It is scary that so much personal information can be found out about anyone for a price, through the small but well-developed industry that specializes in obtaining all manner of details from confidential and usually inaccessible sources. In May 2006, the UK's Information Commissioner exposed this trade in personal details and said that journalists were among the main customers of these shadowy techniques. His report revealed that 305 journalists had been identified during one investigation as customers who were driving the illegal trade in confidential personal information.

The 'suppliers' of this information usually work within the security industry as corporate sleuths, private investigators and tracing agents. Most investigators operate within the boundaries of the law. Others, who are often able to obtain the most interesting information, do not. Investigators use several methods to obtain confidential information, of which the most widely used (ignoring the many euphemisms) are bribery, pretexting (also known as 'blagging') and hacking.

Bribery does still takes place, although the most useful information – that contained on government computers – is increasingly inaccessible. In days gone by most Fleet Street journalists knew a few policemen who would provide the occasional nugget of information, but this has all but died out. The Police National Computer does not allow anonymous logins so any police officer obtaining information (for example, whether someone has a criminal record) leaves a clear audit trail, which could result in them both losing their job and getting a prison sentence. The risk is seldom worth it.

Knowingly or recklessly obtaining or disclosing personal data or information without the consent of the data controller is an offence in most jurisdictions, and in the UK is contrary to Section 55 of the Data Protection Act 1998. This Act however offers a defence that is available to anyone who shows that obtaining the information was in the public interest. Investigators are used extensively by lawyers looking at the resources of those suspected of fraud and civil crimes as a prelude to taking action against them: the justification being that taking action against fraudsters is in the public interest.

Most investigative journalists will use undercover methods to obtain information, and indeed the most groundbreaking modern stories have been obtained only through subterfuge. The BBC, for example, is governed by editorial guidelines that set out that any invasion of privacy must be proportionate and justifiable as having a clear public interest.

Hacking and blagging

> '"Investigative journalists are very often chasing after villains
> or paedophiles, or someone who has committed crime – if
> the only way to get information is through blagging then I
> think it's acceptable,"' said the reporter, who asked to remain
> anonymous.
>
> But he added there was a "grey area" where the public
> interest was not so clear. "In terms of all of the Gordon
> Brown stuff, I think it's completely unacceptable," he said.'
>
> Former *News of the World* journalist[68]

Hacking means to manipulate a computer to gain unauthorized access. Hacking takes place to obtain unlawful access
to emails and voicemails. (In the context of voicemails,
for example, many users simply do not change the default
password – so anyone with a knowledge of the phone
number, and the default settings of the network, can access
voicemail in the same way as the user.)

Pretexting or blagging relies more on 'social engineering',
or persuasion. Blagging is the practice of pretending to be
someone else in order to get personal information about
them – for example, from their bank, doctor or the tax
office. Often it is done by impersonating the individual
themselves, or someone else who has a legitimate need
for the information, making up a multitude of devious and
imaginative stories.

Hewlett-Packard: Blagging in the Boardroom[69]

In September 2006, the chair of the HP board was forced to
step down after it emerged that investigators looking into a
leak in the HP boardroom had obtained the phone records of
a number of journalists and fellow directors.

In a classic case of pretexting, the investigators impersonated the subjects to dupe the phone companies into providing the personal information.

The damage to the reputation of Hewlett-Packard and the subsequent senior-level resignations clearly demonstrate the risks that any reputable company takes in making use of private information obtained by illegal means.

Information Commissioner Christopher Graham, describes blagging as a 'modern scourge'. The Criminal Justice Act 2008 provides for a maximum two-year sentence for illegally obtaining personal information without its owner's consent.

The *News of the World* scandals

> 'The *News of the World* doesn't pretend to do anything other than reveal big stories and titillate and entertain the public, while exposing crime and hypocrisy.'[70]

The *News of the World* (NOTW) was a UK national Sunday tabloid newspaper published by News International, a subsidiary of Rupert Murdoch's News Corporation. With a reputation for celebrity sex scandals, it had the largest circulation of any UK newspaper. It was also known for pushing the boundaries of data protection laws, making use of a network of police officers who accepted bribes, impersonators used to fool interviewees and hacking.

The 'Fake Sheikh', Mazher Mahmood, became Britain's most notorious undercover reporter during his time at the newspaper, exposing the activities of celebrities. One of his highest-profile stings was the Countess of Wessex, who was exposed as abusing her royal connections as head of her PR firm, from which she later resigned.[71]

In 2004, the newspaper's royal editor, Clive Goodman, wrote a story about Prince William injuring his knee. The information was not in the public domain and Buckingham Palace suspected that the Prince's voicemail was hacked to get the story. After a police investigation, Goodman was jailed for four months for instructing a private investigator, Glenn Mulcaire, to intercept voicemail messages on royal aides' phones. Mulcaire was jailed for six months.

The NOTW maintained that only Goodman had been involved and hacking was an isolated practice, but allegations and problems started to mount. The paper settled actions brought by Gordon Taylor (the former chief executive of the English Professional Footballers' Association) and publicist Max Clifford that, if they had gone to trial, could have revealed the identity of other journalists involved with phone hacking. The hacking revelations moved outside the celebrity circuit, with allegations that relatives of dead UK soldiers and of terrorist bombings may also have had their phones hacked. The police now apparently have a list of 4000 possible targets of hacking, including celebrities, sport stars, politicians and victims of crime. The worst incident involved the missing schoolgirl, Milly Dowler, later found dead, whose voicemail messages were alleged to have been accessed.

The NOTW finally admitted to intercepting voicemails in April 2011 after years of rumour that the practice was widespread, and amid intense pressure from those who believed they had been victims. In the wake of the resulting massive adverse publicity, advertisers withdrew from the paper, which soon became unviable. It ceased publication in July 2011. Along with several other former executives, CEO and former editor Rebekah Brooks and former editor Andy Coulson were arrested in connection with 'suspicion of conspiring to intercept communications, contrary to Section 1(1) Criminal Law Act 1977 and on suspicion of corruption allegations contrary to Section 1 of the Prevention of Corruption Act 1906'.

At the date of publication, the scandal is far from over. However it pans out, it is certain that the various enquiries now taking place will result in a dramatic reduction in bribery and blagging by the media, and for more criminal severe penalties for those who continue to do or request it.

Further reading

BBC News, Phone hacking scandal. Available from: http://bbc.in/n7eC1f (http://www.bbc.co.uk/news/uk-14045952).

Federal Trade Commission, FTC publishes final guides governing endorsements, testimonials. Available from: http://1.usa.gov/pzCamx (http://www.ftc.gov/opa/2009/10/endortest.shtm).

I didn't pay for 80 per cent of my wardrobe, *The Times*, 23 August 2011. Available from: http://thetim.es/qzjuYO (http://www.thetimes.co.uk/tto/life/fashion/article3142047.ece).

Information Commissioner's Office, *What Price Privacy Now? The First Six Months Progress in Halting the Unlawful Trade in Confidential Personal Information*, 2006. Available from: http://bit.ly/nyOMZ7 (http://www.ico.gov.uk/upload/documents/library/corporate/research_and_reports/ico-wppnow-0602.pdf).

Chapter 3

What Are the Key Sets of Rules that Govern International Bribery?

Introduction

Some countries – most notably the US – have been vigorously and successfully prosecuting bribery for over 20 years. Other countries – in fact, almost all the rest – have been much less active, despite the fact that most have now enacted their own anti-bribery laws.

There are clear differences between each country's laws, and it's not therefore possible to describe in a single book – at least not one designed to be easily portable and have a modicum of readability – the detail of every single anti-corruption statute. That in any event is something for the specialist lawyer. All is not lost, though, for the purposes of this book. At heart, most of the various laws have the same basic message: don't pay bribes to get things done. For the needs of an international business or compliance specialist, I have found that there are really only three variations on that theme you need to be familiar with, and those rules set the bar as to how companies should be behaving in almost all situations.

The US Foreign Corrupt Practices Act 1977

The first set of rules is the US Foreign Corrupt Practices Act, or FCPA. Enacted in 1977, but not vigorously enforced until the 1990s, it is one of the most aggressively policed and feared pieces of US legislation. The FCPA is designed to deter and punish individuals and companies that make payments to foreign officials to assist in obtaining or retaining business.

The FCPA prohibits the bribery of foreign officials (and of course, being a US statute, this means officials foreign to the US). It applies and is enforced against the worldwide activities of all individuals and companies with a US nexus.

Fines and penalties under the FCPA have recently become massive, with Siemens (a German company found to have been bribing in places like Vietnam) having paid the current record of $800m to settle the FCPA charges brought against it.

The FCPA is not, however, just an anti-bribery statute. It also imposes record-keeping and internal control requirements that can be entirely separate grounds for liability and need not have a link to bribery or corruption. Hence, there are two fundamental and quite separate elements to the FCPA that the government usually pursues simultaneously.

The UK Bribery Act 2010

The second set of rules is the UK Bribery Act, which received Royal Assent on 8 April 2010 but did not become fully operational until 1 July 2011. The wording of the statute is arguably even stricter than that of the FCPA, although official guidance published subsequently softens its tough exterior. The Act applies to both giving and receiving bribes, in both the public and private sectors, in the UK and worldwide. Although the UK authorities are not generally prosecuting as harshly as those in the US, all companies carrying on business in any form in the UK need to comply with the provisions of the Bribery Act.

The OECD Convention of 1997

The third set is the OECD Convention. The mission of the Organization for Economic Co-operation and Development is to promote policies that will improve the people's economic and social wellbeing. Its members comprise 34 of the highest-income countries in the world – Estonia became the OECD's latest member in December 2010. The OECD Convention on Combating Bribery of Foreign Public

Officials in International Business Transactions (abbreviated here as the 'OECD Convention') is not a law that applies to companies or individuals, but rather an agreement between nations to enact domestic legislation to prohibit the bribery of foreign public officials. The OECD Convention was signed in 1997 and became effective once properly ratified in 1999.

Because though there is flexibility in the form that the enabling legislation takes, the national bribery laws within each signatory country will differ, and will depend on each country's constitution, legal system, existing laws and procedures. The laws expected to be enacted in response to a convention can certainly be tougher than the OECD requirements (as is the case with the Bribery Act), but the OECD Convention sets out the minimum requirements that the law must take. Each country's progress towards enacting the requirements of the Convention is monitored by a regular system of self-evaluation and mutual evaluation by its peers from the OECD.

In the US, Congress enacted the OECD Convention through the International Anti-bribery and Fair Competition Act of 1998, which became part of the FCPA. The UK was some way behind; although it enacted legislation to criminalize foreign bribery, it did not fully comply with its obligations until the Bribery Act was finally enacted in 2011.

The OECD Convention has now been adopted by 38 countries at the date of writing (the 34 full members of the OECD plus Argentina, Brazil, Bulgaria and South Africa).[72] In May 2011 the OECD invited the Russian Federation to join its Working Group on Bribery and accede to the Convention, although this is not yet ratified.[73] The rules set out in the OECD Convention therefore provide an excellent grounding as to the minimum that a company is likely to find in those countries that are signatories of the OECD Convention.

The approach that I have therefore taken in this book is to look in some detail at those three sets of rules. If a company complies with all these rules, which substantially overlap anyway, then its executives are likely complying with best practice internationally.

An Essential Summary of the FCPA

Congress enacted the FCPA in 1977, and slotted it into the United States Code (USC) at Title 15 §§ 78dd-1 onwards. There are five main sections that deal with bribery:

- 78dd-1 prohibits foreign bribery by issuers (also known as Section 30A Securities & Exchange Act 1934)
- 78dd-2 prohibits foreign bribery by domestic concerns
- 78dd-3 prohibits foreign bribery by persons other than issuers or domestic concern (this clause amended the FCPA to include the 'any person' provision and was added in 1998, to give effect to the OECD Convention)
- 78m contains the accounting provisions (also known as Section 13 Securities & Exchange Act 1934)
- 78ff deals with penalties for bribery.

The FCPA's two key clauses are 78dd-2 (anti-bribery provisions) and 78m (accounting provisions), both of which are reproduced in Appendix 1. Clauses 78dd-1, 78dd-2, and 78dd-3 are substantively identical in the things they prohibit, differing only in who they apply to.

The FCPA has a two-pronged reach. Not only does it prohibit paying bribes, but with its accounting provisions it attempts to cut off the lifeblood of bribery by outlawing the accounting tools that are necessary to conceal it. To make things even more complicated, the bribery elements and accounting elements apply to different classes of persons and companies. Furthermore, breach of the anti-bribery provisions amounts to a crime, whereas a breach of the accounting provisions amounts to only – although it can become a very expensive 'only'! – a civil wrong.

I deal in detail with the companies and persons that are subject to the FCPA in Question 10.

Let's now look at the two 'prongs' of the FCPA in turn.

What are the anti-bribery provisions of the FCPA?

The recent trial of American Rice Inc.'s executives David Kay and Douglas Murphy (see page 76) is unusual in that it is one of the few FCPA cases that has been taken all the way to trial and then appeal. Most FCPA cases against companies end up settling as part of a plea bargain well before trial; this case is instructive as the US Court of Appeals reviewed the case for the second time in October 2007 and, in doing so, gave a great précis of the essential components of an FCPA case.

The court held that an individual or company commits a crime under the FCPA if they:

'wilfully and corruptly offer, authorize, promise, or give money, or anything of value to any foreign official for purposes of either:

- influencing any act or decision of such foreign official in their official capacity [or]
- inducing such foreign official to do or omit to do any act in violation of the lawful duty of such official [or]
- securing any improper advantage

in order to assist such [company] in obtaining or retaining business for or with, or directing business to, any person.'

What types of payments are covered by the FCPA?
The FCPA does not only apply to paying cash bribes. The legislation is widely drafted and prohibits paying, offering,

promising to pay, or authorizing to pay or offer money or anything of value – directly or indirectly. This could include all manner of tangible and intangible property. I have seen cases where bribes have comprised:

- cash and cash equivalents
- loans
- promises of future employment
- travelling costs and holidays
- donations to favourite charities
- scholarships and school fees for children
- vehicles and fuel
- paying for shopping trips
- information
- special discounts
- testimony of a witness
- the services of prostitutes
- frozen chickens[*]
- pairs of shoes.[†]

'From early 2004, Avery China's then-national manager for the Reflectives Division ... sought to obtain business through the Wuxi Institute. As part of that effort, in January 2004, an Avery China sales manager accompanied four Wuxi Institute officials to a meeting and bought each a pair of shoes with a combined value of approximately $500.'

---

[*]One ruse in African customs departments in particular is to find a reason to delay shipments of perishable food, which, if not cleared quickly, will spoil. The bribes sought by the corrupt customs officers are a portion of the shipments that are taken for personal consumption by the customs officials, their families and friends.
[†]There is no lower limit to the value of the payments. In the SEC's 2009 Cease and Desist Order against Avery Dennison, although dealing with a number of different types of bribes and kickbacks, the issue of shoes was brought into the equation. (Without admitting or denying the SEC's allegations, Avery paid a civil penalty of $200,000, and disgorged gains of $319,000.[74])

As will be seen in Questions 12–14, it matters little whether the payments are made directly or indirectly through agents.

What is the FCPA's 'business purpose test'?
The FCPA prohibits payments made in order to assist a company or person to obtain, retain or direct business to any person. The term, however, deals with much more than obtaining supply contracts from foreign governments. We see in the Kay case below that the court considered that American Rice was 'obtaining or retaining business' by minimizing taxes in order for it to remain competitive.

US v. Kay : The FCPA's 'Business Purpose' Test[75]

David Kay and Douglas Murphy were senior managers of American Rice Inc., a US-based importer of rice into Haiti. During 1998 and 1999, Kay admitted to managing a scheme whereby customs officials were bribed over $500,000 to charge less import duty on rice than would normally be payable. The bribery scheme saved American Rice some $1.5m in duty and tax, and this allowed it to retain its competitive price advantage when compared to its competitors who either smuggled rice into the country and paid no import taxes at all, or paid bribes to officials in the same way. The former president, Murphy, was accused of being aware of the bribery scheme but did not stop it.

The defendants did not deny paying the bribes, but claimed that the FCPA did not apply to such payments, because the law was vague and the payments were not to 'obtain or retain business'.

The court rejected Kay's arguments, and held that bribes paid to foreign officials to unlawfully evade tax *were* covered by the FCPA. Here, by paying bribes, the company sold rice without having to pay the full amount of tax and duty, which it believed was necessary to compete with other companies, and this came within the definition of 'retaining business'.

A jury then found both men guilty. Kay was sentenced to 37 months in prison and Murphy to 63 months.

More recent cases however, such as the Panalpina-related matters (see page 440), have stretched the definition even more thinly. Many of the payments here were made to customs officials to reduce duties, expedite customs clearances or evade import regulations. In the GlobalSantaFe case, for example, the SEC alleged that by making a number of suspicious payments for these reasons, the company 'avoided costs and gained revenue'. The trend seems to be that the US government equates any behaviour that gains revenue or reduces costs generally as coming within the ambit of the FCPA.

What is corrupt intent?
To constitute a crime under the FCPA, the person making or authorizing the payment must have *corrupt intent*, and the payment must be intended to induce the recipient to misuse their official position. This can include influencing any act or decision of an official in their official capacity or in violation of their lawful duty, or inducing an official to use their influence to affect any governmental matter.

The FCPA does not require that a corrupt act succeed in its purpose, but it does require that the official who received a benefit must have been in a position to assist in some way. So entertaining a foreign official who occupies a position entirely unrelated to the activities of the company would not be a violation of the FCPA. Corrupt intent is inferred from the circumstances, regardless of direct evidence, and is often apparent from the lavishness or unusual nature of the largesse bestowed upon the official. If it relates to remuneration, for example, the fact that it was higher than market rates or could not be justified by the work performed or expertise involved, or by the fact that it was subsequently disguised or concealed, would suggest a corrupt intent.

What are the accounting provisions of the FCPA?

The record-keeping and internal control requirements of the FCPA apply only to 'issuers'. Issuers are US or foreign companies whose shares are traded on US exchanges, or which for some other reason are required to submit periodic reports to the SEC. The accounting provisions also apply to directors, employees, agents and shareholders of issuers who might be responsible for improper accounting or circumventing controls.

It is important to appreciate that the accounting provisions do not just relate to foreign corrupt payments: they relate to all payments to all recipients, and can be used against many crimes – not just against bribery.

The FCPA 'pincer'
The idea behind the accounting provisions of the FCPA is a clever one: it requires precise and accurate accounting for all payments, including bribes, which means that companies are caught between a rock and a hard place. They can't pay bribes and account accurately for them (without admitting what they are doing).

In many instances, bribes are charged not only under the anti-bribery provisions, but also under the accounting provisions, given that the payments are often falsely characterized and accounted for. A conviction under the accounting provisions does not require the prosecution to first prove that the defendant engaged in a specific act of bribery; proving that false accounts or other false documents were maintained is sufficient to convict. This makes civil prosecution under the accounting provisions potentially easier and more attractive than a criminal prosecution under the anti-bribery provisions.

The accounting provisions do not contain a materiality or lower threshold limit, which means that any transaction, however small, can trigger a breach of the accounting provisions if it is reflected incorrectly. Inadvertent mistakes in record-keeping, or insignificant or technical accounting errors that management was not aware of, would not result in prosecution. On the other hand, if management *knowingly* avoids controls, fails to put in controls in the first place or deliberately falsifies records, then this is a crime and can be dealt with under the criminal law.[76]

The accounting provisions are in two parts: 'books and records' provisions, and 'internal controls' provisions.

The 'books and records' provisions
15 USC §§ 78m (b)(2)(A), the books and records provisions, require issuers to 'make and keep books, records, and accounts, which, in reasonable detail, accurately, and fairly reflect the transactions and dispositions of the assets of the issuer.' The legislation defines records incredibly widely, to include 'accounts, correspondence, memorandums, tapes, discs, papers, books, and other documents or transcribed information of any type'.[77]

Under this provision, records must be not only quantitatively, but also qualitatively correct. This means that everything, down to the last piece of paper or last expense receipt, must be sufficiently detailed so that a third party would be able to get a complete understanding of all the significant aspects of a transaction. There must be no omissions or inaccurate or overly vague descriptions.

The 'internal controls' provisions

15 USC §§ 78m (b)(2)(B) requires issuers to devise and main-tain an adequate system of internal accounting controls so that transactions are executed in line with management's authorization.

The FCPA does not specify any particular kind of internal controls systems or give any real guidance as to how com-panies should comply with this part of the statute. It sim-ply states that the test for compliance is 'whether a system, taken as a whole, reasonably meets the statute's specified objectives'. The Act states that the accounting provisions were not designed to put an added accounting burden on businesses, but 'reasonable detail' and 'reasonable assur-ances' means such level of detail or assurance as would sat-isfy prudent officials in the conduct of their own affairs.

Lucent Technologies: Lavish Holidays for Officials Accounted for Incorrectly as Legitimate Sales Expenses[78]

Lucent Technologies was a US-based global telecoms com-pany that merged with French company Alcatel in late 2006. In December 2007 it entered into a settlement with the DOJ, paying a $1m fine, and with the SEC, paying $1.5m in civil penalties for accounting violations.

Lucent admitted that between 2000 and 2003 it paid the travel costs for approximately 315 'pre-sale' trips for Chinese government officials. Lucent spent over $10m on trips to the US for senior government officials to attend seminars and visit Lucent facilities, but included substantial elements of sightseeing, entertainment and leisure activities. They included locations such as Disneyland, Universal Studios and the Grand Canyon. Each trip typically lasted two weeks, and some cost up to $55,000.

Lucent improperly accounted for these as legitimate corpo-rate expenditure, improperly recording many of them to a

'Factory Inspection Account' (although many of the officials involved did not visit Lucent factories, or if they did, it was not a major part of the trip), or alternatively as sales, marketing, international transportation or shipping expenses.

Further reading

Question 10.

Appendix 1: The FCPA (extracts), page 484. The full text is available from: http://1.usa.gov/p8ysqQ (http://www.justice.gov/criminal/fraud/fcpa/docs/fcpa-english.pdf). You can also get the text on your smartphone – see page 525.

DOJ, Layperson's guide to the FCPA. Available from: http://1.usa.gov/qc40EJ (http://www.justice.gov/criminal/fraud/fcpa/docs/lay-persons-guide.pdf).

An Essential Summary of the Bribery Act

The Bribery Act 2010 does three things:

- It creates the core offences of bribing and being bribed, which apply equally to bribery in the public and private sectors.
- In a separate section it prohibits bribing a foreign public official with the slightly lower test of intending to influence them in order to obtain or retain business.
- It creates a brand new corporate offence of failing to prevent bribery by a commercial organization.

As to who it applies to, there is more in Question 12.

What are the core offences of the Bribery Act?

The two core offences in the Act are that of 'active bribery' [bribing] (found at Section 1 of the Act), and 'passive bribery' [being bribed] (at Section 2). Specifically, these core offences prohibit an individual, company or other incorporated entity from:

> 'offering or accepting ... directly or indirectly ... a financial or other advantage ... in connection with the improper performance of a recipient's functions.'

Like the FCPA, the Bribery Act deals with much more than just cash changing hands. The Act defines bribery in terms of giving 'an advantage'. What this means is not defined but left to the court to decide as a matter of common sense. It is likely that its reach will be wide and will be potentially be even wider than the FCPA's 'money or anything of value' described on page 484.

The core offences involve a shift from the previous law and indeed the FCPA. The Bribery Act now focuses on *intention* to produce *improper performance* of someone's duties, rather than the question of whether a payment was made *corruptly*. It does not matter whether the bribe had the intended effect; merely that the briber or the recipient intended it to cause the improper performance of the recipient's functions. Indeed, a corrupt mindset does not form a part of the Bribery Act at all.

What is 'improper performance'?

'Improper performance' is enigmatically defined as performance in breach of a 'relevant expectation'. What this means is that for an offence to be committed, the person being bribed must be:

- expected to perform the function or activity in good faith; or
- expected to perform the function or activity impartially; or
- in a position of trust.

However, the intention of the Act is to avoid catching simple breaches of contract or minor torts: so paying a security guard a higher salary to leave their existing job in order to work for a competitor would not be a bribe, because there would be no breach of impartiality or trust. Paying the same security guard to turn a blind eye while a robbery takes place would be caught, because there would be a breach of a position of trust.

The offences under the Bribery Act are divided into six separate 'cases' or scenarios. The Act itself uses these six vignettes, with the actors being:

- P – the person making the bribe
- B – the bribee, or person being bribed
- R – the requestor of a bribe
- F – the foreign public official
- C – the company or commercial organization
- A – the person associated with the company.

The Bribery Act: The core offence of paying a bribe
Section 1 of the Act defines the offence of bribery in terms of the person making the bribe, and requires an individual to know or intend that the recipient has improperly performed, or will improperly perform, their functions.

Section 1, Case 1 deals with the scenario where the person making the bribe intends it to bring about an improper performance by another person of a relevant function or activity, or to reward such improper performance.

Section 1, Case 2 is where P knows or believes that the acceptance of the advantage offered, promised or given

in itself constitutes the improper performance of a function or activity.

The Bribery Act: The core offence of being bribed

Section 2 of the Act makes it an offence to request, agree to receive or accept an advantage, whether or not the requestor, R actually receives it. It deals with four cases, labelled 3 to 6. In Cases 3, 4 and 5 there is a requirement that R takes explicit action linked with the 'improper performance' of an activity; in Case 6, there is merely the expectation that something will be received in the future.

In Section 2, Case 3, R intends improper performance to follow as a consequence of the request.

In Section 2, Case 4, the request itself amounts to improper performance of the relevant function or activity.

In Section 2, Case 5, the request is made in terms of a reward for performing the activity improperly.

Section 2, Case 6 is slightly different because it does not involve an explicit request – at least, not to start with. Instead it involves the improper performance of duties improperly, with the *expectation* that an advantage will be given at a later stage.

Those duties have just been performed improperly. I hope he gives me something

Bribing (Section 1) and receiving a bribe (Section 2) are both subject to the improper performance test. The prosecution will therefore be looking to prove that:

- a payment or advantage was made or offered
- there was the expectation of good faith, impartiality and trust in the relationship between the parties, and
- the conduct was in breach of that expectation.

In offences relating to being bribed (Cases 3–6) it does not matter whether it is R or someone else through whom R acts who requests, agrees to receive or accepts the advantage; and the advantage can be for the benefit of R or of another person.

Bribing a foreign public official

Section 6 of the Act creates a separate and discrete offence of bribing a foreign public official. The section was specifically inserted to allow the UK to comply with its obligations under the OECD Convention and closely follows the Convention's requirements.

This section makes it an offence to provide an advantage to a foreign public official with the intention of influencing them in the performance of their function as a public official, and to obtain or retain business or a business advantage.

Unlike in the case of active bribery under Section 1, the action expected from the recipient need not be improper. So the difference between Sections 1 and 6 can be summarized as follows:

- Section 1: intending to bring about an *improper* performance of duties.
- Section 6: the lesser test of intending to *influence* the performance of a public official, and intending to obtain or retain a business advantage.

The offence of bribery of a foreign public official only covers bribing, not being bribed. The offence will still be committed if the advantage is offered to someone other than the official, if it happens at the official's request or with the official's acquiescence, or if the bribe is made through a third party.

So far as bribing a foreign public official is concerned, there is the requirement to show that whatever advantage was made or promised to the official was not legitimately due under the law of the country in question. The defence – which is narrow, and will be seldom seen in practice – is where the written law applicable to the foreign official either permits or requires them to receive the advantage. Note that it refers only to the *written* law, so will exclude local customs, practice or tolerance.

Offset scenarios
An exception applies in so-called 'offset' scenarios, where a company pays for an infrastructure project, or carries out work in the local community either under the terms of a contract or simply to engender relations with the local community. Many oil companies, for example, will fund the building of schools and local amenities close to their projects. What the law is trying to do here is to make sure that payments that improve standards and living conditions are allowed, but that payments that simply line officials' pockets are not. So any offset project that incidentally benefitted an official alongside other members of the public is likely to be acceptable.

The DOJ advised in one of its Opinion Procedure Releases in relation to the equivalent test under the FCPA. The case concerned a company that had been required to provide training to officials under a Pakistani law as part of a joint venture with the government of Pakistan. The DOJ permitted the company to provide training up to the value of $250,000 per year to the officials.[79] (For more on Opinion Procedure Releases generally, see Question 19).

The corporate offence of failing to prevent bribery

Section 7 is the most important, radical and controversial provision of the Act. It creates a brand new corporate offence of failing to prevent bribery by a commercial organization.

Although corporate criminal liability is a feature of a number of jurisdictions, and there are some strict liability offences in the UK (such as health and safety, and money laundering), the test has historically been very different. In the UK, a company could only be convicted for a crime if a director who acts as its 'controlling mind' is responsible for key elements of the offence. It is very challenging to demonstrate the '*mens rea*' of an international group and prosecute successfully under this principle; it is the same under the Bribery Act. The offences under Section 1 (bribing), Section 2 (receiving a bribe) and Section 6 (bribing a foreign public official) are not strict liability offences, so in order to prosecute a company for these offences the prosecution must prove significant involvement by a controlling mind.

However, under the Bribery Act's new Section 7, an offence is committed where an associated person (A) who is associated with a company (C) bribes another person with the intention of obtaining or retaining business or an advantage in the conduct of business for C.

For the corporate offence to apply, an individual offence has to have already been committed contrary to Sections 1 or 6, and the prosecution must show that the person giving or receiving the bribe has either been found guilty or would be guilty of the offence if that person was prosecuted.

There is no corresponding corporate offence of failing to prevent taking bribes. This offence only applies to corporates *making* bribes.

The relationship between A and C

Section 8 provides that A is *associated* with C if they *perform services for* C, including as employee, agent or subsidiary.

It should be noted that the Section 7 offence does not replace the direct corporate liability for a substantive bribery offence. If it can be proved that someone representing the company's 'directing mind' causes the company to bribe, then the company might be charged under Section 1.

What is the adequate procedures defence?

The Section 7 offence is a strict liability offence, meaning that once an offence has been committed by A, then C is automatically liable. With one proviso: a company charged under Section 7 with failing to prevent bribery can defend itself by showing that it had 'adequate procedures' in place to prevent persons associated with it from paying bribes. In other words, if it can show that the bribery was carried out by a rogue employee or agent, acting alone and unauthorized, and contrary to an adequate compliance regime, then this would be an absolute defence to Section 7.

The burden for this defence is on the company to show – on the balance of probabilities – that it *did* have adequate procedures in place to prevent bribery.

As a result of considerable disquiet from business as to what exactly this meant in practice, it was one of the prerequisites of the Act (under Section 9) that corporate liability would not come into force until the UK government had published guidance on what constituted 'adequate procedures'. There is much more on adequate procedures on page 146.

Further reading

The Bribery Act 2010: http://bit.ly/piSG63 (http://www .legislation.gov.uk/ukpga/2010/23/contents). You can also get the text on your smartphone – see page 526.

The Bribery Act Guidance: http://bit.ly/nTdQB0 (http://www.justice.gov.uk/downloads/guidance/making-reviewing-law/bribery-act-2010-guidance.pdf).

Bribery Act 2010: Joint Prosecution Guidance of the Director of the Serious Fraud Office and The Director of Public Prosecutions, March 2011. http://bit.ly/ughqFa

(http://www.cps.gov.uk/legal/a_to_c/bribery_act_2010/
index.html).

An Essential Summary of the OECD Convention

What does the OECD convention provide?

The Convention prohibits the bribery of foreign public officials and, like the FCPA, also attempts to eliminate the ways
that companies conceal bribes. It therefore has both 'anti-
bribery' and 'accounting' provisions.

Anti-bribery provisions

The Convention deals only with 'active bribery'; in other
words, giving or promising a bribe. It does not deal with
any offence of receiving or soliciting a bribe. It makes it an
offence for any person or company, as well as those acting
on their behalf to:

> 'intentionally to offer, promise or give ... any undue pecuniary or
> other advantage ... to a foreign public official ...
>
> - in order that the official act or refrain from acting in relation to the
>   performance of official duties ...
> - in order to obtain or retain business or other improper advantage
>   ...
>
> in the conduct of international business.'

There is an exemption for payments permitted or required
by the written law or regulation of the foreign public official's
country, including case law.

Small 'facilitation' payments do not constitute payments made
'to obtain or retain business or other improper advantage'
within the meaning of paragraph 1 and, accordingly, companies are not required to criminalize facilitation payments.

Accounting provisions

The OECD Convention also contains recommendations concerning accounting, independent external audit and internal company controls. The precise requirements that a country might take are wisely not set out.

The OECD's further recommendations

In November 2009, the tenth anniversary of the OECD Convention, the OECD council adopted a paper entitled *Recommendation for Further Combating Bribery of Foreign Public Officials*. This sheds light on the OECD's view of current best practice. As well as encouraging countries to keep up their anti-bribery efforts, these Further Recommendations strengthen the original Convention with some key developments, as discussed below.

Facilitation payments and passive bribery

Permitted in the OECD Convention itself, the OECD has tightened its position on facilitation payments, describing them as having 'a corrosive effect'. The Further Recommendations encourage countries to prohibit their use and move to prevent solicitation of them by their public officials through an awareness-raising programme.

Tax deductibility of bribes

In order to eliminate any indirect support, the OECD recommends that countries no longer allow bribes to foreign public officials to be deductible for tax purposes.

Persons subject to the rules

Companies and other legal entities should be able to be prosecuted regardless of whether the person who originally paid the bribe or carried out the offence is prosecuted or convicted. A company cannot avoid responsibility by using intermediaries, group companies or agents to bribe on its behalf.

Further reading

Appendix 4: The OECD (extracts), page 494.

Appendix 5: Which countries have ratified the OECD?, page 496.

OECD Convention: http://bit.ly/pRsFoq (http://www.oecd.org/document/21/0,3746,en_2649_34859_2017813_1_1_1_1,00.html). You can also get the text on your smartphone – see page 526.

OECD Recommendation for Further Combating Bribery of Foreign Public Officials in International Business Transactions: http://bit.ly/oLYxQO (http://www.oecd.org/document/13/0,3746,en_2649_34859_39884109_1_1_1_1,00.html).

Chapter 4

Frequently Asked Questions

1. Is Bribery the Same as Corruption?

Short answer

Bribery can be generally thought of as a particular type, or subset, of corruption.

Longer answer

There is no universally accepted definition of either bribery or corruption. Because of the different legal environments, social histories and ethical and political values between different countries and different sets of stakeholders, it is unlikely that a single definition would ever be agreed upon anyway. In many ways, it is similar Justice Potter Stewart's 'I know it when I see it' standard of assessing what constitutes hardcore pornography.[80]

However, it is important to at least try to define bribery and corruption in some way so that society can judge people's actions as being corrupt or not. But while there has been a considerable amount written on both the legal and ethical aspects of bribery and corruption, little consensus has emerged on a good definition. Even the United Nations, when it was putting together its Convention against Corruption in 2002, could not reach agreement on a comprehensive definition of corruption during the negotiating process and moved forward by simply setting out different examples of corrupt activities.

To start with the blindingly obvious, both bribery and corruption have clearly negative connotations. (The word 'corruption' itself is derived from the Latin 'corrumpere', which means to break up, destroy, annihilate, spoil or weaken). From here, there are two principal ways of looking at it:

- The first focuses on the behavioural aspects, where corruption is seen as some sort of abuse of authority. This is the approach used by many of the anti-corruption organizations. Definitions falling into this camp include the following:
  - 'The misuse of entrusted power for private gain.' (Transparency International)[81]
  - 'Corruption is behaviour which deviates from the formal duties of a public role because of private-regarding (personal, close family, private clique) pecuniary or status gains; or violates rules against the exercise of certain types of private-regarding influence.' (Nye)[82]
  - 'The abuse of public power and influence for private ends.' (Waterbury)[83]
  - 'The abuse of public office for private gain.' (The World Bank)[84]
  - 'Actual abuse of public office for private advantage.' (OECD)[85]
- The second focuses on the relationship between the parties involved and is most commonly described as the betrayal of trust between a principal and agent if the agent makes a secret profit by keeping something of value from the principal. In this context, agents are primarily state officials, the principal is the state administration that sets the rules and entrusts the official to carry out the tasks, and the corrupters are people giving things of value to the official in the hope that they will bend the rules to favour them. This agent/principal definition formed the basis of the UK's 2003 Corruption Bill that ultimately floundered. Definitions of this type include:
  - 'Corruption ... may be defined as A) the sacrifice of the principal's interest for the agent's, or B) the violation of norms defining the agent's behaviour.' (Alam)[86]

Many of the definitions suffer because they are either overly narrow (for example, confining corruption to the public or political sector) or are too broad to really make sense to anyone interested in getting to the bottom of what corruption actually is.

The definition of the Anti-Corruption Trust of Southern Africa is one I particularly like and so I give it particular prominence.

> 'The abuse, or complicity in the abuse, of private or public power, office or resources, for personal gain.'[87]

Senior makes a similar definition, which is based on five conditions, all of which must all be satisfied simultaneously:

> Corruption occurs when a corruptor *covertly* gives a̲ *favour* to a corruptee or to a nominee to influence *action(s)* that *benefit* the corruptor or a nominee, and for which the corruptee has *authority*.

I like this because it is not limited just to the public arena and it does not refer to power as being entrusted in the official by the people. (Many of the dictators in the world are scarcely acting as agents on behalf of their people, yet would be described as notoriously corrupt.) It also incorporates an element of both the exchange of favour for something and the state of mind towards that transaction.

Corruption versus theft

In a case of simple theft, there are primarily only two parties involved: the thief and the one deprived. Corruption differs from theft in that it is a tripartite relationship, involving the corruptor, the corruptee and, crucially, others affected by the behaviour. Those directly affected are often the taxpayers and citizens in the country concerned who suffer increased taxes or sub-standard public resources.

Types of corruption
There are several distinct types of corruption:

- Conflicts of interest, which are often seen through favouring supporters (patronage), relatives (nepotism) or friends (cronyism) with business or employment. It can lead to capable and honest workers being replaced by people not up to the role. It can be combined with bribery when the official demands that a business should employ one of their friends or relatives in return for granting favours. Generally, corruption occurs when the appointments are concealed or there is no method of removing the (often incapable) appointees. Patronage is a widespread practice, because loyalty, trust and the ability to work together are key in politics. Assuming that the candidates are able to do the job, defining what constitutes an abuse depends on how much favouritism a society finds acceptable. A good counterbalance to nepotism in public life is that there should be an effective veto over the appointment of unsuitable staff.
- Extortion – the illegitimate use or threatened use of force in order to damage either property or people.
- Embezzlement – diverting funds and assets.
- Kickbacks – the official's 'share' of misappropriated funds, often seen in conjunction with allowing the price of contracts to be inflated.
- Trading in influence occurs when a person sells their influence over a third party to influence a decision made by that third party in favour of the payer. The essential difference between this and bribery is that trading in influence involves more parties in the relationship. It is not necessarily illegal: the OECD, for example, uses the term 'undue influence peddling' to distinguish it from lobbying, which is the is the attempt to influence government decisions and an accepted part of the democratic process.

Indeed, the distinction between influence peddling and lobbying is often blurred.
- Bribery.

Bribery as a subset of corruption

Bribes are one of the main tools of corruption, being used by individuals and companies to 'buy' many things provided by the organization that an official or person in power controls access to. Although there is again no widely accepted single definition of bribery, the various commentators agree on its essential features. The UK government's working definition of bribery is derived from that in the venerable legal textbook *Russell on Crime*. This provides a good starting point that has become the accepted general statement of bribery under UK law. It is based on offering or accepting an advantage in connection with the improper performance of the recipient's functions, specifically:

> 'The receiving of or offering/giving of any benefit (in cash or in kind) by or to any public servant or office holder or to a director or employee of a private company in order to induce that person to give improper assistance in breach of their duty to the government or company which has employed or appointed them.'[88]

A similar definition which seems to tick all the boxes is:

> 'The offering, giving, receiving, or soliciting of any item of value to influence the actions of an official or other person in charge of a public or legal duty.' (*Black's Law Dictionary*)[89]

Further reading

'Bribery in politics', page 46.

Senior, I., *Corruption – the World's Big C: Cases, Causes, Consequences, Cures*, The Institute of Economic Affairs, 2006. Available from: http://bit.ly/noZkix (http://www.iea.org.uk/sites/default/files/publications/files/upldbook324pdf.pdf).

2. Why Is Corruption Bad?

Very short answer

'Corruption hits hardest at the poorest in society.'

Mary Robinson, President of Ireland (1990–1997) and UN High
Commissioner for Human Rights (1997–2002)[90]

Short answer

'As a result of corruption, private mansions are being built
instead of bridges; swimming pools are dug instead of irri-
gation systems; funds destined to run hospitals and buy
medicines find their way into the pockets of corrupt officials;
economic growth is held back; and public trust in government
is undermined.'

OECD/ADB, Curbing Corruption in Public Procurement in Asia
and the Pacific[91]

But . . . .

'In terms of economic growth, the only thing worse than a
society with a rigid, overcentralized, dishonest bureaucracy
is one with a rigid, overcentralized, honest bureaucracy. A
society which is relatively uncorrupt – a traditional society
for instance where traditional norms are still powerful – may
find a certain amount of corruption a welcome lubricant
easing the path to modernization.'

Samuel Huntington, Political Order in Changing Societies, 1968[92]

Longer answer

The exponential growth in cross-border trade and investment
over the past 50 years has been matched by an increase in
international bribery. But nowadays the work of organizations
like Transparency International has made attitudes such as
Huntingdon's above seem almost heretical. It is important

though to avoid a knee-jerk reaction and examine why this is so. In a capitalist society, what role should governments have in regulating who pays what to whom?

The effects of bribery

Corruption creates economic distortions because it causes officials to make their decisions based on what gives them the largest personal profit, rather than what is in the public interest. One thing that most economic commentators seem to agree on is that these distortions slow economic development, it being generally observed that corruption is associated with lower GNP per capita, lower investments and lower growth rates.

These economic inefficiencies occur through various mechanisms:

- Political corruption reduces the accountability of elected officials and erodes the people's faith in the democratic process as due process is disregarded.
- Judicial corruption compromises the rule of law as due process is subverted.
- Corruption in public services results in the unfair provision of welfare and community benefits, and denies citizens their basic rights if a bribe is required to gain access to them.
- Corruption makes businesses suffer extra costs, making them inefficient. Corruption may ultimately determine the viability and health of a business in any given country, and leads to good businesses moving elsewhere.
- Corruption can siphon millions of dollars of the country's wealth, which in turn handicaps the government from fulfilling its duty to protect and respect the rights guaranteed to its people.
- If looking for bribes is more profitable than 'real' work, talented people will be encouraged to take the easier, corrupt option.

- Corruption leads to the needless increase in the number of employees assigned to do a particular task, driving up costs and sidetracking workers who could be used to do more productive tasks.
- Countries known to be susceptible to corruption experience reduced aid because donor countries focused on ethics and good governance scale back assistance to known violators.
- Public investment is diverted into those projects where bribes and kickbacks are most plentiful, not necessarily the most needed – this leads to lower quality of infrastructure and public services.

Some quick-fire numbers

Front page stories about the excesses of a few despots tell us little about how pervasive bribery and corruption really is. Even though all of the above phenomena can be demonstrated through case studies and examples, the secretive nature of corruption means that it is difficult to get concrete figures about its true prevalence. Here is just a selection of statistics that well-regarded commentators have compiled to show the negative effects of corruption in less developed countries:

- More than US$1 trillion is paid in bribes worldwide each year.[93]
- 25% of African states' GDP is lost to corruption each year.
- Public officials in developing and transition countries are estimated to receive 20–40% of official development assistance to those countries in the form of bribes.
- 50% of allocated funds do not reach clinics and hospitals in Ghana.
- Bribery adds up to 10% to the total cost of doing business globally.[94]
- 15% of all companies in industrialized countries pay bribes to win or retain business. In Asia this figure is 30%; in the former Soviet Union, 60%.[95]

- In developing countries, corruption raises the cost of connecting a household to a water network by as much as 30%.[96]
- The money looted by the former president of Nigeria could have provided anti-retroviral therapy for two to three million HIV- and AIDS-infected people over a 10-year period.[97]
- $50bn in corrupt money is deposited each year into western bank accounts and tax havens.

China and the East Asian paradox – predictable corruption

Although we have lots of anecdotal data showing how corruption slows economic growth, these findings are inconsistent with countries in East Asia including China, Vietnam, Indonesia, South Korea and Thailand, where we have relatively high corruption but also high growth. China for example is currently the fastest-growing major world economy, and has attracted a large inflow of private capital from overseas despite high levels of corruption.

Why the apparent inconsistency? Looking at the data more closely, it is apparent that corruption is correlated with slow growth in most small developing countries, *except* in the large, newly industrializing economies in East Asia. Of course, growth might well have been higher or more equally distributed in the absence of corruption; but this East Asian paradox certainly makes understanding corruption more complicated.

What seems to be important is the scale and, most importantly, the *predictability* of the bribery. Research suggests that while lower levels of corruption do indeed seem to lead to higher levels of investment, *predictable* corruption does not stifle growth nearly as much as *unpredictable* corruption. Therefore, the best situation is to have low levels of corruption: but the second best by far is to have corruption that is as predictable as possible. In such an environment firms are confident that they will be able to obtain the product or service they are seeking, albeit for the price of a small, known bribe. Corruption in East Asia is well recognized and has a relatively high degree of predictability, thus can still lead to high levels of growth.

One problem with more predictable corruption, however, is that it becomes more ingrained and institutionalized – and so more difficult to change.

Are there any compelling arguments in favour of corruption?

'We would have to go without the services of some of our ablest men, sir, if the country were opposed to – to – bribery. It is a harsh term. I do not like to use it.'[98]

Mark Twain and Charles Dudley Warner, *The Gilded Age: A Tale of Today*

Can corruption ever be a good thing? Or put another way, can countries ever *benefit* from a well-established exchange of government privileges in exchange for bribes?

Some free market economists argue that badly designed or badly implemented regulations distort efficient markets, and that low-level, contained corruption can help to correct this. Bribery thus serves a similar function as taxation, although it is much more focused in that money paid to obtain public services is paid by the people that most value that particular service. It is acknowledged that bribery does increase the price of a transaction, but it would have to increase anyway if the government had to pay officials an adequate wage – and this would be funded by levying taxes on the entire population, rather than just on the users of the service.

There are other situations when corruption has been argued to exhibit positive side-effects:

- In some countries not focused on economic growth – for example in some very traditional or revolutionary regimes where the leaders believe it could challenge their power base – corruption encouraged by groups outside the government may actually serve to encourage growth and so counteract repression.
- Public positions where the officials can receive bribes – such as with the police, customs, tax office and immigration – attract good-quality applicants despite low pay.
- If the regulations in a developing country are cumbersome and inefficient, corruption allows entrepreneurs to bypass bureaucracy. The economy can thus respond to current demands rather than rigidly complying with outdated rules.

Behaving ethically
Many of these arguments, though, are theoretical. Very few people still seriously maintain that it is a good thing to give suitcases full of money to officials in developing countries to win contracts. Ultimately, then, one of the challenges for modern companies in their anti-bribery compliance is the question of whether they choose to:

- do whatever they can to make profits, as long as they don't get caught
- behave within the letter of the law
- behave ethically.

The pursuit of profit is clearly a vital corporate goal. But when ethics and profits collide, businesses and managers find it difficult to resist the immediate lure of chasing short-term high profits. However, better education and greater standards of living mean that people are no longer desperate for employment and growth at any cost, and they expect businesses to reflect the ethical standards of the society in which they operate. The media is much more active in investigating and publicizing ethical failings, and consumers take more interest, have their own views and are more willing to let their displeasure be known by boycotting companies. Consequently, businesses and their leaders who get caught acting unethically can suffer much more damage in the medium term than used to be the case.

Ethical businesses have a better image with consumers and therefore better sales, a better ability to recruit the best candidates and better employee motivation, because people are proud of their jobs. In the longer term, this gives rise to greater profits in ethical companies than in unethical ones. Past performance of the world's most ethical companies have significantly outperformed the Standard & Poor's (S&P) 500 over the past five years, according to the research from the Ethisphere Institute. Their research shows that the investment returns from the 2011 World's Most Ethical Companies significantly beat the returns from the S&P 500, as shown in the chart below.

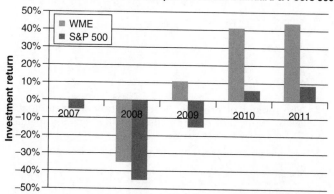

World's most ethical companies versus Standard & Poors 500

Further reading

Bhargava, V.K., Curing the cancer of corruption, Chapter 18 in Bhargava, V.K. (ed.) *Global Issues for Global Citizens: An Introduction to Key Development Challenges*, World Bank, 2006. Available from: http://bit.ly/qpr0hv (http://siteresources.worldbank.org/EXTABOUTUS/ Resources/Ch18.pdf).

Ethisphere Institute, 2011 World's Most Ethical Companies, 2011. Available from: http://bit.ly/rsJfrT (http://ethisphere.com/past-wme-honorees/wme2011/).

Mauro, P., *Why Worry about Corruption?*, Economic Issues no. 6, International Monetary Fund, February 1997. Available from: http://bit.ly/nEwIAi (http://www.imf.org/external/pubs/ft/ issues6/).

Sietsema, E., The upside of corruption: economic benefits of bribery in China, paper, Fall 2005. Available from: http://bit.ly/o5Mrpa (http://www.kentlaw.edu/perritt/courses/ seminar/beth-sietsema-Seminar%20Paper-real-final.htm).

3. When Does a Gift Become a Bribe?

Short answer

Another difficult one, because what constitutes a gift and a bribe varies with social context and is impossible to clearly delineate. Bribes require some sort of specific intent to influence, whereas pure gifts – think of small tips to a taxi driver, or to a server after a meal – are lawful. Tips can stray into the territory of bribes, however, when there is an expectation by the donor of a better standard of service and a breach of a duty of impartiality.

Longer answer

Along the 'bribery spectrum', we see bribery as being morally wrong and deserving of severe punishment, but slipping the maître d' a £20 note to secure a table in a busy restaurant as socially acceptable behaviour. If I send a corporate calendar to a client, that's a business gift, and if I take them to a football match, that's corporate hospitality. If I give money to a waitress at my regular restaurant after the meal, it's a tip. All perfectly accepted, but in all of these cases I am in fact giving something to someone else with the hope of receiving future benefits.[99] Although they are clearly akin to bribes (albeit small ones), they are rarely acknowledged as being morally wrong outside business school ethics classes. So is it simply a question of size, and can a bright line between right and wrong ever be drawn?

Can I draw a line between them?
The difference between bribes, tips and gifts is that the latter two do not involve an immediate and formal exchange of cash in return for illicit favours (or something similar). This complicates the analysis immensely, and the blurring of the distinction between these kinds of transactions represents genuine ambiguity that varies from culture to culture.

There is a widespread train of popular thought that bribery is permitted throughout the less-developed countries of the world. The fact is, though, that bribery is illegal everywhere – particularly in China, where it is prosecuted very harshly (sometimes with the death penalty). I submit that the real question is whether the definition of 'bribe' is the same throughout the world over and across cultures. In fact it varies with social context, and it is impossible to clearly delineate tips, reciprocity and gifts. In many parts of the world what a western compliance officer would call a bribe is, in fact, viewed as being a tip or a gift.

Gifts and reciprocity
John Noonan – Senior Circuit Judge on the United States Court of Appeals – writes that 'the Greeks did not have a word for bribes because all gifts are bribes. All gifts are given by way of reciprocation for favours past or to come.'[100] He suggests that a bribe can only be distinguished from a gift by two factors:

- Its size – does it exceed social norms in the circumstances?
- Is there a covert element, or is it done openly and disclosed?

Most social scientists agree that among all human societies, and within exchanges of every kind, there exists an unwritten rule of reciprocation. Reciprocation is based on social pressure and expectations, because the 'rule' of reciprocation says that we should repay, in kind, what another person has provided us. Not to do so is perceived as morally wrong. So reciprocation can act as a pervasive and subtle form of bribery: no money need change hands, and the quid pro quo – which might be favours, introductions, good service, gifts or invitations – is often more nebulous and anticipatory than with what is seen as a traditional bribe.

The social scientist Marcel Mauss is sceptical as to whether true gifts happen at all in business. He argues that because of reciprocity, gifts are never free because 'there is an obligation to give, an obligation to receive, and an obligation to repay.' Mauss's argument is that solidarity is achieved through the social bonds created by reciprocal exchange, and that a true gift that is not returned is a contradiction because it cannot create social ties.[101] In some cultures, for example in China, giving gifts to your business's web of important relationships – the so-called '*guanxi*', which would include banks, suppliers and customers – is widespread, and is a natural part of any relationship. It shows a relationship is valued and is a means of expressing good will and gratitude to the other party.

The World Bank defines a true gift using a mnemonic GIFT, signifying:

- Genuine (offered in appreciation for legitimate functions without encouragement)
- Independent (with no effect on future behaviour)
- Free (without obligations)
- Transparent (declared openly).

A very safe and increasingly popular position to take is to not give or accept business gifts at all. If you do give small business gifts, and if operating in places like China it is difficult not to, then to avoid allegations of bribery it is important to assess the implied sense of obligation or reciprocity that is likely to be entailed in giving or receiving a particular gift. Exchanging equivalent gifts is not a bad rule of thumb: a mousemat for a mousemat, a T-shirt for a T-shirt, etc. It is vital though to think about whether, through the gift, one is asking the party to engage in behaviour that deviates from being a legitimate part of the transaction. A bottle of wine is unlikely to be seen as anything other than a gift, whereas several crates of finest Champagne, or depositing 1% of a transaction's value in a Swiss bank account, will be construed very differently.

Many businesses now have a clear policy on gifts and hospitality. Normally, such policies demand timely reporting of gifts, sanctioning from the proper authorities and spelling of maximum limits.

Further reading

Balfour, F., You say *guanxi*, I say schmoozing, *Bloomberg Businessweek*, 19 November 2007. Available from: http://buswk.co/p8ULam (http://www.businessweek.com/magazine/content/07_47/b4059066.htm).

Bertok, J., Toolkit for managing conflict of interest in the public sector, issue paper (workshop D), OECD. Available from: http://bit.ly/pZUMmt (http://www.oecd.org/dataoecd/0/6/35592729.pdf).

Cavico, F.J. and Mujtaba, B.G., Baksheesh or bribe: payments to government officials and the Foreign Corrupt Practices Act, *Journal of Business Studies Quarterly*, **2**(1), 83–105, 2010. Available from: http://bit.ly/nSidP4 (http://jbsq.org/wp-content/uploads/2010/12/JBSQ_5G.pdf).

Cialdini, R.B., *Influence: The Psychology of Persuasion*, revised edition, Collins, 1998. Available from: http://amzn.to/riHc3p (http://www.amazon.com/Influence-Psychology-Persuasion-Robert-Cialdini/dp/0688128165).

US v. Harary: http://bit.ly/qukeWl (http://law.justia.com/cases/federal/appellate-courts/F2/555/1113/184456/). Refer to the quote 'The only element which distinguishes bribery from giving a gratuity is the specific intent to influence which is required for conviction of bribery' while looking at this article.

4. If I Pay Someone a Commission, Am I Committing a Bribery Offence?

Short answer

Commissions are a perfectly normal part of business. However, you may be committing an offence if the commission is kept secret and is not properly disclosed.

Longer answer

Many business sectors have a long-standing and widespread practice of paying and receiving commission in return for introducing new business. While the payment of commission remains perfectly legitimate, to avoid problems with bribery laws it is necessary to think carefully about the reasons for the commission and how it is structured and disclosed.

The Bribery Act covers those payments that induce the performance of a business activity to breach the expectations of good faith or impartiality, or breach a position of trust. This could easily capture the payment of commission to intermediaries who owe a duty of trust and confidence to a buyer if the buyer has not consented to such payment.

Take for example a payment of a commission to the external accountant of a company because they assisted you in selling some computer equipment to their client by 'putting in a good word' for you. The company is not aware that you are paying a commission to the accountant, and it had relied on the accountant to provide impartial advice. Like all cases, these are fact-specific – but this could easily fall within the Bribery Act definition, making the difference between a commission and a bribe a very fine one.

The insurance industry is based largely on commissions and brokers have a clear obligation to act in the best interests of the customer and avoid a conflict of interest. Insurers offering brokers increased commission rates for new business must therefore ensure they avoid paying commissions that far exceed those that are usually paid. If the insurer knew or should have realized that the payment to the broker was higher than usually paid and was intended to induce the broker to move away from giving best advice to their client, then this could be construed as a bribe.

Further reading

FSA, Anti-bribery and Corruption In Commercial Insurance Broking: Reducing the Risk of Illicit Payments or Inducements to Third Parties., May 2010. Available from: http://bit.ly/pYRIUx (http://www.fsa.gov.uk/pubs/anti_bribery.pdf).

5. What Are the Causes of Corruption?

'Every man has his price.'

Attributed to Sir Robert Walpole, former British Prime Minister
(1721–42)

'"Every man has his price." This is not true. But for every man there exists a bait which he cannot resist swallowing. To win over certain people to something, it is only necessary to give it a gloss of love of humanity, nobility, gentleness, self-sacrifice – and there is nothing you cannot get them to swallow. To their souls, these are the icing, the tidbit; other kinds of souls have others.'

Friedrich Nietzsche

Short answer

There is no single cause of corruption, but many things that contribute to it. Corruption tends to be high where there are well-meaning yet unwieldy and unyielding regulations, coupled with underpaid and inadequately supervised bureaucrats.

Longer answer

Corruption is rife in countries with high levels of state ownership and bureaucracy. A simple formula has been widely adopted to describe the conditions in which corrupt officials thrive:[102]

Corruption
$$= Monopoly + Discretion - Accountability - Salary$$

The formula suggests that bribery tends to be high where public officials have a monopoly on the exercise of power, with lots of discretion, limited accountability and low salaries.

Conversely, countries where businesses do not need to deal with government restrictions – either because there are few of them or because there are private sector alternatives – are generally correlated with lower instances of corruption. Unfortunately, these drivers are related to macro-economic and institutional traits that only change slowly.

Several economic factors have been found that make bribery within a country or organization more likely. These include:

- **Trade restrictions:** Import licenses are very valuable to manufacturers, who sometimes resort to bribing those who control their issue.
- **Protectionism:** Domestic industries threatened by importers may bribe politicians to set up import tariffs to keep local monopolies going.
- **Government subsidies:** Studies have shown that corruption thrives where countries provide poorly targeted subsidies to businesses – bribes can divert subsidies to companies that need them less.
- **Rationing:** This creates incentives for companies or individuals to bribe officials to acquire an unfair share of scarce items.

Developing countries that are rich in natural resources often have strict government regulation surrounding their exploitation. Indeed, many oil-rich countries have national oil companies that grant drilling, construction and operation rights to private companies, often in joint ventures with the state. There are many reasons why these private companies need to interact with officials, and therefore many opportunities for mutually beneficial corrupt behaviour. Commonly referred to as the 'resource curse', many countries rich in oil, gas and minerals are associated with poverty, conflict and corruption.

> 'Ten years from now, twenty years from now, you will see: oil will bring us ruin ... Oil is the Devil's excrement.'
>
> Venezuelan politician Juan Pablo Pérez Alfonzo, one of the founders of OPEC[103]

Does increased growth result in increased corruption?
Periods of rapid modernization tend to be the times in most countries' development when the highest rates of corruption occur. Both the US and the UK experienced high levels of corruption during their own industrial revolutions. Researchers have suggested that there are four reasons why this happens:

- It changes values and norms within society, leading to some behaviour that was traditionally tolerated becoming unacceptable and redefined as corrupt.
- It creates new sources of assets and resources that officials have access to, and can therefore supply to the highest bidder.
- It creates demand among officials who aspire to better standards of living.
- As countries modernize, their governments tend to expand; thus there are more bureaucrats and more people in a position where they can take bribes.

Paradoxically, this is also the time when societies start to become aware of the problems that corruption can cause and start to strengthen anti-corruption laws and enforcement. If not managed carefully, though, this can backfire: as more bureaucrats are employed to monitor corruption, more people have government jobs that give them the opportunity to be corrupt.

We still have a long way to go in figuring out how to fight corruption. As economists Raymond Fisman and Edward Miguel point out:[104]

> 'Governments tend to make lots of changes simultaneously: Salaries are doubled, enforcement increased, and governments made transparent all at the same time, making it hard to sort out which improvements are really the result of any specific policy. ... Perhaps the answer is that governments should become more experimental, quite literally, in how they deal with their corruption.'

Which came first – supply-side or demand-side bribery?
Is corruption caused entirely by economic conditions or is there a cultural element to it? Are some cultures or societies intrinsically more corrupt than others? Government power alone would not seem to be the over-riding cause of corruption because there are some relatively uncorrupt countries with intrusive governments, such as in Scandinavia. Certain social values (most notably personal honesty) seem to be much more important than the level of governmental control.

In a fascinating experiment to try to disentangle the two factors, Fisman and Miguel looked at an observable proxy for corruption, and chose the incidence of parking tickets in New York given to diplomats from around the world.[105] Prior to 2002, staff of embassies and consulates and their families from 146 countries benefited from diplomatic immunity, including the ability to avoid paying parking fines. These economists examined differences in the behaviour of government employees from different countries, all living and working in New York, and all of whom could act with impunity in illegally parking their cars. It turned out that there was a strong correlation between illegal parking and measures of corruption in the diplomats' home country: diplomats from high-corruption countries (based on commonly used indices) had significantly more parking violations than those from low-corruption countries. This suggests that cultural or social norms related to corruption are deeply engrained; even when living thousands of miles away, diplomats behave in a manner highly reminiscent of officials in the home country.

Negative preconceptions
Once people arrive at the view that it is necessary to pay bribes to do business in a particular country or sector, they will offer unsolicited bribes to officials to get thing done – even when a bribe is not needed. Politicians and public officials in Italy, for example, have reported that they have received money without asking or knowing exactly why. Although some element of corruption must

be in place anyway – otherwise the bribe would be quickly returned – this phenomenon can make widespread reporting of corruption into a self-fulfilling prophesy. It is easy to see why a vicious spiral can arise, with corruption being encouraged not by the local culture but by inward investors and purchasers from developed countries.

Taking the easy way out
The Indian blogger T.R. Ragunandan, founder of ipaidabribe.com – a website devoted to exposing facilitation demands by officials for basic services – bemoaned the prevalence of corruption in his country and was frustrated by the unwillingness of citizens to stand up to it. He modified the equation to bring in other social factors:[106]

$$\text{Corruption} = \text{Monopoly} + \text{Discretion} - \text{Accountability}$$
$$- \text{Salary} + \mathbf{I} + \mathbf{LoD} + \mathbf{LoS} + \mathbf{LoG}$$

Where:

+ I = ignorance of the rules by the public, and an awareness of their own right to insist on due process. This is correlated with high levels of illiteracy.

+ LoD = lack of discipline by the public. Doing the right thing requires discipline, and some people find it easier to pay a bribe than go through the correct procedures.

+ LoS = lack of scruples by the public who would rather do what is convenient than what is right, and are happy to pay a bribe for what they are not entitled to with no consideration given to the wider picture, and the position of other people.

+ LoG = lack of guts by the public, when they are submissive when facing someone perceived as 'superior' to them can set themselves up for exploitation as a potential victim when facing government officials.

Further reading

Fisman, R. and Miguel, E., *Economic Gangsters: Corruption, Violence and the Poverty of Nations*, Princeton University Press, 2008. Available from: http://bit.ly/orFkb9 (http://www.economicgangsters.com/thebook.php).

Gurgur, T. and Shah, A., Localization and corruption: panacea or Pandora's box?, policy research paper, World Bank, January 2005. Available from: http://bit.ly/qmSLDl (http://info.worldbank.org/etools/docs/library/206958/Localizationandcorruption.pdf).

I Paid A Bribe, The corruption formula, 23 March 2011. Available from: http://bit.ly/p7JfB6 (http://ipaidabribe.com/content/corruption-formula-0).

Svensson, J., Eight questions about corruption, *Journal of Economic Perspectives*, **19**(3), 19–42, Summer 2005. Available from: http://bit.ly/onlk4B (http://www1.worldbank.org/publicsector/anticorrupt/Svensson%20Eight%20Questions%20About%20Corruption%20(JEP%20Vol%2019,%20No%203%202005).pdf).

Varese, F., Pervasive corruption, in Ledeneva, A. and Kurkchiyan, M. (eds) *Economic Crime in Russia*, Kluwer Law International, 99–111, 2000. Available from: http://bit.ly/qx2nEL (http://www.sociology.ox.ac.uk/documents/people/materials/varesef/Pervasive_corruption.pdf).

6. Who Polices and Prosecutes International Bribery?

Short answer

The US Department of Justice is responsible for enforcing the criminal anti-bribery provisions of the FCPA. The US Securities and Exchange Commission is responsible for enforcing the federal securities laws, which includes the FCPA accounting rules for issuers.

The UK's Serious Fraud Office is charged with enforcement of the Bribery Act. The Financial Services Authority is also active, and can take both criminal and civil action against companies in the financial sector.

Some of the other active prosecutors who I think we will see more of in the next few years include the French, German, Swiss, Nigerian and Chinese, as well as greater involvement by the formative 'European police force', Eurojust.

Longer answer

The DOJ
The US Department of Justice (DOJ) is the agency responsible for the enforcement of the criminal law, and administration of justice in the US. Its job is to enforce and prosecute federal criminal laws, to deter crime and exact appropriate punishment. The Department is led by the Attorney General, who is nominated by the President. Within the Fraud Section of the Criminal Division of the DOJ sits the FCPA Unit. Based in Washington DC, this group of lawyers (and seconded FBI agents) is responsible for investigating and prosecuting FCPA matters. The FCPA group grew significantly under Mark

Mendelsohn, who became the face of FCPA prosecution for many years before moving into private practice.

FCPA fines accounted for nearly half of the $2bn in settlements and judgements secured by the DOJ's Criminal Division in 2010 – the highest in the FCPA's 33-year history.[107]

The SEC
The US Securities and Exchange Commission (SEC) has a dual role: it is both a financial regulator responsible for the protection of investors and the public, and also responsible for the enforcement of the federal securities laws. The SEC's Enforcement Division has lawyers, accountants and other staff based in Washington DC and in 11 other regional locations. Like the DOJ, the SEC has made the FCPA a centrepiece of its enforcement efforts.

The SFO
The investigation of the majority of fraud in the UK is the responsibility of local police forces, with prosecution being carried out by a specialist unit within the Crown Prosecution Service (CPS). The Serious Fraud Office (SFO) is the agency responsible for the investigation and prosecution of serious and/or complex fraud. Established by the Criminal Justice Act 1987 after a series of failed prosecutions by non-specialist forces, the SFO can take cases where:

• there is a significant international dimension
• the case is likely to be of widespread public concern
• the alleged fraud or corruption is concerned with amounts greater than £1m.[108]

The SFO is the lead agency in prosecution of the Bribery Act, and most significant bribery cases will come within the SFO's remit. The SFO team comprises lawyers, forensic accountants and seconded police officers. It has allocated resources to bribery cases and is publically committed to vigorous enforcement in this area, although most commentators still see it as having work to do to elevate it to the standard of the US prosecutors. David Green will take up the role as Director of the SFO when the Richard Alderman steps down in April 2012.

The City of London Police Overseas Crime Unit

The unit consists of about a dozen police officers experienced in economic crime, and is the group that would become involved with investigating any bribery matter that does not fall within the SFO's remit or requires more traditional policing skills.

The FSA

The Financial Services Authority (FSA) is the UK's financial regulator, with statutory objectives to:

- maintain confidence in the UK financial and insurance markets
- educate and protect consumers
- reduce financial crime by taking enforcement action when its rules and principles are broken.

It also has the ability to prosecute and it takes the lead in cases that pose a risk to financial markets and the interests of consumers. It will typically refer more mainstream fraud to either the SFO or the police, while taking steps to exclude those concerned from regulated business.

Criminal prosecutions do form a key part of their deterrence strategy, but where the evidence does not support a criminal prosecution they can bring civil cases for market abuse, impose regulatory fines and, most importantly, require disgorgement of any illegally obtained profits. The FSA does not need to suspect bribery in order to take enforcement action. Cases can be settled by a form of 'plea bargaining' under a leniency programme where those who come forward and self-report and then cooperate can be dealt with through the regulatory process rather than being prosecuted.

The FSA published a report in May 2010 about anti-bribery and corruption in commercial insurance broking, and bribery has featured in its thematic investigations into investment banks' procedures designed to contain the risk of staff or agents paying or receiving bribes.[109] The FSA has not been promoting its anti-bribery work as effectively as the SFO, although it did fine insurer Aon £5.25m in 2009 for a failure in its systems and controls to counter bribery.[110]

More recently, in 2011, Willis received a penalty of £7m for rule breaches when it was found to have not taken reasonable care to establish and maintain effective systems and controls for countering the risks of bribery and corruption associated with making payments to overseas agents who had helped it win business. Willis won business worth £60m, and paid 50% of this revenue in commission to these agents. Although there was no proven bribery, the FSA determined that that between 2005 and 2009:[111]

> '[a] lack of adequate controls led to an unacceptable risk that payments made by Willis Limited to Overseas Third Parties may have been used to bribe individuals connected with the overseas clients in order to secure business.'

Two new agencies take over from the FSA in early 2013: the Prudential Regulation Authority and the Financial Conduct Authority, which will take forward the FSA's financial crime remit.[112]

The UK's National Crime Agency
When the Conservative–Liberal Democrat coalition came into government in 2010, it pledged to create an 'Economic Crime Agency' that would bring together the SFO, FSA, HM Revenue and Customs, the Office of Fair Trading, and the various other agencies who work investigating and prosecuting

serious crime. George Osborne, currently Chancellor, but then still in opposition, said:

> 'We are very, very bad at prosecuting white-collar crime. We have six different government departments, eight different agencies – a complete alphabet soup – and the result is that these crimes go unpunished. There is £30bn worth of fraud taking place in the British economy each year.'[113]

The Home Secretary published the now-renamed 'National Crime Agency' plan in June 2011, which sets out the vision for the new agency to 'tackle organised crime, defend our borders, fight fraud and cyber crime, and protect children and young people'. The NCA is scheduled to be set up in 2013.

Although Richard Alderman, Director of the SFO, had publicly spoken out again the plan to separate investigators and prosecutors, the Home Secretary was reported to favour SFO lawyers moving into the Crown Prosecution Service and its investigators into the new NCA.[114] The SFO appears though to have earned a reprieve. The Home Secretary said in mid-2011 that:

> '[i]nstead, the NCA will house a co-ordinating board for the agencies that tackle economic crime, including the SFO. This will be set up in the next few months, while the NCA should be fully functional by 2013. Other structural changes will be postponed.'[115]

Some other prosecutors to watch
Clearly, each country has its own group of regulators and law enforcement personnel tasked with investigating and prosecuting white collar crime and bribery. Again, in a book of this type, I cannot possibly deal with each one – even if this information could ever be obtained and collated. Some of these

agencies are more active in the international bribery arena than others, and I set out below some of the groups that I think will be increasingly in the news over the next few years.

French magistrates[116]

The French justice system is what is referred to as 'inquisitional', as opposed to the 'adversarial' US and UK systems. This means that in France, as in many European countries, all criminal cases are investigated initially by an independent investigating magistrate, who considers all the evidence, decides whether there is sufficient evidence against the accused to warrant a trial and produces a report to the court that contains all the evidence that supports both the prosecution and defence cases. The investigations are frequently long – two years in straightforward cases is normal – and much of the obtaining and testing of the evidence is done in secret by the investigating magistrate. The investigating magistrates appear to have a good relationship with the DOJ, and have been active in investigating several high profile French-based companies in conjunction with the US prosecutors, including, Alcatel-Lucent,[117] Alstom and Technip.

German regional prosecutors' offices[118]

In Germany, regional prosecutors have a central role throughout the investigation stage of any major criminal process to either investigate reported crimes or request the police to do so. The prosecutor has the power to compel witnesses and experts to appear and testify, and can request a judge to perform inspections of evidence on their behalf. The prosecutors' offices have been active enforcers of the German bribery law.

In its settlement with the Munich Prosecutor's Office, which was done in conjunction with the DOJ and the SEC, Siemens pleaded guilty to charges related to a corporate failure to supervise its officers and employees, and paid a total of €596m in fines and penalties. They have also carried out purely domestic prosecutions, such as Man Group, where in May 2009 the Munich Public Prosecutor's Office opened an investigation into allegations that unlawful commissions were to its customers in order to obtain contracts; and Deutsche Bahn, which in 2009 self-reported its ongoing bribery investigation in Algeria, Rwanda and Greece to the Frankfurt Public Prosecutor.[119,120]

Swiss prosecutors[121]

An inquisitorial system also exists at the pre-trial stage in Switzerland. For the conduct of investigations, the Office of the Attorney General calls on the services primarily of the Federal Criminal Police. Criminal cases are prosecuted before the Federal Criminal Court in Bellinzona, with a right of appeal against decisions of this court to the Supreme Court in Lausanne. Switzerland has a comprehensive anti-bribery law, and has recently been active in the investigation of allegations that a Swiss government official was bribed for confidential information by a client of UBS, as well as Ericsson[122] and Alstom.

Eurojust[123]

Eurojust was established in 2002 as an agency of the European Union to deal with cross-border cooperation in serious crime. It is composed of national prosecutors, magistrates or police agencies assigned from across the EU. In addition, through cooperation agreements, the US, Norway and Iceland each also have a delegate. While Eurojust does not initiate investigations, its current task is to serve as a central point where information, evidence and investigative leads can be exchanged, and so lengthy formal requests for cooperation between national authorities are eliminated. The plan appears to be to turn Eurojust into an investigator, with the power to order arrests and trials, which will be the first step to creating an EU-wide public prosecutor. Eurojust played a role in the investigation of alleged bribes in the sale of JAS Gripen fighters, and prosecutors, magistrates and police officials from six countries coordinate their investigations at Eurojust's headquarters in The Hague.[124]

China People's Procuratorate[125],[126]

The Public Procurator has a role in China as both investigator and prosecutor. Within the Procuratorate, specialist Anti-Corruption and Bribery Bureaux investigate and prosecute corruption, bribery and embezzlement by state personnel. In recent years, the offices have carried out a series of industry-targeted crackdowns on corruption and bribery to try to snare a number of officials all at once. These crackdowns have tended to be short but intense, and combined with calls on the public to report corruption and incentives to catch officials who inform on their colleagues. These campaigns have seen some success. More than 60,000 people have been sentenced for bribery and corruption since 2008, receiving in many cases severe sentences, including the execution of at least 25 officials.[127]

Rio Tinto: Alleged Bribery in China[128]

Four Rio Tinto executives were arrested in 2009 on suspicion of espionage. Chinese prosecutors initially claimed that the executives had tried to procure secrets about the Chinese steel industry that could be useful to Rio Tinto, although when the charges were eventually filed, they were downgraded to bribery and the theft of commercial secrets.

Subsequently, they admitted to *receiving* several millions of dollars in bribes as well as stealing commercial secrets. It transpired that China's steel makers, most of them controlled by the state, had paid bribes to the Rio Tinto executives, most probably to try to get bigger allocations of iron ore. This though is not clear, because Chinese officials have yet even to announce an investigation into the bribers.

According to press reports, the arrests came a month after Rio Tinto cancelled a major transaction with state-owned

Chinalco, and there was widespread speculation that the arrests constituted possible retribution.

On 1 May 2011, China enacted a law providing terms of up to ten years' imprisonment for anyone paying bribes to foreign officials outside China and to officials of international public organizations. Bribes paid locally to Chinese government officials had already been illegal prior to this new law. The law specifically applies to a joint venture between a Chinese and non-Chinese company formed pursuant to Chinese law, and will have an impact on many US and UK companies doing business in China operating through joint ventures.[129] The Chinese authorities have also been active in investigating Johnson & Johnson, Nike, Areva, Mitsui, and Rio Tinto.

Nigeria's EFCC[130] and ICPC[131]

The Economic and Financial Crimes Commission (EFCC) is a Nigerian law enforcement agency. The EFCC was established in 2003, partially in response to criticism from the international Financial Action Task Force on Money Laundering, which at that time named Nigeria as one of the world's non-cooperative countries. The EFCC works closely with the Independent Corrupt Practices (and other Related Offences) Commission (ICPC) to investigate complaints of allegations of corrupt practices and, in appropriate cases, prosecute the offenders. It also has a role to educate and raise awareness of bribery and corruption.

Nigeria has been active in several recent headline cases, including Daimler and Tidewater, which paid $6.3m to settle Nigerian claims that its Nigerian subsidiary had participated in bribes to customs officials. (This formed part of the Panalpina-related investigations.) In November 2010, the EFCC arrested Halliburton employees in Lagos relating to the Bonny Island scheme and subsequently filed corruption charges against Halliburton and its executives.[132] Technip,

Snamprogetti and JGC Corp. were reportedly also charged on the same day. According to reports, Halliburton and the EFCC reached a $250m settlement agreement to resolve the charges – Halliburton will pay $120m in penalties and $130m in frozen assets in Switzerland will be repatriated to Nigeria.[133]

The role of financial investigator in Nigeria is not without risk. In 2010, the head of the Forensic Unit of the EFCC was assassinated. He had been actively involved in the trials of several heads of banks.[134]

The World Bank[135]

The World Bank is a source of financial and technical assistance to developing countries around the world, and provides low-interest loans, interest-free credit and grants to developing countries for education, health, infrastructure, communications and many other purposes. The Bank is also important as an information provider and promoter of good ethical practice, regularly publishing its 'Worldwide Governance Indicators'.

The Bank, together with other multilateral and regional development banks, has stepped up its efforts to fight corruption in any organization involved with any of its projects. Sanctions include both fines and debarment. Its 'Listing of Ineligible Firms' details companies and individuals that are ineligible to be awarded a World Bank-financed contract because they were found to have violated the fraud and corruption provisions of the Procurement Guidelines or the Consultants Guidelines.

In 2009, Macmillan, a publisher of educational and scientific books, was banned by the World Bank from any of its projects for six years after one of its sales staff made a payment to a local official in Sudan in an unsuccessful attempt to secure a contract for an education project.[136]

Further reading

City of London Police overseas anti-corruption unit:
http://bit.ly/qZi6ER (http://www.cityoflondon.police.uk/
CityPolice/Departments/ECD/anticorruptionunit/).

DOJ FCPA portal: http://1.usa.gov/nNbat4 (http://www.justice
.gov/criminal/fraud/fcpa/).

FSA financial crime portal: http://bit.ly/pNkpqd
(http://www.fsa.gov.uk/pages/About/What/financial_crime/
index.shtml).

National Crime Agency: http://bit.ly/nyi1jf (http://www
.homeoffice.gov.uk/crime/nca/).

SEC Enforcement Manual: http://1.usa.gov/q2fA1S (http://www
.sec.gov/divisions/enforce/enforcementmanual.pdf).

SFO bribery and corruption portal: http://bit.ly/mPWh1n
(http://www.sfo.gov.uk/bribery–corruption.aspx).

US Attorney's Manual: http://1.usa.gov/pj0T7M (http://www
.justice.gov/usao/eousa/foia_reading_room/usam/index.html).

7. What Is the Difference in Focus Between the DOJ and the SEC?

Short answer

The DOJ prosecutes companies for criminal breaches of the anti-bribery provisions of the FCPA. The court levies fines on those defendants being found guilty or those admitting guilt.

The SEC is responsible for civil breaches of the accounting provisions of the FCPA and, as such, its targets are issuers. It can seek civil penalties and force the disgorgement of illegally obtained gains.

Longer answer

There are two distinct elements to the FCPA:

- All companies with a nexus to the US must comply with the anti-bribery provisions.
- Only issuers are obliged to comply with the accounting provisions.

The anti-bribery and the accounting provisions of the FCPA can result in either criminal, or civil penalties, or both. Generally speaking, though, breaches of the anti-bribery provisions are treated as a criminal offence, and breaches of the accounting provisions (unless breaches were deliberately deceptive) as a civil offence. The SEC and DOJ often work on investigations together because they address these different enforcement priorities and consequently are able to impose different penalties.

Historically, there has been a convenient delineation of duties with respect to FCPA enforcement:

- The DOJ investigates and prosecutes anti-bribery provisions, and seeks criminal penalties.
- At the same time, the SEC prosecutes issuers for breaches of the accounting provisions of the FCPA. Remedies here are civil penalties together with disgorgement of any illicit profits made.

The DOJ

A criminal proceeding begins with a complaint, information or indictment. If the DOJ desires an indictment, and it is the right of every citizen to have a grand jury consider the evidence against them before being charged, then it tries to convince a grand jury that there is enough evidence to warrant the filing of formal charges. (It rarely declines.)

A defendant, however, can voluntarily waive that right, so then a prosecutor can skip the indictment and bring charges by way of an 'information' – a simple court filing that details the charges. Each offence is usually set out in a separate count.

The SEC

Although the SEC can bring criminal charges on its own for violations of the FCPA accounting provisions that are 'wilful', the SEC normally restricts itself to civil and regulatory actions. The largest 'stick' that is normally employed by the SEC is a federal court injunction against future acts and practices that violate securities laws. If the injunction is violated there is the avenue open for an action in contempt. To obtain an injunction, the SEC must prove that a company or its officer, director, employee, agent or shareholder has broken the securities law, and – unless prevented by an injunction – is likely to break the law again.

Civil injunctions are used by the SEC for what it considers particularly serious misconduct. The alternative is the cease-and-desist order, which is an administrative proceeding. It is considered to be more moderate than a full injunction, and its effects and impacts are consequently less. There need only be 'some risk' of future reoffending in the case of a cease-and-desist order. Administrative proceedings are generally seen as appropriate in the context of settlement agreements, where there has been no criminal intent.

Allied to either of the above orders, or on a standalone basis, the SEC has the power to request courts to impose civil penalties and to order the disgorgement of profits.

Working together
On most current investigations, defendants will find that the DOJ and SEC attorneys will sit together in meetings and will almost act as one team that sometimes crosses the 'traditional' delineations. In the 2009 Panalpina investigation, for example, the SEC prosecuted a non-issuer.

Panalpina: SEC Prosecutes a Non-Issuer As Being an Agent of An Issuer

Panalpina World Transport (Holding) Ltd is a Swiss-based freight forwarder. A number of its global subsidiaries were alleged to have paid bribes between 2002 and 2007 to customs officials in a number of countries to expedite freight clearing processes. Several of Panalpina's clients, on whose behalf the bribes were made, were US issuers, and were included in the series of settlements.

As is now the norm, both the DOJ and the SEC played an active part on the Panalpina investigation and settlements. However, none of the Panalpina group companies was an issuer, and this was the first time that the SEC had charged a company that was not a US issuer with FCPA violations. The SEC asserted jurisdiction over Panalpina by charging it as acting as an agent of its customers who were US issuers, and with knowingly and substantially aiding and abetting violations by these customers.

As a result of the civil procedure filed against Panalpina, the SEC was able to extract a settlement comprising disgorgement of profits of $11.3m. Panalpina World Transport (Holding) Ltd and Panalpina Inc. agreed in addition to pay a further $70.5m to resolve related criminal proceedings brought by the DOJ.

Further reading

'Panalpina and customs violations', page 440.

8. Why All the Fuss About the Bribery Act?

Short answer

The UK Bribery Act 2010 received royal assent on 8 April 2010, having received all-party support in the last few days of Gordon Brown's Labour government. It was widely hailed as the toughest bribery legislation in the world, introducing laws prohibiting the giving and receiving of bribes in the both the public and private sector, and introducing a new strict liability offence of corporate failure to prevent bribery. The Act did not however come into effect until 1 July 2011. This is because its implementation depended on the publication of governmental guidance to businesses on how to comply with the Act.

This Guidance was eventually issued by the new Conservative–Liberal Democrat coalition government, but was issued in a form that significantly watered down the impact of the original legislation. Although business groups have never really warmed to the Act, they cautiously welcomed the more commercial guidance that they had lobbied hard for. Ethical groups though roundly condemned it. Transparency International called it 'deplorable', saying that 'parts of it read more like a guide on how to evade the Act, than how to develop company procedures that will uphold it.'[137]

Longer answer

UK bribery before the Act

Bribery had been an offence under the common law for many years. Before the Bribery Act was even conceived, the police and prosecutors had several very powerful laws at their disposal:

- Common law offences of bribery, fraud, and misconduct in public office.
- Corruption offences that were found in at least 12 statutes, including the Public Bodies Corrupt Practices Act 1889, Prevention of Corruption Act 1906, Prevention of Corruption Act 1916, and the Criminal Law Act 1977.
- Anti-Terrorism, Crime and Security Act (ATCSA) 2001.
- Proceeds of Crime Act 2002.

The ATCSA in particular was far-reaching legislation that could be used to prosecute UK companies and nationals living abroad for far more than simply 'terrorist' offences. ATCSA enacted parts of the OECD convention and made two main changes to the existing law:

- It made clear that the existing offences of bribery and corruption applied to the bribery of foreign public office holders, including foreign MPs, judges, ministers and 'agents'.
- It gave the UK courts jurisdiction over certain offences of bribery and corruption when they were committed overseas by UK nationals or by bodies incorporated under UK law.

Prior to the Bribery Act being finalized there had been one successful prosecution for overseas bribery when in 2008 an English lawyer, Nigel Heath, was sentenced to six months' imprisonment for conspiring to corrupt authorities in the US so that they would unblock assets that had been frozen after 9/11.[138] Nevertheless, the law was muddled and confused. Few individuals and almost no companies had been prosecuted in recent times under the pre-existing bribery legislation.

Mabey & Johnson: Criminal Plea in the UK Pre-Bribery Act[139]

Mabey & Johnson Limited, the UK-based bridge-building company, finalized a criminal plea agreement with the SFO in

2009. As such, this represented the first successful criminal prosecution for bribery by the SFO.

Mabey & Johnson pleaded guilty under S1 Criminal Law Act 1977 (Statutory Conspiracy) to paying bribes between 1994 and 2001 to government officials in Ghana and Jamaica. In addition, it admitted making payments to officials in Iraq in breach of UN sanctions and the 'Oil-for-Food' rules.

Penalties of approximately £6.6m were imposed (which incorporated fines, a sum for confiscation, reparations to the countries impacted and a contribution to the SFO's costs), in addition to a compliance monitor for three years.

Three of the directors – Charles Forsyth, David Mabey and Richard Gledhill (who pleaded guilty and gave evidence the others) – were subsequently jailed for 21 months, eight months and eight months suspended for two years respectively.

The OECD was losing patience with the UK; not because it did not have laws in place, but principally because bribery often went un-investigated and unpunished.

> 'The OECD has in October 2008 ... already threatened to blacklist British companies if they remained under-regulated, and patience is running out fast. Competitors are getting ready to take robust action against the UK in the light of continued lack of compliance with international law.'

> Professor Mark Pieth, Chairman of the OECD Working Group on Bribery[140]

Implementation of the Bribery Act delayed

Although the Bribery Bill had been around in draft form in various guises since 2003, the final version was passed with all-party support, although it was done in the final 'wrapping up' business of the outgoing Labour government with no time for debate. Politics and lobbying delayed its implementation. The government had undertaken, pursuant to Section 9 of the new Act, to provide official guidance on what was meant by 'adequate procedures', and the corporate offence of failing to prevent bribery could only come into force three months after this guidance had been issued.

After draft guidance and a consultation period in late 2010, it had been anticipated that the final guidance would be published in January 2011 at the latest, in substantially the same form as the draft, and the Act would have come into force by April 2011. On 31 January 2011 the coalition government announced a delay in publication, claiming it needed further time to make the guidance workable for business.[141] Some business groups said the rules were unclear in areas such as the permitted levels of corporate hospitality. Others lobbied for a removal of the ban on facilitation payments:

> 'In a cut and thrust world of exporting what we don't want is the British playing with a straight bat and we find some of our competitors are not. If this is going to work it has to be policed globally.'[142]

The Confederation of British Industry claimed that the Act was 'not fit for purpose' and could harm British exports at a time when the economy needs all the help it can get. The same thing had happened when the FCPA was enacted, when there was also considerable disquiet from US businesses who feared that the FCPA would damage their interests.

Misinformation and feeding frenzies
The SFO made it clear in public statements that its targets were those businesses involved in real wrongdoing, but misinformation and newspaper scare stories led to the popular but incorrect belief that the Act would mean the end of business hospitality and small business courtesies.

'Players at Sprowston Recreation Ground Bowls Club, near Norwich, have for years given staff £20 in cash or vouchers at Christmas to thank them for their efforts. But now the club has received a letter from the local parish council warning that if they continue, they could be in breach of the Bribery Act 2010.'

The Daily Telegraph, 20 February 2011[143]

Lawyers and forensic accountants – whether experienced in the field or not – all became Bribery Act experts, warning clients that they would face jail unless they embarked on expensive remediation programmes.

The Act becomes law
The final Bribery Act Guidance was eventually published on 30 March 2011, and the Act therefore became effective on 1 July 2011. The Bribery Act Guidance was controversial, welcomed by business organizations and criticized by anti-bribery activists. Global Witness said that it 'opens a huge loophole'.[144] Transparency International called it 'deplorable', saying 'parts of it read more like a guide on how to evade the Act, than how to develop company procedures that will uphold it.'[145]

Areas where the impact of the legislation was 'softened' include:

- A non-UK company listed on the London Stock Exchange is not subject to the Bribery Act simply by virtue of the listing.
- Having a UK subsidiary will not automatically mean that a parent company is carrying on business in the UK.
- A UK company is only liable for the actions of subcontractors with whom it had direct contractual relationships.
- Debarment is discretionary, not mandatory.

The Act may create challenges for UK businesses at its
introduction, but as outlined in Question 39, once there is a
groundswell of support against bribery and most companies
refuse outright to entertain bribery, then it will start to be
properly eliminated.

Further reading

'An essential summary of the Bribery Act', page 81.

Questions 10 and 29.

Documents of the Parliamentary Joint Committee on the Draft Bribery Bill: http://bit.ly/plb9v9
(http://www.publications.parliament.uk/pa/jt/jtbribe.htm).

Leys, D., Debate on 17 March: bribery, tax avoidance,
corruption and money laundering, House of Lords Library
Note, 14 March 2011. Available from: http://bit.ly/pjcd6G
(http://www.parliament.uk/documents/lords-library/LLN%
202011-009%20BriberyFP.pdf). This document provides
statistics on bribery, tax avoidance, corruption and money
laundering in the UK, provides an overview of legislation and
policy in these areas, and outlines various perspectives on
the UK's record on legislation.

9. Is the Bribery Act Stricter Than the FCPA?

Short answer

On the face of it, the wording of the Bribery Act is tougher than the FCPA, as its scope is far more expansive. Like the FCPA, the Bribery Act has a global reach, but also applies to active and passive bribery in purely private sector activities, and has fewer exemptions.

The associated Bribery Act Guidance though seems to reassure businesses that only blatant and egregious breaches of the Act will be prosecuted. Furthermore, the SFO is still unable to do wide-ranging and high-value plea agreements, which the DOJ and SEC have been doing for years, and the US prosecutors are currently well-resourced and at the top of their game. All things being equal, I think it's still a win for the US.

Longer answer

Although both pieces of legislation are designed to deter and prosecute major acts of bribery, they do so in subtly different ways. There is a difference in both breadth and reach between the Bribery Act and the FCPA (and the OECD – whose provisions are extremely similar to those of the FCPA).

FCPA
The FCPA prohibits bribery involving foreign officials. The essence of the offence is 'corruptly' giving or receiving anything of value to a foreign official to influence any official act. The word 'corruptly' is not defined in the Act but implies an intent to wrongly influence the recipient to misuse their

position in order to benefit the business of the payer or their client.

The FCPA includes three affirmative defences under its anti-bribery provisions:

- reasonable and bona fide expenditures related to certain promotional activities
- payments that are lawful under the written law of the foreign jurisdiction
- facilitation payments.

Separately, the accounting provisions require all US issuers to keep accurate books, records and accounts so that the true nature of transactions are properly recorded, and to maintain a system of adequate internal accounting controls.

Bribery Act
The core Bribery Act offences require only an intent to influence a person to perform their duty 'improperly'. (Or in the case of a foreign public official, intent to influence in their official capacity and intent to obtain or retain business.) There is an exception for reasonable and proportionate promotional expenditures.

Essential differences
The Bribery Act also goes beyond the FCPA in five main areas:

- It prohibits bribery in the private sector and doesn't just apply to bribing foreign officials.
- It prohibits both the offer and acceptance of a bribe.
- The Bribery Act contains no 'corrupt intent' requirement.
- It has no exception for facilitation payments.
- It has no statute of limitations. (The FCPA has five years).

Balanced against this are some of the weaknesses in the Bribery Act introduced by the Guidance:

- A non-UK company listed on the London Stock Exchange is not automatically caught by the Bribery Act simply by virtue of its listing.
- A subsidiary will not necessarily be an 'associated person' of its parent company (for example, if it merely remits dividends to its parent).
- A UK company is only responsible for the acts committed by contractors or business partners with whom it had a direct contractual relationship. A 'chain' of subcontractors would likely shield it from liability.

The Bribery Act also creates a tough strict-liability corporate offence. Under Section 7, a company is liable if it does not have 'adequate procedures' in place designed to prevent bribery by an 'associated person'. While this offence seemingly goes beyond that of the FCPA, US companies are effectively liable for the acts of employees and agents acting in the course of their duties, under the 'respondeat superior' doctrine, for which there is no adequate procedures defence. (The adequacy of a company's procedures may ultimately overlap with the internal controls requirements of the FCPA's accounting provisions.) Instead, adequate procedures are considered only at the sentencing stage. In respect of corporate liability, then, this is stronger in the case of the FCPA.

The Bribery Act does not have a 'books and records' aspect; however, adequate internal controls may be even more important because they must be present and functioning if a company is to assert an 'adequate procedures' defence to a Section 7 charge.

In practice
Much has been made of the Bribery Act being tougher than the FCPA. A side-by-side comparison, like I do below, demonstrates how fines are potentially larger and the scope is indeed more expansive. But many other OECD member states also have well-drafted anti-bribery laws. While the Bribery Act has no facilitation payments exception, for

example, the FCPA definition of facilitation payments is defined very narrowly. The key is whether, in practice, these differences will translate into quicker and more effective prosecutions, and increased deterrence, post-July 2011.

	FCPA 1977	Bribery Act 2010
Prohibitions	Bribery of foreign officials. Deceptive books and practices.	Bribery of any person to induce them to act improperly. Bribery to influence a foreign public official. Failure to prevent bribery by companies.
Corporate liability	The doctrine of 'respondeat superior' effectively means strict liability if an employee or agent's actions were within the scope of their duties, and were intended to benefit the company.	Strict corporate liability if a person 'associated with' the organization commits bribery, unless the company had 'adequate procedures' in place to prevent bribery.
Commercial bribery	Not covered by the FCPA (but see the Travel Acts).	Prohibits paying or receiving bribes in the private sector.
Passive bribery	Not covered by the FCPA.	Prohibits requesting, agreeing to receive or accepting a bribe.

	FCPA 1977	Bribery Act 2010
Definition of a bribe	'Anything of value'.	'Financial or other advantage'.
Corrupt intent	A bribe has to be made with the corrupt intent to obtain or retain business, or a competitive advantage.	A bribe has to be made to bring about an improper performance of duties or to influence the performance of a foreign government official, and must intend to obtain or retain a business. No corrupt intent is needed.
Defences and exceptions	Facilitation payments (exception). Bona fide expenditures related to promotion of products or services, or performance of a contract (defence). Payment lawful under the written laws of the foreign country (defence).	No exception or defence for facilitation payments. No exception or defence for bona fide expenditures.

	FCPA 1977	Bribery Act 2010
Accounting provisions	Issuers must have an adequate system of internal accounting controls, and make and keep books, records and accounts that should accurately and fairly reflect, in reasonable detail, the transactions and dispositions of the assets of the issuer.	Not covered by the Bribery Act (but see S386 Companies Act 1989).
Penalties	Criminal penalties up to $2m and five years' imprisonment per violation.	Criminal Statute only.
	Additional penalties may be levied under other laws.	Up to 10 years in prison; unlimited fines; confiscation of benefits.
	Civil fines, debarment, disgorgement of gains; private actions also likely.	Discretionary debarment under UK Public Contracts Regulation 2006. Civil recovery orders.

	FCPA 1977	**Bribery Act 2010**
Enforcing authority	DOJ (criminal) SEC (civil).	SFO (criminal and civil).
Effective compliance procedures	Guidance on 'the establishment of an 'effective compliance and ethics program' is contained in the US Federal Sentencing Guidelines.'	Bribery Act Guidance on 'adequate procedures' has been published by the Ministry of Justice.
	An effective programme is considered at the sentencing stage only, and might reduce a corporation's culpability score under the sentencing guidelines.	The procedures considered at the liability stage, and having adequate procedures is a complete defence to a corporate action.

Further reading

'An essential summary of the FCPA', page 73.

'An essential summary of the Bribery Act', page 81.

'The US authorities will use other legislation to expand the reach of the FCPA', page 456.

Dogra, S. and Armao, J.P., Anti-bribery enforcement: FCPA v Bribery Act – a practical comparison, *Bloomberg Law Reports*, **3**(1). Available from: http://bit.ly/qAh3Jd (http://www.linklaters.com/pdfs/mkt/newyork/A13007805.pdf).

10. Who Is Covered by What? The Scope of the Various Laws

Short answer

Sorry, but there isn't one this time.

Longer answer

When thinking about bribery, or on finding a potential instance of bribery, companies need to think about several sets of potentially interlocking laws. It's necessary to consider the following:

- Is the offence illegal in the country where it took place? The answer to this is usually going to be yes. Although the person doing the bribing (or their employer or principal) might not be resident in that jurisdiction, the laws of most countries provide that acts of bribery taking place within that territory are covered by that country's criminal law. This is the case under the FCPA, the Bribery Act, and the OECD.
- Is what happened illegal under the domestic laws where the company and/or individual is resident? This will very much depend on the circumstances. In the case of all those companies and individuals resident in countries that have signed up to the OECD, then bribery by nationals and companies incorporated in that country is likely to be unlawful regardless of where in the world it took place. So for example, in the case of a UK employee of a German company who has paid bribes in France:
  - the British employee will be subject to the UK Bribery Act
  - the German company will be subject to the German anti-bribery law
  - the bribe itself could be prosecuted under French law.

- Additionally, for non-US residents, is the offence potentially covered by the FCPA?
- Additionally, for non-UK residents, is the offence potentially covered by the Bribery Act?
- Is the offence potentially covered by the expanded jurisdictions of other countries? (At the date of writing there are few jurisdictions with an active expanded jurisdiction as great as the FCPA and Bribery Act, and I do not consider these further in this book.)

To whom and where does the FCPA apply?

The FCPA applies to three basic classes of people and businesses entities:

- US nationals and companies.
- Non-US issuers – non-US companies that have their securities listed on a US exchange, or are otherwise required to file periodic reports with the SEC. (Overseas companies often list their shares on US exchanges through American depository receipts (ADRs).) There are currently several hundred non-US issuers.
- Any persons, including non-US nationals and companies, carrying out some part of the bribery scheme in the US.

It also applies to people acting on behalf of these three categories, such as their directors, officers, employees, agents and shareholders.

US nationals, US companies and foreign issuers

The US government can exert jurisdiction on US nationals, US companies and foreign issuers on nationality-based principles. This means the following:

- US nationals and companies and non-US issuers may be held liable for a corrupt payment made by them anywhere in the world. Foreign issuers are covered in exactly the same way as US companies. There need be no action in the US relating to the payment.

- Employees or agents of US entities or issuers, regardless of their nationality, are also criminally liable themselves if they commit any corrupt acts anywhere in the world.
- US companies and foreign issuers are also liable for bribes authorized by their employees or agents, regardless of their nationality, operating entirely outside the US.

In other words, a bribe made by a US national on behalf of a non-US company, using money from foreign bank accounts and without any involvement by anyone located within the US, would fall within the ambit of the FCPA. Such jurisdiction does not extend to non-US nationals. In the case of non-US persons, the behaviour needs to have some (albeit small, as we will see) territorial link to the US.

Any person
As it was originally drafted, foreign nationals or companies (other than those that were classed as issuers above) were generally not subject to the FCPA. Amendments were made to the FCPA in 1998 to comply with the OECD Convention requirement to make it a criminal offence for 'any person' to bribe a foreign official. These amendments expanded the Act to assert new territorial jurisdiction over foreign companies and nationals.

- A foreign person or company is now subject to the FCPA if it causes, directly or through agents, an act in furtherance of a corrupt payment within the territory of the United States.
- Non-US officers, directors, employees or agents of foreign nationals or businesses are liable in exactly the same way.

This territorial test for jurisdiction needs to be broadly interpreted; only the briefest physical connection between the corrupt act and the US is required. A payment in dollars that is made via a US bank account is likely to be sufficient to give the US authorities jurisdiction. In a recent submission to the OECD monitoring commission, the US suggested that the term includes just about everything except merely thinking about paying a bribe. Modern methods of communication and funds transfer therefore make it increasingly difficult for any business of substance working internationally to avoid falling within the jurisdictional ambit of the FCPA.

Statoil: First US Prosecution of a Foreign Issuer[146]

Statoil is an international oil company headquartered in Norway. In 2006, the DOJ and SEC announced that Statoil had agreed to pay fines and penalties totalling $21m to settle FCPA actions.

It was the first time that US authorities had instituted criminal proceedings under the FCPA against a foreign issuer. The government asserted jurisdiction because Statoil was an issuer and it had its ADRs listed on the New York Stock Exchange.

Statoil admitted to making payments totalling $5.2m to an offshore intermediary company with ties to an Iranian government official to induce the official to help Statoil obtain participation interests in the massive South Pars oil and gas field. In its accounts, Statoil characterized both payments as being made for consulting services under a contract with another offshore company.

To whom and where does the Bribery Act apply?

The Bribery Act applies to individuals, companies and other incorporated entities, with broad extra-territorial application. This can be summarized as follows:

Bribing, being bribed or bribing a foreign public official

- If any part of the conduct takes place within the UK, then an individual of any nationality is subject to the Act.
- If the actions take place abroad, they still constitute an offence under the Act if the person performing them is a

UK national or ordinarily resident in the UK, or a company incorporated in the UK.

The corporate offence in Section 7 of the Bribery Act
This imposes strict liability on organizations if a person associated with the organization pays a bribe. The corporate offence applies to:

- any company (or partnership) that is incorporated in the UK
- any non-UK company that *carries on a business*, or part of a business, in any part of the UK.

It is immaterial where the predicate bribery offence takes place.

Section 8 defines 'associated person' as 'a person who performs services for or on behalf of [the organization]' and provides examples of employees, agents and subsidiaries.

So a foreign company that carries on any 'part of a business' in the UK could be prosecuted under the Bribery Act for failing to prevent bribery committed by any of its employees, agents or other representatives, even if the bribery takes place outside the UK and involves non-UK persons.

There has also been concern among commentators that every entity in a chain of subcontractors or suppliers might be an associated person of the entity at the top of the chain. However, the Guidance explains that a contractor or a supplier will generally be deemed to perform services only for the entity with which it has a direct contractual relationship.

What is 'the UK'?
Strictly, the Act applies to UK citizens in both the UK and elsewhere, British Overseas Territories citizen, British Nationals and Commonwealth Citizens. Many offshore jurisdictions – including the British Virgin Islands, Turks

& Caicos, Cayman, and Bermuda – are British Overseas Territories. This means that the Act will apply to many offshore companies and their directors, who can be prosecuted in the UK for bribery offences committed anywhere in the world.

Despite Scotland having a different legal system to England, Wales and Northern Ireland, the Scottish Parliament has specifically adopted the Bribery Act so that it also applies in Scotland. In Scotland it is the role of the police forces to investigate bribery and the Crown Office & Procurator Fiscal to prosecute, not the SFO.

The Bribery Act does not directly apply to the other key offshore centres, Guernsey and Jersey – the Channel Islands are Crown Dependencies – and nor to the Isle of Man. However, it may well be the case that companies and residents of these jurisdictions are either carrying on business in the UK, or retain UK nationality, which will bring them within its ambit anyway.

Further reading

'An essential summary of the FCPA', page 73.

'An essential summary of the Bribery Act', page 81.

Questions 11 and 12.

11. Are Companies Liable for Bribes Paid by Their Employees, Agents, Subsidiaries and Affiliates?

Short answer

Usually, yes. In the US, the legal doctrine called 'respondeat superior' makes companies criminally liable for crimes committed by agents and employees. In the UK, an overseas subsidiary can make a UK parent liable, and a UK subsidiary can make a UK or overseas parent liable unless the subsidiary can be shown to be acting entirely independently.

Longer answer

Companies are legal entities in their own right and are capable of suing and being sued, and of committing crimes. Because companies generally have deeper pockets than individuals and are able to pay much higher fines, prosecutors like to take action against the company itself as well as the person who actually paid or authorized the bribe.

FCPA
The US legal doctrine by which companies are criminally liable for crimes committed by agents and employees is called 'respondeat superior' (literally, 'let the master speak'). To make a company liable, the prosecutor must establish that an agent's actions were:

- within the scope of the agent's duties; and
- intended, at least in part, to benefit the company.

It is normally clear that direct employees of a company are covered by the respondeat superior rule. An agency relationship with a non-employee is more difficult to establish, and requires a mutual understanding that the principal is to be in control of the undertaking and that the agent is acting on behalf of the principal. The respondeat superior rule means that once an employee or agent admits to an FCPA violation or is found guilty, the company has a very hard task to distance itself from the activities and is usually automatically presumed to be guilty as well. The presence of a corporate ethics and compliance programme may be relevant to the question of whether an agent was acting strictly within the bounds of their duties, but the fact that the company specifically instructed them not to engage in the behaviour is not usually enough to escape liability. Therefore an entire organization – despite its best efforts to prevent wrongdoing in its ranks – can still be held criminally liable for any of its employees' illegal actions.

There have been calls to relax the respondeat superior doctrine to allow something akin to the UK's 'adequate procedures' defence.

The FCPA also makes companies potentially liable for the acts committed by its group companies. The rules differ depending on whether the group company is a subsidiary (i.e. the parent owns more than half the shares in the company or exercises control over its activities).

US companies
US companies and Issuers are not necessarily liable for the acts of their foreign subsidiaries with respect to the anti-bribery provisions of the FCPA. But the prosecutor may assert various legal theories to try to establish vicarious liability of the parent:

• The parent authorized the improper payment or gave money to its subsidiary with knowledge that some of the money would be used to make improper payments. (Of course, to do so, there must be evidence of such authorization or proof that an officer, director, employee or agent of the parent corporation had such improper knowledge.[147])

- The 'piercing the corporate veil theory', which assumes that the two separate entities (parent and subsidiary) are essentially the same. Courts generally recognize a presumption of separateness between a parent corporation and its subsidiary; this is a difficult standard to overcome, particularly if the parent and the subsidiary observe appropriate corporate formalities.
- That the subsidiary is an agent of the parent. In order to establish an agency relationship:
  - there must be an understanding between the parties that the principal is to be in control of the undertaking;
  - there must be a manifestation by the principal that the agent shall act for and on behalf of him; and
  - the agent must accept the undertaking.

Recent (settled, not litigated) cases suggest that the DOJ will aggressively claim jurisdiction over 'any person' under the FCPA.

Syncor: US Issuer Charged Over Violations by Its Overseas Subsidiary[148]

Syncor International Corporation Inc. was a manufacturer of radioactive pharmaceuticals based in California. It shares were listed on Nasdaq. In 2002, it resolved an FCPA action brought by the SEC and paid a $500,000 civil penalty. Its wholly owned subsidiary Syncor Taiwan settled a related case with the DOJ, paying a criminal fine of $2m.

Syncor Taiwan pleaded guilty to paying doctors employed by government-owned hospitals in Taiwan in an effort to boost sales. The money was paid in cash in Taiwan via hand-delivered, sealed envelopes. The total payments to doctors averaged over $30,000 per year from 1989, increasing to an average of over $170,000 per year to 2002.

The DOJ asserted jurisdiction because the payments were authorized by the company's board chairman while he was in California.

The SEC charged the US company because the Taiwanese subsidiary had sent financial information to the parent company in California that included line items reflecting corrupt payments. These were then incorporated into the financial records of the parent.

The SEC also charged also Monty Fu, the founder (and at various times the CEO) of Syncor International Corporation, with aiding and abetting Syncor's FCPA books and records, and internal control violations. He consented to a permanent injunction against FCPA accounting violations and paid a $75,000 civil penalty.

Foreign subsidiaries
Foreign subsidiaries (or their officers, directors, employees and agents) of issuers or domestic concerns are not automatically liable under the FCPA. Non-US companies and individuals come within the FCPA only if they commit an act in furtherance of an FCPA violation 'while in the territory of the United States'. However, again using agency theory, the DOJ has tried to extend this by asserting that employees of foreign subsidiaries are either employees or agents of the parent company, and therefore personally liable. Recent cases brought by the government suggest that it will aggressively claim jurisdiction over 'any person' under the FCPA. Nevertheless, no courts have ruled on this issue, and all cases so far have settled out of court.

Non-US firms
A non-US firm can be liable for the acts of subsidiaries, although the act itself must have some connection back to the US.

ABB Vetco Gray: Non-US Subsidiaries of Non-US Issuer Faced Prosecution Under the FCPA[149]

ABB Ltd is a Swiss-based freight forwarder with its ADRs listed on the New York Stock Exchange. Between 1998 and 2003 its US and overseas subsidiaries paid bribes to foreign officials in Nigeria, Angola and Kazakhstan totalling some $1.1m.

Most of the payments were made directly in the US in the form of cash and gifts by an employee of ABB Vetco Gray, Inc. (a US subsidiary). The money came from cash advances on the employee's corporate credit card and were reimbursed by the operating companies, which listed them as consulting fees.

ABB Ltd (Swiss issuer), ABB Vetco Gray Inc. and ABB Vetco Gray (UK) Ltd all settled charges. Jurisdiction was asserted as follows:

- **ABB Ltd:** Some of the payments happened after ABB Ltd became an issuer and the payments were improperly consolidated, recorded as ordinary business expenses in its books.
- **ABB Vetco Gray, Inc.:** Domestic concern; some acts were performed in Texas.
- **ABB Vetco Gray (UK) Ltd:** An employee of ABB Vetco Gray, Inc. (US) acted as an agent for ABB Vetco Gray UK when the employee provided payments and benefits to Nigerian officials and was reimbursed by ABB Vetco Gray UK by cheque or wire transfer.

Bribery Act

Any company that is incorporated in the UK or carries on a business or part of a business in the UK can be liable under the corporate offence under Section 7. Therefore, the test is not where the act of bribery occurs, but where the company conducts business. This means that overseas subsidiaries of UK and non-UK companies can be liable under the corporate offence if they carry on a business or 'part of a business' in the UK, and a person or company 'associated' with them bribes someone.

Companies subject to Section 7
The threshold of 'carrying on business' is potentially a very low one. Under the strict interpretation of the statute, even a business based outside the UK but selling goods in to the UK through the internet might be held to be 'carrying on business'. Such an approach would be consistent with the way the FSA has interpreted similar legislation.[150] The Ministry of Justice's guidance notes that it would not apply to a foreign company that did not have a 'demonstrable business presence' in the UK.

The Guidance acknowledges that a UK listing of itself is unlikely to be sufficient, in contrast to the FCPA, which may be engaged simply by having a US listing. It also states (at paragraph 36) that neither is having a UK subsidiary necessarily enough to cause a company to carry on business:

> 'Having a UK subsidiary will not, in itself, mean that a parent company is carrying on a business in the UK, since a subsidiary may act independently of its parent or other group companies.'

Quite what this means in practice has still to be tested. One strict interpretation is that only very rarely will subsidiaries act entirely independently of their parents; the phrase 'in itself' is likely to be irrelevant, and the actions of most UK subsidiaries will cause both UK and overseas parents to have liability for its actions under Section 7. The SFO has said this:

> 'Many have asked, over the last few months, about whether having a subsidiary in the UK is sufficient to enable the test to be satisfied.

We have certainly had discussions in the SFO with a number of corporations based in the US and in other countries and, of course, the position becomes particularly complex where business structures operate under wholly different systems of law. We have to look at the simple test in the Bribery Act and ask whether or not that foreign corporation is carrying on business here. If it is, then corruption that it commits anywhere else in the world is within our jurisdiction.'[151]

What is an 'associated person'?
A subsidiary will not always be an 'associated person' of its parent company. So an overseas subsidiary can cause a parent company (being any UK or overseas company that is 'carrying on business in the UK') to become liable under the corporate offence at Section 7 where it commits an act of bribery in the context of performing services for the parent. But if the non-UK subsidiary is acting entirely on its own account, it would not make the parent liable under Section 7. So neither the non-UK entity nor the parent will *automatically* be liable following overseas bribery; it depends on the level of interaction and involvement that the parent company has with the overseas entity.

On the other hand, if the entity performs extensive services to a company carrying on business in the UK, there is likely to be liability.

The Guidance explains that an organization is only liable for the actions of its associated person if the bribe was intended (by such an associated person) to benefit the organization directly and intended to obtain or retain business or an advantage in the conduct of business. So a bribe paid by an employee of a subsidiary or joint venture is normally intended to benefit the subsidiary and not the parent company, even though the parent clearly benefits indirectly. If all the parent company does is receive dividends and no more, then the Guidance states that the UK entity will not have liability.

The Guidance considers two different types of joint ventures. In the case of a joint venture through ownership of a separate legal entity, the Guidance notes that an employee of the joint venture entity is likely to be performing services for that entity only and will not be associated with the participants in the joint venture. In addition, a bribe paid on behalf of the joint venture may be deemed to benefit the joint venture entity only, even though the owners may benefit from it indirectly. Thus shareholders may not be held liable for all activities of the joint venture company. The situation becomes more complicated if the employee of the joint venture entity was seconded by (and remains an employee of) one of the joint venture participants.

Where the joint venture is conducted through a contractual agreement, the Guidance states that an employee of one of the parties is likely to be associated with their direct employer only, and a bribe paid by the employee is probably paid for the benefit of that party only. The degree of control that each party has over the joint venture arrangement will be a relevant factor in this respect.

Paragraphs 41 and 42 of the Guidance are as follows:

> 'The degree of control that a participant has over that arrangement is likely to be one of the "relevant circumstances" that would be taken into account in deciding whether a person who paid a bribe in the conduct of the joint venture business was "performing services for or on behalf of" a participant in that arrangement.'

> Even if it can properly be said that an agent, a subsidiary, or another person acting for a member of a joint venture, was performing services for the organisation, **an offence will be committed only if that agent, subsidiary or person intended to obtain or retain business or an advantage in the conduct of business for the organisation**. The fact that an organisation benefits indirectly from a bribe is very unlikely, in itself, to amount to proof of the specific intention required by the offence.' [My emphasis]

The UK parent could still become liable for the actions of its subsidiary in other ways, depending on the facts and its knowledge of the subsidiary's wrongdoing. The UK parent could be liable for false accounting offences if the accounts of the subsidiary are consolidated with its own and contain deliberate and material errors; it could be liable for money laundering offences if it knowingly received the proceeds of contracts tainted by bribery.

Undermining another UK company
The General Counsel of the SFO was asked this question in January 2011:[152]

> 'Q:' Suppose company X, a US company, has two subsidiaries, Y and Z, where Z is located in the UK and Y in Mexico. Could bribery by Y in Mexico create liability to X under the Bribery Act?
>
> A: Yes it could, if the bribery in Mexico could be linked in any sense to a UK operation (i.e., the bribery did, or had the potential to, undermine a UK 'company).'

Joint ventures
Joint ventures (JVs) are risky, because your company is potentially liable for bribes made by an entity that you don't entirely control – all the risks, without all the rewards! The reasons that JVs are attractive in certain situations make them intrinsically risky, for example:

- operating in a risky country where the company does not want to expose its core brand
- local rules making it favourable for enterprises to have some with local ownership
- the political advantages in being in business with a state-owned organization.

Here are some key things to think about when operating a JV:

- Get management control, including the key financial positions.

- Put in place the same procedures in the JV as you would put in a UK company.
- Get veto power over personnel decisions, because you want trusted people in key positions.
- Rotate your people with other expats on a regular basis (18 months to three years is right) to stop them getting too used to things.
- Ensure that internal audit can and does visit.

Further reading

'An essential summary of the FCPA', page 73.

'An essential summary of the Bribery Act', page 81.

'World class internal controls', page 362.

'Properly managing high-risk transactions', page 368.

'There will continue to be calls for the FCPA to be modified', page 461.

The Bribery Act Guidance: http://bit.ly/nTdQB0 (http://www.justice.gov.uk/downloads/guidance/making-reviewing-law/bribery-act-2010-guidance.pdf).

12. Can a Parent Company be Liable Under the FCPA for Accounting Violations Committed by an Affiliate or Subsidiary?

Short answer

Yes. The subsidiary of a US issuer is also subject to the accounting provisions of the FCPA.

Longer answer

Although the FCPA's accounting provisions technically apply only to issuers and not to subsidiaries, in situations where an issuer holds 50% or more of the shares of a company and/or exercises de facto control of its activities, the parent issuer will generally be liable for false entries on any accounting record that is ultimately consolidated with its own.

Even in cases where the parent has less than 50% of the voting power, it may nevertheless have de facto control if the remaining shareholdings are fragmented or it has particular rights such as the ability to appoint directors. In this case, the SEC is likely to infer that the parent does indeed have control and its obligations are akin to those in the case of a subsidiary.

Non-controlled companies

In the case of affiliates, joint ventures and other group companies where the parent company issuer does not exercise complete control, the FCPA requires that the issuer must use 'good faith' to cause the affiliate to devise and maintain a system of internal accounting controls to the extent 'reasonable under the circumstances'.

Exactly what is reasonable under the circumstances is not specified, and will presumably depend on the degree of control and the laws and environment of the country in which the group company is located. As a minimum, it will be expected that a US parent will take prompt action upon any suspicion of accounting irregularities, and use its influence to the greatest degree possible.

Bear in mind that the SEC may also charge officers personally for 'causing' the misstatement of the company's books and records.

The cases suggest that any time there is a questionable payment involving a subsidiary, the SEC's position is that the adequacy of the parent's internal controls is subject to scrutiny and doubt.

13. Can Company Managers be Personally Liable for Bribery?

Short answer

Company managers who personally 'consent or connive' in bribery commit a criminal offence under the Bribery Act. Those exhibiting 'wilful blindness' can be guilty under the FCPA.

Longer answer

Both the Bribery Act and the FCPA make the main actors in any bribery scheme personally liable. Both, however, go further. Section 14 of the Bribery Act makes life difficult for senior managers and directors of companies involved in bribery. It is aimed at individuals who 'consent or connive' in bribery where the bribery is committed by a company. This means that if it has been established that an offence under Section 1 (active bribery), Section 2 (passive bribery) or Section 6 (bribing a foreign public official) has taken place, then a senior officer of the company is guilty of the same offence if they have consented to or connived in its commission.

The words used in the Act are 'senior officers'. This is defined to include a director, manager, secretary or other similar officer. The term 'manager' has a variable meaning within the workplace and, depending on the company in question, could potentially include quite junior levels of employees. We will have to see how the SFO and courts interpret this.

It should be noted that this is different from, and does not apply to, the offence in Section 7. Senior officers are not automatically liable for failing to put in place adequate procedures under Section 7; they are liable only if they *consent or connive* in the acts of bribery themselves.

'Conniving'

While the test for consenting is clearer, conniving is more difficult. Conniving involves knowing that something may occur but to do nothing to prevent it. It may occur through recklessness, but needs something more than simply negligence.

Wilful blindness under the FCPA: 'What if I didn't know that payments were in fact bribes?'

There is a similar personal liability of company executives under the FCPA mandating that any violation must be 'wilful'. Wilful means that:

- the defendant's actions were intentional and not the result of an accident or mistake; and
- the defendant knew that their actions were in some way unlawful – the defendant does not have to be aware of the existence of the FCPA itself, but they must have proceeded with the knowledge that they were doing a 'bad' thing under the general principles of law, or taken the action without reason to believe that it was lawful.

That, however, is not quite the extent of it. A person or company may be guilty under the FCPA not only if they fail to act upon their *knowledge* of a bribe, but knowledge also covers the concept of 'conscious avoidance' or 'deliberate ignorance'. This means that if a defendant was aware of a high probability of the existence of corrupt arrangements yet deliberately avoided confirming that fact by putting their 'head in the sand' because they wanted to be able to deny knowledge, they would still be guilty. Thus, knowledge may be implied if people deliberately insulate themselves from, or consciously disregard, suspicious actions or circumstances, or 'red flags'. On the other hand, knowledge is not established if the person merely failed to learn the fact through negligence, or if the person actually believed that the transaction was legal.

'Corruptly'
An act is done 'corruptly' if done voluntarily and intentionally, and with a bad purpose. It can be aimed at accomplishing either an unlawful result or a lawful result but by an unlawful method.

This issue, and the question of whether the DOJ's evidence was specific enough to show a defendant's 'conscious avoidance', is central to the conviction of Frederick Bourke, summarized below.

US v. Frederick Bourke: Knowledge and Conscious Avoidance[153]

A further element of the Frederick Bourke trial (see also page 184) centres on Bourke's state of knowledge.

The prosecutor's position is that that Bourke either knew the deal was tainted by bribery and ignored the facts, or deliberately avoided learning the truth. During his trial, prosecutors said that if Bourke didn't know that Kozeny's scheme depended on bribing Azeri officials, it was because Bourke deliberately stuck his head in sand. Bourke certainly seems to have been aware of both Kozeny's colourful background and the risk generally of investing in Azerbaijan. And the prosecution contends that he played a role in coordinating US medical treatment, combined with tourism and shopping trips, for Azeri officials.

After the trial ended, the jury foreman was quoted as saying about Bourke: 'We thought he knew and he definitely should have known.'[154]

'But I'm only a non-executive director – I don't have any responsibilities'

Sorry, but you do. Both the DOJ and the SEC have both recently put independent directors under investigation for failing to properly discharge their duties as board members. In March 2010, for example, the SEC filed a settled action against Vasant Raval, former Chairman of the Audit Committee of InfoGroup, Inc. The action alleged that Raval failed to respond appropriately to various red flags surrounding Vinod Gupta, the company's former CEO and Chairman of the Board, in particular his expenses and transactions with parties related to him.[155]

Further reading

Covington, J.P., Bennett, I.E. and Hartigan, S.J., U.S. v. Bourke FCPA prosecution highlights dangers of turning a blind eye to red flags, White Collar Practice Alert, Jenner & Block LLP, 17 July 2009. Available from: http://bit.ly/ux6hcj (http://www.jenner.com/files/tbl_s20Publications%5CRelated DocumentsPDFs1252%5C2553%5CU.S.%20v.%20Bourke %20FCPA%20Prosecution%20Highlights%20Dangers%20of%20 Turning%20a%20Blind%20Eye%20to%20Red%20Flags_072009 .pdf).

US v. Jewell: http://bit.ly/qi8tGU (http://openjurist.org/532/ f2d/697/united-states-v-jewell). A US Court of Appeals case dealing with the meaning of 'wilful blindness' and 'connivance'.

14. Does the Bribery Act have Retrospective Application?

Short and long answers

No. It only applies to behaviour occurring after the Act became effective, which was 1 July 2011. Behaviour occurring wholly before this date would have to be charged under the old law.

However, the SFO may take into account corrupt behaviour occurring prior to 1 July 2011 if it continued after that date, thus providing evidence of an ongoing and pervasive way of doing business.

Sections 19(5) and 19(6) of the Bribery Act 2010 set out its transitional provisions:

Section 19 (5) This Act does not affect any liability, investigation, legal proceeding or penalty for or in respect of –

(a) a common law offence mentioned in subsection (1) of section 17 which is committed wholly or partly before the coming into force of that subsection in relation to such an offence, or

(b) an offence under the Public Bodies Corrupt Practices Act 1889 or the Prevention of Corruption Act 1906 committed wholly or partly before the coming into force of the repeal of the Act by Schedule 2 to this Act.

Section 19 (6) For the purposes of subsection (5) an offence is partly committed before a particular time if any act or omission which forms part of the offence takes place before that time.

Further reading

Alderman, R., TRACE: anti-bribery compliance solutions, speech at the TRACE partner firm symposium, 30 June 2011. Available from: http://bit.ly/nI3EOp (http://www.sfo.gov.uk/about-us/our-views/director's-speeches/speeches-2011/trace – anti-bribery-compliance-solutions.aspx).

15. Who Are Foreign Officials?

Short answer

The FCPA defines a 'foreign official' extremely widely, including an officer or employee of any department, agency or instrumentality of a foreign government or public international organization. Although still controversial, this is interpreted as including employees of state-owned organizations and candidates for foreign political office.

The Bribery Act refers to a 'foreign *public* official'. This definition is limited to those who exercise a legislative, administrative or judicial position or public function. It apparently will not include employees of state-owned organizations. Bear in mind, though, that bribes to *any person* for commercial purposes are included in the core bribery offence in Section 1 of the Act, so the precise definition of 'foreign public official' is arguably less relevant in the UK.

Longer answer

FCPA
The FCPA covers corrupt payments to any foreign official, foreign political party or party official, or any candidate for foreign political office. A foreign official is an officer, employee or person acting in an official capacity for or on behalf of:

- a foreign government
- any department, agency or instrumentality of a foreign government
- a 'public international organization'.

'Public international organizations', such as the World Bank or United Nations, are designated specifically by executive order of the US President. Currently, more than 80 organizations are on the list, but not all international bodies are included: one high-profile exception is the International Olympic Committee.[156]

An employee of a foreign company has been deemed to be a foreign official because they had a parallel position or appointment with a government entity or political party, although the bribe does needs to be connected with the foreign official's job or duty in some way.

DOJ Opinion Procedure Release 10-03. Foreign Consultants[157]

The Requestor – a US limited partnership – was working with a foreign government on 'an innovative natural resources project with a novel approach' and needed help dealing with that government. It proposed retaining a consultant who was a registered agent of the foreign government. The consultant was a US citizen, who also performed some marketing services on behalf of the foreign government in the US.

The DOJ stated that the consultant and its employees could be held to be 'foreign officials' for purposes of the FCPA. But in this case, the consultant was not acting on behalf of the foreign government: he fully disclosed the relationship, made sure the relationship was permitted under local law and put in place the various contractual obligations to limit the consultant's work for the foreign government. The situation therefore fell outside the ambit of the FCPA.

Instrumentalities

Employees of organizations that are an 'instrumentality' of a foreign government come within the FCPA. Instrumentality is not defined in the FCPA, but once a foreign entity has been deemed an 'instrumentality' of a foreign government, then all of its employees will be considered foreign officials. Remember that the FCPA applies to payments to any public official, regardless of rank or position, so relatively junior people come within this definition. In many countries, particularly those with more centralized economies, the government is an owner or partial owner of all sorts of organizations and it is not always clear that a company is in government hands.

The DOJ has charged many companies based on its view that state-owned companies are 'instrumentalities' of foreign governments and that their employees therefore should be considered as foreign officials. Their interpretation means that all interactions with employees of national oil companies are a particular risk area (for oil and oil services companies in particular). Also, in many countries where the healthcare system is socialized to some degree (including the UK and Canada), doctors in hospitals and surgeries will be regarded as foreign officials (an FCPA risk for healthcare companies).

Diagnostic Products Corporation, Inc. (DPC): Doctors in China as Foreign Officials[158]

DPC is a US-based medical equipment firm. In May 2005 a wholly owned Chinese subsidiary, DPC (Tianjin) Co. Ltd, pleaded guilty to criminal charges brought by the DOJ; DPC itself settled a parallel SEC action at the same time by agreeing to pay nearly $4.8m in penalties.

The case was based on DPC (Tianjin) admitting to making improper payments totalling some $1.6m to medical personnel employed by Chinese government-owned hospitals in order to generate business. The doctors were treated by the US prosecutors as instrumentalities of foreign governments, and therefore within the ambit of the FCPA.

The Control Components/Carson case
There have been challenges to the US government's expansive interpretation of 'foreign official', all of which have so

far failed. The most recent was in the Control Components, Inc. case, where Stuart Carson (former CEO) and others were charged with paying bribes to employees of state-owned customers in China, Korea, Malaysia and the UAE (more on page 181).

In May 2011, the defendants argued that:[159]

> '[s]tate-owned business enterprises ["SOEs"] may, in appropriate circumstances, be considered instrumentalities of a foreign government and their officers and employees to be foreign officials. But Congress (i) knew about SOEs when it enacted the FCPA, (ii) knew that some of the questionable payments in the pre-FCPA era may have been made to employees of SOEs, and (iii) knew how to include SOEs in the definition of "foreign official" if it had wanted to do so. Clearly, Congress did not do so, and contrary to the Government's arguments, there is no evidence that Congress intended SOEs to be covered by this criminal statute, or intended the word "instrumentality" to encompass broadly anything through which a foreign government achieves an "end or purpose." In fact, the plain language of the statute and its history illustrate that the FCPA was aimed at preventing improper payments to traditional government officials. If Congress had wanted SOEs to be included in the definition of "instrumentality," it would have expressly said so – just as it did in 1976 when it enacted the Foreign Sovereign Immunities Act ("FSIA")...
>
> Having no statutory authority for its sweeping position, the Government is thus unable to define the "appropriate circumstances" when an SOE allegedly falls within the FCPA. The Government states only that it is a "fact-based determination." But facts in isolation are irrelevant unless analysed in the context of a legal framework.'

The court denied the defendants' motion to dismiss and held that an SOE may be considered an 'instrumentality' under the FCPA. It acknowledged that the FCPA does not define the term 'instrumentality', but considered that the term was intended to capture entities that are not 'departments' or 'agencies' of a foreign government, but nevertheless carry out governmental functions or objectives. The judge considered that whether a particular SOE constitutes an 'instrumentality' under the FCPA is a question of fact. Several types of evidence are relevant:

- the foreign state's characterization of the SOE and its employees
- the degree of control by the foreign state
- the purpose of the entity's activities
- the extent of government ownership, including level of financial support.

Does the official need to be identified?
It is not even necessary for the intended recipient of the bribe to know anything about the matter at all. In their arguments in the Gun Sting case (see page 452), the DOJ alleged that the defendants intended – via agents, who were DOJ 'plants' – to bribe Gabon's president and the former defence minister, even though the minister himself had not been approached by any of the defendants. The DOJ claimed that the FCPA's anti-bribery provisions do not require that bribe offers be either successful or fully consummated; nor do they require the involvement of an *actual* foreign official. All they require is proof that a defendant intended to bribe a foreign official.

Bribery Act
While the FCPA deals with 'foreign officials', Section 6 of the Bribery Act deals with the bribery of 'foreign *public* officials'. Although the definition very broadly matches that in the FCPA above, the precise definition is an individual who:

- holds a legislative, administrative or judicial position of any kind, whether appointed or elected, of a country or territory outside the United Kingdom (or any subdivision of such a country or territory)

- exercises a public function:
  - for or on behalf of a country or territory outside the United Kingdom (or any subdivision of such a country or territory); or
  - for any public agency or public enterprise of that country or territory (or subdivision)
- is an official or agent of a public international organization.

Significantly, though, the Bribery Act is unlikely to be held by the courts to cover employees of state-owned enterprises. According to the former general counsel of the SFO:

> 'We are not regarding employees of a state-owned company as falling in the ambit of Section 6. People can rest assured that is not what we are looking at at all.'[160]

OECD
Under the OECD, a 'foreign public official' is also defined broadly: any person that holds an office (whether elected or appointed) or any person exercising a public function for a foreign country is considered a foreign public official.

Unlike the FCPA, neither the OECD nor the Bribery Act applies to members of foreign political parties unless that individual has executive or governmental powers.

How do we know we are doing business with foreign officials?
From a bribery risk perspective, companies need to understand who they are doing business with, and whether they have any links with active foreign officials or people with close relationships with foreign officials – in risk parlance these are known as 'politically exposed persons' (PEPs). The risk list will include:

- ministers, ministry employees and government consultants
- members of ruling or opposition parties
- judges, magistrates, and other employees of the local judiciary
- customs and immigration officials
- police and the military
- members of regulatory committees
- members of quasi-governmental organizations and state-sponsored committees
- UN and World Bank representatives
- employees of state-owned health services, including doctors.

Discovering who is a PEP is another issue. Unfortunately there are no publicly available lists, but many business information providers are now researching and selling PEP lists in electronic format (which can also used in your due diligence and compliance reviews).

Further reading

FCPA Professor, posts with label 'Carson'. Available from: http://bit.ly/opPVMh (http://fcpaprofessor.blogspot.com/search/label/Carson).

Fox, T., Reading a crystal ball? Guidance on instrumentality under the FCPA, FCPA Compliance and Ethics Blog, 19 August 2011. Available from: http://bit.ly/pajxtZ (http://tfoxlaw.wordpress.com/2011/08/19/reading-a-crystal-ball-guidance-on-instrumentality-under-the-fcpa-part-ii/).

Some PEP databases include the following (note that this list is far from comprehensive and in no particular order):

- World-Check: http://www.world-check.com

- Dow Jones: http://www.dowjones.com
- Compliance Solutions: http://www.worldcompliance.com
- Metavante Risk and Compliance Solutions: http://www.primeassociates.com
- Governance, Risk and Compliance: http://accelus.thomsonreuters.com.

16. What Are the Affirmative Defences and Exceptions Under the FCPA?

Short answer

A payment does not violate the FCPA if it is:

- legal under local written laws
- legitimate promotional expenditure
- a bona fide facilitation payment.

True instances of extortion are also likely to be exempted.

Longer answer

The FCPA doesn't ban all payments to foreign officials. The anti-bribery provisions contain three statutory defences; if a payment falls within any of these three scenarios, it will not be unlawful under the FCPA.

Lawful under local laws

A person cannot be guilty of violating the FCPA if the payment was lawful under foreign law. Having said this, the defence stipulates that the payment has to have been lawful under the *written* laws and regulations of the foreign country, and not merely local business customs, practices or norms. To be an offence under the FCPA, a payment has to be made 'corruptly', rather than in the normal course of business; since no written laws of countries permit corrupt payments to local officials, I cannot conceive of many situations where this exception would be used.

The criminal codes of many oil-producing nations criminalize bribery but relieve the briber from criminal liability if there was extortion involved, or if the briber reported the bribe to authorities. This is because the country has a strong interest in prosecuting the foreign official who received the bribe, and so for policy reasons encourages bribers to report their acts. This is the position in Azerbaijan, Kazakhstan, Ukraine, Saudi Arabia, Kuwait, the United Arab Emirates, Bahrain, Oman, Qatar and Yemen.

Put another way, while foreign law may provide the briber with a safe harbour, the FCPA does not.

US v. Frederick Bourke: Bribes are Not Lawful Under Azeri Law

The DOJ's evidence was that Frederick Bourke, a successful entrepreneur and multi-millionaire, knowingly backed rogue investor Viktor Kozeny in a corrupt plan to purchase SOCAR – the state-owned Azerbaijani oil industry – in secret partnership with the president of Azerbaijan and his family. The Azeri state privatization programme gave the president of Azerbaijan the ability to choose if and when to privatize SOCAR, and so the plan was to corruptly influence the president to exercise his, and other Azeri officials', discretion.

Bourke's defence team argued that the scheme was lawful under the written laws of Azerbaijan because while the Azeri Criminal Code criminalized bribery, it pardoned the briber if the payment was the result of extortion, or if the person voluntarily reported the bribe to the authorities. Bourke claimed that his payments were legal under both of these provisions.

The US court disagreed, however, holding that the payment itself (that is, the act of bribery) remained unlawful under Azeri law, even though the briber had been relieved of personal liability.

Legitimate promotional expenses
The FCPA is not transgressed if a payment to a foreign official was a reasonable and bona fide expenditure, such as travel

or accommodation expenses, that was directly related to the demonstration or explanation of a product or service, or performance of a contract with a government agency.

This exemption is specific and it is most unlikely that general hospitality or client entertainment come within this exemption.

Facilitation payments
Additionally, the FCPA includes an exception allowing 'facilitation or facilitating payments' – payments made to expedite or secure performance of a routine, non-discretionary governmental action.

Extortion?
This is not one of the stated exemptions, although here seems a good place to put it. The FCPA is only transgressed if there was corrupt intent, and where the payer of a bribe had little realistic chance but to pay it, this test is unlikely to be satisfied.

Is giving in to extortion different from paying a bribe?
Many of the reported bribery cases do not involve grand bribery schemes. In fact, many arise from situations where the company never intended to pay money to receive something to which they were not entitled, but merely gave in to extortion demanded by government officials to supply a basic and efficient service that they should have been entitled to receive.

Anecdotally, one hears many stories of companies being asked for petty bribes. With many smaller companies trying to gain a foothold in developing countries, being asked for petty bribes and kickbacks is par for the course. Many companies report that if you don't pay, you don't do business – regardless of the strength of your product. And with wages so endemically low in developing countries, it's unlikely that this will change any time soon.

Blackmail is demanding something from someone and then gaining from this demand. The demand must be unwarranted and 'with menaces' – a threat from the blackmailer to do something for not agreeing to the demand. But the threat doesn't have to be something illegal. Neither does the demand have to be made in terms of a requirement or obligation. Indeed, it can be couched in terms which are by no means aggressive, and the more suave and gentle the request, the more sinister in the circumstances it might be. Paying ransoms and blackmail payments is not generally illegal, and in many cases is a rational response. The example is often cited of the captain of a ship who, when seeking to have its cargo of fruit unloaded, was told by the stevedores at the port that it would be unloaded only on the condition that a payment was made to someone nominated by the stevedores, not necessarily to the stevedores themselves. If the captain doesn't pay, and pay quickly, the cargo will spoil. That is a very difficult position for the captain of a ship to be in, and yet, if they paid, the Bribery Act would criminalize the payment. US companies may of course be permitted to make such payments under the facilitation payments exception of the FCPA.

The judge in Bourke's case noted that if Bourke could 'provide an evidentiary foundation for the claim that he was the victim of true extortion' then she would instruct the jury that they would have to find that Bourke possessed 'corrupt intent' to the criminal standard of beyond reasonable doubt. The FCPA makes clear, she stated, that 'true extortion situations', such as one where the Azeri government threatened to blow up an oil rig if it did not receive bribes, would not be a violation of the FCPA, because the briber had no realistic choice but to pay the bribe and thus did not possess the required criminal intent.[161]

Further reading

Question 18.

Keneally, J.M. and Park, S.E., 'Kozeny': foreign laws and the FCPA – limits to your defences, *New York Law Journal*, **240**(109), 1–2, 5 December 2008. Available from: http://bit.ly/qRgyFJ (http://www.kelleydrye.com/publications/articles/0442/_res/id=Files/index=0).

17. Can I Do Business in Some Parts of the World Without Paying Bribes?

'43% of respondents believe that they failed to win new business in the last five years because a competitor had paid a bribe, and one-third had lost business to bribery in the last year.'[162]

Short answer

Yes, although no one should pretend that there will not be challenges in certain high-risk countries. Companies with a zero-tolerance approach to bribery can find themselves losing deals to competitors that are more willing to pay, and they will certainly find some services more difficult to obtain in the short term if they are not willing to make facilitation payments. Please don't let that put you off! In the medium term, the positives far outweigh the negatives.

Longer answer

When going into a new market, the only sound way nowadays is to refuse to pay any bribes, kickbacks or facilitation payments. You will face problems, but if you have a product or service that people want, have other partners and alternatives, and plan effectively, then although you might occasionally face delays, shortages and non-supply, eventually people will get used to it and stop asking.

If you give in to demands, people get to hear that you are willing to pay, and you will be faced with all sorts of demands: utilities will 'accidentally' be cut off and require money to be turned back on. And it will happen time and time again. If you refuse to pay from the outset, you'll feel some short-term pain, but in the long run you'll be much happier. The requests for money will eventually stop, and you'll just be known in the market as someone that won't do it.

Stopping paying
Meanwhile, in the real world, this is an aim that will take time to come to fruition. If you have been 'playing the game' for some time, then an even steelier resolve is needed, because people will have seen you bend the rules in the past, and won't believe initially that you aren't willing to do it again. If you are going through it at the moment, take heart that others have done it before you, have experienced similar aggravations along the way, but got through it successfully and are now in a better place as a result.

A useful strategy that has worked as an interim measure is to stop paying anyone directly and say that you will only pay charges to their office, and if you get a receipt. That usually help things slow down a bit. Then request the CEO should request internally that all facilitation payment requests must be approved by the CCO. That cuts down the number even further, because no one wants to ask the CCO for anything.

But that's not the end of the matter. The real difficulty is ensuring that the person in the region is not simply continuing to make the facilitation payment, without telling the CCO, and accounting for it, or charging it through expenses in a different way. If they are doing this, there is a still a potential bribery violation, and so we're back to having strong controls over accounting for payments and expenses to prevent this as much as humanly possible.

When stopping making facilitation payments or petty bribes, ensure that senior management have bought in, and call on them to demonstrate that 'tone at the top'. There will be disruption and a hit to profits from taking the ethical stance and showing that you are unwilling to engage in any bribery at all. If you have to sue the electricity company to get your electricity switched back on, then that is what you need to do.

It is far from being the panacea, but when communicating the message to business partners there are three points to get across:

- Explain your difficulties using both local and international rules, and explain that sticking to fair business practices is in everyone's interests. Don't just talk about the FCPA. Let your customers and suppliers know that you are aware of their own domestic laws and suggest that exposure would be embarrassing for everyone.
- Set out the valuable alternatives that you can offer. Instead of paying a bribe, you can offer a government official help in other ways: perhaps community projects, marketing local products, or training and other consulting.
- Indicate the other partners and alternatives that you have, and make sure you have them. In many countries, the competition for business is intense – let them know you know, so you don't become boxed in or dependent.

Staying above reproach
The best strategy to staying safe in a high-risk country is to have a comprehensive compliance programme. Also, get reputable local advisors on your side. You need them at all levels and all regions. They can advise you on the local rules, and if they are well regarded they assist in pushing forward your company's ethical credentials.

Further reading

'Designing effective compliance procedures', page 351.

18. Are Facilitation Payments Legal?

'I hope to be reborn as a customs official ...'
CEO of a successful Thai manufacturing company[163]

Short answer

No. Facilitation payments are invariably illegal in the country in which they are paid. Some international bribery laws, however – such as the FCPA – will not prosecute companies for making minor facilitation payments in other countries. In the UK and some other OECD countries, there is no such exception.

Longer answer

Facilitation or 'grease' payments are relatively minor amounts paid to public officials to expedite routine business activities. The sums involved are small, yet the consequences of not paying can be serious. (A delay by a foreign official issuing a permit for example could seriously delay a entire project, which could increase the contractor's costs and result in very severe monetary penalties.) Whilst illegal, they have become a fact of life in many countries to get things done quickly. The question of whether, and to what extent, small facilitation-type payments should really be criminalized is continuing to divide opinion in the business and compliance communities.

The position under the FCPA

The FCPA has a written exception for bona fide facilitation payments. Contrary to popular opinion, though, not all petty bribes are truly facilitation payments.

Facilitation payments have a number of specific characteristics which are set out in the FCPA. A facilitation payment is:

- a payment to a foreign official, political party or party official
- in respect of 'routine governmental action'
- paid to in order to expedite performance of duties of non-discretionary nature that the official is already bound to perform
- not intended to influence the outcome of the official's action, such as awarding new business – only its timing.

A common facilitation payment exception under the FCPA would be slipping an immigration official a few dollars to speed up the processing of a visa. The visa is an automatic entitlement – the official has no discretion whether to grant it – but the payment prevents it sitting at the bottom of an in-tray while other applicants who have paid what is often the going rate have their documents expedited. The issue here is not paying to be advantaged, but paying not to be disadvantaged.

Even within this tight definition, the FCPA further defines and limits 'routine governmental action', specifying it to mean only those actions that are 'ordinarily and commonly performed,' by officials, and limiting them to:

- obtaining permits or licenses that qualify a person to do business in a foreign country
- processing government papers, such as visas
- providing police protection, mail pick-up and delivery, or scheduling inspections or customs inspections
- providing utility service, loading and unloading of cargo, or protecting perishable products from deterioration.

It should further be borne in mind though that the fact that facilitation payments are legal under the FCPA does not make them legal in the country where the payment took place. Most countries will treat the payment and receipt of facilitation payments within that country as a crime.

The DOJ's view on facilitation payments

Not all small bribes are allowed under the FCPA, and the prosecutors apply the rules to the letter. So unless the payment is in respect of a permit that actually 'qualifies a person to do business in a foreign country', as is specified by the wording in the Act, then it is unlikely to be exempted. The enforcement landscape is littered with companies prosecuted heavily for making small bribes (see for example the 'Panalpina' series of settlements that were based around payments to avoid customs formalities).

The DOJ will take the following into account when deciding whether to prosecute:

- The size of each individual payment. There is nothing set out in writing, but my view is that payments over $100 individually are starting to move out of the realm of facilitation payments.
- The total of the 'facilitation payments'. Companies that allow numerous yet individually small facilitation payments may be said to have a pervasive course of conduct involving bribery, which would bring them clearly within the authorities' radar.
- Who the payments was made to. The more senior the individual, the less chance that the action is truly routine and non-discretionary.

The position under the Bribery Act

The Bribery Act, unlike the FCPA or OECD, has no facilitation payments exception. Instead, it criminalizes the making of all bribes, worldwide, no matter how small. There was hope within sections of the business community when the Act was still in its committee stage, and again when the Adequate Procedures Guidance was published, that there would be at least tolerance on the part of prosecutors to facilitation payments – but this did not prove to be the case. The SFO has indicated that it does not approve of any company that does not adopt a 'zero-tolerance' policy to facilitation payments.

Perhaps even more importantly, if companies have a policy of allowing facilitation payments, then the courts may not view a company's policies as constituting 'adequate procedures' under Section 7 of the Act. This will be the case even if it was a US-based entity and thought itself able to make facilitation payments with impunity.

The SFO's view on facilitation payments
Ultimately it will come down to the discretion of the SFO whether it prosecutes a company or person making facilitation payments. Payments that are one-off, small or self-reported to the SFO, or made as a response to extortion or to ensure personal safety, are unlikely to be prosecuted. SFO director, Richard Alderman, stated in 2011:

> 'I do not expect facilitation payments to end the moment the Bribery Act comes into force. What I do expect though is for corporates who do not yet have a zero tolerance approach to these payments, to commit themselves to such an approach and to work on how to eliminate these payments over a period of time.'[164]

The SFO has stated that they would not target a company committed to eliminating facilitation payments, and would consider whether:

- the company has issued a clear policy regarding facilitation payments
- written guidance is available to employees as to the procedure they should follow when asked to make such payments
- such procedures are being adhered to
- there is evidence that all facilitation payments are being recorded by the company
- there is evidence that action is being taken to inform the authorities in the countries concerned that such payments are being extorted

- the company is taking practical steps to stop making facilitation payments.

Key issues that might however lead to a prosecution include:

- large or repeated payments
- planned payments
- those accepted as a standard way of conducting business in the company.

The OECD
The OECD, like the FCPA, has an exemption for facilitation payments. There are some 38 signatories to the OECD convention, but the only countries that permit facilitation payments are the US, Canada, Australia, New Zealand and South Korea. The OECD's 2005 monitoring report for the US expressed disapproval of the FCPA's facilitation payments exception, although US rule-makers contend that its current laws are adequate.[165]

That being said, the OECD now discourages facilitation payments, as does the United Nations Convention Against Corruption and the Inter-American Convention Against Corruption. In November 2009, the tenth anniversary of the OECD Convention, the OECD released its new 'Recommendation for Further Combating Bribery of Foreign Public Officials'. This report, among other things, recommended that OECD member countries prohibit or discourage the use of small facilitation payments, stating that it:

'RECOMMENDS, in view of the corrosive effect of small facilitation payments, particularly on sustainable economic development and the rule of law that Member countries should:

i) undertake to periodically review their policies and approach on small facilitation payments in order to effectively combat the phenomenon;

ii) encourage companies to prohibit or discourage the use of small facilitation payments in internal company controls, ethics and compliance programmes or measures, recognising that such payments are generally illegal in the countries where they are made, and must in all cases be accurately accounted for in such companies' books and financial records.'

What if our staff are stopped at a roadblock in sub-Saharan Africa and asked for a $10 'fine'?
This question is frequently asked, often as an attempt to show that a blanket ban on all facilitation payments is not realistic. Are you serious – critics say – that the correct response is to never, in any circumstances, make any payment?

The reality is that many companies operate in the developing world where the rule of law is not what it should be, and the police and military have been known to stop vehicles at 'checkpoints' for a real or imaginary infraction. Where the personal safety or security of a member of staff or other person is at risk, then they should make a payment in order to get people to safety. Such practices though are only eliminated if reported to the more senior authorities through the proper channels. This is generally though the embassy in the country in which the extortion occurred.

Further reading

Question 17.

OECD Recommendation for Further Combating Bribery of Foreign Public Officials in International Business Transactions: http://bit.ly/oLYxQO (http://www.oecd.org/document/13/0,3746,en_2649_34859_39884109_1_1_1_1,00.html).

19. Can I Obtain Guidance About Whether My 'Novel' Marketing Scheme will be Viewed as Bribery?

Short answer

The DOJ has a formal procedure that companies can use in order to obtain an opinion on whether future conduct by the company would be considered by the DOJ as violating the FCPA's anti-bribery provisions. These 'Opinion Procedure Releases' are published on the DOJ's website.

In the UK, the SFO does not have a similar procedure, although it has frequently said that its 'door is always open'.[166]

Longer answer

DOJ Opinion Procedure Releases

The original text of the FCPA contained no procedure whereby prosecutors would provide guidance to companies about the appropriateness of certain behaviour. Since 1992, however, the DOJ has had a formal procedure whereby companies could obtain an opinion letter from the DOJ as to whether a future course of conduct would violate the FCPA's anti-bribery provisions. This procedure was codified by 1998 amendments to the FCPA.

Under the procedure, companies can seek guidance on actual – not hypothetical – conduct so long as the request is specific and 'all relevant and material information bearing on the conduct ... and on the circumstances of the prospective conduct' is described. If the DOJ issues a favourable opinion, there is a presumption that the conduct as described in the request does not violate the FCPA. The SEC has confirmed that it will not commence any action against a company that has received a favourable DOJ review letter.

Although technically the opinion procedures are fact-specific and can be only be relied on by the company making the request – and only then if the disclosure of facts and circumstances in its request is accurate and complete – the DOJ has referred to its Opinion Procedure Releases as 'precedent'. It has also suggested that the guidance offered in them can be used as guidance by subsequent prosecutors and regulators.

The DOJ has published all of its opinion procedures releases since 1980 online. A list of all the releases can be found in Appendix 6. Interestingly, of the 56 Opinion Procedure Releases issued by the DOJ since 1980, all but one (98-01) have been positive (i.e. the DOJ has approved the course of action). This is unlikely to be pure coincidence, in that the opinion procedure mechanism (at Section 80.15) does provide a route for a request to be withdrawn before a formal opinion is issued; it is likely that when the requestor senses that it will not receive a favourable opinion, it simply withdraws the request.

SFO
The SFO has no equivalent formal mechanism to the Opinion Procedure Releases. It has, however, stated that it will provide informal guidance if requested. In particular, the SFO is keen to discuss merger and acquisition cases, such as where one company is proposing to take over another and, during due diligence, discovers overseas corruption issues in the target. The SFO is able to provide guidance on the scope of remediation and the agency's likely response if the transaction goes ahead.

This path is not yet well trodden: there is a risk that a company goes to the SFO to get guidance on how to comply with the Act and ends up as the target of an investigation.

The SFO is unable to exclude this possibility, although based on past experience its most likely response is to ask the company to conduct an internal inquiry, based on mutually agreed parameters, and then provide a report to the SFO concerning the specific matter in question.

Further reading

Appendix 6: DOJ Opinion Procedure Releases, page 498.

FCPA Opinion Procedure, Electronic Code of Federal Regulations. Available from: http://bit.ly/qRuiDh (http://ecfr.gpoaccess.gov/cgi/t/text/text-idx?c=ecfr&sid=361742e80e420cac62807727ef8aeade&rgn=div5&view=text&node=28:2.0.1.1.34&idno=28).

FCPA Professor, The FCPA mulligan rule?, 19 October 2010. Available from: http://bit.ly/pViyZb (http://www.fcpaprofessor.com/the-fcpa-mulligan-rule).

20. What Are the Penalties for Bribery Under the FCPA?

Short answer

The Federal Sentencing Guidelines set out the parameters of a criminal fine. In the case of bribery, the penalty depends on a number of factors; principally the gain made, but also its egregiousness. The Alternative Fines Act modifies the Sentencing Guidelines and allows a maximum fine of up to twice the loss to the victim or benefit to the defendant, whichever is the higher.

The SEC is able to levy a civil penalty, which is typically less than the criminal fine, but its main weapon is the ability to force the disgorgement of all the gain made from the bribery scheme.

Longer answer

It is a source of wonder to most outside (and many inside) the rarefied environment of US white-collar defence law how fines under the FCPA are assessed. In this question I set out the law and guidelines surrounding fines and penalties.

I set out a worked example, being the penalties levied on BAE Systems pursuant to its settlement – the facts of which are set out in Question 22.

Anti-bribery provisions
There are four sources of statutory guidance for assessing penalties for violations of the FCPA.

1. Under the FCPA itself
This sets the maximum fine levels:

- Individuals who commit wilful violations of the FCPA *anti-bribery* provisions may be punished by up to $250,000 in fines and/or five years' imprisonment. Individuals who violate the FCPA *accounting* provisions may be fined up to $5m and imprisoned for up to 20 years. A criminal fine imposed on an individual cannot be paid directly or indirectly by the company on whose behalf the person acted.
- Companies may be fined up to $2m for violation of the FCPA *anti-bribery* provisions and $25m per violation of the FCPA *accounting* provisions.

2. Statutory civil penalties for the SEC
The SEC focuses its enforcement efforts primarily on the accounting provisions of the FCPA, bringing enforcement actions against issuers or persons acting on behalf of an issuer. The SEC may therefore seek various remedies for violations of the FCPA, including civil monetary penalties, in addition or as an alternative to disgorgement.[167] The maximum amount of penalty for each act wilfully violating any provision of the Securities Act 1933 is $150,000 for a natural person or $750,000 for a company if it can be shown that the violation falls into the most serious tier set out under the rules, which applies to violations that:

> 'involve "fraud, deceit, manipulation, or deliberate or reckless disregard of a regulatory requirement", and "directly or indirectly resulted in substantial losses or created a significant risk of substantial losses to other persons."'

It is likely that the SEC would argue that serious FCPA violations would fall into this tier. It can be seen that this element of the penalty can mount up quickly for a breach that comprises a number of discrete transgressions.

3. Under the Alternative Fines Act
This Act authorizes a *maximum* fine for a federal criminal offence up to twice the loss to the victim or benefit that the

defendant did or sought to obtain by making the corrupt payment, whichever is the higher. In other words, this Act provides that the fines can be much higher than those set out in the FCPA itself.[168]

4. The Federal Sentencing Guidelines

The Sentencing Guidelines inform the DOJ's *actual* approach to calculating fines. The starting point for fines under the Guidelines is the 'gain' made by the defendant. In those cases where no gain was made (which might be the case where the bribery scheme was unsuccessful), the fine can be driven by the amount of the bribe itself.

The largest criminal fine in an FCPA enforcement action has been $450m levied in the settlement with Siemens. The individual given the longest criminal sentence to date has been Charles Jumet, who received 60 months for conspiracy to violate the FCPA, plus 27 months for making false statements to federal agents.[169]

Does the government adhere strictly to the sentencing guidelines?

No. A decision of the US Supreme Court in the case of *US v. Booker* held that the Sentencing Guidelines were not binding, but merely advisory. Notwithstanding this, the DOJ does like to have a scientific basis for its fines; its Guidelines are important and it does not want to set any precedent whereby it deviates from the sentencing guidelines, as this may affect future settlements.[170] But both the DOJ and SEC still have considerable discretion as to the level of fines: the DOJ will routinely agree fines significantly below the lower level dictated by the Guidelines, and companies will be treated very differently by the DOJ depending on their level of cooperation and remediation.

In practice, settled fines are arrived at by a process of negotiation, where the fine calculations are almost reverse-engineered to arrive at an accepted gain that both parties can live with. Clearly, everything needs to be in the right ballpark; but it is an inexact science, and there is much flexibility to the process.

Through a 'carrot and stick' philosophy, judges, and therefore the DOJ, are directed to consider three *aggravating* factors in any bribery case:

- managerial involvement
- prior criminal history
- obstruction of justice

. . . and four *mitigating* factors:

- maintenance of an effective programme to prevent and detect violations of law
- self-reporting of the offence
- full cooperation in the investigation
- clearly demonstrating recognition of, and affirmative acceptance for, its criminal conduct.

In the Siemens settlement, for example (see page 15), the guidelines gave a fine range of $1.35bn to $2.70bn. The fine agreed with the DOJ was $450m. This is still a huge sum, but because of Siemens' cooperation and its lengthy and expensive remediation programme – involving teams of lawyers and forensic accountants undertaking a worldwide review of operations – the DOJ were more lenient on the level of the fine than they could have been.

Other notable settlements coming in below the lower limit suggested by the sentencing guidelines include Universal Corporation, where the fine was 30% below; Technip, where it was 25% below; and Snamprogetti, where it was 20% below. Such reductions are fact-specific – again, this goes to the DOJ not wanting to set a precedent – and are not explained or quantified well in the settlement documents.

One count or multiple counts?
Further, the prosecutors have discretion on how many counts to charge. It is often found that a company that has historically been prepared to bribe to win business has paid not one single bribe, but a number of bribes – often as part of related schemes. Is this one violation or several? Just how many fines should be applied against the same company?

It is bad news here for companies. In cases where there are multiple contracts between a company and consultants making illicit payments, the DOJ will typically want to charge each contract as a separate violation of the FCPA. Indeed, the government may go so far as suggesting that every single payment is a separate offence (and therefore a separate fine). As always, there are few precedents and most cases arise from negotiated settlements – although there is clear precedence for the DOJ eventually agreeing to treat instalment payments as a single violation of the FCPA.

The ABB Vetco Grey entities,[171] for example, were each charged with two counts of bribery for bribes relating to seven contracts. But in the Titan case,[172] the company paid bribes in 'several instalments' but was only charged with one count of violating the FCPA. Similarly, the defendants in the DPC (Tianjin)[173] and Syncor Taiwan[174] cases were only charged with a one-count indictment, despite the fact that payments were made over the course of more than five years.

SEC practice
Similarly, the SEC is not obliged to seek the maximum penalties set out above in every case. The cases where the SEC is most likely to seek corporate penalties are those where the company *and* its shareholders directly benefitted. Where third party shareholders were the victims of the violations, the SEC is more likely to be lenient.[175]

Unfortunately, in most of the settled cases, the SEC does not elaborate on its rationale for selecting the amount of the penalty, and with few cases ever coming to court it is difficult to predict the level of the civil penalty in a particular case. This is even more difficult because the authority to impose civil corporate penalties is relatively recent, and the use of very large corporate penalties is more recent still.

The SEC's decisions generally depend on seven criteria:

- the gain, i.e. the extent to which the company directly benefitted through reduced expenses or increased revenues as a result of the violation (a key driver in the fine calculation)
- the extent of the company's cooperation with the government's investigation
- the extent of tolerance of criminal activity and accepting responsibility for misconduct
- the harm to third parties as a result of any violation
- the extent and quality of the company's remediation efforts
- the need to deter the particular type of offence
- ability to pay – the objective is not to bankrupt the defendant, and evidence here by the forensic accountants about the defendant's cash position now and in the future will carry weight.

Forfeiture
Exceptionally, and in addition to fines and restitution, the DOJ may seek civil and criminal forfeiture of assets. Accordingly, any property, real or personal, that constitutes or is derived from proceeds traceable to a violation of the FCPA, or a conspiracy to violate the FCPA, may be forfeited.[176] While seldom seen in an FCPA context, it was used in the Siemens case to freeze and seize cash in the accounts of consultants, which was intended to be used to pay bribes. The DOJ also looked for forfeiture against agents Jeffrey

Tesler and Wojciech Chodan, (see the Bonny Island case, page 438), and in the case against Gerald and Patricia Green.

Gerald and Patricia Green: overseas bribery, fines and forfeiture[177]

The Greens were Los Angeles film executives. They were found guilty of FCPA violations in connection with kickbacks they paid to the former Governor of the Tourism Authority of Thailand to secure contracts to manage and operate the country's annual film festival. Between 2002 and 2007, the Greens allegedly paid $1.8m through numerous offshore bank accounts that were held in the name of the former Governor's daughter, and his friend. The Greens' businesses earned over $13.5m in revenue as a result of the contracts obtained.

In September 2009, a federal jury found them guilty of conspiracy and violations of the FCPA and money laundering laws. In its December 2009 pre-sentence report for Gerald Green, the US prosecutors argued that his sentence should be life in prison. (Gerald Green was 78 and suffers from emphysema. His wife was 53.)

In August 2010, the Greens were each sentenced to six months in prison followed by six months of home confinement, and were each ordered to pay $250,000 in restitution.

In addition, and at the prosecutors' request, the judge ordered forfeiture of their assets, including their Hollywood home, their bank accounts, company, car and pension assets, effectively leaving them penniless. The judge then waived the fines against them on the basis that they did not have the ability to pay, and ordered them to settle the restitution by paying $50 a month.

At the time of going to print, the DOJ is appealing against the short prison terms and the Greens are appealing against their convictions.

Further reading

Questions 22 and 29.

US Sentencing Commission, 2010 Federal Sentencing Guidelines Manual. Available from: http://1.usa.gov/pZj8zg (http://www.ussc.gov/Guidelines/2010_guidelines/index.cfm).

21. What Are the Penalties for Bribery in the UK?

Short answer

Many and varied. Traditional criminal penalties are fines, plus criminal confiscation orders. Particularly popular with the SFO are civil recovery orders, although they have not received unconditional support from the judiciary in respect of bribery offences.

Longer answer

Section 11 of the Bribery Act introduces the following penalties:

- a fine up to the statutory maximum[178] and up to 10 years' imprisonment for individuals who commit an offence under Section 1 (bribing), 2 (being bribed) and 6 (bribing a foreign public official); and
- a fine up to the statutory maximum for any company or partnership that is convicted of an offence under Section 7 (negligently failing to prevent bribery).

Substitute or ancillary orders
In the UK, an ever-increasing range of sanctions are being used for regulatory offences, some of which were perhaps never intended for such use. A bribery conviction under the Act triggers the court's power to impose:

- confiscation orders under the Proceeds of Crime Act 2002
- civil recovery orders under the Proceeds of Crime Act (which can also be standalone remedies that don't need a prior criminal conviction)
- serious crime prevention orders, which are used to impose prohibitions to protect the public by preventing, restricting or disrupting involvement in a serious crime

- financial reporting order (Sections 76 to 81 Serious Organised Crime and Police Act 2005)
- debarment from competing for public contracts under the Public Contracts Regulations 2006 (which give effect in the UK to EU law).

Confiscation orders under the Proceeds of Crime Act

Confiscation orders are a remedy under Part 2 of the Proceeds of Crime Act 2002, and are only available to judge sitting in a Crown Court, once a criminal conviction has been made. Confiscation orders are designed to prevent offenders from benefiting from crime, and they do this by confiscating an amount equivalent to the 'benefit' obtained from their crime. A confiscation order is not limited to those assets tainted by bribery, although any order is limited to the assets of the defendant.

It is normal SFO policy to apply for a confiscation order once a conviction has been made, unless there are compelling circumstances not to do so.

The confiscation regime is recognized to be both complex and severe, limiting any judicial discretion that might soften its effects. Although it uses the term 'confiscation', the order can be more accurately viewed as one imposing the defendant to pay a sum of money representing the benefit from their criminal conduct.

Civil recovery orders

Civil recovery orders (CROs) under Part 5 of the Proceeds of Crime Act 2002 allow the court to order the return of property that is established to be the proceeds of 'unlawful conduct'. Although CROs were introduced in 2002 by the Proceeds of Crime Act, they have only been available to the SFO since April 2008. (Although the name gives it away, it causes lots of confusion, and so it is worth stressing that these are standalone *civil* claims, which are heard in the High Court. Compare this with confiscation orders, which only come into effect following a conviction for a crime in the Crown Court.)

For a civil recovery order to be made, the claimant agency (in this case the SFO) only needs to establish that:

- criminal activity has taken place
- the funds that it seeks to recover represent the proceeds of such crime.

There is no need to obtain a criminal conviction first. It can therefore be used in situations where the subject cannot be brought to trial or has been acquitted, or there is insufficient evidence to obtain a criminal conviction. As such, the CRO can be used as a means of settling bribery charges without the need for a criminal trial. This can have advantages for all concerned. From the point of view of the prosecutor, it avoids the requirement for due process, court involvement and scrutiny of the settlement. From the point of view of the defendant, it is confidential and it means that there is no criminal conviction, and therefore no automatic debarment.

Another key difference to confiscation is that civil recovery only 'bites' on assets that are allegedly tainted with criminality.

The CRO – being a civil remedy – is subject to a lesser standard of proof than the criminal 'beyond reasonable doubt'; although in regard to evidence, the courts have stated that:

> '[t]he burden of proof is on the claimant and the standard of proof is the balance of probabilities. However, the serious nature of the allegations being made and the serious consequences of such allegations being proved mean that careful and critical consideration has to be given to the evidence for the Court to be satisfied that the allegations have been established.'[179]

The SFO has used the CRO on several recent cases, including Balfour Beatty and AMEC. Balfour Beatty for example was not charged with a criminal offence; instead the company pleaded guilty to not keeping adequate accounting records and accepted a CRO together with a compliance monitor. Following the Balfour Beatty resolution Richard Alderman, director of the SFO, stated that:

> '[t]his is a highly significant development in our efforts to reform British corporate behavior. We now have a range of enforcement tools at our disposal, and a major factor in determining which of those tools is deployed will be the responsibility demonstrated by the company concerned.'

Serious crime prevention order (Part 1, Serious Crime Act 2007)

The serious crime prevention order (SCPO) was created by Part 1 of the Serious Crime Act 2007. It is a civil order, but intended for use against those involved in serious crime. SCPOs can also be made against companies and partnerships, as well as their individual employees or officers, but it should be noted that they can only be made against those convicted of a serious offence. A serious offence is specifically defined in the Act to include bribery and corruption.

Effect of a SCPO

The orders are designed to protect the public by disrupting the defendant's ability to be involved in crime. The terms of the order are almost limitless and could restrict a person's life in almost any respect. An order may contain:

> 'such prohibitions, restrictions or requirements; and such other terms as the court considers appropriate for the purpose of protecting the public by preventing, restricting or disrupting involvement by the person concerned in serious crime in England and Wales.'

The provisions that could be contained in an order against an individual are very broad and include restrictions on financial, property or business dealings, such as:

- working arrangements
- who a person associates or communicates with, and the means used to do so

- the premises they are allowed to use and for what purpose
- the use of any item
- travel both within the UK and abroad.

An SCPO can be for a maximum period of five years, although the court can delay the commencement of the order so that, for example, it commences upon a defendant's release from prison. Breach of an SCPO is a criminal offence, the penalties for which include imprisonment, asset forfeiture under POCA and winding-up in the case of a company.

There has been no use of the SCPO orders as yet applied to bribery cases or, as far as I can see, to companies. But in 2009 the SFO stated that it wants to make increasing use of the SCPO in its efforts to prosecute international bribery:

'Serious Crime Prevention Orders are also a very powerful tool. For instance, if we believe that a corporate is engaged in fraud or corruption in a particular country, then we can apply to the High Court for an order preventing that corporate from continuing to operate in that territory. This would be a very effective weapon for us.'[180]

Financial reporting order (Sections 76 to 81 Serious Organised Crime and Police Act 2005)
On every conviction the SFO must consider the relevance of a financial reporting order (FRO) and its relationship with an SCPO, because there are benefits from obtaining both types of order. A court can impose an FRO following conviction if it is satisfied that the risk of the defendant committing another serious offence is sufficiently high to justify it. The FRO obliges the subject to provide reports of their financial affairs for a set period of time (up to 15 years in the case of fraud). It can only be made against individuals and not corporate entities, and is designed to stop career criminals from carrying out further criminal activity by identifying suspicious and irregular monetary movements.

The order might include, for example, requirements to submit
a report every six months setting out details of income,
assets and expenditure. It could include requirements to
submit copies of all bank statements, credit card accounts
or other documentation detailing financial transactions,
including tax returns and business accounts. If required, the
reports must be audited or otherwise verified.

Further reading

Question 29.

The Chambers of Andrew Mitchell QC, The increasing use
of civil recovery rather than prosecution, 2010. Available
from: http://bit.ly/p4Ci4R (http://33knowledge.com/wp-
content/uploads/2010/07/The-Increasing-use-of-Civil-
Recovery.pdf).

Crown Prosecution Service, Financial Reporting Orders. Available from: http://bit.ly/oY9pFo (http://www.cps.gov.uk/legal/
d_to_g/financial_reporting_order/).

Crown Prosecution Service, Proceeds of Crime Act
2002 – Enforcement. Available from: http://bit.ly/r4B79V
(http://www.cps.gov.uk/legal/p_to_r/proceeds_of_crime_act_
guidance/).

Crown Prosecution Service, Serious Crime Prevention
Orders: Serious Crime Act 2007 – Sections 1–41 and
Schedules 1 and 2. Available from: http://bit.ly/psHV77
(http://www.cps.gov.uk/legal/s_to_u/serious_crime_
prevention_orders_(scpo)_guidance/).

SFO, Financial reporting orders, January 2010. Available from:
http://bit.ly/o53hwr (http://www.sfo.gov.uk/media/99195/
financial%20reporting%20orders%20web%201.pdf).

22. How Is an Actual FCPA Fine Calculated? Worked Example: BAE Systems

Short and longer answer

The DOJ did not charge BAE with violating the FCPA or conspiring to do so. Instead, the charges were formulated as conspiracy to defraud the United States under Section 18 USC 371, which BAE agreed to plead guilty to, and which carried equivalent penalties. Accordingly, the company entered into a plea agreement, which meant that the court accepted the prosecutor's and defendant's agreements on sentence if it accepted the guilty plea. In March 2010, the US court accepted the plea and sentenced BAE to a criminal fine of $400m.

I explain the principles that go into the determination of a fine in the US in Question 20.

The fine was based on the 2009 Sentencing Guidelines. The method set out in the Sentencing Guidelines is by a multi-step process: to first calculate an *offence level*, which is in turn used to calculate a *base fine level*. Then a *culpability score* is calculated, which is used to derive a *multiplier*, which increases that base fine level.

The offence level
The starting point is the offence level, an integer normally between about 10 and 50. The number is derived from tables in the sentencing guidelines and depends on three key factors:

- the amount of gain made by the defendant, or potential loss suffered by victims

- whether high-level personnel were involved in the offence
- the size of the company.

The starting point in calculating a criminal fine for conspiracy or an FCPA anti-bribery violation is usually Section 2C1.1 of the Sentencing Guidelines, a section that deals with economic crimes relating to bribery or fraud. The base level for fines in this category is 12, or 14 if the defendant was a public official. This can be adjusted to reflect aggravating factors:

- If the offence involved more than one bribe or extortion, increase by two levels.
- If the offence involved an elected public official or any public official in a high-level decision making or sensitive position, increase by four levels.

The base level is then augmented by the gain received in return for the payment, as shown in the table below.

Gain		Increase in level
(A)	$5000 or less	No increase
(B)	More than $5000	Add **2**
(C)	More than $10,000	Add **4**
And so on ...		
(N)	More than $100m	Add **26**
(O)	More than $200m	Add **28**
(P)	More than $400m	Add **30**.

In the case of BAE, the offence level was 44:

Base offence level	12	A	§ 2C1 (a)(2)
High-level decision maker	+4	C	§ 2C1 (b)(3)
Benefit received over $200m	+28	B	§ 2B1(b)(I)(O)
Offence level	**44**	**A + B + C**	

The base fine
Using tables in the Sentencing Guidelines, one then looks up the fine amount that corresponds to an offence of level 44. In this case it is $72.5m. The actual base fine to be used in the calculation is the greater of this amount, and the loss or gain from the scheme, which in this case was $200m. So the base fine is $200m.

Greater of the amount of:		
Fine corresponding to base level 44	$72.5m	§ 8C2.4(a)(l) & (d)
Or		
The pecuniary gain/loss from the offence	$200m	G
Base fine	**$200m**	**G**

Culpability score
The next step is to assess what is known as a culpability score. Again, this is taken from tables in the Guidelines, and depends on the type of crime involved. In the case of bribery, the base level is 5.

If the defendant company has over 5000 employees and a high ranking officer of the defendant was in some way involved with the offence (as was the case with BAE), this culpability score is increased by 5. Additional points are added for previous violations and obstruction of the investigation process. There are also steps that a defendant can take to ameliorate the penalty range: points are subtracted for having an effective compliance system in place and 1 point is deducted for acceptance of the conduct, here ending up at 9.

Base score	5	D	§ 8C2.5(a)
5000 or more employees; high-level personnel involvement; pervasive tolerance	+5	E	§ 8C2.5(b)(1(a)(i) and (ii)
Acceptance of responsibility	−1	F	§ 8C2.5(g)(3)
Culpability score	**9**	**D + E + F**	

Multiplier
The culpability score above is used to look up a 'multiplier range' from the table below.

Culpability score	Minimum multiplier	Maximum multiplier
10 or more	2.00	4.00
9	1.80	3.60
8	1.60	3.20
7	1.40	2.80
6	1.20	2.40
5	1.00	2.00
4	0.80	1.60
3	0.60	1.20
2	0.40	0.80
1	0.20	0.40
0 or less	0.05	0.20

So a culpability score of 9 leads to a multiplier **between 1.8 and 3.6**. This is not an unusual place to end up in the case of a major FCPA violation.

Calculation of fine range

The final step is to bring all these parts of the calculation together to come up with an eventual fine range. This is done by applying the multiplier derived from the culpability score to the gain to give a fine range. This is ultimately limited to twice the overall gain, however, by virtue of the Alternative Fines Act.

This gives a fine range of $360m to $400m as follows.

Multipliers, from tables in Sentencing Guidelines, based on a culpability score of 9	1.8 – 3.6x	H	§ 8C2.6: 1.6–3.2
Fine using gain/loss	$360m to $720m	I=GxH	8C2.7
Limited to statutory maximum of 2x gain	$400m		18 USC SS 3571
Fine range	**$360m to $400m**		

The eventual fine agreed was $400m.

Further reading

Question 20.

BAE Systems sentencing memo: http://1.usa.gov/rPEmbC http://www.justice.gov/criminal/pr/documents/03-01-10%20bae-sentencing-memo.pdf).

23. How Is Disgorgement Calculated?

Short answer

In the US, defendants who are found guilty or settle proceedings with the SEC will usually be made to disgorge the 'gain' they made from the illegal corruption scheme. The starting point for this is generally earnings before tax depreciation and amortization (EBITDA) on the business obtained. Here, direct costs can be deducted, but fixed overhead costs cannot.

The confiscation regime is potentially more severe in the UK, but it has not been properly tested yet on a major bribery case. The starting point in a criminal confiscation would be the defendant's 'benefit' from a crime, and this normally means revenue without any deduction of costs. In the case of civil recovery orders the indications are that disgorgement will be assessed as in the US, with the gain/benefit equating broadly to the EBITDA obtained on the contract or business tainted by bribery.

Longer answer

Disgorgement of unlawfully obtained gains is usually sought against defendants by the SEC in securities and FCPA actions. The Securities Enforcement Remedies and Penny Stock Reform Act 1990 (codified as 15 USC § 78u-2) provides that:[181]

> '[i]n any action or proceeding brought or instituted by the Commission under any provisions of the securities laws, the Commission may seek, and any Federal court may grant, any equitable relief that may be appropriate or necessary for the benefit of investors.'

Disgorgement is an equitable remedy designed to deprive a wrongdoer of the 'gain' they made from their crime, and to prevent them becoming unjustly enriched. As such, disgorgement should be remedial and not punitive. Because it is not designed to compensate victims, the defendant's gain may not equal the victims' losses.

Although the SEC has had this remedy available for some time, it has become far more aggressive in using it over the last few years. It asks the court for far higher settlements in the post-Enron and post-Sarbanes Oxley era, rightly viewing high levels of disgorgement as having a significant deterrent effect. The SEC is now willing to ask for disgorgement of very large sums provided they are reasonably related to the alleged misconduct. The SEC began this approach in 2004, yet no court has yet had to opine on its validity, and the methodology used by the SEC in assessing disgorgement (and by both the DOJ and SEC is assessing 'gain') has not been much scrutinized and discussed. Indeed, in some instances, the SEC will look to go beyond established case law and economic principles and as such ends up being punitive rather than purely remedial.

Profits and gains

The DOJ fine and the disgorgement of gain to the SEC are likely to be the largest components of any settlement, and both are driven by the 'gain' number. So the 'gain' made by a company from the bribery scheme is fundamental as a starting point to both the DOJ and SEC penalties. Although both agencies rely on gain, there is no need for the DOJ and SEC to agree on the amount of the gain (although in practice they usually do).

Fundamental to gain is an understanding of the financial effects that the bribe had on the profits of the defendant. Again there is little settled law, but:

$$\text{Gain} = \text{incremental revenues} - \text{direct costs}$$

This does differ (but is related to) an accounting measure of 'profit'. There needs not be absolute precision in the gain calculations – really, 'gain estimation' is a better term – and rough justice prevails. The burden is on the defendant to show that the SEC's calculations are unreasonable and rebut its disgorgement calculations, although the initial calculations will come from the company so it is vital that companies control this process. Courts have failed to alter the SEC's calculations and have upheld their initial claim where the defendant has not offered convincing alternative methodology. This will frequently be done by way of expert evidence submitted on behalf of the defendant by a forensic accountant.

Defendants will challenge the SEC's gain estimates in two ways:

- showing that the SEC has included revenues that are not causally connected to the alleged misconduct
- demonstrating that the SEC has not deducted costs that are directly connected to the revenues.

What is the incremental revenue?
There needs to be a direct link between the illegal activity and the amount to be disgorged. This means that disgorgement calculations need to differentiate between illegally obtained gains (which are potentially subject to disgorgement) and legally obtained gains (which are not). So in the case of a bribery scheme, the disgorgement potentially bites only on the actual gains that were generated from contracts won by virtue of the violations subject to the charges. Contracts untainted by FCPA violations or other alleged bribery schemes not subject to the charges can be excluded from the gain calculations.

In the first instances the calculation requires an estimate of what effect the bribe has in securing any new business or project, and therefore what the revenues would have been 'but for' the bribe. Deducting this hypothetical 'but for' revenue from the actual revenue gives the incremental revenue.[182]

Expected values

It may be argued that a world-class company found to have bribed (which has tended to be the case in recent prosecutions) would have had a chance of getting some revenue even if no bribe had been paid. This implies that the incremental revenue is less than the full revenue earned on the project. Take, for example, a project worth £20m. A company assesses that it would have a 30% chance of winning it.[183] It pays a bribe, to make things certain. An economic analysis looking at expected values would look at the hypothetical revenue 'but for' the bribe as being £6m (30% × £20m). The actual revenue was £20m, leading to incremental revenue of £14m.

Similar arguments are possible when companies are operating at full capacity. If a company pays a bribe to win a project in one location, this is done at the expense of another project, and the company will still potentially be able to remain at full capacity. Again, the incremental revenue might be far lower than the full revenue on the project.

Actual gain or anticipated gain?

In cases where a bribery scheme was not as successful as anticipated, the government may well consider 'gain' to be the benefit that the defendant sought to obtain by making the corrupt payment and not the actual amount realized. Or looking at it another way, a defendant will not be allowed to benefit because their plan failed to work as anticipated.

What costs can be deducted when calculating gain?

Economically speaking, the gain from a project is the incremental revenue earned on the project minus the opportunity cost of using the resources on the project in another way. This means that expenditure that would have been avoided if the project had not been performed can be properly deducted from the incremental revenue.

The next big question is what, if any, costs can properly be deducted from revenue. In other words, what is the appropriate measure of 'profit' that forms the gain? Again, courts in many jurisdictions disagree over the questions of whether (and if so, which) costs are properly deductible.

Cost categories and why they matter – allowable deductions

When approaching gain, it is vital to understand the cost base of the company, and how its costs are related to the revenues generated from the alleged bribes.

Direct costs can usually, at least in the US, be deducted from revenue to arrive at gain. They are the costs of raw materials and other resources that are closely and necessarily associated with generating the relevant revenue. Most of these costs are variable in nature in that they vary with the level of sales activity. For example, buying the raw materials to conduct an oil facility is likely to be variable: the purchase costs are avoided if the contract does not proceed.

Businesses also have various kinds of *indirect and overhead costs*. These costs include the costs of utilities, property and the wages for administrative and back-office staff. Costs of this nature generally cannot be deducted on the basis that they would have been incurred by the company irrespective of whether the project was performed or not.

They also include *non-cash costs*, including the depreciation of assets. These costs are merely accounting entries that slowly charge the acquisition cost of assets against profit over the life of the asset. They do not represent the transfer of cash to anyone.

One term that is often seen in accounting circles is earnings before interest, tax, depreciation and amortization (EBITDA). EBITDA is a good starting point for a calculation of gain. It is greater than net profit and can be derived by adding back interest, financing charges and depreciation to net profit given in the profit and loss account. Because it does not deduct non-cash items such as depreciation in its estimate of earnings, it provides a better estimate than net profit of the amount of cash generated from a particular activity.

Overheads

The government is likely to take EBITDA and then look to add back any indirect costs already deducted from revenue, thus increasing gain. Defendants will look to resist this.

A defendant is unlikely to ever win an argument with a prosecutor that 'overheads' should be deducted from revenue when calculating gain. There is however scope for closely examining exactly where the boundary between direct and indirect costs, and variable and fixed costs, actually sits. The way we classify these costs is not mere semantics. Indirect costs – both fixed and variable – are often a large share of a firm's total cost base and are typically many times larger than a firm's net profit. If it can be successfully argued that some of these costs are in reality directly related to contracts, then this can reduce the disgorgement substantially – and when the multiplier effects are taken into account in the fine calculation, it could reduce the fine even more so. Defendants will also argue (again assisted by their forensic accountants) that overheads and so-called 'fixed costs' might be fixed in the short term, although the majority are actually variable in the medium to longer term: property costs can be reduced if the level of business drops, because the company would be able to move to new, cheaper premises, or extra space can be leased if business increases. The longer the time horizon, the more costs are able to be varied – and in the real world, they vary in a stepped manner. Using these sorts of arguments, defendants can try to maximize allowable cost deductions and thus reduce gain.

Causal links

A further difficulty arises in the real world when estimating gain in that a company normally has several business lines or undertakes several contracts, only some of which are tainted by bribery.

Let's take the example of a US oil services company active in the US, Brazil, Nigeria and Iran. The contract in Iran has been found to have been obtained by bribery. Therefore, for settlement talks with the DOJ it is necessary to estimate the gain just on this contract. Certain costs can be directly associated with the Iranian operations. The wage costs of employees involved on the contract and the cost of materials used on the project, for example, would not have been incurred if the contract had not been undertaken, and it is entirely sensible to deduct these. There is likely to be an Iranian office, and the question of whether these are direct costs, variable costs or fixed overheads is fact-specific. In practice, some are likely to be allowed.

More difficult are the general costs of the organization that are not associated uniquely with any of the contracts or counties. Take, for example, the costs of the Human Resources and IT departments, which are a centralized resources based in the US head office but provide services to all the employees and projects. How do we treat these costs – are they fixed overheads or is there some allowable deductions here? A further interesting cost is the cost of finance: although traditionally viewed as a cost that cannot be deducted from revenue to arrive at gain, there is some limited precedent to allow an element of direct finance costs to be deducted.

Bribes must be added back
The bribes paid are not allowable deductions for the purposes of gain calculations. To the extent that the alleged bribes were paid by the party against whom fines or disgorgement is being sought, then they need to be added back to the measure of accounting profit and not serve as a cost deduction. If the bribes were paid by a third party and have not been deducted in the accounts of the settling party, then no adjustment is necessary.

Netting gains against losses
In securities actions, there is usually netting of gains made on certain share transactions against losses on others. Depending on the timing and nature of these losses, there may be no net gain because the losses wipe out any gain entirely. Netting of losses is seldom allowed in FCPA actions, although there can be situations where a 'net gain' calculation is appropriate. Take for example the following business unit, which undertook two contracts, both of which were obtained by the same bribery scheme:

£m	Contract A	Contract B	Total
Revenue	10	6	16
Costs	(5)	(9)	(14)
Gain	5 gain	(3) loss	2

When assessing the gain, can the losses of £3m on Contract B be deducted from the gain of £5m on Contract A? Is the amount of the gain £5m or £2m?

The starting point generally adopted by the SEC is that netting losses against gains is normally not permitted, and the onus is always going to be on the defendant to demonstrate why it is appropriate. Where the contracts themselves are separate, discrete profit centres, the SEC's position is going to be difficult to shift: if the SEC could properly limit their prosecution to simply Contract A, the court would accordingly only consider the factual matrix and financial position of Contract A when making its award. In cases like this, the SEC is unlikely to accept the netting of Contract A's profits against Contract B's losses.

If, however, the SEC could not without difficulty limit its case to one contract, and would have to prosecute instead the activities of a business unit or entire company – each comprising the consolidated results of several, if not many contracts – then netting might be possible. This would be more likely if the results from each contract were not generally accounted for or managed separately, but instead their revenue and costs were always combined into the results of a larger unit. A complementary way of looking at this is if the loss-making Contract B had to be undertaken as a consequence of entering into Contract A, in effect arguing that the losses on B were inevitable and necessary to gain the benefit of the gains on A. In a case such as this the results from the two contracts could not properly be split.

It must be borne in mind though that this is a potentially risky position for a defendant to take, because they are combining the gross revenues together as well. If the courts did not accept that the full amount of the operating costs here were an allowable deduction and wanted to calculate disgorgement based simply on revenue, then the defendant could be looking a far higher gain figure – here, £16m as the starting point (which incidentally would be the starting point in a UK confiscation order.)

When is prejudgement interest added to a disgorgement?
Disgorgement in respect of an FCPA offence is generally taken to be 'the amount with interest by which the defendant profited from his wrongdoing'. Prejudgement interest is intended to capture the time value of money. It is the notional interest that the defendant could have earned by investing the funds to be disgorged between the date they were received and the date of judgement or settlement. For example, if a bribe won a contract that gave rise to a gain of £10m in 2006, then a settlement in 2011 would include interest on the £10m for five years. Prejudgement interest can add very significant amounts sums to total amount to be disgorged.[184]

Prejudgement interest is discretionary. Courts have routinely awarded it in SEC enforcement actions where the defendant's scheme evidences a high degree of bad intent, but conversely have also declined to award it on the disgorgement amount when there has been extensive cooperation by the defendant.

The SEC's default position seems to be to add it and the onus is on the defendant to argue why it is inappropriate (if the defendant has offered high levels of cooperation, etc.).

How is the prejudgement interest calculation performed?
Courts and the SEC generally look to calculate prejudgement interest by using the Internal Revenue Service (IRS) rates for the underpayment of taxes under 17 USC § 201.600(b).[185]

This again evidences the non-punitive and compensatory nature of the interest, as this is the rate used where a taxpayer owed but had not paid tax. It is, however, a policy rate, and clearly does not match the defendant's actual gain (or the government's loss). The courts are not bound to apply the IRS rate and on rare occasions have utilized their discretion to apply a different rate. Historic rates can be found at http://bit.ly/tvagvZ (http://www.smbiz.com/sbrl004.html).

The calculation is generally a straightforward calculation of interest compounded quarterly. A format that has been acceptable to the SEC for a prejudgement interest calculation is shown in the table below. This shows an assumed gain of $50m made on 31 December 2009, and calculates the prejudgement interest for one year to an assumed date of settlement on 31 December 2010. So here, $2.03m would be added to the estimated gain.

Quarter range		Annual rate	Quarter rate (annual rate/4)	Quarter interest	Principal and interest
Assumed gain on 31/12/09					$50,000,000
01/01/10	31/03/10	4%	1%	$500,000	$50,500,000
01/04/10	30/06/10	4%	1%	$505,000	$51,005,000
01/07/10	30/09/10	4%	1%	$510,050	$51,515,050
01/10/10	31/12/10	4%	1%	$515,151	$52,030,201
				$2,030,201	$52,030,201

Confiscation and disgorgement in the UK
It is too early to draw any meaningful patterns about the level
of fines and disgorgement that will be sought and awarded in
bribery cases under the Bribery Act. Most of the more recent
settlements have been civil recovery orders (CROs) and the
amounts are a very mixed bag:

- Balfour Beatty plc: CRO for £2.25m in October 2008.[186]
- AMEC plc: £4.95m in October 2009.[187]
- Innospec: $12.7m as a UK criminal plea agreement as part
  of a US and UK global agreement resulting in the payment
  of approximately $40m.[188]
- BAE Systems: £30m (strictly £500,000 plus £29.5m
  reparation) as a criminal plea agreement from a $450m
  combined US/UK settlement.[189]
- MW Kellogg (part of the Halliburton case): £7m as a CRO in
  February 2011, which represented funds that the UK
  company was due to receive. The SFO recognized that the
  company took no part in the criminal activity that
  generated the funds, but rather was used by its parent.[190]
- Johnson & Johnson/DePuy: £4.83m as a UK CRO in April
  2011, as part of a global resolution. This includes a US
  deferred prosecution agreement with a financial penalty of
  $21.4m, a civil sanction imposed by the SEC of $48.6m, and
  the Greek authorities restrained €5.7m.[191]
- Macmillan: £11.26m, August 2011.[192]

Both Innospec and BAE received serious adverse judicial
comment, and their fines are unlikely to be useful to gauge
the level of future penalties. It had been rumoured, for
example, that the SFO had been seeking a fine of up to £500m
in the BAE case if it could make the bribery and corruption
charges stick.[193] With Innospec, the judge stated that a fine
comparable to that imposed in the US ($101.5m) would have
been the starting point, in addition to disgorging profits. The
judge indicated that if he was not limited to what had been
set out in the agreement, the fine would have been measured
in 'the tens of millions'.[194]

The settlement in the Macmillan case (£11.2m CRO) seems to point the way for the SFO. The CRO was a consent order under Section 276 Proceeds of Crime Act 2002, and so did not require judicial intervention. As to how the amount was calculated, the SFO press release is vague and there is nothing else out there that elaborates on this. It merely says the following:

> 'Accordingly it was plain that the Company may have received revenue that had been derived from unlawful conduct. Following an accounting examination and taking an aggressive approach to the revenue received in order to capture all potential unlawful conduct the SFO was in a position to determine the appropriate amount to be recovered. The value of the Order made by the High Court is £11,263,852.28. MPL will also pay the SFO costs of pursuing the order which amount to £27,000.'

Confiscation versus CRO
The SFO is keen to see an extensive use of CROs under Part 5 of the Proceeds of Crime Act 2002. These allow the court to order the return of property that is established to be the proceeds of 'unlawful conduct'. The judiciary however is keen to see *criminal* convictions for bribery, as opposed to merely civil settlements. These criminal convictions will lead to confiscation orders under Part 2 of the Proceeds of Crime Act 2002.

Although designed to achieve similar goals, CROs give considerable leeway as to the estimate of gain. The SFO (and therefore the court approving the agreement) is likely to support a gain calculation that reflects a measure of 'profit' made by the defendant and allows the deduction of certain costs.

However, the UK's criminal confiscation regime is recognized to be both complex and severe, limiting any judicial discretion that might soften its effects. The problem from a defendant's perspective is that the starting point for confiscation is 'benefit', which is not profit, but revenue. At least, that's always been the case law to date, as was confirmed by the Court of Appeal in 2010 in the case of *R. v. Del Basso*. This is a major problem for corporates – we have already seen in the cases of Innospec and BAE that the judiciary resists the civil route for obvious criminality, but once confiscation bites the position can be far more severe than that in the US.

R. v. Del Basso: Confiscation Benefit = Revenue

A successful 'park and ride' business had been set up by Mr Del Basso and Mr Goodwin from the car park of Bishops Stortford Football Club and was used by travellers to London Stansted Airport in increasing numbers. Planning permission had been repeatedly refused in relation to the park and ride scheme but the defendants continued to operate it, despite numerous warnings from the local planning authority. Eventually the defendants were convicted and fined for failing to comply with a planning enforcement notice. Confiscation proceedings under POCA were also initiated.

It was submitted by the defence that the two men had not made a significant personal profit from the operation but that the majority of the proceeds had been used to fund the football club and to pay for the everyday running of the park and ride business. The judge found that this was irrelevant and that the key factor to consider in judging any benefit was what benefit had in fact been obtained, and not what happened to that benefit after it had been obtained. The defendants appealed to the Court of Appeal but the appeal was dismissed.

Further reading

Questions 20, 21, 25, 27 and 28.

Basso & Anor v. R., EWCA Crim 1119, 2010. Available from: http://bit.ly/oLkZB6 (http://www.bailii.org/ew/cases/EWCA/Crim/2010/1119.html).

Buckberg, E. and Dunbar, F.C., Disgorgement: punitive demands and remedial offers, *The Business Lawyer*, **63**, 347–81, February 2008. Available from: http://bit.ly/nYYjAx (http://www.nera.com/extImage/PUB_Disgorgement_BusinessLawyer.pdf).

24. What Happens to Fines and Penalties Paid to Settle Bribery Actions?

Short answer

In the US, fines, penalties and disgorgement, either ordered by the court or negotiated as part of an out-of-court settlement, all go to the US Treasury.

In the UK, the position is more complicated. Fines go to the public purse. In confiscation and civil recovery actions, the investigating authorities and prosecuting authorities each take a cut of the proceeds. Where the SFO acts as both investigator and prosecutor, it is entitled to 37.5% of all amounts confiscated: a clear incentive for the SFO to boost its budget through the use and promotion of CROs and confiscation orders.

Increasingly, both the US and the UK are considering restitution to order defendants to send back money to the country where the unlawful conduct took place. But restitution, though good in theory, has practical difficulties such as identifying the victims and determining how the money will be repaid, and what it will be used for. Indeed, countries have reportedly refused to accept it, perhaps seeing taking the payout as an admission of guilt.

Longer answer

US

Fines, disgorgement and penalties go directly to the US Treasury. The amount is not insubstantial; FCPA fines accounted for nearly half of the $2bn in settlements and judgements secured by the DOJ's Criminal Division in 2010, the highest in the FCPA's 33-year history.[195]

UK
Fines imposed by the court go to the Home Office, where they form part of public funds.

In the case of confiscation actions and civil recovery orders, the Home Office has published guidance on how money gathered from confiscation orders is divided up. Under what is called an 'incentive scheme', it is split three ways between the Court Service, the prosecuting authority and the investigating authority (i.e. police, HM Revenue & Customs, SFO, SOCA, etc.) as follows:

- Home Office: 50%
- investigators: 18.75%
- prosecutors: 18.75%
- Court Service: 12.5%.

Because the SFO acts as both investigating authority and prosecuting authority, it is entitled to 37.5% of any confiscation.

There is a potential conflict therefore in the SFO's role if it is recommending to courts how a lump sum settlement should be split between fines and confiscations: it has a clear incentive to maximize the confiscation element of any penalty, which it can keep for itself. This was recognized in the Innospec judgement when the court stated that confiscation orders by the director of the SFO were problematic because such arrangements 'give rise to a very considerable conflict of interest incompatible with his independent duties as a prosecutor'.[196]

Restitution and reparations
There is a restitution mechanism available by which the DOJ can send money back to the identifiable victims of a crime, although it is seldom used currently. The DOJ has discussed

the concept of setting up a system where it would be permitted to divert a portion of fines to global anti-corruption efforts via institutions that encourage and assist developing countries to deter and prosecute their own bribery. As yet, however, this has not got off the ground.

In 2011, Instituto Constarricense de Electricidad (ICE) petitioned for protection of its rights as a victim of Alcatel-Lucent's bribery scheme, claiming that it had suffered massive losses. As a victim, the Crime Victims' Rights Act would entitle it to claim restitution.[197] The position of ICE was unusual in that its directors and employees were the recipients of Alcatel-Lucent's bribes. The US Court of Appeals denied ICE's petition, maintaining the lower court's finding that ICE actually functioned as the offenders' co-conspirator and had failed to establish that it was directly and proximately harmed by the offenders' criminal conduct.[198] Still, expect to see more of these types of claims in the future.

Reparation in the UK
Restitution is more popular in the UK, with the SFO stating that compensating victims of corruption is a priority to them. It has been seen in several recent settlements: in the BAE settlement, for example, BAE agreed to repay £30m in UK penalties, for which £29.5m was earmarked as reparations for the people of Tanzania. This is the highest so far in the corporate bribery cases that the SFO has pursued.

Julian Messent: UK-Ordered Restitution to Costa Rica[199]

In October 2010 Julian Messent, a director at a London-based insurance brokerage PWS International Limited (PWS), was sentenced in Southwark Crown Court to 21 months' imprisonment after pleading guilty to paying nearly $2m in bribes to Costa Rican officials in exchange for reinsurance contracts.

In addition, Messent was ordered to pay restitution of £100,000 to the Republic of Costa Rica. If he fails to do so he must serve an additional 12 months' imprisonment.

Problems with reparation
The BAE case is not the first time that a payment has been made to an affected country. It was seen in the Julian Messent settlement (see above), and both Mabey & Johnson and Weir Group made reparations to the UN Iraq Fund over Oil-for-Food Programme transgressions. NGOs such as the World Bank have initiatives: its Stolen Assets Recovery Initiative is run in conjunction with the UN Office on Drugs and Crime to repatriate misappropriated assets.[200]

Although admirable in theory, making reparatory payments to countries where bribery or related offences has occurred is not without difficulties: for instance, who actually gets the money? Often there is lack of trust in how the payment will be used if it is returned to the government of the country where the bribes were paid, because in many cases it would be going back to the same group of people that took bribes in the first place.

The judge made no comment in the BAE case as to how the £29.5m should be paid and to whom, leaving this for BAE to address. The Department for International Development and the Tanzanian government agreed to use the money on education. After a delay, BAE eventually agreed to pay the money to the UK's Department for International Development to pass on to the Tanzanian government. Further thought at an international level is likely to be needed as to how best to achieve the aims of these initiatives.

Further reading

The Home Office, Asset recovery incentive scheme 2010-11: arrangements for implementation and payment, August 2010. Available from: http://bit.ly/qh99GY (http://www.northants.police.uk/policeauthority/files/docs/Agendas%20Reports%20and%20Meeting%20Dates/Agendas%20and%20Reports/Reports/20110629/ITEM%207a%20-%20Appendix%20A%20-%20Asset%20Recovery%20Incentivisation%20Scheme.pdf).

25. How Does a Settlement or Plea Agreement Work? Part 1: The US Experience

Short answer

Many companies have entered into deferred prosecution agreements (DPAs) or non-prosecution agreements (NPAs) with the DOJ, paying huge fines but technically avoiding prosecution. The SEC now also has this settlement tool, which it is starting to use to resolve FCPA cases.

DPAs (and more unusually, NPAs) are court-sanctioned agreements between the prosecutor and the company whereby charges are formulated but not prosecuted. If the company keeps to its side of the agreement – which most likely involves a major compliance overhaul and possibly the imposition of a compliance monitor, in addition to a significant fine – then the charges are thrown away. DPAs have become the method of choice for settling most corporate FCPA cases where circumstances permit.

Longer answer

Plea agreements
Plea agreements involve the formal conviction of the defendant in court proceedings at an uncontested trial because the defendant has agreed to plead guilty. A plea agreement may include:

- a reduction in the seriousness of the charge
- an agreement to reduce the number of charges in return for a guilty plea for the remainder of the charges
- cooperation and giving evidence against other defendants

- a recommendation to the judge that the defendant receives a lighter sentence than would normally be the case if convicted after a contested trial.

By contrast, a prosecutor has always had the ability in certain circumstances to *defer* the prosecution of certain defendants in an effort to reduce pressure on overcrowded courts and to give the defendants a chance to change their behaviour. These deferments have been common with juveniles or first-time petty criminals. The prosecutor would typically file a criminal charge, but would not prosecute provided that the defendant complied with certain agreed terms. Colloquially known as 'settlements', there are two types:

- deferred prosecution agreement (DPA), where charges are prepared and filed with the court
- non-prosecution agreement (NPA), where no charges are filed with the court – instead, the agreement is maintained by the parties.

Importantly, unlike in plea agreements, DPAs and NPAs do not involve a formal guilty plea – merely an agreed statement of facts.

Corporate DPAs and NPAs

During the early 1990s, prosecutors tended to see the decision of whether to charge a company as a stark choice between either indictment via a grand jury or declining to prosecute. The middle ground, be it a DPA or NPA, was unattractive – partly because there was no formal guidance on the topic within the DOJ, and partly because prosecutors were unwilling to have to get involved in the company's difficult remediation and compliance challenges. Both the DOJ and the SEC prosecutors are more forward-looking than before, trying to reform ingrained cultures and encouraging ethical conduct. Both have a great deal of discretion, but the decision comes down to a number of relatively simple issues that I deal with in the next question.

One of the first corporate deferred prosecutions took place in 1992, when Salomon Brothers settled a claim by the DOJ that it had committed securities fraud.[201] The company carried out extensive remediation and cooperated with the investigation, and its commitment to changing its ethical approach convinced the DOJ not to indict, although substantial fines and forfeitures were still imposed. Although the case did not involve a formal NPA, it provided a message to companies that cooperation, coupled with a willingness to change, could lead to favourable results. DPAs and NPAs proliferated between 2002 and 2005, and the trend has continued to the point where DPAs are how most major corporate cases are now disposed of. Indeed, the first conviction at trial of a company under the FCPA since the law was enacted in 1977 did not occur until May 2011. A California federal jury found Lindsey Manufacturing Company (a privately held manufacturer of electrical transmission towers) and two of its senior officers guilty of by paying bribes to obtain contracts with the state-owned Mexican electricity company.[202] Even then, the conviction was later overturned for government misconduct – which included providing false information to obtain a search warrant, making unauthorized searches and providing incorrect testimony to a grand jury. At the time of going to print, the DOJ has expressed its intention to appeal.[203]

Modern DPAs

The benefits of a DPA when faced with a trial are that the company avoids the collateral consequences of indictment by voluntarily entering a probationary period, during which it will:

- make compliance improvements to prevent bribery happening in the future
- cooperate with the government, possibly to help prosecutors build a case against individuals – this may involve waiving legal privilege and disclosing documents generated during the investigation

- pay a fine and make significant restitution payments
- often agree to the appointment of a compliance monitor.

The prosecutors will dismiss the charges at the end of the deferral period if they are satisfied that the company has fulfilled its obligations. If, the company has failed to abide by the conditions of the DPA, however, then the prosecutor can declare a breach and formally prosecute.

The SEC's new cooperation initiative
Until very recently, DPAs and NPAs were only available to the DOJ. However in January 2010, the SEC issued a policy statement designed to encourage greater cooperation from individuals and companies in the agency's investigations. Robert Khuzami, Director of the Division of Enforcement, introduced it by saying that:

> '[t]here is no substitute for the insiders' view into fraud and misconduct that only cooperating witnesses can provide. That type of evidence can expand our ability to conduct our investigations more swiftly, and to act quickly to file charges, freeze assets, and protect investors.'[204]

The SEC laid out various tools in a revised version of their enforcement manual in a new section entitled 'Fostering Cooperation'. The new options for resolving cases include:

- cooperation agreements – formal written agreements where a defendant receives credit for providing substantial assistance, including information and evidence
- DPAs and NPAs – formal written agreements in which the Commission agrees to drop an enforcement action against a defendant if they to cooperate fully and comply with express prohibitions and undertakings.

In December 2010, the SEC announced that it had entered into an NPA with Carter's, Inc., a children's clothing wholesaler based in Atlanta[205] – the first of its kind for the SEC. However, it was not in respect of an FCPA violation, which came with a DPA for Tenaris in May 2011 when the SEC announced that:[206]

> '[u]nder the terms of the DPA, the SEC will refrain from prosecuting the company in a civil action for its violations if Tenaris complies with certain undertakings. Among other things, Tenaris has agreed to enhance its policies, procedures, and controls to strengthen compliance with the FCPA and anti-corruption practices. Tenaris will implement due diligence requirements related to the retention and payment of agents, provide detailed training on the FCPA and other anti-corruption laws, require certification of compliance with anti-corruption policies, and notify the SEC of any complaints, charges, or convictions against Tenaris or its employees related to violations of any anti-bribery or securities laws. Tenaris has agreed to continue to fully cooperate with the SEC in its investigation.'

Tenaris: First DPA with the SEC in Respect of an FCPA Violation[207]

Tenaris SA was a Luxembourg-based company, with ADRs listed on the NYSE. Its main business was the supply of steel pipes to the oil and gas industry. Tenaris retained an agent to obtain information about competing bids on government energy tenders, which Tenaris then used to resubmit winning revised bids. The agent was paid 3.5% of the value of the four contracts on which he was involved, some of which was paid to government officials in exchange for the confidential information.

In May 2011 it was announced that Tenaris had entered into an NPA with the DOJ, paying a $3.5m criminal penalty. At the same time Tenaris entered a DPA with the SEC, disgorging $5.4m in gains and interest.

Further reading

Question 26.

Ethisphere DPA/NPA Database: http://bit.ly/sjK1x7 (http://acstage.ethisphere.com/?page_id=84). Free, but requires registration.

SEC Enforcement Manual: http://1.usa.gov/q2fA1S (http://www.sec.gov/divisions/enforce/enforcementmanual .pdf).

Spivack, P. and Raman, S., Regulating the 'new regulators': current trends in deferred prosecution agreements, *American Criminal Law Review*, **45**, 2008. Available from: http://bit.ly/nrB2BF (http://papers.ssrn.com/sol3/papers.cfm? abstract_id=1096726).

26. How Does a Settlement or Plea Agreement Work? Part 2: The Holder, Thompson and McNulty Memos, the Filip Principles, and the Seaboard Decision

Short answer

This series of memos and policy documents set out the DOJ's and SEC's approaches to prosecution and settlements, and are essential reading for anyone thinking of self-disclosing potential FCPA violations.

Longer answer

Filip Principles

The first guidance to DOJ prosecutors on the recommended approach to prosecutions and settlements came in 1999 in the form of a memorandum issued by then Deputy Attorney General Eric Holder entitled 'Federal Prosecution of Corporations'. What became known as the 'Holder Memo' outlined various factors that prosecutors should take into account when deciding whether to prosecute a company for misconduct. Holder's principles were updated several times. The 2003 Thompson memo was probably the toughest guidance, and its requirements on matters such as waiving privilege as a precondition of settlement have since been eased. It was replaced in 2006 by the McNulty memo. In August 2008, the then Deputy Attorney General Mark Filip released the a revised set guidelines (the 'Filip Principles'), which represent the rules on which all current settlements are based.

Overview of prosecutorial factors

The Filip Principles sets out nine factors that federal prosecutors must take into account when approaching settlement discussions. These factors were formalized in the DOJ's 'Principles of Federal Prosecution of Business Organizations' as follows:

- The nature and seriousness of the offence, including the risk of harm to the public and applicable policies and priorities, if any, governing the prosecution of corporations for particular categories of crime.
- The pervasiveness of wrongdoing within the corporation, including the complicity in, or condoning of, the wrongdoing by corporate management.
- The corporation's history of similar misconduct, including prior criminal, civil and regulatory enforcement actions against it.
- The corporation's timely and voluntary disclosure of wrongdoing and its willingness to cooperate in the investigation of its agents.
- The existence and effectiveness of the corporation's pre-existing compliance programme.
- The corporation's remedial actions, including any efforts to implement an effective corporate compliance programme or to improve an existing one, to replace responsible management, to discipline or terminate wrongdoers, to pay restitution, and to cooperate with the relevant government agencies.
- Collateral consequences, including whether there is disproportionate harm to shareholders, pension holders, employees and others not proven personally culpable, as well as impact on the public arising from the prosecution.
- The adequacy of the prosecution of individuals responsible for the corporation's malfeasance.
- The adequacy of remedies such as civil or regulatory enforcement actions.

A good positive score on the above factors mean that the DOJ is likely to want to settle.

The SEC's Seaboard decision

Commonly called the 'Seaboard decision', the SEC's guidance is similar in substance to the DOJ's, and gives a similar message about what the government requires for cooperation. The Seaboard decision was issued in 2001 though, before formal SEC non-prosecution agreements were brought in. Nevertheless, the Seaboard principles are still instructive.

The Seaboard decision explains why the SEC chose not to take action against Seaboard Corporation – the parent company in this investigation – given the nature of the conduct and the company's responses. The decision can be broadened to the SEC expressing a 'willingness to credit' cooperation by a company that discovers and discloses wrongdoing. The SEC further stated that, in evaluating the extent of a corporation's cooperation, it would consider the following questions:

- What steps did the company taken upon learning of the misconduct?
- What process did the company follow to seek out necessary information?
- Did the company commit to learning the truth, fully and expeditiously? and
- Did the company do a thorough review of the nature, extent, origins and consequences of the conduct and related behaviour?

Both the Filip memo and Seaboard decision reflect the DOJ's and SEC's expectation that companies will conduct prompt and thorough internal investigations when faced with a potential FCPA violation.

Further reading

Questions 25 and 34.

Corporate Compliance Prof Blog, Compliance 101 – the Seaboard report, 11 July 2005. Available from: http://bit.ly/ njzm6s (http://lawprofessors.typepad.com/compliance_prof/ 2005/07/compliance_101_1.html).

Federal Evidence Review, Corporate prosecution princi-ples resource page. Available from: http://bit.ly/qGc5NH (http://federalevidence.com/corporate-prosecution-principles#holder-memo). A library of key materials concerning criminal and civil enforcement issues involving corporations and other business organizations.

Filip memo: http://bit.ly/oKVUMq (http://federalevidence.com/ pdf/Corp_Prosec/Filip_Letter_7_9_08.pdf).

Holder memo: http://bit.ly/mOSbtp (http://federalevidence .com/pdf/Corp_Prosec/Holder_Memo_6_16_99.pdf).

McNulty memo: http://bit.ly/pgjTy5 (http://federalevidence .com/pdf/Corp_Prosec/McNulty_Memo12_12_06.pdf).

Principles of Federal Prosecution of Business Organiza-tions: http://1.usa.gov/octgSt (http://www.justice.gov/opa/ documents/corp-charging-guidelines.pdf).

SEC, The Seaboard decision, Release No. 44969, 23 October 2001. Available from: http://1.usa.gov/omhGqM (http://www.sec.gov/litigation/investreport/34-44969.htm #P16_499).

Thompson memo: http://bit.ly/nnrRyE (http://federalevidence .com/pdf/Corp_Prosec/Thompson_Memo_1-20-03.pdf).

27. How Does a Settlement or Plea Agreement Work? Part 3: The UK Experience

Short answer

To date, the UK's efforts to follow the DOJ's lead in using out-of-court settlements has gone far less smoothly than has been the case in the US. Judges in the UK believe it is unacceptable for the SFO to agree a fine or sentence (or do this in all but name) with a defendant, as this is strictly a decision for the court. They also have real problems with the SFO dealing with serious crimes such as bribery as a civil rather than a criminal matter.

Longer answer

The UK approach to settlements

There is clearly a difference between the US and UK settlement and plea bargaining process. Settlements and plea bargains are far more common in the US, but it is incorrect to think that pleas doesn't happen in the UK. Indeed, it has been common for many years in criminal cases for the prosecution and defence to hold informal and confidential discussions and agree to charge less serious offences in return for a guilty plea. Furthermore, there is a well-recognized discount by the courts for a guilty plea, commonly:

- one-third discount for saving the cost of the trial
- more if a guilty plea introduces other mitigating factors
- more still (half to two-thirds, but exceptionally more) where defendants have agreed to assist the investigation or prosecution of offences committed by others, under Sections 71–75 of the Serious Organised Crime and Police Act 2005.

The criminal enforcement regimes in the UK and US are vastly different. Until recently there has been no real corporate criminal liability in the UK, and so no culture of self-reporting had emerged. Defendants were individuals, who were more prepared to take their chances with the SFO, knowing that the downside on conviction was less than it would be in the US. Two practical factors need to be borne in mind when looking at differences between the US and the UK:

- Sentences are typically far more severe in the US, where white collar criminals in their fifties or sixties who get convicted are unlikely to ever get out of jail. Bernard Madoff received a sentence of 150 years for masterminding his well-reported Ponzi fraud.[208]By contrast, the UK Crown Prosecution Service's Sentencing Manual, in its guidance on fraud and false accounting, give even the most serious crime under this category (a large advanced fee fraud or deliberate targeting of a large number of vulnerable victims) a starting point of six years' custody, with a range of five to eight years.
- There is at least a chance of getting acquitted if the case goes to trial in the UK: the SFO simply doesn't have the same reputation of always getting a conviction that the DOJ does. Going in front of a jury in a fraud case in the US is a high-risk strategy because an individual defendant may well not see freedom again, or a corporate defendant could face a penalty in the billions if it goes against them – which makes a plea much more attractive to get certainty.

The Attorney General's Guidelines on plea discussions
The UK Attorney General published the 'Guidelines on Plea Discussions in Cases of Serious or Complex Fraud' in March 2009. This document encouraged the use of plea discussions to try to narrow down the issues and try to reach a quick resolution of a case. This could include reaching an agreement about acceptable pleas of guilty and preparing a joint submission as to sentence, although the Guidelines do make

clear that the prosecutors are not about offering discounts, immunity or incentives (which obviously raises the question: what's in it for me?).

The steps in a plea agreement under the Attorney General's Guidelines are as follows:

- The prosecutor can initiate discussions once it is reasonably satisfied of the suspect's guilt.
- The defendant must be legally represented.
- Discussions will take place on a 'without prejudice' basis.
- Where agreement is reached as to pleas, the parties should discuss the appropriate sentence with a view to presenting a joint written submission to the court.
- The document should list the aggravating and mitigating factors in the case.
- The prosecution should also send the court sufficient material to allow the judge to assess whether the plea agreement is fair.
- The court retains an absolute discretion as to whether or not it sentences in accordance with the joint submission.

In both the US and the UK, the contents of any settlement and plea agreement needs to be disclosed to and approved by the court, and a judge has the power to accept or reject it.

The SFO published its 'Approach of the Serious Fraud Office to Dealing with Overseas Corruption' in July 2009. It explained that it asks the following questions in considering any decision to settle:

- Is the board of the corporate genuinely committed to resolving the issue and moving to a better corporate culture?
- Is the corporate prepared to work with us on the scope and handling of any additional investigation we consider to be necessary?

- At the end of the investigation (and assuming acknowledgement of a problem) will the corporate be prepared to discuss resolution of the issue on the basis, for example, of restitution through civil recovery, a programme of training and culture change, appropriate action where necessary against individuals, and at least in some cases external monitoring in a proportionate manner?
- Does the corporate understand that any resolution must satisfy the public interest and must be transparent? This will almost invariably involve a public statement, although the terms of this will be discussed and agreed by the corporate and us.
- Will the corporate want us, where possible, to work with regulators and criminal enforcement authorities, both in the UK and abroad, in order to reach a global settlement?

One real advantage that the SFO has is that it is possible to get a judge in the UK to indicate what sentence they would pass if there was a guilty plea to a particular offence: this can really assist parties in reaching settlement, but is not usual in the US.

At least in respect of criminal claims against individuals, many defence lawyers are privately very sceptical of agreeing to settle cases with the SFO – as paradoxically, defendants may well find themselves in a worse position by entering this process. There are three main drawbacks with pleading:

- defendants have to make a formal confession before the trial begins
- they have no certainty as to what sentence they might receive, even if it has been tentatively agreed with the SFO
- although there is mutual confidentiality during the negotiations, it is unclear whether these override other disclosure obligations – information provided by the defendant may find itself subsequently disclosed.

Going down the civil route

The SFO will want to settle self-referral cases through the civil route unless the offending is too serious. 'Serious' would include cases where, for example, board members of the corporate had engaged personally in the corrupt activities, particularly if they had derived personal benefit from this. In these cases the SFO would be left with no alternative to a criminal prosecution. Examples of the questions the SFO would ask are as follows:

- How involved were the individuals in the corruption (whether actively or through failure of oversight)?
- What action has the company taken?
- Did the individuals benefit financially and, if so, do they still enjoy the benefit?
- If they are professionals should we be working with the appropriate disciplinary bodies?
- Should we be looking for directors' disqualification orders?
- Should we think about a serious crime prevention order?

Confiscation orders versus civil recovery orders

Confiscation orders are not the same as civil recovery orders. The recent use of CROs to settle bribery cases has been criticized heavily – see, for example, Innospec, where the judge said that it would 'rarely be appropriate' for a company that is guilty of bribery to receive a CRO instead of (rather than in addition to) a criminal fine, and:

> '[i]t is of the greatest public interest that the serious criminality of any, including companies, who engage in the corruption of foreign governments, is made patent for all to see by the imposition of criminal and not civil sanctions. It would be inconsistent with basic principles of justice for the criminality of corporations to be glossed over by a civil as opposed to a criminal sanction.'[209]

This reflects the legislation, which is that the powers in POCA should be exercised to reduce crime and that criminal proceedings have precedence over civil proceedings.

But where criminal prosecution cannot result in a conviction, there will be a greater use of CROs. The advantage for the State is clear: assets can be recovered on the balance of probabilities, even in the event of an acquittal. Joint guidance was given by the Home Secretary and the Attorney General to the prosecuting authorities in November 2009 on the use of civil recovery under the Proceeds of Crime Act 2002. It states the following:

- Criminal prosecution must be considered first.
- If the case does not meet the criteria for prosecution (sufficient evidence plus the case is in the public interest), then civil recovery can be considered.
- In deciding whether the public interest criteria is met, the prosecuting authorities are entitled to take the view that the public interest is better served by civil recovery.
- A criminal investigation does not need to be completed before civil recovery can be considered.
- A criminal investigation or prosecution can continue in tandem with a civil recovery investigation, but criminal and civil proceedings cannot be carried on at the same time in relation to the same criminality.
- A prosecution that fails can result in civil recovery.
- Civil settlements may be entered into to compromise civil recovery proceedings, but a potential defendant cannot buy their way out of prosecution by making a civil payment. If the case justifies a prosecution, criminal proceedings should be brought.

What have judges thought of some SFO civil settlements?

Criticism   The SFO has shown a clear move in recent cases towards a more 'US-like' approach, involving the use of DPAs, civil penalties and recovery, and serious crime prevention orders that enable a prosecutor to obtain court orders regulating the future conduct of those who have engaged in serious crime. It is hampered slightly though in that the SFO is unable to agree a sentence with a defendant for simple rubber-stamping by the courts. In the US, the judge is unlikely to question a settlement too deeply: this is not the case in the UK, particularly if the SFO is suggesting going down the civil route.

If there was any doubt about this previously, the Innospec case made clear that in cases of serious fraud or bribery, the SFO may enter into a settlement, but the court is not bound by any agreement that it might tentatively float. It does want assistance from both parties as to sentencing, but in the courts' view, sentencing decisions are a matter for them alone. Crown court judges, however – who have to approve settlements – have been highly critical of civil agreements, saying in no uncertain terms that the criminal route is the most appropriate to proceed to prosecute serious criminal activities.

The UK courts handed down some scathing views on how they view plea agreements and CROs in the case of Innospec, Robert Dougall and BAE. The Innospec judgement, handed down in March 2010, contains some very strong views of how the court it would like to see prosecutions being handled in the future, and some undesirable features of recent civil settlements negotiated through the SFO.

Innospec: UK courts criticize SFO civil recovery order[210]

Innospec is a specialty chemical maker listed in the US. It has a significant operation, using a UK limited company, Innospec Ltd, based in Ellesmere Port in the UK. Executives of Innospec were charged with conspiring to give corrupt payments to executives of Pertamina, an Indonesian state-owned refinery in return for contracts to supply its old-technology anti-knock fuel additive tetra-ethyl lead between 2002 and 2006. Prosecutors also investigated making payments to Iraqi officials under the UN Oil-for-Food Programme, and in the US, selling some $20m of chemicals to Cuba without a licence from the Treasury Department's Office of Foreign Assets Control (OFAC). This was still a violation of the US Trading With the Enemy Act.

The US authorities began to investigate Innospec in 2005 and the SFO began to take a serious interest in 2007. The directors decided to admit wrongdoing in late 2008 and, following the usual protracted negotiations, a deal was eventually struck with all the prosecutors whereby the company would agree to pay a lump sum by way of penalty. The settlement was heralded as the first formal joint SFO–DOJ settlement, with the agreed penalty being divided between the UK and US authorities, and the appointment of a joint UK–US compliance monitor.

After some behind-the-scenes machinations, the UK's share of the penalty was eventually agreed at 31% of the total amount, which amounted to $12.7m. Of this, $6.7m was planned to be allocated to a criminal and confiscation order to be imposed in the Crown Court (in respect of Indonesia transgressions) with the balance being the subject of a civil settlement (in respect of Iraq Oil-for-Food Programme transgressions).

The SFO had suggested that a civil recovery order would be appropriate for part of the agreed penalty. Accordingly it presented proposals to the court for $12.7m of the total fine to be paid in the UK, of which $6.7m was to be allocated to a fine or confiscation in the Crown Court, and the balance being subject to a CRO.

This represented the first use of the Attorney General's Guideline on Plea Discussions in Cases of Serious or Complex Fraud and as such, the judge gave formal written sentencing remarks setting a steer on the Guidelines for future use. The judgement contains some strong views of how the court would like to see prosecutions being handled in the future, and some undesirable features of recent civil settlements negotiated through the SFO. He concluded though that the SFO does not have power to enter into plea arrangements such as this and unequivocally stated that 'no such arrangements should be made again'.

The SFO's agreement with Innospec was rejected by the judge, who sentenced the company to a fine of the full $12.7m, with no element under a civil settlement. He stressed that those who commit crimes of corruption 'must not be viewed in any different way to other criminals' and that it would 'rarely be appropriate' for a company that is guilty of bribery to receive a CRO instead of (rather than in addition to) a criminal fine.

The judge made it clear that he considered the level of the fine much too low, in part because the profits made in the UK by Innospec alone may have been as high as $160m, all of which could have been subject to disgorgement. Both the SFO and DOJ agreed that the fines and other penalties that might be imposed in the US and the UK might exceed $400m in the US and $150m in the UK. If it had been up to him to decide, the penalty would have been in the tens of millions.

The judge was seemingly also unhappy with the agreed split, thinking that there was scant rationale for deviating from an equal split between the penalty to be paid in the UK and the US.

Robert Dougall was a marketing executive at a Johnson & Johnson subsidiary who pleaded guilty to participating in a bribery scheme with Greek doctors. He cooperated fully with the SFO, who described him as 'the first cooperating defendant in a major SFO corruption investigation'. He handed documents to the SFO prosecutors and undertook to give evidence in any future trials against other individuals. He had signed an agreement with the SFO under s73 of the Serious Organised Crime and Police Act 2005, which allows the court to take into account the extent and nature of the assistance given or offered when considering what sentence to pass on the defendant. Accordingly, the SFO looked for a light sentence, and at the sentencing hearing, both the prosecution and the defence asked that a suspended sentence be given. But Justice Bean at Southwark Crown Court thought otherwise and went again the SFO's wishes. The judge said that he accepted the public policy consideration of prosecutors being able to promise/recommend more lenient sentences in return for cooperation:

> 'But it does not justify a suspended sentence in a case where corruption was systemic and long-term and involved several million pounds in corrupt payments.'

Dougall was accordingly sentenced to a year in jail. The case was the first major SFO fraud case involving a 'cooperating defendant', but Dougall's sentence threatened to deter future whistleblowers. The Court of Appeal however recognized the importance of having someone assist an investigation at a very early stage, and reduced the conviction to a suspended sentence after all. It warned however that there would be no automatic expectation of suspended sentences for bribery whistleblowers in the future.[211]

Approval   Only a handful of cases in the UK have involved formal plea discussions, and some of the earliest – Innospec, Dougall and BAE – were subject to the harshest criticism by the judges. Notwithstanding this, though, I think that it is likely that the UK will inexorably move towards more formal DPAs – in time we will see the majority of bribery cases resolved this way in the UK as in the US. As also explained in Question 21, by August 2011, there had been five civil settlements by the SFO, all of which have been approved by the court.

- Balfour Beatty plc, October 2008, £2.25m
- AMEC plc, October 2009, £4.95m

- MW Kellogg Ltd, February 2011, £7m
- DePuy International Ltd, April 2011, £4.83m
- Macmillan. August 2011. £11.26m.

The Macmillan CRO seemed to go very smoothly indeed ...

Macmillan: A Model SFO Civil Recovery[212]

Macmillan Publishers Limited is a leading technical publisher. Its attempted bribery came as it tried to win part of a $45.9m project in 2008 and 2009 to develop a new school curriculum, train thousands of teachers and build 100 new schools in southern Sudan. The project was financed by the World Bank, which commenced its own investigation. Acting on this initial report, the City of London Police executed search warrants in December 2009.

In March 2010 Macmillan self-reported the corporate case to the SFO. The first stage of the full investigation process involved Macmillan instructing external lawyers to conduct a review of its books and records with a view to identifying areas of corruption risk. This work enabled the City of London Police, the SFO and the World Bank, to identify the limited area within the business that potentially presented the greatest risk. Three jurisdictions (Rwanda, Uganda and Zambia) were selected for detailed investigations.

As a result of this investigation, it was concluded by all parties that '[i]t was impossible to be sure that the awards of tenders to the Company in the three jurisdictions were not accompanied by a corrupt relationship'.

There does not seem to be any definitive admission or finding of corrupt conduct to the criminal standard.

As a result of its investigation and admissions made by Macmillan, in 2010 the World Bank debarred Macmillan from being awarded contracts financed by the Work Bank for a minimum of three years. In August 2011 the company settled with the SFO and undertook a CRO. A number of relevant features that have informed the resolution of this enquiry, include the following:

- Macmillan approached the SFO with a view to cooperation, and fully cooperated with all parties.
- The company had, in response to learning of the allegations of bribery and corruption, reacted appropriately by first reviewing its internal anti-bribery and corruption policies and procedures, appointing external consultants to recommend and help implement an internal appropriate anti-bribery and corruption compliance regime.
- The company decided to cease all live and prospective public tenders in its Education Division business in east and west Africa, regardless of the source of funds.
- The actual products supplied were of a good quality and not overpriced.

The SFO asked for, and got, a CRO for £11.2m by consent. Macmillan escaped a criminal prosecution and none of its employees were prosecuted. A compliance monitor was imposed.

Further reading

'Serious bribery cases will increasingly require admissions of bribery', page 468.

Attorney General's Office, Attorney General's guidelines on plea discussions in cases of serious or complex fraud, 18 March 2009. Available from: http://bit.ly/ox8Pga (http://www.attorneygeneral.gov.uk/Publications/Documents/AG's%20Guidelines%20on%20Plea%20Discussions%20in%20Cases%20of%20Serious%20or%20Complex%20Fraud.pdf).

Attorney General's Office, Attorney General guidance to prosecuting bodies on their asset recovery powers under the Proceeds of Crime Act 2002, 15 November 2009. Available from: http://bit.ly/pKCfZy (http://www.attorneygeneral.gov.uk/Publications/Pages/AttorneyGeneralissuedguidancetoprosectuingbodiesontheir assetrecoverypowersunder.aspx).

Crown Prosecution Service, Queen's Evidence – Immunities, Undertakings and Agreements under the Serious Organised Crime and Police Act 2005. Available from: http://bit.ly/qA3fK4 (http://www.cps.gov.uk/legal/p_to_r/queen_s_evidence_-_immunities_undertakings_and_agreements_under_the_serious_organised_crime_and_police_act_2005/).

Sentencing Guidelines Council, *Reduction in Sentence for a Guilty Plea*, definitive guideline, revised edition, 2007. Available from: http://bit.ly/nvvLD9 (http://sentencingcouncil.judiciary.gov.uk/docs/Reduction_in_Sentence_for_a_Guilty_Plea_-Revised_2007.pdf).

SFO, Approach of the Serious Fraud Office to dealing with overseas corruption, 21 July 2009. Available from: http://bit.ly/qvMkWd (http://www.sfo.gov.uk/media/128701/approach%20of%20the%20serious%20fraud%20office%20v6.pdf).

28. What Is a Compliance Monitor?

'Corporate monitors are not going away. But I think we've become more sophisticated and refined with our use of them. We're wary of corporate monitors gone wild. We don't put monitors in to ruin a company.'

Chuck Duross, Head of the FCPA Section, DOJ[213]

Short answer

A monitor, who historically has tended to be a US lawyer experienced in regulatory dispute resolution and compliance, can be appointed under the terms of a DPA or NPA to ensure that a company is complying with the agreement. Historically, slightly less than half of DPAs imposed some sort of external monitor.

A key role of the monitor is to evaluate the company's internal control and compliance regime to reduce the risk of it reoffending. Compliance monitors have been seen in corporate settlements under the FCPA for several years, and are not uncommon now in the UK. The first joint UK–US monitor was appointed to Innospec in April 2011.

It is likely that we will continue to see compliance monitors being used, but in a focused way. The judiciary in both the US and UK is keen to limit their roles, and companies see them as intrusive and are unwilling to pay their costs. Gone are the days when compliance monitors insisted on becoming involved in all aspects of a company's commercial activity, costing companies tens of millions of dollars.

Longer answer

Monitors are appointed under the terms of a court-sanctioned agreement and as a condition of probation. They are therefore subject to court oversight.

Practice has evolved as to who they are appointed by and who they report to. Early monitors worked for the government; the DPAs in September 2007 involving medical device companies DePuy Orthopaedics, Biomet, Smith & Nephew, and Zimmer, stated that:

> 'the Monitor works exclusively for and at the direction of the [United States Attorney's] Office.'[214]

Monitors are generally now appointed and paid by the company, subject to DOJ veto. The DOJ and the monitor, in conjunction with the company, are guided by principles set out in a document known as the 'Morford memo' to establish a detailed plan about how the monitorship will work.

The Morford memo
In March 2008, then Acting Deputy Attorney General Craig Morford issued guidance about the use of corporate monitors in connection with DPAs and NPAs. The so-called 'Morford memorandum' set out the principles that the DOJ adopts for appointing and interacting with monitors. The principles are listed below.

Monitor's independence A monitor is 'an independent third party, not an employee or agent of the corporation or of the government'. The monitor does not act for the company and so cannot give legal advice to it. This also means that information gathered by or provided to the monitor is not protected by privilege.

The monitor's duty A monitor's primary responsibility is to assess and monitor a corporation's compliance with those terms of the DPA or NPA that are designed to reduce the risk of misconduct. This includes evaluating internal controls and ethics, compliance programmes, and, where appropriate, proposing changes and enhancements. Final responsibility for designing an effective ethics and compliance programme is the company's – subject to the monitor's input, evaluation and recommendations.

The monitor's mandate is not to investigate historical misconduct. Nevertheless, the memo states that in appropriate circumstances, an understanding of historical misconduct may guide a monitor's assessment of the state of the internal controls.

Reporting to the DOJ   The monitor must have the discretion to communicate with the government as they deem appropriate, and it is usual for the monitor to make periodic written reports to both the government and the company. Recent monitoring agreements have generally required an initial report – for example, within 120 days of being appointed – and annual follow-up reports thereafter. These reports would be provided contemporaneously to the DOJ and board of directors of the company.

If the company chooses not to adopt recommendations made by the monitor within a reasonable time, either the monitor, the company or both should report that fact to the government, along with reasons. The government may consider this when evaluating whether the company has fulfilled its obligations under the prosecution agreement.

Discretion to disclose previously undisclosed conduct   DPAs and NPAs should specify the type of undisclosed or new conduct that must be reported to the DOJ. In some instances, the monitor should immediately report misconduct directly to the government and not to the company when it:

- poses a public health, safety or environmental risk
- involves the corporation's senior management
- involves obstruction of justice
- involves criminal activity that the DOJ hopes to proactively and/or discreetly investigate
- poses a substantial risk of harm.

Duration of agreement DPAs and NPAs typically have had terms of between 18 months and three years. The following criteria should be considered when determining the agreement's duration:

- the nature, seriousness and pervasiveness of the underlying misconduct
- the corporation's history of similar misconduct
- the nature of the corporate culture and senior management involvement
- the scale and complexity of any remedial measures contemplated by the agreement, including the size of the entity or business unit at issue.

Flexibility of monitor's term There should be flexibility in the term of the monitorship that allows an extension if the company has not satisfied its obligations and early termination if there is a change in circumstances sufficient to eliminate the need for a monitor. Cutting the appointment short might arise on the termination of business lines subject to the agreement, or if an entity merges with another corporation with an effective ethics and compliance programme.

Resolving disputes – the Grindler memo

The DOJ issued a press release in May 2010, comprising a memo written by Acting Deputy Attorney General Gary Grindler. The memo provides a supplemental provision that prosecutors should also explain in DPAs the DOJ's role in resolving disputes that may arise between the monitor and the company. The DOJ policy provides examples of dispute-resolution language that might be included in the agreements.

Selecting a monitor

While the Morford and Grindler memos don't provide a selection process for monitors, they do address certain aspects of the process. The DOJ will allow companies to choose their monitors in the first instance, as opposed to having the government make the choice. This is good news for companies, because they can interview monitor candidates and find one they feel comfortable with. Companies pick three candidates for the monitoring position, one of which is approved by the DOJ. If none of the candidates are suitable from the DOJ's perspective, companies must go back to the drawing board. The company's choice though will still be subject to the DOJ's veto if they don't meet certain criteria, such as:

- sufficient FCPA experience
- sufficient independence from the company
- a good reputation in the professional community
- the quantity and quality of resources needed to carry out the tasks expected of monitors.

It should not be a challenge for a company to find a FCPA practitioner who it will be happy working with, and who the DOJ will accept. However, companies should realize that the DOJ, by virtue of being involved with every FCPA case in the country, is probably in a better position than anyone else to know which alleged FCPA experts really are qualified. To avoid the risk of a veto, companies thinking about a monitor should ask as many questions as possible to gauge the like-lihood that the DOJ will accept them. This happened in the case of the BAE monitor, where the DOJ rejected all of the first three candidates put forward by BAE. The DOJ informed BAE that it should continue looking because, among other things, the candidates appeared to lack experience in estab-lishing compliance programmes, the specifics of the defence industry, and a background in relevant criminal law, includ-ing US and UK anti-corruption and export control. Finally, the company and DOJ settled on David Gold, a former senior partner at lawyers Herbert Smith.

The DOJ is not involved in agreeing the fees for monitors; companies work out the cost of the contract with the monitors themselves. Historically, monitors were very expensive with fees running into the tens of millions because they brought in a whole compliance team from their own law firm, together with 'Big 4' forensic accountants, to give the company a detailed inspection. Thankfully, their roles are now more limited and pre-agreed.

Non-US monitors
Monitors increasingly have the challenge of how to deal with information across an international group, without falling foul of data protection or blocking statutes. Several European companies have found that a non-US monitor is the best way to minimize these challenges.

One of the less-reported aspects of Siemens' record-breaking settlement with US authorities was an important 'first': the DOJ allowed Siemens to appoint a non-US compliance monitor. The monitor, Dr Theo Waigel, was a highly experienced politician and a former German Minister of Finance,[215] although as a banking lawyer his expertise in the factors above that the DOJ looks for in a monitor (and caused them to reject several BAE candidates) was unclear.

Subsequently, overseas monitors have been used by Technip and Alcatel-Lucent. They have tended to be well-regarded and experienced business and finance professionals from that country (rather than FCPA specialist lawyers). However, they will typically undertake to work with an FCPA specialist lawyer who is approved by the DOJ, can advise on more technical aspects of the assignment and provide an interface with the DOJ.

The Alcatel-Lucent DPA: A Non-US Monitor

Alcatel-Lucent is a global telecommunications corporation, headquartered in Paris, that provides voice, data, and video services around the world. In December 2010, Alcatel-Lucent announced agreements with the DOJ and SEC to resolve allegations of payments to foreign officials in Costa Rica, Taiwan and Kenya to obtain contracts for network equipment and services.

Alcatel-Lucent entered into a three-year DPA in which the DOJ charged the company with violations of the accounting provisions, and three subsidiaries with violations of the FCPA's anti-bribery and accounting provisions. The company agreed to pay a $92m criminal fine (in four instalments over the course of three years), as well as $45m in disgorgement of profits and prejudgement interest to the SEC.

The DPA included a three-year monitorship by a French national. His role was strictly limited to monitoring the effectiveness of Alcatel-Lucent's internal controls, record keeping, and financial reporting policies and procedures, with a view to avoiding violations of US laws.

The monitor will report any future infractions to French authorities who, in turn, will report them to the DOJ. This indirect disclosure does not violate the French blocking statute, because through mutual legal assistance treaties French authorities are permitted to report violations to the US authorities directly. The French monitor, on the other hand, is not permitted to do so.

UK monitors

Monitors have not been routine in the UK. The SFO does not have the power impose a corporate monitor upon a company, so any appointment would have to be part of either a civil agreement between the parties or ordered by the criminal court. There are only a handful of cases to date where a UK monitor has been appointed.

According to the SFO guidelines, one of the aspects that the SFO will consider following a self-report is whether:

'[a]t the end of the investigation ... the corporate [will] be prepared to discuss resolution of the issue on the basis, for example, of restitution through civil recovery, a programme of training and culture change, appropriate action where necessary, and at least in some cases external monitoring in a proportionate manner.'

The guidelines explain further that:

- the monitor would be an independent, well-qualified individual nominated by the company and accepted by the SFO
- the scope of the monitoring would be agreed with the SFO
- the monitor's work would be proportionate to the issues involved.

Balfour Beatty plc: UK Civil Recovery Order and Monitor[216]

In a consent order agreed before the High Court, Balfour Beatty agreed to a settlement of £2.25m plus costs as part of civil recovery order proceedings. It also agreed to introduce certain compliance systems and to submit these systems to a form of external monitoring for an agreed period.

Balfour Beatty had self-reported payment irregularities by its subsidiary during the construction of the Bibliotheca Project in Alexandrina, Egypt. The project was undertaken by a Balfour Beatty subsidiary in a joint venture with an Egyptian company.

Balfour Beatty plc accepted that the documentation prepared in connection with these payments did not comply with the requirements for accurate business records to be kept in accordance with Section 221 of the Companies Act 1985.

Criticism of monitors

Whilst widespread, compliance monitors have also become controversial in recent years as companies have complained about their fees and the scope of their work, over which they have almost no control. The judge in the US Innospec hearing in 2010 expressed concern over the sometimes exorbitant costs of monitors:

> 'It's an outrage, that people get $50m to be a monitor. ... I'm not comfortable, frankly, signing off on something that becomes a vehicle for someone to make lots of money.'[217]

The UK judge also had major concerns – not only with the way the settlement had been handled, but also with the appointment of the compliance monitor at all. The judge considered that imposing a compliance monitor on a company with a new management team in place is an expensive form of checking, some of which can be done by its auditors. He thought the huge cost of an Innospec compliance monitor would be far better used for fines, confiscation or compensation. Nevertheless, a joint US–UK monitor (a US compliance lawyer, assisted by a UK QC) was finally appointed in April 2011.

Working with a monitor
Companies that need to enter into settlement discussions are advised to:

- think early about the profile of potential monitors
- (if a European company) look for a suitably qualified national
- carefully set out these lines of communication – blocking statutes might be a reason why the monitor should not have unfettered access to report back to the DOJ
- try to limit the role of the monitor to simply reviewing the compliance strategy and plan, not the detail of the compliance efforts
- try to do their own remediation and review work in advance of the monitor coming – it should not be the role of the compliance monitor to do detailed in-country interviews and audits.
- have a single point of contact for the monitor.

Self-monitoring
As both courts and prosecutors have cast a more critical eye over the benefits of an independent monitor, in the right circumstances, some companies may be allowed to self-monitor. Since 2009 – when Helmerich & Payne settled FCPA charges and the DOJ allowed it to self-monitor – the US government has begun to give credit to companies that were seriously committed to improving their compliance programmes by enabling them to regularly self-report on their compliance programme improvements.[218] The DOJ appears to be increasingly keen to do this, as the expertise and experience of lawyers and compliance professionals, as well as the DOJ, has increased; all parties increasingly know what the compliance goals should be, and these are formalized in the DPA.

Self-monitoring often goes hand-in-hand with enhanced compliance commitments beyond those customarily required. (See for example the pretty onerous Johnson & Johnson DPA, which did though come with the benefit of self-reporting.)

Further reading

'How Do I Set Up Proportionate Yet Effective Anti-Bribery Compliance Procedures?', page 343.

'Document review and e-disclosure', page 412.

Appendix 7: Johnson & Johnson's enhanced compliance undertakings, page 518.

Grindler memo: http://1.usa.gov/mSruon (http://www.justice .gov/usao/eousa/foia_reading_room/usam/title9/crm00166 .htm).

Low, L. Analysis: Alcatel-Lucent's $137 million FCPA set- tlements reflect expansive jurisdiction, new compliance standards, international cooperation, and collateral risks,

Mondaq, 15 March 2011. Available from: http://bit.ly/vytGCV (http://www.mondaq.com/unitedstates/article.asp?articleid =126032).

Morford memo: http://1.usa.gov/qlZv84 (http://www.justice .gov/dag/morford-useofmonitorsmemo-03072008.pdf).

29. What Is Debarment?

Short answer

Public procurement projects are an important revenue stream for many companies, particularly those in the sectors that have faced the greatest FCPA enforcement action. One of the main concerns for a company being found guilty of (or admitting to) bribery is debarment from contracts awarded by national bodies. Fines are bad and always unwelcome, but usually a company can pay them and move on. But an inability to do any government-sponsored or government-funded work would put many companies out of business. Both the US and EU have rules providing for debarment following conviction for bribery offences.

To date, few companies have faced debarment. This has been through the use of well-crafted settlement agreements that do not admit bribery in any of the important parent companies or those needing to contract with public bodies.

Longer answer

Do governments really want to debar?
Debarment is draconian, and the fact that it is in place for bribery offences regardless of the seriousness of the offence or the any mitigating factors makes it especially damaging. But is this actually what governments want? Many of the large, private sector companies in high-risk industries are key suppliers of equipment and services to governments, and many FCPA violators – Siemens, Halliburton, BAE and many more – are *still* major suppliers to governments and have not been debarred. Most of the recent plea US agreements focused on accounting breaches only and did not contain admissions of bribery in key companies specifically to avoid debarment. In the case of the Siemens settlement, for

example, the fact that the charges and guilty pleas were structured against Siemens Argentina, Siemens Bangladesh and Siemens Venezuela – all non-European – insulated the parent Siemens AG and key European entities from potential debarment.

Several collateral consequences to governments make debarment unattractive, including:

- loss of government flexibility in its contracting process by the removal of contractors through debarment
- injured diplomatic relations with foreign allies
- threats to national security from the removal of key contractors
- disproportionate harm to shareholders
- other political risks.

Nevertheless, in a relatively unconcerned report, the Project on Government Oversight found that between 2007 and 2009 the US Department of Defense awarded work worth $270bn to 91 contractors who had been found liable in civil fraud cases and $682m to 30 contractors convicted of criminal fraud, as well as 43 cases where companies and individuals received government contracts in 2009 after actual suspension or debarment.[219]

US
Companies violating the FCPA or committing bribery come within the ambit of the Federal Acquisition Regulations. According to Part 9.406 of the Regulations, companies committing any 'offense indicating a lack of business integrity or business honesty' can be debarred from participating in any procurement or non-procurement activity with any executive agency.

The rules are not mandatory; active intervention by a federal official is required to debar a particular company.

In September 2010 the Overseas Contractor Reform Act was passed by the House of Representatives. But because the House was suspended before the Act could pass into law, it was not enacted and lapsed. (However, members often reintroduce bills that did not come up for debate under a new number in the next session – it might yet reappear.) The Act provided that a corporation found to be in violation of the FCPA's anti-bribery provisions *shall* (as opposed to 'may' under the existing Regulations) be proposed for debarment from any contract or grant awarded by the federal government within 30 days after a final judgement of such a violation.

Whether the Overseas Contractor Reform Act would have had much impact anyway is a matter for debate. The draft legislation suggests debarment for even minor infractions, as the Act's trigger is 'found to be in violation' of the FCPA's anti-bribery provisions. Because a company entering into a DPA or NPA is never 'found to be in violation' of the FCPA's anti-bribery provisions, the trigger would not be reached in most carefully drafted settlement agreements. Further, there is debarment 'unless waived by the head of a Federal Agency'. Nevertheless, companies need to be even more acutely aware of what they admit to when negotiating such agreements.[220]

US export bans   The State Department must ensure that no licences to export sensitive US-made products are granted to companies involved in corrupt or illegal practices. A person or firm found guilty of violating the FCPA is normally ineligible to obtain export licences, although bans can be carefully crafted and largely discretionary where US jobs and security is at stake. As with debarment, bans can have a significant impact if they apply to holding companies and US entities, although they can be largely inconsequential if they apply only to minor non-US vehicles.

In the BAE case, after a year-long investigation following the FCPA settlement, BAE agreed to pay a further $79m civil penalty – the largest in State Department history – for more than 2500 alleged breaches of rules governing military exports, although that is set to be reduced by $10m if the company maintains compliance standards. As part of this settlement, the State Department had to consider whether to ban BAE from exporting military items from the US. In a very convoluted fashion, the Department issued a ban and then rescinded it, saying it was satisfied with changes BAE had made to senior management and its board of directors. Then, following a detailed review, three BAE subsidiaries – including two that are no longer in business and one that had been folded into BAE's Saudi Arabian unit – were denied permission to export US-controlled items. The deal does not apply to the company's US subsidiary, which accounts for more than half of the parent company's revenue, because the US operation was not a part of the criminal wrongdoing.[221]

Further knock-on effects that we have not seen yet – but if the US government was really throwing the book at an FCPA offence, they might also factor in – would include US security clearances, which could all be taken away, and the Bureau of Alcohol, Tobacco and Firearms could also deny all ability to possess commercial explosives. The latter may seem insignificant until you realize that most defence, mining and airline companies make use of them (for example, aeroplane doors have actuators triggered by explosives), and licence-removal would make life very hard indeed.

EU
The EU debarment policy was set out in the 2004 EU Procurement Rules, codified as European Union Directives 2004/18/EC and 2004/17/EC. These contain provisions debarring companies or persons found guilty of corruption from participating in public tendering contracts in the EU.

The Directives were enacted into UK law as the Public Contracts Regulations 2006 and the Utilities Contracts Regulations 2006. These state that a public authority that has actual knowledge of a company or its directors or certain representatives having been convicted of a fraud, bribery, corruption or money laundering offence should treat that company as ineligible to be selected in a tending process.

Putting companies completely out of business was not the aim of the Bribery Act. The Bribery Act Guidance provides that the conviction of a commercial organization under Section 7 of the Act in respect of a failure to prevent bribery will attract *discretionary* rather than mandatory exclusion from public procurement.[222]

At the date of writing this book the Public Contracts Regulations 2006 have been amended, meaning that there is now automatic debarment from public tendering for offences under Sections 1 and 6 of the Bribery Act (as was the position under the old corruption laws). Section 7, the corporate offence, is not mentioned in this amending instrument, meaning perhaps that Section 7 is not viewed as a pure dishonest 'bribery' offence. It is still unclear though how, and by whom, the discretion under the Regulations will be exercised.

Further reading

Federal Acquisition Regulations System, Part 9 – Contractor Qualifications, Subpart 9.4 – Debarment, Suspension, and Ineligibility: http://bit.ly/nfiJz9 (http://law.justia.com/cfr/title48/48-1.0.1.2.9.4.1.10.html).

'The Public Contracts Regulations 2006 (unamended): http://bit.ly/o08dSZ (http://www.legislation.gov.uk/uksi/2006/5/contents/made).

Stevenson, D.D. and Wagoner, N.J., FCPA sanctions: too big to debar?, *Fordham Law Review* (forthcoming), 15 April 2011. Available from: http://bit.ly/omFS08 (http://papers.ssrn.com/sol3/papers.cfm?abstract_id=1811126).

30. How Much Does It Cost to Fully Respond to an International Bribery Investigation and Prosecution?

> 'Alas! The small discredit of a bribe – Scarce hurts the lawyer, but undoes the scribe.'
>
> Alexander Pope, Epilogue to Satire

Short and longer answer

Even leaving aside the fines, civil penalties, disgorgements and prejudgement interest, the fees that companies will end up spending on lawyers, forensic accountants, IT, e-disclosure and other specialists to investigate, defend, negotiate the pleas, added to the costs of a monitor, and the fees in carrying out a worldwide compliance review and remediation exercise, can be huge.

The law firm Debevoise led the Siemens's investigation, which it described as follows:[223]

> 'The Siemens investigation, among the largest of its kind in scope, was completed in two years. It included 1750 interviews; over 1000 informational briefings; 82 million documents electronically searched and 14 million documents reviewed; 38 million financial transactions analysed; and 10 million bank records reviewed.'

Debevoise instructed forensic accountants and e-disclosure professionals from Deloitte, and the extensive and sustained participation of the hundreds of lawyers, accountants and support staff totalled well over 1.5 million hours of billable time, at a reported cost of $850m in fees and expenses. The investigators spent an additional $5.2m for translation services and $100m more on document collection, review, processing and storage, bringing Siemens' investigation cost to nearly $1bn, not including fines.[224] Furthermore, 75 PricewaterhouseCoopers professionals provided support in implementing an 'Anti-Corruption Toolkit' at 162 Siemens locations, at a total cost to Siemens of more than $150m.

Siemens hired Theodor Waigel, a former German finance minister, as its monitor, at a projected cost of $52m over, potentially, four years. This price did not include the cost of the FCPA expert retained to guide and mentor him.

Although Siemens was a vast exercise, smaller international investigations hardly come cheap. The five-year internal investigation at Daimler, for example, was reported to have cost at least $500m. The recent investigation in Avon was reported to have cost $95m in 2010 alone.[225]

The best approach is to think of an unfeasibly large number, which is way above your wildest expectations. And then double it. It needs to be borne in mind throughout the investigation, though, that the cost of a full investigation is going to be less than the cost of not doing one, taking into account the extra enforced costs and damage to the business when you are caught and prosecuted.

Further reading

DOJ's Siemens sentencing memo: http://1.usa.gov/raA9bM (http://www.justice.gov/opa/documents/siemens-sentencing-memo.pdf).

31. When Do Old Bribes Become Ancient History?

Short answer

Although crimes are statute-barred after five years in the US, a charge of conspiracy is an effective way to extend the time limits – all that's needed is that any part of the conspiracy took place within the last five years.

In the UK, there is no criminal state of limitations. Civil recovery orders can look back over the preceding 20 years.

Longer answer

US

The FCPA itself does not contain a statute of limitations provision. Instead, the 'catch-all' provision in the US Constitution sets a five-year statute of limitations. A further extension of up to three years can be applied for by the government if it needs to obtain evidence from other jurisdictions.[226] The US statute of limitations for civil cases is also five years, although certain claims (such as for injunctive relief and disgorgement) are not subject to the same limits.

Because the statute of limitations in criminal cases begins to run when the crime is 'complete', prosecution for an FCPA bribery violation would normally be time-barred five years after the bribe scheme has ended (usually after the payment of the last bribe). The government therefore routinely charges companies and individuals with *conspiracy* to violate the FCPA in place of or in addition to substantive FCPA charges. It does this in part because limitation is effectively stretched if just one act in furtherance of the conspiracy occurred during the limitation period.[227]

By using conspiracy charges the DOJ was able to include conduct that occurred as far back as 1997 in the recent charges against Siemens' subsidiaries – some 11 years prior to the date that the criminal information was filed. Similarly, in the recent KBR/Halliburton matter, the DOJ was able to include conduct that occurred as far back as 1994, even though the five-year period generally applicable to those acts would ordinarily have expired in 1999.

The use of conspiracy charges can be used to avoid jurisdictional problems that come up with substantive FCPA charges. In the case of a company that is neither a domestic concern nor an issuer, establishing jurisdiction under the FCPA requires some part of the bribery scheme to have taken place in the US. Using a conspiracy charge avoids having to prove this.

The OECD Convention does not mandate a specific statute of limitations. This can affect the extent of due diligence required on an acquisition or agent, or the time period that should be covered by representations and warranties. While the FCPA's statute of limitations on an acquisition's past corporate conduct may have expired, the acquired entity could be devalued as a result of subsequent local enforcement actions if other applicable anti-corruption laws have longer limitation periods.

UK

The UK has no statute of limitations with regard to criminal offences; in theory, you can be arrested and taken to court for an indefinite time after an offence was committed. For civil recovery orders (CROs), POCA originally provided for a 12-year limitation period. In other words, SOCA could seek CROs for property that was obtained as long as 12 years before the proceedings were issued (S27A of the Limitation Act 1980). However, not content with 12 years, from January 2011 SOCA now has a 20-year limitation period.[228]

What is a tolling agreement?
By signing a tolling agreement, the potential defendant agrees not to assert a 'limitations' defence in the enforcement action for a specified time period. Such requests are occasionally made by the DOJ and SEC in the course of settlement negotiations to extend the five-year window to allow time for further investigation.

In fact, the government often asks companies for such agreements during the course of the investigation and will consider them to be part of the company's cooperation. Many companies believe that they have little realistic alternative but to agree to the tolling. The government also routinely makes tolling agreements part of its DPAs, so the government has the ability to prosecute the company should the DPA be violated by the company after the original statute of limitations has expired.

32. Should I Self-Report?

Short answer

Sorry, but there isn't one. The decision on whether or not to disclose evidence or allegations of misconduct to prosecutors is one of the most difficult decisions that a company can face.

> 'But I can offer you this: If you come forward and if you fully cooperate with our investigation, you will receive meaningful credit for having done so. In talking about "meaningful" credit, we are not promising amnesty for doing the right thing. But, self-reporting and cooperation carry significant incentives – by working with the Department, no charges may be brought at all, or we may agree to a deferred prosecution agreement or non-prosecution agreement, sentencing credit, or a below-Guidelines fine. Ultimately, every case is fact-specific and requires an assessment of the facts and circumstances, as well as the severity and pervasiveness of the conduct and the quality of the corporation's pre-existing compliance program. But, in every case of self-disclosure, full cooperation, and remediation, the Department is committed to giving meaningful credit where it's deserved to obtain a fair and just resolution.
>
> US Assistant Attorney General Lanny Breuer[229]

Despite promises of leniency if companies self-report, the extent of the credit has never been quantified; indeed, some researchers question that demonstrable leniency exists at all. With fines increasing and in the face of such uncertainty, some companies make the conscious business decision that – faced with the huge cost and disruption of an investigation and a certain high fine, or the risk of doing nothing, which is so much less costly – they will do nothing until they are caught and deal with it all then.

The smart companies immediately start an extensive compliance review and remediation programme, regardless of the decision.

Longer answer

The settlement and plea negotiation mechanism must provide a sufficient incentive for the defendant to admit guilt at the earliest opportunity. The most important factor in this calculation is the likely sentence and the discount that a defendant will receive. Yet this is the one that is the least certain.

The Filip Principles provide insight into the current practices and sentiment within the DOJ. They explain that there are benefits to the government when companies cooperate, in that the prosecutor is often able to conserve court and prosecution resources and avoid delays. There are also likely to be benefits for the company and its shareholders and employees, in that it may be able to avoid serious reputational harm and move quickly past a potentially difficult time. They also make it clear that companies:

- are not required to self-disclose potential misconduct, but early self-disclosure may be taken into account when assessing sentences
- are expected to conduct internal reviews to discover and properly remediate any wrongdoing, particularly if they decide not to self-disclose.

The Filip Principles outline the benefits of self-reporting in terms of sentencing credit. They state that:

'[s]o long as the corporation timely discloses relevant facts about the putative misconduct, the corporation may receive due credit for such cooperation, regardless of whether it chooses to waive privilege or work product protection in the process. Likewise, a corporation that does not disclose the relevant facts about the alleged misconduct – for whatever reason – typically should not be entitled to receive credit for cooperation. ... A corporation's failure to provide relevant information does not mean the corporation will be indicted. It simply means that the corporation will not be entitled to mitigating credit for cooperation.

The 'benefit' is not quantified, however. This is a problem for companies: without knowing the 'upside', it is difficult to make an informed decision as to whether the potential sentencing credit outweighs the downside of almost certain prosecution. And a downside it most certainly is, even if the self-disclosure leads to a plea bargain:

- Following a guilty plea there may be debarment issues, which in certain sectors would bring down the business. A negotiated settlement means that the company is better able to resolve the issue without admitting bribery and/or triggering debarment; whereas without the credit that self-reporting brings, debarment is more likely.
- In addition, most bribery schemes are international in scope. Once a settlement is reached in one jurisdiction, other countries want to share in the spoils and bring their own prosecutions.
- Once prosecutors are involved, the company's potential problems become part of the public domain and subject to disclosure to investors. Follow-on civil suits are easy to launch if the company has already admitted to bribery.
- The directors need to be careful of their personal position. While a commercial settlement and a fine might make sense from the company's perspective, no executive wants to open themselves up to extradition to the US to face personal criminal liability.

A recurrent item on the SFO's agenda is that UK companies should make quick and voluntary disclosure to the SFO as soon as they spot a potential bribery problem. This is clearly modelled on the US approach, where corporates come to the DOJ on a voluntary basis. If it works, great – it's a lot easier than having to hunt to find companies breaking the law. But the SFO has not got a steady stream of companies knocking on their door making voluntary disclosure. Of the handful of cases 'self-disclosed' to the SFO, many were cases that had been under investigation by someone, somewhere for some time anyway. Of course if the wrongdoing is going to come out anyway, there is little downside to self-disclosure to try to pick up as much credit as possible; but most defence solicitors are making sure companies fully understand the issues, potential benefits and the downside before even thinking of self-disclosure to the SFO.

Is there a really penalty reduction following self-disclosure?

Anecdotally, there is a growing list of companies that have gone through extraordinary remediation efforts and level of cooperation, all of which had been recognized by prosecutors, only to still face record fines (Baker Hughes[230] and ABB/Vetco[231] spring to mind). In the Mabey & Johnson case, three board members received custodial sentences. Would the situation really have been dramatically worse if these companies had not self-disclosed?

The perceived wisdom, and the quotes coming out of the prosecutors' offices, is that there is a clear (albeit unquantified) reduction in sentence for self-reporting. It is very much a rule of thumb that has never been confirmed or tested, but many enforcement lawyers will privately talk about self-disclosure resulting in a 50% reduction in fines.[232]

Research done in the US by Bruce Hinchey, however, contends that these claims are not backed up with firm evidence. Based on the publicly reported information in 40 FCPA cases between 2002 and 2009, he compared the ratio between the bribes paid and fines levied for companies that did and did not voluntarily disclose. Hinchey concluded that there doesn't appear to be a demonstrable benefit to voluntary disclosure. The amount paid as a bribe is only one of the factors taken into account under the sentencing guidelines when assessing fines, which also factor in company size, senior management involvement in the conduct, compliance history, corrective actions, the number of illegal payments and, crucially, the profit made from the scheme. It is impossible to factor these into a statistical analysis, however, because the amount of the fines and bribes are the only figures that the DOJ publishes consistently.

Still, Hinchey's models do demonstrate that there is a relationship between fines and bribes, and the relationship seems to differ depending on whether the company self-reported or not. He found that, on average, companies that voluntarily disclosed an FCPA violation faced a penalty of $4.53 for every dollar given as a bribe. Companies that didn't voluntarily disclose faced a penalty of just $3.22 per dollar. Excluding disgorgement of gains and prejudgement interest, the self-disclosure group faced a $2.45 fine-to-bribe ratio, compared with a $1.70 fine-to-bribe ratio for the non-disclosure group.

When to self-report
If the decision is made to self-disclose, companies should not rush into it. Before finalizing the decision, and indeed to allow a company to satisfy itself that there is something substantive to self-disclose – not simply a malicious allegation or a misinterpretation of some raw data – it is necessary to conduct some sort of review and evaluation of the problem.

The prosecutors say that they want to see almost immediate disclosure to them, and the SFO has let it be known that holding off reporting while instructing forensic accountants to carry out a review is leaving it too long. As to the vexed question of how much of a delay is too long (at least to qualify for leniency), consensus in the UK at the moment is that regulators want to see self-reporting certainly within three months of first spotting a potential problem. Feedback from DOJ insiders suggests that taking three months to conduct a preliminary investigation to evaluate a company's initial concerns is an entirely sensible and rational step, and unlikely to constitute an unreasonable delay. After all, why invite an investigation if the initial suspicions prove groundless?

In high-risk situations it is possible for the company's solicitors to make an approach to the SFO to discuss particular issues of concern on a 'no names' basis, in order to get a sense of the SFO's likely response to self-reporting on the facts in question.

Going for a chat
Recent practice is for prosecutors to write to companies, inviting them to go in for a meeting with a view to self-reporting. This is normally done when the prosecutor has some intelligence or a tip-off that there are issues, but does not necessarily have firm evidence. Often the target company does not have any real evidence either. This often takes place at the screening stage, when considering whether to open a full investigation.

With both parties acting in the dark, there is no firm answer on how to respond: it depends on the likelihood of problems in the target company, and its attitude to risk and adverse publicity. A company that goes into the SFO positively might be able to agree a timetable of six months to one year to carry out an internal investigation with full disclosure to the SFO. Experienced criminal defence lawyers are likely to be able to understand how to speak to the SFO to get an idea from them about the business areas that they are focusing on and what their intelligence is, which will allow the internal investigation to be properly targeted.

It is a brave company, though, that rejects an invitation of this type. It might go away, but more likely it will lead to a fully-fledged raid.

Further reading

Questions 26, 36 and 37.

Hinchey, B., Punishing the penitent: disproportionate fines in recent FCPA enforcements and suggested improvements, George Washington University, 2010. Available from: http://bit.ly/oOEZ7H (http://works.bepress.com/ bruce_hinchey/1).

33. How Do the Money Laundering Laws Change the Approach to Self-Disclosure in the UK?

Short answer

The Proceeds of Crime Act 2002 defines money laundering very broadly. In effect it includes possession, handling or becoming concerned in an arrangement involving any proceeds of any crime committed at any time in any place. So a shoplifter stealing a shirt from a shop is guilty of both theft and money laundering, because they have possession of the proceeds of a crime (the shirt that they stole). So money laundering need not involve either money or laundering.

Company directors who know that their company has laundered money have committed a criminal offence. The prospect of a custodial sentence under POCA provides a strong incentive to self-disclosure.

Individuals outside the regulated sector – essentially, financial institutions and professional advisors – have no obligation to report money laundering *by others*, except for terrorist offences. Professionals operating within in the regulated sector – if not covered by privilege – must report any illegal activity, however small, to the Serious Organised Crime Agency.

One of the problems with criminalizing all facilitation payments is that it puts pressure on professionals. Facilitation payments appear to come under the 'money laundering' definition; accountants, lawyers (other than those covered by privilege) and other professional advisors have an obligation under the POCA to report suspicions of the most trivial offences to the authorities.

Longer answer

The Proceeds of Crime Act 2002 ('POCA') provides that a money laundering offence is committed when someone possesses criminal property. If a company is involved, a director can become personally liable for aiding and abetting this offence. 'Criminal property' refers to a person's benefit from criminal conduct and embraces benefit from any conduct constituting an offence in the UK or – where the conduct is committed abroad – any conduct that would constitute an offence in the UK if it occurred in the UK. This clearly includes bribery, so possession of money that represents the benefit of a contract obtained by bribery constitutes money laundering.

There are reporting obligations under POCA that depend on whether or not your business is in the 'regulated sector'. The regulated sector comprises banks, financial institutions, a firm of accountants, insolvency and tax advisors, external lawyers, trust or company service providers, estate agents, casinos and high-value dealers who may sell items worth more than €15,000.

Will my accountant turn me in?
Under POCA, there is an obligation on all those working in the 'regulated sector'. They are under a positive obligation to report their suspicions about money laundering committed by *other people* to the Serious Organised Crime Agency (SOCA). (Compare this to those in the unregulated sector, who in effect are only required to report their own money laundering.) Individuals in the regulated sector must report to SOCA if certain conditions apply and there are serious penalties for not doing so: the maximum penalty is five years' imprisonment and a fine.

Specifically, POCA requires:

> '[a] person engaged in an activity in the UK which falls within the "regulated sector" to make a report whenever, based on information

which comes to them in the course of relevant business, they know
or suspects, or have reasonable grounds for knowing or suspecting,
that another person is engaged in money laundering.'

When deciding whether a report must be made, there are two
questions that a professional must ask themselves:

1. Did the information come to me in the course of *an
   activity* falling within the regulated sector?
2. Do I have knowledge or suspicion of money laundering by
   another person?

It is not the individual or company that falls within the first
test, but the activity.

For lawyers, a provider of legal services will be in the 'regulated sector' when, and only when, engaged in an activity that
'involves participation in a financial or real property transaction (whether by assisting in the planning or execution of any
such transaction or otherwise by acting for, or on behalf of, a
client in any such transaction)'. In other legal work, such as
acting for a client in connection with civil or criminal litigation, a provider of legal services is not within the 'regulated
sector'. A provider of legal services in general practice might
move in and out of the 'regulated sector' numerous times in
the course of a typical day's work.

For accountants, the nearest regulated activity is the
'provision to other persons of accountancy services by a
firm or sole practitioner who by way of business provides
such services to other persons'. Companies proving these
activities are within the ambit of POCA. Some boutique
companies that provide forensic accounting services as
part of their consulting and compliance services will not
be faced with reporting obligations, but most of the larger
accounting companies take a policy view that, because
they are in the regulated sector so much, everything
they do comes within POCA and they report on client's
activities accordingly.

If a report is made, it is an offence to tell the client about it, so the client will never know. (Although they may eventually wonder why SFO investigators are standing in reception.) Some information about potential money laundering will be obtained under privileged circumstances, so this section should be read in conjunction with the question about privilege, in which the news is not all bad.

Do I need to report my own money laundering?
If your business is not in the regulated sector, Parliament has stipulated – as a trade-off to encourage reporting criminal activity – that no offence is committed where a person discloses to SOCA that they are acquiring, using or possessing criminal property. But this means that if SOCA is *not* told that a company holds funds that are the proceeds of bribery, individuals who are aware of the fact face prosecution for money laundering. The penalty for this is up to 14 years' imprisonment and an unlimited fine. It should be noted that this is a personal, criminal penalty against those individuals with knowledge.

One of the main drivers towards self-reporting on Mabey & Johnson was money laundering concerns. The route by which this case arrived at the SFO appears to have stemmed from an employee telling all during an employment dispute, following which a full internal investigation was carried out and a number of bribery problems were uncovered. Knowing that they were in possession of funds that were the proceeds of a criminal activity, the directors faced a choice between making a disclosure under the money laundering legislation, or keeping quiet – whereupon they were potentially committing and continuing to commit a criminal offence. If a declaration was going to be made to SOCA, then the SFO would soon be told by SOCA – so why not make a disclosure to both agencies at the same time?

Further reading

Crown Prosecution Service, Proceeds of Crime Act 2002 Part 7 – Money Laundering Offences. Available from: http://bit.ly/nGxxKF (http://www.cps.gov.uk/legal/p_to_r/proceeds_of_crime_money_laundering/).

Winch, D., Money laundering made simple, Accounting Evidence, May 2006. Available from: http://bit.ly/otDGoz (http://www.accountingevidence.com/documents/articles/Money%20laundering%20made%20simple.pdf).

34. What Is Privilege and Why Is It Important?

Short answer

Parties in dispute and under investigation are obliged to disclose all documents relevant to the case. There are very limited grounds for withholding documents, and one of them is that the document is 'privileged'. If privileged circumstances exist, the documents do not have to be disclosed to third parties during litigation or an investigation. In a bribery context, losing the privileged status of an internal document means that the document will have to be disclosed to a prosecutor – potentially with damaging consequences.

Generally, communication between lawyers and clients is confidential and subject to privilege. The protection is intended to encourage complete disclosure of information between the lawyer and client, and to further the interest of justice. Most jurisdictions have a mechanism for legal privilege, but privilege varies from country to country. Usually, US privilege is broader than that in the UK.

Longer answer

Privilege in the US

In the US, privileged documents and other communications are immune from discovery. This automatically also covers communication between the company's lawyers and other professionals who may be assisting in the investigation or resolution of a claim, such as forensic accountants and data collection professionals.

Privilege protects only the communication and not the underlying facts. A client cannot, for example, shield documents from disclosure simply by sending them to a lawyer. 'Communication' though can cover a wide variety of things:

- paper records (letters, faxes, manuscript notes, jottings)
- electronic records (emails, word documents, spreadsheets)
- disks and back-up tapes
- recordings of telephone conversations and voicemails.

US jurisdictions recognize several legal privileges, the two most common being the attorney–client privilege and the work–product doctrine.

Attorney–client privilege

Attorney–client privilege protects confidential communications between attorneys and their clients that are made:

- in the course of legal representation
- for the purpose of providing legal advice to the client by the attorney.

US courts disagree about how far down the corporate chain the privilege extends. Some courts have held that the privilege extends only to communications between attorneys and those employees who have actual control over legal decisions; others consider that it applies to most employees within the client company.

Work–product doctrine

The work–product doctrine protects documents and tangible things prepared in anticipation of litigation by an attorney or an attorney's agent. It does not provide absolute protection, and does not prevent disclosure of an attorney's mental impressions, conclusions, opinions or legal theories with respect to actual or reasonably anticipated litigation.

Privilege in the UK

Legal advisors have a duty to keep all communication between themselves and their clients confidential. However, the material is disclosable in certain circumstances, including under some of the money laundering rules. Solicitors are not in breach of their professional duty of confidentiality if they do so.

Some communication, said to be protected by legal professional privilege (LPP) between a lawyer and client, cannot be disclosed – even under the money laundering provisions. For the purposes of LPP, a lawyer includes solicitors and their employees, barristers, and in-house lawyers. It does not include accountants or other professionals assisting on a case. LPP does not apply all the time: it only protects confidential communications falling under either of the two categories of privilege – legal advice privilege or litigation privilege.

Legal advice privilege   Communications between a lawyer and a client are privileged if they are:

• confidential
• for the purpose of seeking or providing legal advice.

Conversations, correspondence or meetings with other lawyers or third parties are not privileged, as the content of the communication is not confidential.

Litigation privilege   This privilege (which is wider than legal advice privilege) protects confidential communications made after litigation has started, or is reasonably in prospect, between either:

• a lawyer and a client
• a lawyer and an agent, whether or not that agent is a lawyer
• a lawyer and a third party.

These communications must be for the sole or dominant purpose of litigation, for one of:

- seeking or giving advice in relation to it
- obtaining evidence to be used in it
- obtaining information leading to obtaining such evidence.

So a solicitor and a forensic accountant, for example, can communicate on a privileged basis. Their correspondence is immune from disclosure if it relates to contemplated proceedings.

Litigation privilege is limited to adversarial proceedings and is not extended to inquisitorial proceedings. Generally speaking, however, it will depend on whether the purpose of the investigation or inquiry is adversarial (as it might well be with a bribery case) or merely fact-gathering.

Privileged circumstances   Quite separately from LPP, POCA recognizes another type of communication that is given or received in 'privileged circumstances'. This is not the same as LPP; it is merely an exemption from certain provisions of POCA, although in many cases the communication will also be covered by LPP.

'POCA privilege' can be viewed as extending legal advice privilege: it applies to lawyers *and other relevant professional advisors* where information is received from a client who is seeking legal advice, or legal proceedings are underway or in prospect.

Privileged circumstances exempt communications regarding advice to be provided to representatives. This may include communications with a junior employee of a client and other professionals assisting in a transaction, such as accountants or surveyors.

POCA privileged circumstances exemption exempts professionals from certain POCA reporting provisions. It does not provide any of the other LPP protections to those communications: a communication that is only covered by POCA privilege, not LPP, will still remain vulnerable to seizure or production under a court order or other such notice from law enforcement.

Without prejudice   As a matter of public policy, the courts want to encourage parties to resolve their disputes without the matter going to trial. Therefore, all genuine attempts to settle a dispute will, in the absence of any indication to the contrary, be treated as 'without prejudice' and be privileged from production to the court or any other party.

US versus UK differences

US privilege is wider than that in the UK. In the US, attorney–client privilege can apply to communication with third parties if the purpose of the communication is to help the attorney to provide legal advice to the client. By contrast, these communications would not be protected under UK law unless litigation was reasonably in prospect at the time.

In the UK, it is possible to confidentially share a copy of a privileged communication with a third party without losing privilege. This is not the case in the US, where disclosure of a single copy of a privileged document to third parties, including regulators (even if that disclosure takes place abroad), generally results in loss of privilege as to the entire subject matter of the privileged documents.

In the US, a privileged email and its attachments may be withheld in its entirety if it is privileged; whereas in the UK, the non-privileged elements would be disclosed, and the privileged components specifically identified and redacted.

Privilege elsewhere

Civil law countries in mainland Europe also have laws that prohibit lawyers from disclosing information about their clients. For example, in Germany, the relationship between a lawyer and client is protected by regulations that prohibit a lawyer from divulging any confidential information or documents obtained in the course of their professional activities. Compare this with the approach of common law countries such as the UK and US, whose laws seek to protect the *specific communications* rather than the entirety of the relationship.

In the context of international investigations, there is an issue about whether courts in the US or UK would consider privileged those communications between the company and lawyers and other non-lawyer professionals (some of whom may be giving legal advice) in overseas jurisdictions. Because of the relatively strong privilege that exists in the US, there are good arguments for appointing a US lawyer to coordinate investigations with a predominantly US nexus.

In France, the attorney–client privilege does not apply to discussions with business executives, as is the case in the US. Accordingly, a memo circulated between US and French corporate counsel providing advice to management could be withheld as privileged in the US, and disclosed in France.

Maintaining privilege

There are some basic steps that need to be taken to ensure privilege is maintained during a bribery investigation or response to prosecutors' enquiries.

Limit the production of documents Minimize the creation of unnecessary, non-privileged documents. Do not write about critical matters in emails or memos without being absolutely sure that the communication is privileged. For very sensitive issues, pick up the phone.

Communication through lawyers   Only lawyers have privilege. Accountants have many qualities, but inherent privilege is not one of them. Use lawyers to instruct the accountants, thus ensuring as far as possible that the accountant's reports are privileged. Once proceedings are likely, get advice from your lawyers about who you should and should not discuss the matter with, both internally and externally, and how to do it. Remember that comments made in memos at the very outset of an investigation may be particularly interesting and potentially helpful to the prosecutor.

Who is the client?   Communication between a lawyer and the employees of a corporate client may not be protected by legal advice privilege if the employee cannot be considered to be 'the client'. As such, some employees will be 'clients' while others may not. Client staff should be designated specifically for the purpose of representing the company as 'the client'. If there is no litigation in prospect, only the communication between the lawyers and the particular individuals in the 'client team' are privileged.

Losing by forwarding   Those within 'the client' must take care that privileged communications do not cease to be privileged as a result of copying them to others who are not 'the client'. Privilege generally is lost unless the communication is forwarded on to another party 'in confidence'.

Marking documents   Documents such as internal notes regarding a particular matter are generally not covered by privilege. An exception would be if they are produced at the request of lawyers for the purposes of obtaining legal advice, when they may arguably be covered.

If you want to indicate that you think an internal document you are creating is privileged, then marking it 'Privileged and Confidential. Attorney Work Product – Produced in Contemplation of Litigation' covers all the bases. Just using that label, however, does not itself guarantee protection; it is the substance of the document, not its label, that will determine whether it is protected by privilege.

Don't mix privileged and non-privileged documents   Keep them separate. If there are matters to discuss with lawyers that relate to both legal advice and commercial issues, put them in different documents. Similarly, don't attach privileged documents to non-privileged documents, as they might all become non-privileged.

Don't have informal 'off-the-record' discussions   They don't really exist.

Does privilege have to be waived following a DPA?
One of the key aspects in the Filip Principles concerned the treatment of attorney–client privilege and work product protection in the context of assessing a company's cooperation.

The Thompson memo required waiver of privilege, which came in for considerable criticism. A number of former senior Justice Department officials wrote to the Attorney General in 2006 to ask for attorney–client privilege and the work–product doctrine to be preserved. They wrote:[233]

> '[W]e believe that the 'Thompson Memorandum' is seriously flawed and undermines, rather than enhances, compliance with the law and the many other societal benefits that arise from the confidential attorney–client relationship. Therefore, we urge the Department to revise its policy to state affirmatively that waiver of attorney–client privilege and work–product protections should not be a factor

in determining whether an organization has cooperated with the government in an investigation.'

The Filip Principles state that, 'waiving the attorney–client and work–product protections has never been a prerequisite under the Department's prosecution guidelines for a corporation to be viewed as cooperative.' The Principles make clear that, although a company is always free to waive privilege on its own accord, prosecutors need to base their cases on firm evidence and not legal advice obtained from privileged documents – 'prosecutors should not ask for such waivers and are directed not to do so.'

The SEC has followed suit, initially prohibiting its staff from requesting work–product or attorney–client waivers. The Commission later revised its position: the 2010 Enforcement Manual instructs that the 'staff should not ask a party to waive the attorney–client privilege or work–product protection without prior approval of the Director or Deputy Director.'

Although historically in the UK agencies including HM Revenue & Customs have always respected a defendant's right to privilege, the SFO has indicated that it expects companies that self-report to waive privilege over certain documents, including internal factual investigations, as well as waive privilege against self-incrimination. In Mabey & Johnson – which did waive privilege when it self-reported – the SFO stated that where self-reporting companies in the future failed to waive privilege, 'the SFO will not regard the cooperation as a model of corporate transparency'.

Further reading

For the treatment of privileged material by the SFO, see Question 37.

The Council of Bars and Law Societies of Europe, The professional secret, confidentiality and legal professional privilege in Europe: an update on the report by D.A.O. Edward, QC. Available from: http://bit.ly/qMybu3 (http://www.ccbe.org/fileadmin/user_upload/NTCdocument/update_edwards_repor1_1182333982.pdf).

Dugan, J.B., Cowman, J.W. and Sheedy, A.W., Negotiating the privilege minefield: some differences between attorney–client privilege in the U.S. and Europe, *State Bar of Texas Corporate Counsel Section Newsletter*, **6**(2), Spring 2011. Available from: http://bit.ly/pL3dmP (http://www.akingump.com/files/Publication/3fe7773d-5f97-4421-919b-f4176443f0c2/Presentation/PublicationAttachment/6543a6a3-3b48-480a-9576-00e994345b33/Negotiating_the_Privilege_Minefield).

Herbert Smith LLP, *Guide to Privilege in Asia*, 2010. Available from: http://bit.ly/oW56GL (http://www.herbertsmith.com/NR/rdonlyres/8121AB29-EA2D-481A-8F51-93B9E8BEB2EC/17648/GuidetoprivilegeinAsia2011.pdf).

304 Frequently Asked Questions in Anti-Bribery and Corruption

35. Can I Acquire Bribery Problems During a Corporate Takeover?

Short answer

Yes. If there's a bribery violation lurking in the target company, its valuation can certainly go down very significantly. Even worse, though, the acquiring company can assume full liability for the target's transgressions. A significant proportion of bribery prosecutions have arisen as a result of acquisitions, where problems were discovered in the company being taken over.

An essential way to reduce the risk of successor liability and subsequent regulatory enforcement action is to conduct thorough anti-bribery due diligence on the target company before a transaction completes, and remediation immediately thereafter. Anti-bribery due diligence is now a regular feature of any merger or acquisition.

Longer answer

If you buy a company with pre-existing bribery problems, one immediate consequence is that it is worth far less than you anticipated because it has potential liabilities for fines, penalties, profit disgorgement and the associated investigation and remediation costs. At worst, though, successor liability means that acquiring companies can themselves be held liable (in the US by the doctrine of respondeat superior) for the conduct of companies that they acquire. Successor liability may also attach in an asset purchase, but it would involve a fact-specific investigation into the facts and circumstances regarding the specific transaction.

The DOJ has agreed that an effective post-completion due diligence and compliance programme can shield a company from successor liability for the acts of a newly acquired business unit and even, in some circumstances, provide a limited grace period for post-acquisition wrongful conduct. On the other hand, a new owner that turns a blind eye or fails to expend the necessary time, energy, and money to implement adequate controls will be held liable for such ongoing activity – even activity that takes place very shortly after the transaction closes.

Being alive to these sort of issues, recent purchasers in uncontested merger and acquisition (M&A) transactions commonly insist that the target's compliance problems are reported and resolved before the transaction completes.

Bribery due diligence
Although buyers and sellers have competing goals, transactions are only consummated when the goals of the buyer and seller overlap. In a bribery context, these are as follows:

• **Buyer's goals:** To avoid acquiring liability for past or ongoing bribery problems (successor liability), and ensure that the seller covers any costs of violations.
• **Seller's goals:** To ensure that disclosures regarding material contractual provisions such as representations are not misleading, and reduce the possibility of a challenge to the sales price due to unknown bribery problems.

Bribery-related provisions should be included in the purchase agreement, including the right to pull out if any representations are materially untrue or if other covenants are breached, and the right of indemnifications for any liabilities caused by bribery.

When M&A activity increases, so do bribery prosecutions and settlements. This is because all acquisitions involve due diligence either before or after the deal is done, and this is one important way that bribes are discovered. Once bribes are discovered in an M&A context, most are now self-reported as the acquiring directors seek to insulate themselves from successor liability through disclosure.

Halliburton's due diligence plan
The steps that an acquirer should address to insulate itself from liability to the DOJ's satisfaction was addressed in the hostile takeover by US firm Halliburton for the UK-listed company Expro. Like most oil and gas services firms, Expro operates in high-risk countries and deals directly with government-owned customers. But because it could not get adequate access in advance to the hostile target's books, Halliburton couldn't determine whether Expro had undisclosed FCPA-compliance problems. Also, under the terms of a confidentiality agreement entered into with the target, Halliburton would not have been able to disclose to the DOJ any pre-completion problematic conduct anyway.

If its bid succeeded and Expro had compliance problems, Halliburton could have been held responsible. It therefore went to the DOJ and proposed an aggressive post-acquisition compliance plan. In return it received the green light in Opinion Release 08-02.[234] If Halliburton acquired Expro, it was committed to undertaking an aggressive post-completion plan to 'scrub' the target company by:

- meeting immediately with the DOJ and disclosing whether any information made available to it during the takeover negotiations suggested that any corruption or accounting issues existed
- presenting to the DOJ within ten days of closing the deal a comprehensive, risk-based FCPA due diligence work plan, including the use of agents and other third parties; commercial dealings with state-owned customers; any joint venture, teaming or consortium arrangements; customs and immigration matters; tax matters; and any government licences and permits
- reporting to the DOJ the results of:

- high-risk due diligence within 90 days of closing
- medium-risk due diligence within 120 days of closing
- low-risk due diligence within 180 days of closing
• retaining external counsel and third-party consultants to conduct FCPA due diligence
• signing new contracts with the target's agents and other third parties, incorporating FCPA representations, warranties and audit rights, and terminating contracts with agents and other third parties who were unwilling to re-sign.
• imposing and implementing at the target its own Code of Business Conduct and FCPA policies and procedures, and training all target employees within 60–90 days of closing (depending on position)
• not selling Expro if the DOJ investigated Expro or any of its officers, directors, employees, agents, subsidiaries and affiliates
• ensuring that Expro and all its subsidiaries and affiliates retain their liability for any past and future violations of the FCPA.

So Halliburton essentially agreed to help the DOJ prosecute Expro's personnel if their pre-acquisition behaviour might have violated the FCPA. This was not attractive to Expro, who in the event found a buyer that did not expose it to such US liability.

This was a very high due diligence and review burden; I suspect that such a level is not required in every case. However, it is usually necessary to ensure as a minimum that an acquirer:

• undertakes reasonable risk-based due diligence in advance
• ensures that reasonably rigorous compliance procedures and controls are in place soon after the acquisition
• undertakes appropriate remedial action immediately upon learning of any issue.

Post-completion

Integration is crucial and the acquirer should have a 'Day 1' plan in place, similar to Halliburton's above. A compliance review should always be carried out following an acquisition in much the same way as a routine compliance review on a business location or sector, ideally between the signing of the purchase agreement and completion. It's of vital importance to determine whether the acquired company's existing anti-bribery policies are complete and can be effectively integrated into those of the new parent (and if not, what changes are necessary).

Compliance training and unifying internal controls should also take place as soon as possible.

Private equity

Private equity firms may also face liability under bribery legislation, even if a corrupt act occurred prior to the acquisition by the fund. Not only may liability be inherited for a company's past actions through the concept of successor liability, but a firm may also be under fire for any ongoing consequences of corrupt acts – even if there is no direct evidence that the fund or its officers knew of them.

The list of associated persons to whom a fund may be linked to is so wide that either or both the fund vehicle, its limited partners, and the general partner may face liability if an agent in a portfolio company has provided services and acted in a corrupt manner – even though there has not been direct knowledge of the bribery taking place.

Further reading

Question 19.

DOJ Opinion Procedure Release 08-02: http://1.usa.gov/vJwjcu (http://www.justice.gov/criminal/fraud/fcpa/opinion/2008/0802.pdf).

36. What Do I Do If I Discover a Potential Bribe?

Short answer

Consider from the start, and throughout the process, what the prosecutors will think of the scope and thoroughness of your investigation. Get advice. Ensure rigorous notes are kept that backs all this up and supports the decisions you make.

Longer answer

Ensure that the questionable conduct has stopped
If it involves potential bribe payments, put a hold on anything potentially questionable. Suppliers won't like it if payments due to them are delayed, but the alternatives are far worse. Change suppliers to ensure continuity of supply if there is any doubt at all.

Ensure that an independent and thorough investigation is carried out
The US Sentencing Guidelines provide that a meaningful compliance programme requires, among other things, that when criminal conduct is detected, the company implement 'reasonable steps to respond appropriately ... to prevent further similar criminal conduct'.

The investigation that needs to take place to respond to an allegation of bribery is similar to the routine compliance review that I set out later in the book. Clearly, though, it must be more expansive in scope, and will include email reviews. I won't repeat all the steps here – they will come later – but here are some of the essential points to reiterate:

Instruct lawyers Early instruction of lawyers gets privilege in place. Ensure that communication passes through the lawyers and thus becomes – as far as possible – confidential.

It's far better to get the services of one seasoned and experienced lawyer with criminal and regulatory experience than ten bright and keen graduates with experience in document review.

Potentially relevant evidence should be preserved Obtain a basic understanding of the company's electronic document architecture. Cast the net as wide as possible during the initial collection of evidence to include emails and recordings of phone conversations, if they exist.

If there are single individuals acting alone who are believed to be responsible, remote access to the organization's systems, files and information will need to be disabled to the targets once the investigation has been initiated. Once their computer hard drives have been over-written or physically moved, recovering files becomes much more difficult, if not impossible. Imaging drives using forensically sound backups provides the best scenario for finding electronic evidence.

Data protection and privacy laws may impact the ability to move documents. Lawyers should have a preliminary understanding of the laws before documents are innocently shipped out of the country – even by email – when forbidden by law. For this reason, it may be necessary to have servers set up in each location to host data. The investigation team can then review the data remotely without breaking data protection laws.

If a governmental investigation has begun or is likely to, then – as with any matter involving a disclosure obligation – any document-retention policy involving deletion of data should be suspended. A preservation or 'hold' notice that clearly states what categories of documents must be preserved should be distributed to employees and managers as soon as possible. Keep a record of the individuals to whom such a notice has been sent, and keep the scope of the instruction and the individuals to whom it has been sent under regular review. Particular attention should be given to automated processes that could inadvertently cause the destruction of data that could be relevant to the matter.

The plan   Once initial documents are gathered, it is time to determine the *scope* of the problem and *how* it should be investigated. Carefully control the scope of work initially in order to avoid an expensive, worldwide fishing expedition by your own team.

The investigative plan should be committed to paper because:

- it allows each team member to understand the scope and their part in the overall structure of the investigation
- it allows the team to track each component's progress
- the government may ask for it – creating a paper trail is essential to anti-bribery compliance.

Documents and people   It is sensible to conduct preliminary interviews as soon as possible. If there is a whistleblower, one of the first interviews is likely to be with them. Preliminary interviews – which will need to be in the local office where it all took place – will provide the team with:

- a sense of the size, scope and nature of the problem
- the culture of the company and how its business works
- personalities of key figures in the investigation.

An effort should be made to collect some key documents, but the team should *not* wait for an exhaustive document collection to be completed before travelling. Many of the principles dealt with in the section about routine compliance reviews can be adopted for use in the circumstances of a more formal, and necessarily more thorough, investigation.

Review insurance Some directors and officers (D&O) liability policies contain coverage for fines and penalties under the bribery legislation, and the costs of defending against the investigations for directors or officers of the company. Siemens reached a €100m settlement with its D&O insurers in connection with the claims arising from the company's bribery scandal – although it was reportedly not an easy claim, and it is necessary for the claim to be notified strictly in accordance with policy wording.

Consider reporting obligations – but don't be hasty In many countries, including the US and UK, there is no general obligation on companies or individuals to report a crime or suspected crime to the police or other authorities. In other jurisdictions – China, for example – there is a general duty to report.

Non-issuers are not usually required to make disclosure of pending or ongoing investigations, and therefore they usually don't. Listed companies, though, are likely to have more onerous obligations. Sarbanes–Oxley § 301 requires that the audit committee be notified of complaints related to accounting, internal accounting controls or auditing matters. As such, when confronted with a potential FCPA problem, it is imperative that a company investigates the complaint appropriately and considers whether to report to the audit committee. Issuers are required to report investigations in SEC filings if they 'are material for investors'. Modern FCPA settlements are of such size, and have such potential knock-on effects, that only the most insignificant settlements may be said to be immaterial for investors.

If the investigation highlights that a bribery offence may have been committed, it might be appropriate to self-report. It is not necessary to self-report immediately, but the investigation cannot continue indefinitely without a decision being made. This should ideally have been made within three months of the investigation commencing, which is likely to be judged sufficient time for the company to have known that there was in fact a real problem, but still soon enough to get credit with the authorities for early self-reporting.

Further reading

Question 32.

'How Do I Carry Out a Review to Detect and Deter Bribery?'

37. I've Just Received a 'Section 2' Notice. What Do I Do?

Short answer

The SFO has wide-reaching powers under Section 2 of the Criminal Justice Act 1987 that allow it to require any person or company to provide documents (even confidential ones) and/or require them to answer questions at the time and place specified in the notice.

Longer answer

Pre-empt enquiries, notices and search warrants

Before I get into the specifics, a note to remind companies – especially those operating in risky countries and sectors – that they should have a crisis policy written in advance to minimize the confusion and uncertainty (and, frankly, panic) that can occur when problems are uncovered. It need not be a long document and will need to remain flexible, but it sets out what happens if there is a dawn raid at your offices in Lagos, or you get a call for a journalist asking for a response to allegations that your company has been paying bribes to senior politicians in Indonesia.

Make sure the receptionists at all locations know who to call immediately if a search warrant or some other similar document is served. It is likely to be the general counsel or some other in-house lawyer. Make sure that all staff know to refer press enquiries to this person. If police or investigators turn up unannounced, receptionists should know that they put them immediately into a room on their own while waiting for this person to come. They are not to start searching or speaking to other staff before this. Legal advice should be taken before a search is allowed. Generally, the police will allow this to happen, although strictly speaking the SFO have no obligation to do this with a Section 2 notice.

The Section 2 notice
As the SFO ramps up its anti-bribery investigations, its main evidence-gathering tool – the 'Section 2 notice' – is being seen much more often.

It is important to bear in mind that the SFO is not a police force and that its lay members have no police powers, such as the power of arrest (although note that police officers on secondment to the SFO can arrest if an investigation requires it). Powers of investigation are given to the SFO by Section 2 of the Criminal Justice Act 1987. So-called 'Section 2 powers' are designed to obtain information to assist an investigation, and are available for bribery and corruption. They are not designed to obtain evidence for direct use in court, although material obtained using Section 2 powers may subsequently be produced. Section 2 powers enable the SFO to:

- require any person or company to provide any relevant documents at the time and place specified in the notice
- require any person to answer any relevant questions at the time and place specified in the notice.

There is no requirement to provide questions in advance and the SFO is not obliged to wait for a solicitor to arrive or to allow a solicitor to be present at an interview.

Importantly, Section 2 notices can only be issued once a case has been accepted for investigation by SFO. The power to use Section 2 endures until the case is fully investigated, even after charge.

Section 2 powers are known as 'compulsory' powers because:

- failure to comply with a Section 2 notice, without a reasonable excuse, is an offence
- giving false or misleading information in response to a notice is an offence
- the 'right to silence' does not apply to information obtained under Section 2, because it cannot generally be used in evidence without a witness statement.

Section 2 notices are designed to obtain information during an investigation. Recipients will often be professional advisors who owe a duty of confidence that would otherwise preclude them from cooperating without a court order. In many cases, it is advantageous to be operating pursuant to a Section 2 notice, as it overrides any obligations of confidentiality or secrecy attaching to the information or to the holder, other than legal professional privilege.

Section 2 notices do not require a court order. The usual route is simply for the SFO to serve a notice on the person concerned, which states on a date by which the action should be carried out. (If necessary, it can require immediate action.) If a person fails to comply, if it is not possible to serve a notice or if the SFO has reasonable grounds to believe that serving a notice would seriously prejudice the investigation, the SFO may apply to a court for a warrant to search the relevant house or business premises and seize documents.

Additional powers granted to the SFO in overseas corruption investigations

Extended powers were given to the SFO in July 2008. The new powers, inserted as Section 2A of the Criminal Justice Act 1987, grant the SFO the ability to use Section 2 powers at a 'pre-investigation stage' in relation to overseas bribery and corruption. For practical purposes, this allows the SFO to screen allegations it receives and gather evidence in order

to determine whether it wishes to open an investigation
or not.

It may now be particularly important in corruption cases to
establish with the SFO whether there are exercising Section
2 powers as a consequence of an investigation having been
commenced or whether it is part of a screening process using
Section 2A.

If you have received a Section 2 notice
It is important for recipients of a Section 2 notice to seek
legal advice wherever possible because far-reaching sanctions
exist if the notices are not complied with. Often, though, SFO
case managers are prepared (in fact, will be keen) to agree
the scope and logistics of complying with a lengthy document production request, and agree the form in which the
production will take. If the document production request is to
be carried by identifying emails or documents using search
terms, it is important to try to agree the scope of this with
the SFO.

It might not be that bad ...
The fact that a notice is sent to an individual or company
does not always mean that person is suspected of an offence.
Although Section 2 notices can be used against suspects,
many practitioners believe that the SFO is reluctant to issue
notices against suspects themselves. Historically, Section 2
notices tended to be confined to people merely who had
information, and/or who could be potential witnesses.

'It's a raid!'
Sometimes, when there is reasonable suspicion (a relatively
low standard of proof) that there has been bribery, the SFO
will carry out a raid. These are most unwelcome, and should
be avoided at all costs – for example, by cooperating with an
invitation to self-report. Although the US approach to bribery
enforcement is normally more aggressive than that in the UK,
in the area of the raid, the SFO do not mess about!

The raid will normally involve teams of investigators and police in multiple locations at once. They will have lots of bags to take away documents with them. They can take original documents and forensic images of digital media, regardless of relevance, to review later.[235] Bear in mind that these documents might be gone for many months, if not years, while the investigation progresses. The company will be allowed access to make copies but, as you can imagine, the documents will soon be in storage and will not always filed as well as they might.[236] Computers will be imaged, or will be taken away if this proves impossible in the time available and the SFO technicians do not have the necessary equipment to image in situ. This means there will inevitably be massive disruption to the business, and companies who see this coming must copy business-critical documents and electronic files.

The SFO is not allowed to remove legally privileged material, but usually this cannot be determined at the time. Documents subject to a claim of privilege will be placed in clearly marked blue bags, sealed in the normal way at the scene of the search, for later review by a lawyer person not involved in the case.[237]

Executives will often be interviewed at the same time under Section 2. Many appreciate the seriousness of the situation only when they get a call in the middle of the interview from their spouse, telling them that ten people from the SFO have just turned up at their home, are rifling through their underwear drawers, and have imaged all their home computers and mobile phones. (Many go very sheepish at this time, knowing that their personal SMS texts and internet browsing history will soon come under scrutiny.)

Further reading

Question 34.

38. Do I Share in the Fine If I 'Blow the Whistle' on My Employer?

'We get thousands of tips every year, yet very few of these tips come from those close to the frauds as they are occurring. We hope that this new whistleblower program will change that.'

Mary Schapiro, SEC Chair[238]

Short answer

One consequence of the regulatory reform legislation introduced in response to the fraud perpetrated by Bernie Madoff was that the SEC's little-used Whistleblower Bounty Program was extended to cover people coming forward with evidence of any type of securities fraud. Specifically, the new Dodd–Frank Wall Street Reform and Consumer Protection Act 2010 now means that individuals coming forward with information about FCPA violations stand to receive 10–30% of amounts recovered by the SEC through subsequent enforcement actions.

The Dodd–Frank Act has few, if any, equivalents in other jurisdictions.

Longer answer

Speaking up is not easy

For most people, fear is a more common cause of corrupt behaviour than greed. People want to avoid conflict and speaking up can taint a person's career, even if the person is vindicated. Even the terminology used can send an important message: 'speaking up' has a far more positive connotation than 'whistleblower'.

So many people keep quiet. It takes courage to report wrongdoing. Besides, there is also a chance that you may be wrong and might be embarrassed, because there will always be opinion and shades of grey. But you have to take the risk.

Qui tam

For many years the US had had a mechanism whereby whistleblowers could share in the bounty. The False Claims Act 1863 is a long-standing US federal law that allows citizens to file actions against contractors committing fraud against the government. Claims under the False Claims Act have been filed by people with inside knowledge of false claims that have typically involved healthcare, the military or other government spending programmes.

People filing claims under the Act stand to receive a portion (usually 15–25%) of any recovered damages under what is called the 'qui tam' provision. ('Qui tam' is an abbreviated form of the Latin legal phrase, 'qui tam pro domino rege quam pro se ipso in hac parte sequitur' – roughly translated as 'He who brings a case on behalf of the King, as well as for himself'.) To pursue a qui tam suit, the whistleblower must demonstrate knowledge that the defendant knowingly presented false bills or other information to the government, either to swindle it into paying more than it owed or to cheat it out of monies it is owed.

The Dodd–Frank Act

The Dodd–Frank Wall Street Reform and Consumer Protection Act 2010 is a US federal statute signed into law by President Obama in July 2010. (The law was initially proposed by Barney Frank and Chairman of the Senate Banking Committee Chris Dodd.) The Act makes a number of changes to financial regulations, but we focus here on Section 922 of the Act, which promotes whistleblowing by authorizing the SEC to pay rewards for information that leads to successful enforcement actions.

Under the new rules, a whistleblower (defined as someone who provides information to the SEC relating to a potential violation of the securities laws) could receive 10–30% of amounts recovered through enforcement actions. The SEC decides the final amount based on the originality and value of the information provided and how directly it led to the financial penalty being levied against the defendant. To be considered for an award, a whistleblower must do the following.

Voluntarily provide the SEC ... In general, a whistleblower provides information voluntarily if they provide it before the government, a self-regulatory organization or the Public Company Accounting Oversight Board asks for it.

... with original information ... Original information must be based upon the whistleblower's independent knowledge or analysis, not already known to the Commission and not derived exclusively from public sources.

... that leads to the successful enforcement by the SEC of a federal or administrative action ... A whistleblower's information can be deemed to have led to successful enforcement in two circumstances:

- if the information results in a new examination or investigation being opened, and significantly contributes to the success of a resulting enforcement action
- if the conduct was already under investigation, but it is essential to the success of the action and would not have otherwise been obtained.

... in which the SEC obtains monetary sanctions totalling more than $1m The SEC proposed its rules for the whistleblower provision in November 2010. They became effective in May 2011. The Dodd–Frank legislation is nuanced as follows:

- There are higher awards for whistleblowers who report their information through internal compliance channels first.
- Lawyers who obtain information from their clients, accountants who learn of the fraud through audits or compliance staff who receive information through internal reporting mechanisms would not usually be eligible to receive the awards.
- People who uncover misconduct through compliance processes could become whistleblowers in certain instances, such as if their employer does not act on the information within a reasonable time, or acts in bad faith.
- The proposed rules would bar foreign officials from collecting any reward.
- Any sanctions that a whistleblower pays in relation to the fraud does not count towards a reward. Similarly, if a company is sanctioned for conduct the whistleblower directed, that amount also does not count for purposes of a bounty.

Am I protected if I speak up?

A variety of federal and state laws protect employees who call attention to violations or help with enforcement proceedings, or refuse to obey unlawful directions. Unfortunately, however, when passing the Sarbanes–Oxley Act 2002, the Senate Judiciary Committee found that whistleblower protections were dependent on the 'patchwork and vagaries' of varying state statutes:

- The False Claims Acts provides reassurance for whistleblowers. It is a further violation of the Acts for an employer to take any kind of retaliation against an employee who reports corporate fraud: the employee

cannot be fired, demoted, or denied benefits. If an employer does take such action to punish a whistleblower employee, the whistleblower is entitled to sue for retaliation as part of the qui tam suit.
- The Whistleblower Protection Act 1989 is a US federal law that protects whistleblowers who work for the government and report agency misconduct. A federal agency violates the Whistleblower Protection Act if agency authorities take or threaten retaliatory action with respect to any employee because of any disclosure of information by the employee. Transgressions of the FCPA would be included within this.

Will Dodd–Frank bounties work?

I expect to see an even greater increase in FCPA enforcement activity at both the DOJ and the SEC as, for the first time, people who come across evidence of suspected corrupt behaviour will have a real financial incentive to report it to prosecutors. Given the large fines in foreign bribery cases in recent years, there could be some big rewards for those prepared to speak out. The SEC has reported many more whistleblower tips since the Dodd–Frank reforms were publicized, including some high-value ones.

Just as importantly, though, the whistleblower incentive risks changing the dynamic of internal investigations. Compliance people worry that the SEC bounty programme will undermine their internal compliance programmes – employees who once approached them with their suspicions may decide instead to go straight to the SEC in the hope of a reward.

Is there a UK equivalent of Dodd–Frank?

No – and there is unlikely to be one soon. However, there is strong employment protection for employees who speak up. In the UK, if there is malpractice or wrongdoing happening in a workplace and you make a disclosure in the public interest, then as long as you follow the correct procedures your employment rights are protected.

Some employment experts do caution however that the law cannot entirely remove the risk to employees. According to UK employment tribunal statistics, the number of people citing whistleblowing as a factor in the dispute increased from 157 cases in 1999 to 1791 in 2009. Each of these cases is evidence of a breakdown in relations between employer and employee, where those claiming to have spoken out have been undermined or removed from their jobs.[239] People are more likely to take action with respect to unacceptable behaviour if there is a formal policy in place that offers near-absolute confidentiality.

Informing as part of a settlement

The DOJ is likely to give considerable credit, meaning a reduced sentence, if defendants inform on other players in the same scheme, or on competitors who are also involved with corrupt schemes of their own. In the DPA by pharmaceutical company Johnson & Johnson, the company was reported to have saved at least $17m in fines by identifying improper practices in the life sciences industry and informing the DOJ of similar allegations involving its competitors.[240] This is one of the first instances where sentencing credit relied heavily on informing. The DOJ press release stated that:

> '[i]n addition, J&J received a reduction in its criminal fine as a result of its cooperation in the ongoing investigation of other companies and individuals, as outlined in the US Sentencing Guidelines.'[241]

Further reading

'Speaking up and whistleblowing', page 402.

Dodd–Frank Wall Street Reform and Consumer Protection Act 2010: http://1.usa.gov/pjCofQ (http://www.sec.gov/about/laws/wallstreetreform-cpa.pdf).

DOJ, False Claims Act cases: government intervention in qui tam (whistleblower) suits. Available from: http://1.usa.gov/o796UC (http://www.justice.gov/usao/pae/Documents/fcaprocess2.pdf).

SEC, Office of the Whistleblower. Available from: http://1.usa.gov/p1Q1XL (http://www.sec.gov/whistleblower).

SEC, SEC adopts rules to establish whistleblower program, 25 May 2011. Available from: http://1.usa.gov/qfDhDp (http://www.sec.gov/news/press/2011/2011-116.htm).

Whitaker, L.P., The Whistleblower Protection Act: an overview, CRS report for Congress, Congressional Research Service, 12 March 2007. Available from: http://bit.ly/qcU2l7 (http://www.fas.org/sgp/crs/natsec/RL33918.pdf).

39. How Can I Deter Bribery?

Short answer

Bribery – in common with any crime – occurs when an individual has:

- motivation to do it
- opportunity to do it
- the ability to rationalize that what they have done was morally justified.

Taking away any of these can stop the crime taking place. In the case of bribery, the removal of opportunity is generally the easiest thing to eliminate. This occurs when there are strong compliance structures in place.

Longer answer

Deterring bribery involves eliminating those factors that lead to it taking place. Before you can set up a truly effective compliance procedure, you need to understand an even more fundamental question: why do people become involved in bribery in the first place?

In common with all types of frauds, there are three key drivers that lead to people bribing or accepting bribes. These come from the famous 'fraud triangle' made popular by criminologist Donald Cressey in the 1940s:[242]

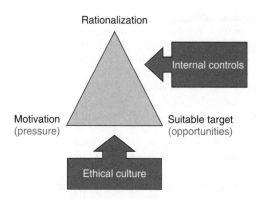

Motivation or pressure
Crimes always have motives. Corruption feeds off a requirement for the perpetrators to meet their financial obligations,
achieve budgets, win commissions, satisfy the spouse or
impress the neighbours. In brief – need or greed.

The slippery slope People tend to become comfortable
with bribery when it starts out small and grows by small
increments. In this way, they can easily find themselves
engulfed in a major bribery scheme that they would never
have become part of had it happened all at once.

Motivation can also involve saving face: individuals can
become swept into a sequence of behaviours that go from
ethically borderline to outright corrupt in just a few years.
To start with, they might see or do something that's just on
the edge of permissibility, and don't say anything. By the
time this practice has grown to something that is clearly
wrong, challenging it would involve admitting their past
mistakes. The person becomes actively engaged in a cover-up
to prevent their own earlier cover-up from being discovered.

Rationalization

Individuals involved with bribery need to feel that their actions were something other than criminal conduct. Many people pay bribes because they think that:

- everyone else is doing it
- it's not a big deal
- they are getting back at their unfair employer or the evils of capitalism
- they are assisting in the wellbeing of people or organizations within a developing economy.

Not everyone is doing it – minimizing prevalence and social acceptability

News headlines highlighting the prevalence of bribery can be a double-edged sword. Although drawing attention to its widespread nature can work to bring its damaging effects into people's consciousness, it may not always prevent bribery occurring in the workplace. This is because social pressures contribute heavily to bribery. Although many people's initial reaction to individuals involved with bribery is that they are morally flawed, the reality is that social and work situations are very powerful – many otherwise good individuals can easily become caught up in it.

Research into cheating, for example, has shown that in any group of people there are some that are simply dishonest and would cheat in virtually any circumstances given the opportunity. But there is a much larger proportion who are deeply conflicted about what to do when other people are involved in dishonest behaviour: most either keep quiet or 'go with the flow' and become involved themselves.

You are probably familiar with Rudy Giuliani spearheading a 'zero-tolerance' response to crime when he was Mayor of New York. His idea was based on social scientists Wilson and Kelling's 'broken windows theory', which suggested that focusing police attention on remedying small but powerful

signs of disorder and petty crime, such as graffiti, litter and
fare evasion, would be effective in reducing more serious
crimes.[243] The tactics were widely thought of as a success
and demonstrated that if people see that others have violated a social norm, then they themselves are more likely to
feel hesitant about violating one themselves.

Psychologist Robert Cialdini points out the importance of
group dynamics in deterring petty crime. In an experiment in
Petrified Forest National Park in Arizona, researchers placed
signs at entrances asking people not to take home petrified
wood. The sign at one entrance showed three thieves with
an X over them, while at a second entrance the sign depicted
just one thief. The sign at the second entrance was far more
effective in reducing theft. This is thought to be because if
you emphasize how common cheating is, it gives the subtle
message that all of your neighbours and co-workers are doing
it. 'And if there's a single, most primitive lever for behaviour
in our species, it's the power of the crowd.'[244]

Many people will tell you that it's impossible to do business
in country X without paying bribes, without themselves having much experience of ever trying to do it. Allowing people
to see that violations of laws are frequent or widespread
makes them less likely to be followed by others. It is therefore important in communicating an anti-bribery policy to
marginalize those who bribe and subtly portray them as violating moral and social norms. Rather than propagate the
message that 'too many of us are involved with bribery and
we need to cut down', it is far more effective to highlight the
fact that if even one person is involved, it undermines the
principles of transparency and fairness by which business
partners treat each other. The more a myth is perpetuated,
the more that people will still bribe in country X.

Suitable targets and opportunity
People clearly must have some sort of opportunity to become
involved in a bribery scheme. When weighing up whether or

not to do it, a perpetrator of any crime will rationally assess a number of variables, such as how easy it is to do, the risk of being caught, the severity of expected punishment and the 'moral cost' of being dishonest. Opportunity generally arises from a lack of internal controls, checks and balances, and operational transparency.

Breaking the 'fraud triangle'
Deterring bribery means breaking the bribery triangle by removing at least one (and ideally all) of its elements. Of the three elements, removal of opportunity is most directly correlated with an effective compliance procedure and so generally provides the most actionable route. Much of the rest of this book consists of tangible steps to put together and review just such a compliance policy.

Just bear in mind, though, that the 'right' structure is the sweet spot between too few controls with empowered staff and overly cumbersome regulation that breeds inefficiencies and resentment, and so – paradoxically – increases corruption.

Further reading

Minogue, R., Working with rationalizations, Richard's Blog, Septia Group, 16 February 2011. Available from: http://bit.ly/nmqEb8 (http://septiagroup.com/blog/?p=74).

Steen, M., How to prevent cheating, *Stanford Business Magazine*, August 2008. Available from: http://bit.ly/n8cHFt (http://www.gsb.stanford.edu/news/bmag/sbsm0808/feature-preventcheating.html).

40. What Accounting Records Must I Keep?

Short and longer answer

It is important to bear in mind that the FCPA is not just an anti-bribery law. There are also penalties to US and foreign issuers for failure to properly maintain adequate accounting records, and put in place adequate internal controls. These infractions, however, may not be related to bribery, and can form an entirely independent source of liability. It is therefore vital that any effective anti-bribery policy deals with financial controls and accurate and transparent accounting. Under the FCPA, issuers must:

- keep books in reasonable detail that 'accurately and fairly reflect the transactions and dispositions of the assets of the issuer'
- devise and maintain a system of internal accounting controls to provide reasonable assurances that the company has accurate books and records, and GAAP-compliant financial statements.

So how much detail is reasonable? Unfortunately all we get from the FCPA is the enigmatic guidance that 'reasonable detail' means 'such level of detail and degree of assurance as would satisfy prudent officials in the conduct of their own affairs'. The requirement is not limited to accuracy in accounting systems or to specifying the correct cost codes into which payments might be allocated, but it applies widely across all business records and even internal documents. It would include for example inaccurate notes, memos and schedules, and even diary items. Companies need to ensure the position is replicated through all companies in which it has control or influence.

Unlike the FCPA, the Bribery Act does not mandate that accurate books and records and control systems must be maintained by a company. Instead, the duty of UK companies to keep adequate accounting records is set out in both the Companies Act and tax legislation. Section 386 of the Companies Act is attached as Appendix 3. The test is lower than the FCPA, and mandates that 'adequate' accounting records means records that are sufficient to show and explain the company's transactions, and to disclose with reasonable accuracy, at any time, the financial position of the company.

Most other OECD countries have laws governing accounting books and records, and prohibiting falsification. However, in many countries, penalties are limited to criminal sanctions, often with an accompanying knowledge requirement; corporate liability for inaccurate books and records is often limited or non-existent.

What does this mean in practice?
Again, operating on the principle that it is best practice to work to the tightest set of rules, a company's books and records must be not only quantitatively but also *qualitatively* correct. Documentation must be reasonably current and in reasonable detail to give a third party a complete understanding of the significant aspects of a transaction.

Companies do not need to go overboard and produce documentation more extensive than is typical in the ordinary course of business. However, they must maintain and record not simply the bare financial facts (such as the invoice number and the amount), but must have full transparency regarding date, recipients and purpose of payment. Literally true descriptions that are misleading owing to lack of detail are not sufficient. A bribe accounted for as a 'sales cost', for example, would be misleading – although it was literally true (in that the bribe was paid to increase sales), it was inaccurate in that it did not sufficiently specify the nature of the payment.

How should facilitation payments be recorded?
There is no facilitation payment exception under the accounting rules, which makes them exceedingly difficult to account for. The only way to properly account for them under the FCPA is truthfully, as something like 'FCPA-permitted facilitation payments'. This raises all sorts of problems, however. For one thing, you need to hope that all your staff understand the difference between a facilitation payment and a bribe, to stop bribes being accounted for in this account (which is tricky, as even experienced FCPA lawyers disagree on what a true facilitation payment is). This will mean that you need controls to have everything that goes into that account properly approved: if you ever do get into trouble, that is the first account that will get scrutinized – because it has red flashing lights all over it. Furthermore, it is a brave company that explicitly admits to bribing in its accounts – in the US it might be legal, but it won't in other places. Far easier not to pay them at all!

If an entity concludes that its business requires it to make facilitation payments, a record should be kept of all of them. This is because the onus of establishing that a payment was a facilitation payment, not a bribe, lies on the company, not the US government. There is no alternative then but to set up cost codes within the accounting systems for 'facilitation payments', supported with information on each that specifies:

- the value of the benefit concerned
- the date on which the conduct occurred
- the identity of the foreign official or other person in relation to whom the conduct occurred
- particulars of the routine government action that was sought to be expedited or secured by the conduct
- (ideally) the official's signature or some other means of verifying the official's identity.

The best way of doing this is by a standard document that should be filled out by all staff as soon as they have had to make a facilitation payment. The form should be completed by the employee and passed to the CCO as soon as reasonably possible.

Further reading

'An essential summary of the FCPA', page 73.

Questions 17 and 18.

Appendix 3: Section 386 of the Companies Act 1989: accounting provisions (extract), page 492.

41. What Are the Main 'Red Flags' of Bribery?

Short and longer answer

So-called 'red flags' are not necessarily evidence of corruption; nor do they automatically disqualify a supplier or business partner. They do, however, raise concerns that must be addressed, so you can be comfortable that the 'red flags' are not pointing towards real problems. This list is by no means exhaustive and the ingenuity of those involved in corruption knows no bounds, but here is my top 15.

1. Large, unusual or unexplained cash payments, including payments to vendors in cash.
2. Round sum payments (e.g. $100,000 exactly).
3. Payments being made through a third party country, i.e. goods or services are supplied to Country A but payment is made to Country B, often a shell company in an offshore jurisdiction.
4. Small suppliers and consultants – with no web presence, a serviced office and no other clients – being paid large amounts of money for uncertain services.
5. Advances to vendors or credit balances with suppliers; long-standing entries in suspense and temporary accounts.
6. Lavish entertaining and gifts to clients, including paid travel.
7. Missing documents or records regarding meetings or decisions to retain suppliers; one-time transactions, or payments to vendors not approved in the company's master vendor file.
8. Doing business directly with government officials, associates of government officials, politicians or the police.

9. Transactions with unusual or enigmatic descriptions, such as 'extraordinary costs'.
10. A third party's refusal to participate in due diligence, identify a beneficial owner or certify anti-corruption compliance.
11. Convictions or allegations of illegal or unethical conduct by suppliers.
12. Recommendation of the use of particular suppliers by a governmental official.
13. An agent's requirement of an usually high commission or a deficient invoice lacking details of the tasks performed.
14. A middleman or local is involved in a public contract and their addition has no obvious value to the performance of the contract.
15. Supplier invoices – especially freight forwarders – include claims for disbursements without supporting receipts.

42. Are Any of My Employees Receiving Kickbacks from Suppliers?

Short and longer answer

The majority of this book has looked at active bribery and the position of the company who has been (potentially) paying the bribes. Sometimes of course the position is reversed, and an employee in the purchasing organization privately receives a bribe or kickback from a vendor. How does this change the approach to an investigation?

Overbilling by suppliers

In a kickback scheme, a complicit employee authorizes an additional illegal payment to a supplier. The supplier might be bogus, but it is usually providing some legitimate business supplies or services. The cooperative supplier then forwards or 'kicks back' an element of the overbilling, usually in cash, to the complicit employee.

Overbilling can include:

- increased price – amount that the eventual price varies from the agreed or market price
- reduced quantity – deliveries fall short of the amount invoiced
- reduced quality – delivery of sub-standard goods, or supplying inferior goods but charging for best quality
- services allegedly performed that weren't needed in the first place, or services never performed at all
- extras and penalties charged by the supplier
- tender-rigging – only the related party vendors are selected
- non-payment and writing off the payable
- payments being made to entities or persons that do not exist by establishing fictitious vendors.

Kickback arrangements are difficult to detect because they are 'off-book', which means that there is a totally legitimate order, delivery and payment, but the bribe is not recorded in the accounts of the purchasing company. While not easy, they certainly can and should be investigated. There are three possible approaches to it.

Looking at the vendor company

If you have audit rights, use them, because the most effective means of concluding a successful investigation of a suspected kickback is an on-site audit of the supplier's financial records. This examines if they are selling material that is overpriced or under-specified compared to what they are supplying to others, and paying kickbacks from the excess profit. So an investigation will focus on:

- reviewing the cash disbursements of the vendor, identifying:
  - any payments to your employees
  - any payments to employee controlled entities
  - excessive owner distributions
  - other unusual transactions
- ascertaining the gross profit of the company on sales made to your company compared with the norm.

Looking at the circumstances of the individual

Explore links between the suspect and the vendor company. Company databases and Google are invariably the first point of call. Is your employee, for example, a Facebook friend of the salesperson from the supplier? Imaging their laptop/desktop and looking for evidence is a good first start. Investigators can do more of the on-the-ground digging, in particular by examining your employee's wealth and assets: what's new, and can it all be explained by the person's legitimate salary?

Using data mining in the buyer company
Data mining and accounting analytics are key to uncovering these schemes. Specialist forensic accountants are experts in obtaining and crunching the financial data that pinpoints the suppliers at high risk of paying kickbacks. The overbilling forms the key to an investigation and analysis of the purchase ledger will highlight accounts whose behaviour does not match underlying trends. So look at:

- higher-than-normal cost of raw materials or excessive purchases relative to stock
- irregularities in inventory accounts, including excessive write-offs
- an unusually high volume of purchases from one vendor or unexpected switching between vendors
- when and who from your organization authorized the procurement and payments (e.g. is there anything unusual about the way they treated this particular supplier?)
- whether there are purchase amounts just under review limits or multiple purchases in a short period of time
- accelerated payment of invoices
- increases in vendor charges and penalties
- total billing exceeds budgeted or anticipated amount
- whether cost of goods sold increase disproportionately compared to sales – most kickback schemes start small and grow over time as individuals become emboldened and greedier
- contracts written to limit competition (for example, sole-source contracts)
- bypassing normal tendering/contracting procedure
- whether the same vendor always wins contracts by small margins or the contract always goes to the bid received last.

These schemes can transform into extortion if the vendor decides to take advantage of the corrupt buyer. They threaten to expose the buyer if they do not continue to accept fictitious invoices for products that were never shipped. Such a stalemate can result in inventory shortages in the buyer, and so it's there where you can also look.

Preventing kickback fraud

An effective three-way match of the key purchase documents can prevent most kickback schemes. These three key documents are:

- purchase order
- delivery note
- invoice.

This means that before paying any invoices, an independent employee must match all three documents to ensure that the company has been billed for the right number and quantity of items/services delivered, and which corresponded to the specifications of what was ordered. This simple accounting control cuts out all but the most determined collusive schemes.

This should be allied with segregation of duties to separate:

- vendor approval
- purchase requisitions
- purchase approval
- receiving and payment.

Except in those situations where there is a sole supplier of a product – in which case, the need for a kickback is a moot point – an organization should monitor and compare prices among suppliers. Obtain competitive bids on an annual basis and involve more than one individual in the approval of bids from key suppliers.

Also, to prevent excess ordering, companies should determine an economic reorder quantity for inventory items and carry out periodic physical inventories, reconciling these counts with the inventory on the balance sheet.

An effective quality assurance programme is invaluable to deal with the substandard goods issue.

43. How Can I Stay Up To Date?

Short and longer answer

These are some of the key blogs that should be essential regular reading to all in the field.

- Main Justice's Just Anti-Corruption website: http://www.mainjustice.com/justanticorruption/ (excellent, but quite pricey and subscription-only)
- FCPA Professor: http://www.fcpaprofessor.com/
- The FCPA Blog: http://www.fcpablog.com/
- thebriberyact.com: http://thebriberyact.com
- FCPA Compliance and Ethics Blog: http://tfoxlaw.wordpress.com/
- Howard@OpenAir: http://openairblog.wordpress.com/
- The European Anti-Bribery Blog: http://www.antibriberyblog.eu
- TRACE International Case Compendium: http://bit.ly/qM2lEZ (https://www.traceinternational2.org/Knowledge/ Compendium/Search_Compendium.html)
- Ethisphere Anti-Corruption Resource Center: http://acstage.ethisphere.com/

Chapter 5

How Do I Set Up Proportionate Yet Effective Anti-Bribery Compliance Procedures?

'We have yet to bring a case where we've had a company come to us with a meaningful compliance program.'

Mark Mendelsohn, former Deputy Chief, Fraud Section, US Department of Justice, March 2006[245]

Introduction

Even though Siemens had voluminous anti-corruption policies, the government charged it with having only a 'paper programme' that it failed to properly implement. As a result, it paid the largest foreign bribery fine to date and, furthermore, has said that the cost of addressing its compliance failings was nearly as much again as its $1.6bn penalty.

Companies are now getting the message that although it has historically been difficult to satisfy prosecutors that procedures are adequate, it is now vital to get anti-corruption compliance procedures in place in advance of any investigation – particular with the Bribery Act and the Dodd–Frank Act newly enacted.

I focus here on what the Bribery Act and the US Sentencing Guidelines think about what constitutes adequate compliance procedures, before moving on to more practical steps that a company can take.

The 'six principles' under the Bribery Act

Section 7 of the Bribery Act 2010 creates the criminal offence of a failure to prevent bribery by commercial organizations. The same section, though, provides a defence for a company accused of such a violation if it can show it had 'adequate procedures' in place to prevent a person associated with it from engaging in bribery. While it may at first glance appear inconsistent for a company to have adequate procedures yet still be involved with bribery, the legislators have sensibly recognized that it is possible for a business's procedures to be circumvented by a rogue employee. In such cases, the company would not be guilty of a Section 7 offence.

The Ministry of Justice published Guidance with help for companies struggling to put in place 'adequate' procedures. The Guidance is based on six general principles aimed at assessing the risks of a violation of the Act and implementing a programme of prevention and monitoring. A first consultation paper on adequate procedures was published in September 2010.[246] The final version was published in March 2011 in a somewhat different form, with a far stronger commercial focus and a more lenient view on the interpretation of several of its provisions.

Status of the Bribery Act Guidance

The Bribery Act Guidance is not mandatory and there is no positive onus on companies or their boards to put in place 'adequate procedures'. However, there is personal liability for senior officers of a company who 'consent or connive' in bribery, and it is possible that blatant disregard of these procedures when operating in high-risk jurisdictions could expose a director to personal liability, or claims of negligence or misfeasance.

Although broadly applicable, the principles lack detail, in many cases are self-evident and are frankly vague. Nevertheless, they are still important in that they will be the starting point for prosecutors and a court trying to assess the adequacy of the steps taken by a defendant in any given case. The six principles are listed below.

Proportionate procedures

This is actually an addition from the earlier consultative document, which had listed risk assessment as principle 1 (now moved to principle 3). The final Guidance now stresses that systems and procedures need to be bespoke: there is no 'one size fits all' solution, but above all, large organizations will require more complex and developed controls than smaller ones. This sentiment is echoed by the US Sentencing Guidelines, which also focuses on size. It states that '[i]n general, the formality and scope of actions that an organization shall take ... depends on the size of the organization'.

The Bribery Act Guidance describes it as follows:

> 'This is to allow each commercial organisation to tailor its policies and procedures so that they are proportionate to the nature, scale and complexity of its activities. ... [S]mall and medium sized organisations will, for example, face different challenges compared to large multi-national enterprises.'

Everything else being equal, large companies have more risk than small companies, because one person or a small group of people are less able to know and control everything happening within the company as it grows in size. It must be borne in mind, though, that the anti-bribery programme that is put in place, and all the subsequent steps, should really be guided by the bribery risk involved in the business rather than on size. In my view, bribery risk depends on where the company is operating and what it is doing, not on its size. This means that despite the guidance here, companies acting in riskier business sectors and areas need more controls to prevent bribery.

The challenge that smaller, riskier companies have – take for example a small, newly incorporated company acquiring oil exploration rights in sub-Saharan Africa – is to put in place an adequate programme of controls that adequately address the country and sector risk, yet are still proportionate and do not stifle or bankrupt a small company.

Top-level commitment
This is all about establishing a culture across the organization in which bribery is acknowledged to be unacceptable. The commitment must be made by the most senior management (the so-called 'tone at the top'). The ethos of operating without resorting to bribery should be clearly and regularly communicated to all staff and business partners, both inside and outside the organization.

Whatever the size, structure or market of a commercial organization, top-level management's commitment to bribery prevention is likely to include:

• communication of the organization's anti-bribery stance
• an appropriate degree of involvement in developing bribery prevention procedures.

Risk assessment
The company must assess the nature and extent of its exposure to potential external and internal risks of bribery. The assessment is periodic, informed and documented.

Due diligence
This is about knowing who a business is working with; knowing why, when and to whom it is releasing funds; seeking reciprocal anti-bribery agreements; and being in a position to feel confident that its business relationships are transparent and ethical. The approach is again risk-based and means that a business must have due diligence policies and procedures that cover all parties to a business relationship, including the organization's supply chain, agents and intermediaries; all forms of joint venture and similar relationships; and all markets that the commercial organization does business in. This is not only so that a business can assess its compliance risks, but also to properly manage them.

Communication (including training)
This is about how a business implements its anti-bribery policies and procedures, and ensures they are embedded throughout the organization in areas such as internal controls, recruitment and remuneration policies, operations, communications, and training. The Guidance encourages a business to regularly communicate its ethics and anti-bribery programme, using all the different channels available.

The procedures should be documented, setting out not only what will not be tolerated, but also providing guidance on what to do in difficult situations when faced with blackmail or extortion, or when an allegation of bribery comes to light. The Guidance covers particular high-risk areas such as:

- political and charitable contributions
- gifts and hospitality
- promotional expenses
- facilitation payments.

Monitoring and review
This relates to instituting monitoring and review mechanisms – possibly using external experts – to ensure that the business and persons associated with it are complying with its policies and procedures, and that any issues can be identified and remediated as they arise.

The Federal Sentencing Guidelines

A company's compliance regime is addressed during an FCPA case. However, it is considered at a very different phase of the criminal process. Under the Bribery Act, as we have seen, a company's compliance procedures are considered during the liability phase of the case; if they are adequate, this forms a substantive defence to Section 7.

In the US however, the adequacy of a compliance programme is only considered at the sentencing stage. The Federal Sentencing Guidelines provide that if a company is found by the court to have had an effective compliance and ethics programme in place, there can be a reduction in sentence – sometimes by up to 95%.

Under the Sentencing Guidelines, an 'effective compliance and ethics program' requires a company to carry out seven key tasks. These are substantively the same as those set out in the 'adequate procedures' section earlier, but for completeness:

- Establish standards and guidelines to detect and prevent criminal conduct.
- High-level personnel are assigned overall responsibility to oversee compliance with such standards and procedures.
- Due care should be taken to avoid delegation to individuals whom the organization knew, or should have known, was engaged in criminal or unethical activities.
- Effective communication to all levels of employees – training all employees, officers and directors on the compliance programme's standards and guidelines.
- Monitoring, auditing and reporting systems should be established, including a reporting hotline system whereby employees can report criminal conduct anonymously and without fear of retribution.
- Standards should be enforced through appropriate mechanisms, including, as appropriate, discipline of individuals responsible for the failure to detect an offence.
- Appropriate responses to offences should be developed, taking all reasonable steps to respond appropriately and to prevent further similar offences, including any necessary modification of the compliance programmes.

DPAs and NPAs

Any settlement with the DOJ will require that the company modifies its internal controls, policies and procedures so that it maintains:

- a system of internal accounting controls designed to ensure that it makes and keeps fair and accurate books, records, and accounts
- rigorous anti-corruption compliance code, standards and procedures designed to detect and deter violations of the FCPA and other applicable anti-corruption laws.

DPAs generally contain details of the elements of an anti-bribery compliance programme that the DOJ considers adequate.

The Johnson & Johnson DPA of April 2011 contains several further and fairly onerous conditions not even found in recent settlements, indicating that the DOJ is getting stricter with FCPA compliance. It was an important document because it set out steps that the DOJ actually approved as being adequate. The DPA required a system of annual certifications by senior managers in each of the company's overseas business units, confirming that their local standard operating procedures adequately implements the company's anti-corruption policies and procedures, including training requirements, and that they are not aware of any FCPA or other corruption issues that have not already been reported to corporate compliance. (As an upside, however, there was no external compliance monitor and the company was allowed to 'self-monitor'.)

Other sources of guidance

Many organizations have published their own guidance on the components of an effective compliance system. Most contain little that is really different to the legislation already described, although several go into far more detail. The Bribery Act and Sentencing Guidelines need studying because they are going to be the starting point for a prosecutor, but in the following sections I set out some more practical steps that companies need to do to implement this.

Further reading

'An essential summary of the Bribery Act', page 81.

Question 28.

'Designing effective compliance procedures', this page.

'Johnson & Johnson', page 30. For the extended compliance terms under the terms of Johnson & Johnson's DPA, see Appendix 7, page 518. For slightly less onerous terms in a modern DPA, see Fiat's DPA at http://1.usa.gov/uhDmMK (http://www.justice.gov/opa/documents/fiat-dpa.pdf).

DOJ, FCPA Opinion Release 04-02 (ABB): http://1.usa.gov/t5z5Ym (http://www.justice.gov/criminal/fraud/fcpa/opinion/2004/0402.pdf). A detailed DOJ statement considered to be the paradigm for establishing a corporate FCPA compliance programme and accompanying internal controls.

Designing Effective Compliance Procedures

Compliance can be daunting before it starts and challenging once underway. But apart from minimizing legal risk, it is also a positive opportunity to improve performance throughout the whole organization. All organizations have a different structure and different ways of operating, needing their own tailor-made programmes; here I look at the essential elements common to all compliance regimes.

Three essential prerequisites, that have to be right before anything else can start

- Top-level commitment
- A chief compliance officer/'bribery czar'
- A risk-based approach.

World-class internal controls

- Control activities, particularly with high-risk transactions
- Properly managing high-risk transactions
- Due diligence on business partners
- Communication and training
- Speaking up and whistleblowing.

Compliance reviews

These are regular and appropriately targeted reviews. Depending on risk, they may require elements of:

- talking to people – interviewing
- looking at the company's electronic and hard-copy documents and data – document review and e-disclosure
- looking at the company's financial and business records – forensic accounting and data mining.

Three Essential Prerequisites

Top-level commitment

One of the most important things to get right is to ensure that your company, its board and shareholders have the right top-level commitment. It's easy to say, but actually difficult to fake. Although everybody in a company is responsible in one way or another for ensuring that controls are put in place and observed, the process has to start with the directors, who should ultimately assume ownership of the system and set the 'tone at the top'. If this doesn't happen, the compliance regime will always be a 'paper process' that prosecutors will quickly see through – just ask Siemens.

The 'tone at the top' means that the board and senior management team – from the CEO downwards – must truly buy in to the need to do business ethically. They need to commit their organization to rejecting bribery and corruption, lead by their actions, and communicate and manage this throughout the organization.

To get the tone at the top right does not need a lot of steps or a lot of bullet points, so this is a short section. It simply requires that top management:

- act ethically and transparently, and reject a 'do as I say, not as I do' attitude
- oversee the preparation of a statement of commitment to having zero tolerance towards bribery and carrying out business fairly, honestly and openly
- appoint and fully resource a chief compliance officer
- oversee the development of an internal code of conduct and an anti-bribery compliance programme
- ensure that there are ethical metrics on all the key business reports
- ensure that there are ethical metrics on all employee performance reviews
- provide leadership and direction to middle managers from where the message can filter down to the remainder of the organization
- have a reporting/whistleblowing and question channel where any employee can report concerns or get advice
- keep talking about exercising good business judgement and 'doing the right thing'.

It is vital that ethical behaviour is not subordinated to the drive to make money. In an environment where middle managers have a 'results at all costs' philosophy, staff may perceive that senior management is giving them the message to focus on the quantifiable at the expense of ethics. It is also important that senior managers recruit and promote only those behaving ethically.

People tend to be most comfortable in organizations where ethical standards are similar to theirs. It can be very damaging for an organization if senior managers are seen to cut corners or cheat – even a little bit – because those who are opposed to the behaviour they see will eventually move or be moved out.

The True Test of the Tone at the Top

You are the CEO of an international company. The company's star salesperson has been negotiating a major contract in Africa. If obtained, it would be a great piece of work, and be highly profitable. Just before signing, the salesperson comes to you to tell you that their contact in Africa has said that to secure it, the company needs to transfer $100,000 for 'special consulting fees' to a bank account in the Cayman Islands.

What do you do?

A. Tell them to pay it via an offshore subsidiary, where it might stay hidden.
B. Construct a paper trail with some basic 'due diligence' and try to convince yourself that the payments might actually be for genuine services. Get your highly-paid but relatively tame lawyers to write to you stating that they found no evidence that they are a bribe.
C. Make yourself unobtainable. Ignore all calls and emails, but do nothing to stop the payment happening. (They can take the blame if anyone ever finds it.)

D. Refuse to make the payment, lose the contract and curse the salesperson for bringing this problem to you rather than just 'sorting it out' (i.e. paying it) locally. (This is a typical response.)

E. Refuse to make the payment, lose the contract and publicly praise the salesperson, letting them have the commission they would have made had the contract been won.

Senior management choosing anything but E have not yet got tone at the top. Go back to the beginning of the book and start again.

A chief compliance officer / 'Bribery Czar'

The board of directors is ultimately responsible for the design, implementation and oversight of a company's compliance programme – but practically, in any medium or large company this is achieved by delegating these tasks to a chief compliance officer (CCO). The job of the CCO is a positive one: they are there to change behaviour and promote an ethical way of doing business, not to stop managers making money. The CCO has traditionally been a lawyer, but increasingly we are seeing former forensic accountants and other professionals making some of the best CCOs. Some organizations place the compliance function in the legal department, while others (particularly those in high-risk or regulated industries) create a separate corporate compliance department.

Smaller organizations will not need a dedicated compliance professional, although I would still recommend that even in the smallest companies a senior person should become the 'bribery czar' and take responsibility for ensuring that the company does what it needs to do to remain ethical, by doing precisely the sort of things that I set out in this book – although perhaps on a slightly more modest scale, depending of course on risk.

To whom should the CCO report?
The CCO should report directly to the board, or a sub-committee of the board, such as the audit committee.
In particular, they should have the express authority to communicate personally to the organization's board. This helps ensure that a board receives clear and direct communication from the individual with day-to-day responsibility for the programme, and enhances the CCO's role in the organization.

If this point was ever in doubt, it was made clear in the 2010 amendments to the Federal Sentencing Guidelines, which now encourages a 'direct reporting' structure for compliance officers. CCOs should report immediately to the board on any matter involving criminal conduct or potential criminal conduct, and every six months (certainly no less than annually) on the implementation and effectiveness of the compliance and ethics programme.

There should be a link between legal, audit and compliance departments, with an interlinked system of control throughout the group. There must be a flow of information in two directions:

• Information should flow downward from senior management to staff and provide accurate information, expectations and procedures.
• Feedback about what is and isn't working should flow back up through both formal and informal communication channels.

They should have adequate 'clout,' resources and independence
Less controversially, the CCO must be given adequate resources and the appropriate authority to perform their compliance duties. This means that the compliance

department must have personnel and financial resources appropriate to the company's size and risk profile.

Siemens' compliance organization now totals more than 500 full-time compliance personnel worldwide. Control and accountability for all compliance matters is managed by a CCO who, in turn, reports directly to the General Counsel and the CEO. (This is in addition to a Chief Audit Officer and a team of 450.)

It is beneficial for the CCO to have a written job function that has been circulated throughout the senior management team and expressly sets out their authority with respect to compliance.

A risk-based approach

As it relates to bribery deterrence, risk assessment involves the identification of internal and external factors that could potentially defeat the organization's internal control structure and conceal any divergence from management. It requires identifying as many potential threats as possible and evaluating them in a way to determine which require action, and their respective priorities.

In the real world, money, time and resources are very limited, especially for those tasked with anti-bribery compliance, which vies for attention with all the other types of compliance risks faced by the enterprise. Key questions are:

- What proportion of your compliance department's time and money do you devote to bribery risk, rather than other types of risk?
- Once you have that decided, how do you prioritize the locations and activities competing for anti-bribery attention?

These decisions all need to be documented so that if there is subsequently a problem and your anti-bribery compliance efforts are criticized, you can show that this was not because you didn't do any compliance at all but that in that particular year other risk areas were prioritized.

The risk committee
I personally dislike committees; however, I do think that risk is one area where a committee is really warranted, and I would advise all businesses to set up a small risk committee. It is very different from an audit committee staffed by non-executives because it should have representatives from all levels of the organization, with sales, operations, legal and compliance representation. It would include those who have current operational exposure and are junior enough to know how transactions actually happen in practice (i.e. who might request a bribe and when), as well as those who are senior enough to force things to happen.

The purpose of the committee is to discuss the real, on-the-ground risk areas of your business and its various operations, rather than simply the theoretical risk areas obtained by comparing a map of your operations with a corruption perceptions index and asking people to fill in questionnaires. The most important thing is to understand what bribes and facilitation payments you are making within your company. If your employees in sub-Saharan Africa tell you that they have never made facilitation payments and have never been asked for them, then either they are lying or you are not asking the right questions.

So the main agenda items for the committee are straightforward:

- Who has been asking us for bribes?
- Who might ask us for bribes in the future?
- Where might outsiders think we are paying bribes?

- Redrafting some of the compliance team's policies.
- Date of next meeting.

Regular review
Risk assessments have a short shelf life, because each time there is a significant change in the business – new markets, joint ventures, acquisitions, new services – the risk profile changes. I would suggest that your risk committee meets quarterly.

The Anti-Bribery risk profile
There are literally dozens of factors that move a company or transaction from low risk to high risk. Commonly encountered external risks can be categorized into five broad groups:

- company
- country
- sector
- transaction
- business partnership.

Company risk
This is only likely to be relevant when assessing a number of different companies – either when managing a portfolio of companies from the perspective of the head office of a conglomerate, or a private equity house – but some companies are inherently more difficult to control and manage than others. Higher-risk companies involve:

- private companies with a close shareholder group
- large, diverse and complex groups with a decentralized management structure
- autocratic top management
- a previous history of compliance issues or regulatory actions
- poor marketplace perception.

Often it is not possible to assess internal risks without getting deeper into the company as part of a due diligence or review process. But for companies that are already known, it may be possible to form a view on some of the other key internal risks:

- deficiencies in employee training, skills and knowledge
- bonus culture that rewards excessive risk-taking
- lack of clarity in the organization's policies on, and procedures for, hospitality and promotional expenditure, and political or charitable contributions
- lack of clear financial controls
- lack of a clear anti-bribery message from the top-level management.

Country risk
This involves reportedly high levels of corruption, an absence of effectively implemented anti-bribery legislation and a failure of the foreign government to convince outsiders that they have transparent procurement and investment policies.

A company that is seeking business in a high-risk country must view compliance somewhat differently to one operating where there is a lower corruption risk. The source of most of this type of information is Transparency International's corruption perceptions index or a similar service. Also useful is to search previous enforcement actions, using resources like the TRACE Compendium.

Sector risk
Some sectors are higher-risk than others. Higher-risk sectors include those with a history of FCPA cases or perception of corruption, which tend to be those getting business from, or requiring licences and permits from, governmental instrumentalities. These include:

- extractive industries
- oil and gas services
- large-scale infrastructure

- telecoms
- pharmaceutical, medical devices and healthcare
- financial services.

Transaction risk
Transaction risk first and foremost identifies and analyses the financial aspects of a payment or deal. This means that it is necessary to think about where your money is ending up: is there money being spent in a non-transparent way or is there one party that's getting far more than the assets or service they provided are worth? Risks here arise in projects that:

- are high-value
- involve many contractors or intermediaries
- are not apparently undertaken at market prices
- do not have a clear legitimate objective.

Companies seldom have management reports that are sufficiently detailed to allow an accurate assessment of these risk factors. Forensic accountants can help unpick complex corporate acquisitions and data mining usually helps at the risk assessment stage to scan the accounts for the highest-risk transactions.

Business partnership risk
A company must consider how it does business. Certain relationships involve higher risk, including:

- the use of intermediaries in transactions with foreign public officials
- consortia or joint venture partners
- relationships with politically exposed persons.

Of course, the Bribery Act specifies that risky business partners go beyond the government, into the exclusively private sector. Currently few if any companies routinely put their private sector business partners who do not interact with the government through due diligence, but this is an area of compliance that will become important in the future.

Using risk analysis
The risk assessment should be performed on each business unit and region separately. The goal is clearly to identify all those circumstances that may put the organization at risk, so that each of these risk areas can be addressed in the next phase of the compliance exercise. Management can determine what type of compliance programme is appropriate for each particular area of the organization.

An organization with extensive dealings involving foreign officials in high-risk countries will need a more robust programme than an organization with comparatively few overseas operations. This is best done in any business unit by combining the results the five markers described earlier into a rudimentary risk-scoring system that ranks the things to review using risk indicators of potential bribery. This ensures that the high-risk exposures are done first and/or are given more time. As with all populations of this type, there is likely to be a normal or 'bell curve' distribution of risks around the mean. So 10–15% of exposure falls into the relative low-risk category; the vast majority (70–80%) into the moderate-risk category; and the final 10–15% would be high-risk.

Further reading

'Properly managing high-risk transactions', page 368.

World-Class Internal Controls

Can you say with confidence that your no one in your organization can sign a cheque for £10,000 to pay for services that were never provided? What are the controls that prevent this happening?

Controls are the tangible policies, procedures and practices that ensure management's objectives are achieved and risk mitigation strategies are carried out. All companies have some controls over financial and business processes. They are not just there to stop people doing bad things; they are an essential positive part of any business, and without them the business would not be in business for very long. Many of the rudimentary controls in small businesses are neither documented nor sophisticated, but they do the job. For example, keeping the petty cash box in a locked safe is a good, effective control that mitigates the risk that people may steal it.

The three primary objectives of an internal control system are to ensure that:

- operations are efficient and effective – 'efficient' means that they provide the best 'bang for your buck', while 'effective' means that they achieve their required objectives
- financial reporting is accurate and reliable
- the company achieves compliance with external laws and regulations.

Focusing on the compliance aspect, controls form the front line in a company's efforts to ensure that:

- assets are safeguarded
- things can only be paid that have been properly approved
- all transactions are aligned with the company's business
- accurate records surrounding payments are maintained to allow review and audit.

The absence of proper internal controls is a key factor in a prosecutor's enforcement decision, so it is vital that controls are documented and can be evidenced. Beyond this, internal controls:

- enable a company to identify compliance problems early
- can prevent a potential violation from being completed

- can reduce or avoid costs of investigation or remediation, and act as a possible defence
- demonstrate a commitment to lawful and ethical business practices.

Although they will need some additional tweaking to take bribery risk into account, almost all of the financial controls in an organization will contribute in some way to preventing bribery and it is important that they are therefore documented as part of an anti-corruption programme. A company must think about and put in place *specific* anti-corruption controls rather than relying entirely on its existing accounting controls. This is because:

- General accounting controls are biased towards preventing problems in the larger financial balances, and this can easily overlook small bribes. (Remember that the bribery laws do not have a materiality threshold, and serious problems tend to lurk in the smaller, more remote locations, which are not the greatest contributors to revenue and are bottom of internal audit's list.)
- Typical Sarbanes–Oxley controls will not catch many bribery payments. For example, a corrupt charitable contribution or political donation may be duly processed through the accounts department with the required documentation and authorizations.

Control activities

In the context of anti-bribery compliance, the two main control activities are:

- adequate segregation of duties
- proper authorization of transactions and activities.

Adequate segregation of duties
A fundamental element of internal control is the segregation of certain key duties. The basic idea is that no employee

or group of employees should be in a position to both perpetrate a fraud or make a mistake, and then to be able to conceal it – there should always be independent checks. This means, for example, that a person who requisitions the purchase of goods or services should not be the same person who makes the purchase, who in turn should not be the person who makes the payment. In general, the principal incompatible duties where responsibility should be divided are:

• custody of assets
• authorization or approval of transactions affecting those assets
• recording or reporting of the transactions affecting those assets
• reconciliation of accounting balances affecting those assets.

Specifically, in the procurement business cycle, the following steps should be separately performed:

• initiating an internal purchase requisition
• reviewing and authorizing the purchase requisition
• initiating a purchase order to a vendor (this should ideally be done by a separate purchasing function)
• reviewing and authorizing the purchase order
• modifying the vendor master file
• receiving goods physically from the vendor
• recording vendor invoices, where a three-way match of purchase order, receiving document and vendor invoice should be performed
• modifying inventory records
• reconciling inventory records.

Ideally, no individual employee should handle more than one of the above-noted functions in a process – but in a small organization, that does not mean that it is essential that you have at least nine people in your procurement/payment section. In a department of three people, just make sure that employees are not responsible for consecutive actions: so have employee A do the first task, employee B do the second, employee C do the third, and back to A again who does the fourth task, and so on. When employees share the above tasks, it is less likely a perpetrator can succeed in a fraudulent or bribery scheme. It is one thing to commit a fraud by yourself, quite another to ask someone to aid in your scheme.

A similar principle applies with rotating employees: job-shares, for example, are great in a control context because there is always someone checking the work, even if this only happens during holiday periods. Many international companies ensure that their expats only stay in a position for two years or so, which means that corrupt behaviour cannot become too ingrained.

Proper authorization of transactions and activities
All transactions should be properly authorized and approved. Individual transactions should be authorized by signature or electronic approval by a person with approval authority. 'Approval' of a transaction means that the approver has reviewed the supporting documentation, questioned unusual items and made sure that necessary information is present to justify the transaction, and is satisfied that the transaction is appropriate, accurate and complies with applicable laws, regulations, policies and procedures.

Approval authority is usually linked to specific monetary limits. Transactions that exceed a manager's specified level require approval from a more senior authority. A department's approval levels should be specified in a departmental policies and procedures manual, or an accountability matrix.

Approval rules include the following:

- Signing blank forms should never be allowed.
- Under no circumstance should an approver tell someone to sign their name on their behalf.
- Under no circumstance should an approver with electronic approval authority share the password.

Further reading

The COSO model
One of the best ways of looking at systems and controls is given by the COSO model. COSO is an independent private sector initiative to develop recommendations and guidance on internal controls, risk management, and fraud deterrence. COSO stands for the 'Committee of Sponsoring Organizations' of the Treadway Commission. It was formed by the five major US accounting and auditing associations in 1985 to sponsor the National Commission on Fraudulent Financial Reporting, under the chairmanship of James Treadway, former Commissioner of the SEC. COSO's 'Internal Control – Integrated Framework' model describes five interrelated components of internal control that provide the foundation for deterring fraud and illegal acts – including bribery. These elements of internal control are the means by which the 'opportunity' factors in the fraud triangle can be removed to most effectively limit instances of fraud.

The COSO model outlines five essential components of an effective internal control system, which will be familiar to readers of the Bribery Act and the Sentencing Guidelines.

- control environment
- risk assessment

- control activities
- information and communication
- monitoring.

For more information, see http://www.coso.org/.

Properly Managing High-Risk Transactions

No system of internal controls can completely prevent all improper payments or inaccurate records. But if key controls as set out in this section are properly applied, then you will have a great balance of adequacy and efficiency – easily enough to satisfy a regulator. Again, the most important internal control is the one over the procurement and payment process: if you can stop bribes being made at the approval and payment steps, you have (almost) won the battle.

The majority of bribes fall into several well-defined categories. You will find that if bribes are being made in one of these areas of the business, they are made in others. The high-risk areas are:

- sales agents and consultants
- hospitality and client entertainment
- client travel and trips
- gifts and other forms of benefit
- employing public officials as consultants
- charitable and political contributions
- freight forwarding, visa, licences and permits
- petty cash.

Most of the published guidance on anti-bribery compliance contains some ideas about steps to take in managing high-risk payments. The Bribery Act Guidance, for example, contains case studies dealing with many of the areas above. Frankly, though, the Guidance doesn't always help. (If you use sales agents, you might of course 'request that the agent company trains its staff on resisting facilitation payments' – but I'm not sure having emailed your guy in Zimbabwe and even documenting it will get the DOJ off your back.)

The problems with some salespeople is that if they are trying to make a sale and there is a requirement to pay a gift to secure it, they can quickly persuade themselves that a particular gift with a particular value is 'appropriate'. So please read the Bribery Act Guidance and then get your CCO and risk committee to take responsibility for setting out tangible compliance policies and guidance in each of these areas. The policy should not be written by a lawyer, but by the risk team, to appeal to people on the front line of the business making the day-to-day decisions. It should provide tangible guidance with actual numbers, not just lots of 'reasonables' and 'adequates', with consideration of what's common in the market in that region. As always, rigorous notes should be kept.

Sales agents and consultants

Are all commercial agents dodgy?

Good ones ...   Many businesses selling into countries where they don't have their own local operation retain the services of sales agents, distributors and commercial consultants. These agents usually provide an invaluable service – making introductions to local businesses, keeping clients happy, filling in tedious paperwork and resolving problems in the local language, providing in-country translation and logistical support, and ensuring the overseas company complies

with the necessary rules and regulations. A good agent
will have:

- understanding of local business practices and an
  established presence in the local business community
- good access to information (within the government, private
  industry and financial sectors)
- good access to public officials and relevant business
  persons in the local community
- adequate staff and resources
- financial stability
- an understanding of your business
- a good reputation for ethical behaviour, competence and
  reliability
- knowledge of customs procedures, permit and licences,
  importing, and tax laws
- no conflicts of interest.

Dodgy ones ...   Paying cash bribes directly to public officials
is now rarely seen: cash is difficult to generate, transport and
spend without drawing suspicion. Also, cash transactions are
difficult to deduct as business expenses for tax purposes.

Using fake 'consultants' is far easier. These agents and consultants have given the profession a very bad name indeed,
because they are used as front companies for paying bribes
to government officials and other senior employees of the
bribing company. The practice has meant that the prosecutors and therefore compliance professionals have had to get
very hot on consultants generally.

Agents and consultants can act for either the company trying to get the work or the corrupt officials. In the case of the
former, the broker approaches officials of government organizations with bribes to leak bid data, tailor bid specifications
or offer other favours to help its clients win contracts. With
the latter, the agents will typically present themselves as a
legitimate 'procurement advisor' or business consultant, and

sometimes as an affiliate of a substantial business organization. These consultants will typically operate behind front
companies and launder the bribe payments through several
offshore jurisdictions, making proof difficult.

They may:

- on bigger projects, approach large corporate bidders
  around the world to solicit kickbacks
- on smaller projects, set up and operate front companies on
  behalf of project officials
- rig the award of smaller office supply, vehicle and IT
  contracts through a network of 'competing' suppliers that
  they control
- collect the profits from the above schemes, taking their
  cut, sending the balance to their clients and then
  laundering the funds through a network of other shell
  companies and accounts in offshore banks.

Retaining agents
The key to minimizing the risk of retaining commercial agents
is to ensure that you understand the transaction risk and
that you:

- are only contracted to pay market rate for the services
  they provide
- make sure that you only actually pay that amount
- make sure you got the contracted-for services
- make sure they are not paying anything 'extra'.

The 'extras' happen when you are paying more than they
have to pay to give the service. If you pay an agent £100 to
obtain a visa for which the set government charge is £20,
then there is an £80 'profit'. That might all comprise profit to
the agent, or £60 profit for the agent plus a £20 bribe to the
official to get it done quickly. It is vital that you know – as
far as possible – how much profit they have to play with and
where that is going.

If the decision has been made to use a particular sales agent, it is critical that:

- complete due diligence has been done and documented
- there is an appropriate contract in place
- the relationship is carefully managed
- you insist they do receive some anti-bribery training (although whether they actually do it or take any notice of it is another question)
- the file is maintained
- this is all reviewed regularly.

What if you find something unusual?

If you have a suspicion that your agent has paid bribes, then you need to act. First, withhold any payments due until any alleged breach of compliance obligations is investigated and resolved to the satisfaction of the CCO. Then, investigate by exercising your audit rights. If you still have a reasonable belief, then you have little alternative but to terminate the relationship. If you don't, your defences to any subsequent investigation will not look very impressive.

Maintaining the file

The due diligence file should be rigorously maintained, and should contain as a minimum copies of:

- the application and questionnaire submitted by the consultant
- the due diligence report
- the agreement with the partner or agent and any amendments
- reports of business activity, meetings, marketing efforts or specific projects by the agent
- business justification.

It should also be signed off by the CCO.

Monitoring
There needs to be ongoing oversight of the activities of commercial agents:

- Changes in the agent's personnel, especially at senior levels, need to be authorized by the company.
- All of the agent's invoices and expenses reports should be properly completed by the agent, matched to the contract and approved by a senior company official.
- There should be periodic written activity reports submitted by the agent.
- The company should conduct periodic audits of the books and activities of the agent, as provided by written agreement.

Hospitality and client entertainment

Corporate hospitality is a legitimate way of building business relationships. Although lavish hospitality in certain circumstances can amount to a bribe, sensible, moderate expenditure is entirely legitimate and is not outlawed by either the FCPA, the Bribery Act or the OECD.

The difficult areas come when the entertaining or hospitality has less business purposes, is overly extravagant and has a significant pleasure mixed in with the business. Although the authorities have prosecuted entertaining costs in the past, this is normally as part of a larger overall scheme – it is unheard of for isolated examples of modest entertaining to be prosecuted. Companies certainly need not direct staff to always choose the cheapest dish on the menu during a corporate lunch. No one has ever been to prison for ordering steak!

Set specific guidelines

The SFO has made it clear that in the UK, reasonable and proportionate business hospitality that seeks to showcase products or services, or cement relationships, will fall outside the scope of the offence. The Bribery Act Guidance provides examples of acceptable hospitality, where the bar is set at a fairly lavish level: it mentions entertaining at Wimbledon, the Grand Prix and the Six Nations rugby championships, or flying a public official to New York (with spouse) for a meeting with 'fine dining' – all of which are stated to be acceptable. The provision of a luxury family holiday to Disneyland, though, is where the line has been crossed.

Meanwhile, back in the in the real world, it is unrealistic to expect sales staff to interpret or second-guess what the SFO defines as 'reasonable'. People need tangible limits so they know where they stand and managers and compliance teams are not forever being asked 'Can I take Harry for a steak?' In turn, managers must set limits: ideally by country, authorized by the country manager and reviewed annually. The limit should be set not to create exceptions for a decent lunch or dinner, but will catch crazy excesses. Something like £100 per person for a meal would be appropriate, and then everyone knows where they stand. The limit should be for both government and non-government people.

I view entertaining at an event or function in the same category as meals, provided that there are hosts from the company accompanying the guests. Tickets to events fall into this same category. For functions, it's also necessary to provide the constraints: sporting, musical or cultural events are all OK, and it is appropriate to bring spouses to occasional events. No strip clubs, or worse, and nothing that you would not tell your spouse or want to see on the front page of the trade magazine – even if the client demands it. Limits will clearly be more, but limits of £250 for a day out – such as a round of golf or a top-flight football match, with a couple of drinks and dinner – should be adequate for approval by first-level managers. As the event gets larger, the approval process gets higher. Larger events require more escalated permissions, and compliance needs to approve the guest list.

All entertaining needs to be authorized by the next level of management up. Depending on the company, pre-approval might be appropriate – or if there is a lot of entertaining, approval by monitoring retrospectively, which means that things can be stopped (such as repeated meals with the same recipient) if it looks like they are getting out of hand. Functions or events costing more than £1000 per person including travel make me nervous, particularly if they have become routine – such things should be at the most once a year, and then approved at the most senior levels and coordinated centrally.

Good practice dictates that companies should always ensure that there is a business element or discussion as part of any entertaining and that this is evidenced, perhaps by way of a follow-up internal memo or email referring to the discussions during the event.

Tickets to events where there are no hosts from the company there are simply gifts, and must be dealt with as such.

Record keeping
It goes without saying that all entertaining expenses should be accounted for accurately and transparently, and that adequate records and receipts should be kept. I am a fan of having very detailed expense receipts because it is a great way of keeping entertaining costs in check – not from an anti-bribery perspective, but to avoid staff taking the same group out time after time with little in the way of business in return.

An expense form should have two roles: as an auditable record of gifts and entertainment, and also as an approval form that provides managers with the information they need to determine whether to allow a particular payment.

In addition to the details of the essential facts surrounding the expenditure (date, recipient, nature, of expenditure and value), the form should include:

- a description of the purpose of the expenditure, including why it is required
- a tick box confirming that no cash or cash equivalent (gift card, per diem, reimbursement) was provided to the recipient of the entertaining
- details of whether the recipient has the power to assist or hinder the company's business and how they would do so, including any pending or anticipated business with, or decisions coming before, the recipient
- details of any other entertaining, gifts or benefits provided to this individual within the last 12 months
- the necessary approvals from supervisors and legal/compliance officers (if required).

Employees should of course attach to the expense form the receipts documenting the expenditures.

Expense summaries and reviews
The accounting group should pull out meals and entertaining costs per month, per employee and per meal for review by management. This can normally be done straight from the expense reimbursement system. Remember the accountant's mantra: 'what you can measure, you can manage'.

The Bribery Act covers both public and private sector bribery, and so it is important to do this exercise for all meals and entertaining – not just for entertaining foreign officials. Having said that, because the focus of the FCPA is on interactions with public officials, they still remain higher risk than business-to-business entertaining. For this reason, entertaining foreign officials within the standard limits should be notified to the compliance department.

Client travel and trips

Paying for an official to go on a fact-finding trip to a facility is fine; but when you bring the official, their spouse and their kids, and there are side-trips to theme parks, that becomes a problem. So many inspection tours are often glorified holidays with a bit of business activity thrown in to appease the compliance people. Such trips will violate the bribery legislation, however.

The DOJ has had to consider this question on several occasions in Opinion Procedure Releases. All of them set out strict conditions for the payments – usually limiting very specifically the scope of the relationship with the foreign official. In relation to the question of whether paying for government employees to attend a conference would fall foul of the FCPA, the DOJ stated in Opinion Procedure Releases 07-01 and 07-02 that it would not take action where the following factors applied:[247]

- there was no actual ongoing business with the government agency where the officials worked
- the company played no role in selecting which government employees attended the conference or tour – the choice was made by the government
- the officials did not have direct authority to award future contracts or licences to the company
- the company paid all expenses for travel and accommodations directly or reimbursed the attendees only upon presentation of a receipt
- the company paid, at most, only a modest per diem for expenses
- spouses and family did not accompany the officials
- the total cost was reasonable under the circumstances.

It is best to require pre-approval from the compliance department for all paid travel for foreign officials. The rules that I recommend are:

- if paying for customers or officials, flying them in business class is OK, but not first class
- nice hotels and executives rooms are OK, but not suites
- don't pay the air fare for relatives, although they can both fly economy if you normally pay for business
- cash per diems should not be approved
- costs should all be paid centrally, and the total of the costs for particular events should all be summarized so it is possible to say who received what.

Is there a benefit to the public official?
In cases where companies pay the travel and accommodation for public officials to attend a function or conference, there is no real 'advantage' given to the public officials if the foreign government would have paid for the trip if the host company hadn't done so. If the official would have attended anyway, and wouldn't have paid for themselves in any event, arguably they cannot be said to have received an advantage.

Gifts and other forms of benefit

Gifts are more commonly seen outside the UK and US, but where they are given, they form an ingrained and essential part of the local culture.

In China for example, gifts of 'mooncakes' are often given between business contacts during the Mid-Autumn festival. I understand from several of my Chinese clients that if you don't buy mooncakes for the tax inspector, you are sure to get a tax inspection in short order. Buying mooncakes is almost obligatory.

The first time I did a compliance review in China I thought that there would be no problem with giving a token ritual cake to a client. (Wikipedia said that mooncakes were round pastries with a filling of lotus seed paste and, occasionally, salted duck egg yolks. Yum!) However, digging slightly further, I realized that mooncakes and in particular the packaging have now grown to fairly lavish proportions, and that Western companies such as Häagen-Dazs are popular suppliers of 'new' mooncakes made from ice cream. I then further discovered that physical mooncakes were seldom given; instead, what was given were vouchers to enable the recipient to go and pick up a mooncake. And guess what: there was an active mooncake voucher exchange, and at every metro station there were mooncake agents who would buy unwanted vouchers. It was also clear that few people actually wanted these mooncakes when crispy cash was a ready alternative. So what was actually given as these 'mooncakes' was as good as cash.

As with meals and other entertaining, I think it appropriate to set limits based on the recommendations of the country manager – amounts such as £25 for birthdays, Christmas, Divali, Chinese New Year, etc. As with entertaining, managers should approve all gifts, and all gifts to foreign officials should be reported to the compliance group.

Employing public officials as consultants

'A fair day's wages for a fair day's work.'

This is an area to be managed very carefully indeed. It is not prohibited, though: bribery laws prevents companies and individuals bribing. It does not prevent all payments to all public officials, and there is no prohibition on this per se. But the company needs to ensure that the public official is providing a genuine service and that any remuneration under this agreement is not a bribe by any other name.

Many healthcare companies retain medical professionals as advisors. In China, though, doctors and medical staff are all employed by state-owned institutions and therefore the DOJ considers that they come under the definition of 'public officials'. Many pharmaceutical companies hire doctors to sit on 'advisory boards' and they are paid to do so.

Micrus Corporation: Employing Doctors on Advisory Boards[248]

In 2005, privately-held US -based Micrus Corporation and its Swiss subsidiary entered into a two-year non-prosecution agreement with the DOJ to resolve potential FCPA violations. The settlement involved appointing an independent compliance monitor for three years and a penalty of $450,000.

The DOJ alleged that amounts paid to various doctors in government-owned hospitals exceeded the value of the services that the doctors performed as consultants or advisory board members, and that the excess compensation was intended to cause increased purchases of defendant's medical products.

Micrus made more than $105,000 in improper payments through its officers, employees, agents and salespeople to doctors employed at public hospitals in France, Germany, Spain and Turkey. The company paid additional disbursements totalling $250,000 to public hospital doctors without obtaining the administrative and legal approvals required under the laws of those countries. It disguised these payments in its books and records as stock options, honorariums and commissions.

The key to these types of high-risk transactions is transparent documentation. Keep plenty of records, in one constantly updated file:

- the business case as to why technical input on the project was essential
- why that particular official had the skills required, and how the selection process took place

- the agreement should be documented, with standard 'FCPA clauses'
- the consultants' input should be documented
- the fees paid should be commensurate with the time spent by the consultant, using hourly rates that reflect their expertise, and comparable to market rates.

The agreement should again be signed off by the CCO.

A similar situation exists with employing the children or relatives of clients, perhaps on internships or work experience. Again, there is no prohibition, and indeed there are significant advantages in working with young people whose background is known. But common sense rules apply, and a file should be kept to ensure that:

- it is explained why that particular person had the skills required
- the agreement is documented, with a standard contract, identical to one that any other employee or intern would sign
- remuneration is identical to other employees or interns providing similar services
- they do not work on projects where their family member is involved – they should be in a separate part of the business entirely.

Charitable and political contributions

Charitable and political donations frequently raise bribery concerns, particular if the charity or party is affiliated to a public official that the company is interested in keeping sweet.

Schering-Plough Corp.: Charity Begins at Home[249]

The SEC charged Schering-Plough with violations of the books and records and internal controls provisions of the FCPA, in that its wholly owned subsidiary paid approximately $76,000 to a charitable organization that belonged to the director of a regional government health authority in Poland.

The Commission alleged that these payments were made to induce the director to influence the health fund's purchase of Schering-Plough's pharmaceutical products. The SEC found that the company's policies and procedures were inadequate in that they did not require employees to conduct any due diligence prior to making promotional or charitable donations to determine whether any foreign officials were affiliated with proposed recipients. The Commission also found that Schering-Plough improperly recorded these payments in its books and records.

Political contributions
These always make me very nervous. The good thing, though, is that it is a foolhardy manager who makes donations to a political party without board approval (unless of course it's a bribe). A company's policy should specify that no political donations should be made without board and compliance function approval.

Charitable donations
Far more companies make charitable donations. Again, clear policies are needed to ensure that they only do this when the recipient feels no obligation to purchase products from the donor company:

- The company should specify the amount it wishes to spend at the start of the budget year on charitable giving.
- A small committee of managers and employees should be responsible for disbursing the money. Employees wishing to use the fund make an application to the committee.
- No more than 5% of the budget or one single payment should be made to any particular charity.

- No donations should be made to a charity where a foreign official who is involved in the company's business is a patron.
- The company should not offer 'scholarships' for children of key customers.
- The company should make a claim for a tax relief (if the tax rules permit it – which they usually do) deduction for any charitable payment, to ensure maximum transparency.
- Ensure all decisions are documented.

Freight forwarding, visas, licences and permits

These all represent high-risk situations. Problems usually arise when agents employed by a company pay small bribes or make facilitation payments to officials to 'make things easier' for the client.

Problems have arisen in customs clearance in particular (for example, see the Panalpina story on page 440). Invoices from freight forwarders and customs clearance agents typically have a number of disbursements, representing the out-of-pocket costs incurred by the freight forwarder on the company's behalf bringing the goods from A to B. (These would include things like warehousing, transport hire, labour hire and customs duties.) All of these disbursements should have receipts attached. Some don't, however, and it is these that are the problems, because often these are the facilitation payments and bribes that the freight forwarder has paid to get things done. Companies were caught in west Africa because they paid unreceipted disbursements contained on Panalpina's invoices. Usually these have slightly enigmatic names, such as 'special handling charges', 'other clearance charges' or 'overtime for customs officers'. Once you have reviewed a few of these, they become fairly easy to spot.[250]

Key controls stop this practice:

- Always ensure freight forwarders and customs agents provide a tariff sheet for the various services they provide, and check their invoices against the tariff sheet.
- *Never* pay additional disbursements unless the agent provides a proper, understandable receipt.
- If the disbursement is to a government department, ensure there is an official receipt.
- To reduce the risk of the agent bribing the customs agent to reduce the duty payable, always pay the duty directly to the tax department if possible.

Petty cash

In cash-based economies, heavy use of cash is unavoidable. In most companies there is an opportunity to make, and there should be, a concerted effort to reduce the amount of cash used. Here are the rules:

- Use an impress system, with a monthly reconciliation.
- There should be regular reporting on the amount of petty cash used, and a target for the cashier to reduce it.
- No suppliers should be paid with petty cash. Emergencies need to be authorized at the country manager level and reported retrospectively to the CCO. (That single requirement usually reduces cash payments to suppliers by more than 50%, as 'emergencies' become lessened once employees know they have to email the CCO.)
- Expenses should be reimbursed to employees directly into their bank accounts. (If necessary, to avoid moans by employees having to spend their own money first and suffering a delay in reimbursement, give modest fixed advances to employees using the expenses system, which is taken off their final salary.)

Further reading

Questions 11 and 19.

Herbert Smith LLP, *Gifts and Entertainment: A Guide to Anti-bribery Regulation in Asia*, 2010. Available from: http://bit.ly/nt2KiU (http://www.herbertsmith.com/NR/ rdonlyres/EFD9330D-15F2-440E-927A-F7CBDB5480C2/15770/ Giftsandentertainmentaguidetoantibriberyregulation.PDF).

Due Diligence on Business Partners

Because agents can cause companies to be liable for bribes committed on their behalf, it is vital that companies know exactly who they are dealing with, and trust them. An organization needs to perform a review known as 'due diligence' on all intermediaries, acquisitions and business partners. The purpose of carrying out this due diligence is not to determine if the counterparty has ever paid a bribe (which is impossible), but to allow you to collect information to get to know enough about them so that you can make an informed decision on whether to accept the risk of doing business with them. It is particularly important where the intermediary is operating in a high-risk or regulated environment.

When

The due diligence process begins before you enter into the relationship and continues throughout it. There can be said to be three phases to due diligence. Although the essential tasks performed at each phase are similar, the purpose and objective varies:

- **Before entering into the relationship:** To find out who the business partners are, and whether you want to take on the risk of doing business with them.

- **On completion of the agreement:** Post-acquisition due diligence confirms the findings from the pre-acquisition due diligence, does some further checking of the high-risk areas and makes sure the new operation is properly integrated into your company's compliance structure.
- **On an ongoing basis as the relationship proceeds:** Due diligence becomes a monitoring programme that you must maintain throughout your relationship.

Who

Due diligence should really be carried out at some level on all parties performing services for a business. It need not be done on utilities such as the electricity company or on the entire supply chain – just the people with whom there is a direct relationship. Until 2010, there was little risk in doing business in the private sector: the FCPA applied only to bribing foreign officials. The Bribery Act has changed this, and it is now sensible for businesses to carry out the same level of due diligence on *all* intermediaries, not just those who are interacting with governments.

As with most compliance tasks, due diligence should be risk-based. Vendors should be segmented, with the more risky intermediaries requiring increased due diligence. Those performing less risky services require less due diligence. High-risk business partners include:

- proposed joint venture partners
- external sales and marketing agents, or commercial intermediaries
- distributors
- external lawyers, accountants and tax advisors
- freight, logistics and customs agents
- visa and licence intermediaries, and anyone else retained to procure licences or permits from the government

- major subcontractors
- anyone whose low-risk due diligence below produces a red flag.

Low-risk business partners include:

- any firm in an otherwise high-risk category whose shares are publicly traded or regulated by a government entity (i.e. there's nothing you're going to find out about it that isn't already known)
- everyone else.

How

There are several steps in actually doing the work:

- Get buy-in. Ensure a clear understanding of the process and implication by the people involved, especially the commercial managers. Implementing appropriate due diligence also requires a significant internal marketing effort, because you're going to be delaying (and in some cases terminating) relationships the business thinks it needs.
- Set clear expectations in terms of timing: don't sign or renew a contract without getting the results of the due diligence.
- Collect information.
- Determine in advance a list of red flags adapted to the business sector in question and based on the company's general policies and guidelines.
- Assess the information, setting clear criteria and procedures as to how the red flags should be examined and who will be entitled to decide what the impact on a relationship will be.
- Present it to an impartial management team.
- Act on the decision.

In order to streamline and standardize the process and ensure that all relevant information is considered, companies with a number of relationships usually use a standard vendor take-on form, questionnaire and checklist to be completed as part of the due diligence. Because the information to be obtained from a sales agent differs from the due diligence to be undertaken when entering a joint venture or other business transaction, different checklists may be appropriate. Of course, large corporate transactions – for example, the acquisition of a company with foreign operations – will require a separate due diligence process that exceeds a simple checklist.

Low-risk diligence
Low-risk diligence should include, at a minimum, the following:

- Obtaining a request from the business unit or employee who wishes to engage the business partner, specifying:
  - terms of engagement
  - expected activities and scope of work
  - how the remuneration is to be structured
  - where and how the payment is to be made
  - expected monthly payments
  - how they first became aware of the candidate
  - who the alternatives are, and how this one was selected
  - entity information/documentation.
- Understanding who the key people are – who owns it, who manages it and who is doing the work for your company?
  - directors/officers/key employees with brief biographies
  - identification of known conflicts
  - known relationships with government agencies
  - Internet research (i.e. running the names and addressrd through a search engine), including a news search using Google News, Factiva or LexisNexis if you subscribe to it – save the search so you'll get notified if anything pops up

- whether it has a web presence and is an accommodation address, or a 'real' business is there
- run all names through an OFAC Sanctions check – there are free resources on the internet that you can simply type names into, or paid-for services such as Trace or World Check.
- Call the contact number given by the third party to see how they answer.
- Take notes of everything. Put those notes in an agent file, making one copy for compliance and another for the business manager managing the relationship.
- Review the diligence every two years.

High-risk diligence
High-risk diligence includes everything in the 'low risk' list above, as well as the following:

- Questionnaire to the business partner, asking about:
  - ownership
  - directors/officers/key employees and CVs
  - details of other directorships for the key individuals
  - details of existing partnerships and relationships
  - details of previous employment at government agencies
  - whether anyone is related to a foreign official
  - relevant judicial or regulatory findings
  - business/financial references
  - anti-bribery policies
  - past and present relationships with government agencies
  - if they do business in any sanctioned countries.
- Call the embassy in the country and talk to the commercial attaché.
- Ask the third party for three references. Call them.
- Have the businessperson who wants to engage the third party conduct a site visit.
- Looking at the agent's anti-bribery policies and procedures, and, if applicable, records.

- Be alert to key commercial questions such as whether:
  - the agent is really required
  - the agent has the required expertise
  - the agent going to interact with the foreign official
  - the payment is reasonable.

Even a small company needs to do these steps if it operates in a high-risk venture in a high-risk market.

Red flags

Many companies are now taking the view that they should not be doing business through agents that have any red flags and simply walk away. In any event, if you do proceed, you need to manage incredibly tightly any business relationships where the agent:

- comprise politically exposed persons (PEPs), which means senior foreign political figures including heads of state, senior politicians, government, judicial or military officials, senior executives of state owned corporations, and political party officials – by virtue of their position and the influence that they may hold, a PEP generally presents a higher risk for involvement in bribery and corruption
- is hired or introduced at the request of foreign official
- does not have the credentials you would expect for the business you want to get
- does not have the resources, size or office space to allow them to provide the services
- refuses to certify compliance with applicable anti-bribery laws
- refuses to allow the company to periodically audit their business to check that no bribes are being paid
- provides incomplete or inaccurate information in required disclosures

- requires payment to third parties or to accounts in countries other than where the services are provided, particular in offshore jurisdictions
- has unusually large commissions, or remuneration not tied to tangible services provided
- has been implicated in bribery in the past
- does business in sanctioned countries
- insists on non-disclosure of relationship
- has a reputation for previous criminal or corrupt activity
- was engaged as an 'urgent' matter, which avoided the usual approval channels.

Where you still have concerns

While it is possible to perform low-risk due diligence from the office, when it comes to more challenging situations where there have been one or more red flags, it makes sense to bring in people who do this every day to help you make the difficult decisions. This is the case when you get candidates who throw up red flags during the due diligence but the business unit is pushing hard to have them retained.

In these situations, you need to interview the business partner, along with FCPA-experienced lawyers, and also engage professional investigators to do a full background check with some local 'boots on the ground'. Experienced practitioners will be more used to giving clear, unequivocal advice. (That is what you are paying them for, and should push for.) Be guided by their recommendations.

The contract

Besides obviously setting out the agent's deliverables and compensation, the contract should include terms that make explicit the following factors.

Prohibit bribery and all forms of corruption

- Many agents have come across the FCPA, but they need to be reminded that a prohibition on bribery applies to all parties, not just foreign officials, and it applies to entertaining, gift-giving and the like.
- They should confirm this in writing. While an agent who bribes is unlikely to have qualms about signing an agreement, it is essential to complete the company's file and it might just remind and persuade them that someone is watching.

Duties

- Spell out exact duties and deliverables.
- There should be no assignment of rights or subcontracting.
- The agent has a continuing duty to adhere to training and due diligence.
- The agent has a duty to report immediately changes in their ownership or corporate leadership. (This is particularly important when there are changes in the overseas governmental regime.)

Making payments

- Always try to make payments via electronic funds transfer.
- No upfront payments – unless exceptionally designated for legitimate start-up expenses.
- Pay only the named company, not unknown third parties.
- Payment in local currency, in the agent's country of residence or where the work is done – strictly no payments in dollars to offshore jurisdictions.

- The agent should generate the invoice, not the company.
- The agent's invoice should be fully supported and comply with the terms of the contract.

Right to cancel

- There should be a unilateral right to cancel the contract if there is a compliance violation or breach of contract. You should be able to disclose unilaterally to the authorities and take any other action you think necessary or appropriate, and there should be an allowance for disgorgement of any monies previously paid under the agreement.
- Withhold any payments due until any alleged breach of compliance obligations is investigated and resolved to the satisfaction of the CCO.
- Dispute resolution by arbitration in the company's home country (ideally) or, failing that, in a third country. It should not be on the agent's turf.

Limited term

- The contract should be renewable annually.

Audit rights

- The company should have the right to review the books and records of the agent. The DOJ has said that it expects to see such rights. The main benefit here is that it is an active acknowledgement by the agent that they expect ongoing due diligence during the term of the contract. If at all possible, exercise the audit rights every year, and look at the agent's high-risk categories (i.e. those in this section).

Monitoring

The diligence process continues after the business partner has been brought on board. Key things to look for include:

- when the payments become higher (or lower) than was originally thought
- last-minute requests for more money
- poorly documented invoices and expenses.

Don't ask if you don't need to know

It is tempting to ask potential business partners for more than is necessary, but there is a real risk when you try to over-engineer basic due diligence. If you are sent something but don't properly act on it, you stand to be criticized. This is potentially worse than having taken the rational decision not to have asked for the information in the first place.

For example, what happens if you ask your Chinese agent if they have an anti-bribery policy? If you then after three weeks receive a long document in Chinese that looks like it was downloaded from the internet, you simply can't leave it at that. You must have it properly translated and then you need to read it. If you don't like it (which you won't), again, you can't just leave it at that – and you'll need to point out why you wish to see amendments. Then you get into a debate about their internal policies. In low-risk situations it might have been better not to have asked for a copy of their anti-bribery policy.

You need to take a commercial view on who you are dealing with. Large companies will have compliance departments and anti-bribery policies, but they are low-risk anyway. Smaller companies out of the mainstream won't have anti-bribery policies – and if they are going to bribe anyway, they will be more than happy to download a policy and sign it to keep you happy.

Communication and Training

Written policies and meticulous documentation

It is crucial to have written standards, policies and procedures in place to guide employees and third parties doing business with you. A good way to do this is through three interlinked documents, in increasingly length and complexity:

- a short statement of commitment that a company rejects bribery
- a code of conduct to set out how employees and third parties are expected to act
- a detailed anti-bribery compliance policy that is clearly written, regularly updated and tailored to actual risks.

Furthermore, all compliance efforts should be documented carefully in order to allow the company to demonstrate that it implemented a rigorous programme in practice rather than just on paper. This will include a full paper-trail of policies and standards, training materials and documents circulated, attendance at training sessions, due diligence reports, hotline calls, and regular compliance reviews. Internal investigations also should be documented and preserved.

Statement of commitment
The statement of commitment is the public declaration of a company's commitment to do business without paying bribes. Such a statement will include commitments to:

- carry out business fairly, honestly and openly
- adopt a zero-tolerance policy towards bribery
- avoid doing business with others who do not commit to doing business without bribery.

It should be drafted in clear and straightforward terms, and in simple language that can understood by non-native English speakers. It should be no longer than half a sheet of paper, and three or four sentences is about right. The statement of commitment can be printed out onto glossy paper, posted on the website, stuck onto notice boards in staff kitchens and frequently communicated to staff and business partners.

Code of conduct
While the statement of commitment is unchanging across the corporate group, the more detailed code of conduct contains policies that can vary from business unit to business unit or region to region, and differs between employees and agents. A code of conduct sets out expected standards of behaviour that will be circulated to all staff and business partners, and forms part of the each employee's employment contract.

The precise elements of the code will depend on many factors, including location and sector. In addition to the FCPA and Bribery Act, the local laws of the countries in which the company does business must also be considered during the drafting process. It will typically include the following written components:

- a clear prohibition of all forms of bribery
- guidance on sensitive areas, to include the company's policy and limits on gifts; hospitality, client entertaining and promotional expenses; employment of foreign officials; political and charitable contributions; and facilitation payments
- advice on relevant laws and regulations
- examples of real-world situations, with practical examples of the conduct it expects
- guidance on what action should be taken when faced with blackmail or extortion, including a clear escalation process
- the organization's commitment to speaking up and an explanation of the process
- where to go for further guidance internally.

Certification by front-line employees and agents
Employees who are likely to face bribery-related issues should be required to confirm in writing that they have been advised of the company's code of conduct and that they will abide by those policies. Foreign agents, representatives, consultants and other business partners should be asked to provide a similar written certification, and these certifications should be periodically renewed.

Compliance policy
This is a document that sets out how a particular company is going to assess and manage its bribery risk, and sets out all of the compliance steps and processes in this and subsequent chapters – tailored again to its particular circumstances. It is likely to be a fairly long and detailed document, regularly revised, and maintained internally by the compliance department. It is not circulated to all staff.

Communicating the policies

There needs to be more than simply a written policy. Additional information and detail will need to be communicated to employees and implemented in the business units, so it's necessary to plan:

- who will be responsible for implementation
- how the policies and procedures will be communicated internally and externally
- the nature of training and how it will be rolled out
- the internal reporting of progress to top management
- the extent to which external assurance processes will be engaged
- the arrangements for monitoring compliance
- the timescale of implementation.

Often the first and best method of anti-bribery communication is a presentation during a company meeting, which includes a discussion of the importance of compliance to the company's culture, showing the results of enforcement actions against non-compliant companies, and practical advice on avoiding exposure. Some businesses have successfully used videos and online education to disseminate these messages. This should be followed up regularly with written materials as discussed above, as well as training.

Compliance portal

An extremely effective way to collate and organize the documents and research required is using some sort of 'compliance portal' – a centralized resource on the organization's computer network that allows all staff to access standard documents, and different parts of the organization to add, edit and review areas relevant to their role. Certain parts of the portal will be password-protected and accessible only to senior management or the compliance team. The portal also could be used to support the risk assessment activities. Microsoft SharePoint or a similar record management system is ideal for such a compliance portal.

Running an anti-bribery training programme

The main goal of any anti-bribery training programme is not to create an army of bribery law experts. Clearly one key real-world objective is to be able to demonstrate to regulators that you have 'given the training', but it is slightly defeatist to think that this is all it can be. Instead, it should be your objective to ensure that each employee has sufficient background to be able to identify and report red flags within their areas of responsibility.

The most effective training programmes consist of a combination of the company's values and bribery law. Rule-based training is common, but ineffective, because unless employees can apply the rules to the incredibly wide and ever-changing situations that confront them in the real world, the compliance regime will never succeed.

Formal training can range from 'live' classroom training to a more impersonal online course, or even a taped session that's replayed. In all cases, though, a record of the company's training efforts and attendances should be recorded (in a section of the compliance portal). It is vital that the content of the training is appropriately tailored to the job function and the risks specific to the particular audience being trained. One of the most effective ways to do this is to divide the people to be trained into separate streams, based on risk. For example, there could be three streams:

- **The board and senior-level employees:** The board will expect face to face live training.
- **High-risk employees:** Front-line sales staff and those who interact with foreign officials as part of their duties, logistics staff, or those who have financial approval authority. High-risk employees need live training. There can be a 'basic' core presentation, which is then tailored for every discipline – meaning sales should have a different one from logistics. An hour and a half is a good length, comprising a presentation, scenarios and 'what ifs', and an extensive question and answer session.
- **The rest:** It is possible to use conference calls, or web-based, taped or videoed presentations here. Online training is really useful because it can be rolled out through an international organization, and slides and animations can be translated. It is also useful for its built in record keeping and reminders, which can ensure everyone actually does it.

The training should ideally be led by your compliance department or 'bribery czar'.

How do we know that our training is effective?
Part and parcel of adequately communicating and training on company policies and processes is assessing the effectiveness of the training. Many training professionals suggest a test

at the end of the training that is graded to ensure that the employee has learned at the least the required concepts, and to ensure the content is achieving the desired goals and where it can be clarified or improved. I am not a fan of tests following training, although many better trainers than me swear by them. Exams for things that matter I can understand, but I actually find 'tests' in a business context slightly condescending, and many C-suite executives do too. And tests raise more problems than they solve when employees either don't take or fail the training – which, if the questions are not condescending, people would expect to occasionally fail.

Martin and Daniel Biegelman in the 'Foreign Corrupt Practices Act Compliance Guidebook' suggest the following five informal 'quiz' questions to round off a training session, which I have used successfully.

- What does FCPA stand for?
- What is a facilitation payment and does the company allow such payments?
- How do you report compliance violations?
- What types of improper compliance conduct would require reporting?
- What is the name of your company's chief compliance officer?

But remember, it's better to conduct training without tests than it is to not conduct training because you're evaluating how to administer testing.

Holding individuals accountable

When implementing an anti-bribery compliance programme, management should identify clearly the consequences to employees and agents if they violate the law or company

policy. The Filip Principles place emphasis on appropriate
remedial measures, including the training, suspension or
termination of employees who are guilty of misconduct,
or else a financial penalty (in the case of agents and
third parties).

A tricky question is what happens if people confess or admit
to transgressions during a compliance review. My view is
that if information was received in any manner other than
under an amnesty programme and discipline is warranted,
you should discipline employees for compliance violations
just as you would if the information came in through a mechanism other than a review.

Rethinking goals and rewards

Conversely, employees should be given incentives to perform
in accordance with the compliance and ethics programme.
In short, good enforcement of compliance requires both the
'carrot' and the 'stick'. This is a key, if not *the* key step to
effective compliance.

People with specific goals are more likely to cheat in order
to reach them. This is true even when there is no extra compensation for meeting the goal – the psychological benefit
is enough to make people stretch the truth. A system that
bases people's pay solely on how much they sell provides
little incentive for behaving responsibly, so this means that
sales targets and incentives need to explicitly disallow orders
where bribery is suspected.

Employees are not doing their job well if they embroil the
company in a regulatory issue. Companies should therefore
create explicit links between maintaining good compliance
and compensation for all employees, and so conforming with
the letter and the spirit of ethics policies should factor into
performance evaluations.

Further reading

Question 26.

Speaking Up and Whistleblowing

Involving employees

Many commentators report that the majority of whistleblowers don't speak up out of ill will toward the company. Most report problems outside the company simply because they tried to or wanted to report it internally, but didn't know how to, or got turned away, or worse. With the implementation of Dodd–Frank 'bounties', it is even more important that employees know that companies take employee concerns seriously. Any would-be whistleblower should be encouraged to report to the company and not directly to the government.

Although it raises tricky questions of corporate culture, companies may consider offering incentives to employees who report unethical behaviour. I expect to see more of this, in an attempt to deflect Dodd–Frank claims.

Reporting mechanism for violations

Employees must be given adequate opportunity to report violations and to do so anonymously if they wish. For companies subject to the Sarbanes–Oxley Act, this anonymous reporting requirement also must be extended to third parties. Accordingly, companies often establish an anonymous telephone hotline or use an internet-based mechanism for anonymous communications to encourage employees to express concerns.

There is of course the potential for misuse, and to use whistleblowing to settle or escalate private arguments. It is therefore extremely important both to safeguard the confidentiality of the whistleblower and to properly investigate all allegations made.

This is often best achieved by being able to get in touch with a designated member of the compliance department, or even the board. While many people will be reluctant to directly go to their boss (who might be involved), it can be easier to go to the very top.

Overseas challenges

It is vital that employees in overseas branches are trained and treated the same way as US and UK employees, and that means having the opportunity to speak up in their own language. Despite its apparent simplicity, though, it is not straightforward to put in place and operate a worldwide helpline. There are clear logistical, cultural and language issues.

It is also important to understand the cultural aspects: in Japan, for example, it is often found that employees are very consensus-oriented and reluctant to whistleblow, whereas in China, employees seem far less afraid to voice their criticism. Anonymous reporting can sometimes also raise legal issues. In France, for example, a country with strict blocking statute, the law strongly discourages anonymous whistleblowing, relying instead on assurances of confidentiality.

Further reading

Question 38.

‘Document review and e-disclosure’, page 412.

Chapter 6

How Do I Carry Out a Review to Detect and Deter Bribery?

Introduction

If you don't find any problems during a compliance review, then you're not looking hard enough.

Internal controls are simply not enough on their own to deter bribery and corruption, as all controls can be overridden or circumvented by people with sufficient motivation and imagination. Regular independent compliance reviews by people *outside* of the process are vital as both a deterrent, and as a way of assessing what has gone on. This is done by a properly trained and resourced internal audit group, compliance team or external consultants.

The US Sentencing Guidelines require that a company takes reasonable steps to ensure that the organization's compliance and ethics programme is being followed, including *monitoring and auditing* to detect criminal conduct. A 2010 amendment to the Guidelines mentions compliance reviews as one of the factors that prosecutors should consider when evaluating the effectiveness of a compliance programme.

As set out in Question 34, a compliance review team for any non-routine investigation should be formally instructed by a lawyer to get privilege in place.

Objectives: The Key Questions to Answer

The compliance review seeks to answer the two fundamental questions: 'Is the company's compliance programme well designed?' and 'Does it work?' It does this by a combination of talking to people, observing how things are currently done, and because those who cannot remember the past are condemned to repeat it, a review of transactions.

At the end of a compliance review, the team should be able to answer the following questions:

- Is the location sufficiently focused on compliance? Is it properly resourced?
- What is the level of internal anti-bribery training and awareness?
- Are there regular company meetings, training sessions and get-togethers where anti-bribery is discussed?
- Is there a whistleblowing policy that people are aware of? Are there ever any reports? Are complaints taken seriously?
- Authority levels – do they exist? Are they observed? Are they appropriate? What work-arounds exist?
- Expenditure limits – are they followed and can they be effectively monitored?
- Can the company rapidly detect red flags surrounding high-risk payments?
- Does the company monitor transactions with foreign officials?
- How many third parties have passed and failed the due diligence process?
- Have audit rights relating to suppliers, agents and other third parties been exercised?
- How many employees have been formally commended or awarded a bonus, or disciplined, for corruption-related matters?

The components of a full compliance review

There are three practical components of any compliance review:

- talking to people – interviewing
- looking at the company's electronic and hard copy documents, and data – document review and e-disclosure
- looking at the company's financial and business records – forensic accounting and data mining.

The last 20 years of technological evolution though has deeply and permanently altered business record keeping. In matters involving bribery and corruption, the majority of the facts will now be found inside corporate networks, email servers and electronic devices, and the most important evidence will be found in accounting systems that capture the details of millions of transactions. A modern compliance review doesn't get very far without financial records to examine. Interviewing is crucial, but the core of any compliance review or response to governmental investigation is the review and assessment of electronic and accounting documents.

The precise scope of these activities varies considerably, dependent on the risk and objectives. In less risky business units, the email review is generally not required, which saves a considerable amount of time and money. I look at this further in 'Maintaining proportionality' on page 429. The steps below set out the steps to a full compliance review.

Logistics

Although some of the information-gathering and preliminary work can be performed centrally in order to minimize travelling time, I am a believer in the principle that any meaningful compliance review on a high-risk location needs to involve a trip there. Actually, a full compliance review usually requires an iterative approach, so usually consists of at least two on-site visits:

- the first visit to collect information and understand in overview the risk areas
- a period back in the office where the information collected is analysed
- a final visit where testing can be carried out on red flag transactions and interviews can confirm initial findings.

A good team to travel with is small enough to be able to fit into the single boardroom that the host office typically makes available (two rooms are invaluable, though, and should always be requested):

- a compliance, legal or internal audit person from the company
- an external lawyer with extensive bribery and interview experience, and one of their team to assist and take notes
- two experienced forensic accountants who can start collect and test financial data (one of them will sit in many of the interviews, certainly those touching on financial matters)
- a data collection expert to collect server data and image computers.

Often visits to different locations take place in parallel, if time is of the essence – but if not, do it in phases rather than having teams going to all branches at once and bringing the business to an effective standstill. I have found that it is often better to get a small group of experienced staff to travel the globe if required than to rely on a firm's affiliate offices in every country and spreading the investigation among lots of people, many of whom lack experience and all of whom lack in-depth client knowledge and have got slightly different ideas and approaches.

Interviewing

One of your first thoughts when faced with the prospect of a site visit is figuring out where the useful data and informa- tion might reside. You will already have obtained publically available information giving valuable background about the operation – the more you can get, the better – but now you need to get data and evidence about the operations to give you a reasonable prospect of uncovering instances of bribery, without bringing the local operation or your own team to a standstill.

The review team will perform interviews with the key company staff regarding, among other things:

- corporate culture and attitude toward ethics and compliance
- vetting procedures for, and use of, third parties and agents
- interactions with foreign officials and departments
- red flags and instances where bribes have been requested and paid
- ideas for compliance improvements.

Identifying and selecting custodians

You will want to interview, and collect data from, the key managers at the site. These people are known in electronic discovery circles as 'custodians' of data. Those paying bribes to win work – directly or through agents – tend to be salespeople, with the knowledge and consent of management. Those involved with facilitation payments are typically responsible for freight forwarding, logistics, procurement, licences and visas. Start with the heads of the finance, logistics, sales, procurement, HR and legal departments, with the site manager last, and allow the results of their interviews to shape the rest of the collection strategy.

Don't start with entire departments; that may come with time if problems are found. Instead, work on the basis of scheduling four interviews for each day of the trip. You will find that a couple of these can't make the interview for some reason, so you can find a couple of other people that you hadn't realized would be useful and who are available. (I realize that in an ideal world, the length of the trip would be determined by the number of interviews required to be carried out. But in the real world, logistics and other people's diaries often prevail, and you have to do what you can in the time available.)

The interview team

The interview team should ideally have legal, forensic accounting and IT disciplines all taking part, although there will be a lead interviewer – usually the lawyer. This will negate the requirement for each advisor to perform their own separate interviews, and also allow the different advisors to all have the same big picture approach to the investigation. The other advantage to a group interview is that follow-up questions can be brought up right away, and intelligence gathered will be integrated with the investigation as a whole.

The first thing that the interviewer should stress is that the compliance team is instructed by the company, so that the process is an internal one. The interviewers are not acting for, or reporting to, regulators. This should allow the subject to commit to assisting you and being truthful. Other than to prepare fully, here are some other things that I have learnt from carrying out these interviews:

- The interviewers must introduce themselves, but avoid titles. Less is accomplished if you're formal or ostentatious, and attempt to impress the subject with your authority.
- Demonstrate a lack of bias.
- Don't be afraid to say that you don't understand.
- Keep asking yourself whether what the interviewee is saying makes business sense.
- The interview should be sufficiently long and deep to uncover relevant facts.
- Ask open, closed and leading questions. Use each type in a logical sequence to maximize the development of information.

- Phrase all questions in a non-accusatory manner. Don't try to 'interrogate'.
- Ask them directly if they have ever seen bribes being paid, or seen things that make them uncomfortable.

The interviewer should prepare a memo of the key information furnished by each custodian from contemporaneous notes taken by the interviewer's assistant during the interview. Use clear and concise language. A separate memo should be prepared for each custodian, to safeguard confidentiality and limit potential disclosure.

Further reading

International Competition Network, *Anti-cartel Enforcement Manual – Chapter 6: Interviewing Techniques*, April 2008. Available from: http://bit.ly/qC6C6S (http://www.internationalcompetitionnetwork.org/uploads/library/doc345.pdf).

Kassin, S.M., Appleby, S.C. and Perillo, J.T., Interviewing suspects: practice, science, and future directions, *Legal and Criminological Psychology*, **15**, 39–55, 2010. Available from: http://bit.ly/oGoPGB (http://web.williams.edu/Psychology/Faculty/Kassin/files/K-A-P%20(09).pdf).

Document Review and E-Disclosure

Documents and emails have to be reviewed as part of internally focused compliance reviews, as well as during formal investigations and prosecutions. Compliance reviews will differ in their scope and focus from situations where prosecutors are demanding document production from the target company, as shown in the table that follows.

	Compliance reviews	Investigation or prosecution
Data request from prosecutor	No	Yes. Section 2 notices and subpoenas under time pressure.
Document production to prosecutor	No	Yes. Privilege review required. Prepare your own analysis before disclosing.
Dawn raids	No	Yes. Need to obtain copy of seized evidence.
Process	Focus on the most pertinent and accessible information. The review team defines scope and evolution.	Conduct the internal investigation to enable a better response to external investigation. The prosecutor defines the scope of the production.

Data collection

The first step in the data collection process requires that the review team obtains a complete picture of the way in which data is stored in the organization, the purpose and operation of the IT systems, and how each custodian interacts with it. This is usually done by interviewing the company or region's in-house IT specialists, as well as asking custodians during their interviews how they use email, what documents they typically use and where they store them.

All companies will need professional assistance to collect, process and host electronic documents in a form suitable for review. It is vital though that everyone knows and understands what the IT people/e-disclosure vendors are doing, in order to manage their costs. E-disclosure can be extremely expensive, and the way the team approaches data collection will impact both the cost and speed of the entire compliance review. It is invariably faster (and therefore cheaper) to collect custodians' emails directly from the corporate email server – often a Microsoft Exchange database, but maybe Lotus Notes or another similar system – rather than performing individual collections from desktops and laptops. The different methods of data collection, in ascending order of complexity, cost and time, are:

- obtaining data from servers
- obtaining data from servers and copying files from custodians' hard drives
- obtaining data from servers and forensic imaging of custodians' hard drives – forensic imaging involves taking a bit-by-bit copy of an entire hard drive, including files, deleted files, metadata (i.e. data about data, so information about when a file was last modified and by whom), and 'empty space' that is seldom truly empty and contains deleted files and file fragments that can contain invaluable information in a high-stakes review.

When the data needs to be collected as part of a request from the prosecutor, the standards are higher and forensic imaging of custodians' hard drives is usually appropriate. If disclosure to third parties is not required, the high cost/benefit of imaging is often overkill, and back-up copies of email files and user directories on the server are likely to suffice if indeed it has been decided to review emails at all.

Less accessible forms of data
Other data sources such as archive warehouses and back-up tapes take the debate about excessive volume to a new

level, given the level of effort needed to extract data from them, and the questionable value of the data they may contain. When confronted with such data sources, it is important to preserve them with a litigation hold if there is a formal investigation or dispute. However, a compliance review team should not usually attempt to search such data sources from the outset.

Data privacy and protection

In large corporate reviews and regulatory responses, people, entities and information systems will be found in multiple jurisdictions. Local laws, and the conflicts between them, will play out in a variety of ways. Compliance investigations are never easy, but cross-border ones have particular challenges.

Throughout the collection, data protection rules must be carefully considered. It will often be necessary to work directly with employees to retrieve data from devices, such as their laptops, that they consider personal. People always become nervous hearing that the information they create and manage will be subject to scrutiny – but in some parts of mainland Europe, each custodian should be given the opportunity to consent to the collection of their data for processing and to identify any data that may be personal. Such personal data should be kept separate and excluded from the processing phase. In jurisdictions such as the UK, data collection to investigate wrongdoing is more flexible, although needs to be 'proportionate'.

If there is a concern that a data custodian might destroy any data, it is necessary to proceed to data collection as quickly as possible – preferably without alerting them. If necessary, some types of collection can be completed 'invisibly', while the custodian is connected to the network, or after hours. Similar approaches are also useful if, for example, one or two employees are located in a distant location. To simplify the logistics of travelling to these sites, the data collection can be completed remotely using specialized software.

Cross-border data transfers

Any investigation in two or more countries will likely give rise to requests for information to be distributed among the parties. But data laws in many countries prohibit moving certain types of data, especially into the US, and this needs to be carefully managed. (This also applies to compliance monitors appointed over non-US companies, who may be restricted in what they can pass on to a US prosecutor.)

The details depend on location, and problems are generally experienced in more developed jurisdictions. But investigators may have to understand and contend with the following:

- **European blocking statutes:** Many European countries have taken two measures to reduce what were considered oppressive and burdensome discovery demands made on their citizens by US litigation:
  ○ Blocking statutes that criminalize the act of exporting information requested in the course of foreign legal proceedings. Blocking statutes create difficulties for foreign defendants facing prosecution or litigation under the FCPA, although the US authorities have not always been sympathetic to the necessary quandary from which defendants seemingly cannot escape unharmed.[251]
  ○ Ratification of the Convention on the Taking of Evidence Abroad in Civil or Commercial Matters (more commonly referred to as the 'Hague Evidence Convention'), which provides formal procedures for responding to information and discovery requests through letters of request *(letters rogatory)*. At the date of publication, there are 54 countries that are parties of the Hague Evidence Convention.

- **European data privacy:** The EU's Directive on data privacy sets limits on the transmission of personal data – such as that contained in emails – outside Europe.
- **Secrecy laws and sovereignty:** These include:
  - International Traffic in Arms Regulations prohibits non-US nationals viewing defence-related information that is considered critical to national security.
  - Swiss bank secrecy laws prohibit the disclosure of any banking information.

Managing data in light of legal constraints

After data is collected, it must be stored and managed in a manner that complies with the various local and international rules discussed above. Best practice is to conduct all data processing in the country where the data originated, which avoids the risk of moving data with little downside. In cases where data is deemed particularly confidential, or subject to secrecy laws (such as the Swiss banking secrecy laws), it is often necessary to process and manage the data within the client's corporate network. Fortunately, portable systems are available today that enable such work to be completed at the client site, and at reasonable cost.

If there is a compelling reason to transfer the data to another jurisdiction, this process should be thought through carefully. With the exception of formal document production, such as responses to Section 2 notices or subpoenas, data is commonly removed from its home country only for the convenience of outside professionals who do not have the means to conduct their work locally or who want to host the data in data warehouses in the US. Moving data can cause two problems:

- it opens up the data more easily to seizure by US authorities
- it can often break the laws of the country from where the data is moved.

Finding needles in haystacks

The exponential increase in data volumes means that if data is to be reviewed for, say, 20 custodians between 2008 and 2011, there is going to be a lot of it. The initial data set could involve millions of documents; large investigations featuring terabytes of data with hundreds of millions of documents are now common. This vast volume of data is not however the most significant problem faced by defence and prosecution lawyers, because powerful software is now available that can process a terabyte of data in a few hours. The biggest challenge is the inability to quickly identify relevant documents at the earliest possible stage from the information that has been processed.

From the collection phase the data is put onto a review platform, where it can be accessed remotely by the compliance team. There are many different review platforms, although all have similar features that allow the reviewer to search the population of documents by all manner of metadata and keywords, mark documents as 'responsive' (if they contain relevant information), collate and print them, annotate them, manage queues of documents, and redact (hide words), as well as (more recently) use heuristics to cluster, concept-search and target more precisely documents that are likely to be interesting.[252]

Keyword searching

During any type of detailed investigation, iterative searching electronic data using keywords is still the most common method of identifying relevant documents. Performing searches for names (for example of agents under suspicion or government ministers), dates, locations, and amounts is a vital first step once you have a target or suspicious transaction to investigate more closely.

Searching for 'bribes'

Simply searching for the text 'bribe' is not going to get you very far. When searching emails, one key search that has to be done is for words that suggest either extortion or bribery, and have the potential to lead to 'smoking gun' emails.

Corruption has its own language and bribes hide behind terms ranging from innuendo to elaborate code. Emails should therefore be searched against search strings relevant to the industry and sector under review, including terms such as:

Agent	Bribe	Conflict	Crime
Favor/favour	FCPA	Fraud	Friend
Gift	Intervene/ intervention	Lobby	Minister/ Ministry
Demand	Back hander	Pressure	Scam
Scheme	Slush	Bung	Special
Extort	Facilitation	Grease	Under the table

Each search, however, must be bespoke. I once ran this search against the email server of an oil company, resulting in literally millions of responsive emails. A moment's thought in advance would have led me to realize that every oil engineer uses the word 'pressure' hundreds of times a day – but in a different context to the one that I had in mind. Fortunately, if there are too many or too few responsive documents, the search can simply be run again with different combinations of search terms.

Much of the challenge around FCPA compliance comes from doing business in foreign countries, where the red flag keywords that are so important for FCPA testing are likely to be in a language other than English. Care needs to be taken, though, because as well as the obvious direct translations of the word 'bribe', non-native speakers are in danger of getting entangled in a web of subtext. Many synonyms for bribery downplay the seriousness of the payment: in Egypt people may offer *ashaan ad-dukhaan*, or 'something for your cigarettes'; in France, an innocuous-sounding *pot-de-vin*, or 'glass of wine'. In Russia, you may see 'coming to an agreement' or 'understanding each other'; in India, one may be invited to 'do the needful', or in China, 'go through the back door'.

The limited usefulness of search terms   Confronted with a massive volume of data, is it more effective to dive straight in and start to read documents to learn about their content, or is it better to look at the data as a whole to search for key features that are likely to identify relevant information? The legal industry has historically answered this question in favour of the first: the keyword approach, where you pick some keywords and start to read documents responsive to those terms. (After all, it is good for billing!)

Let's assume that our custodians in one particular country review have 10 million documents between them. A de-duplication procedure might reduce the data down to 5 million documents, and then the keyword searching reduces it to 500,000 documents. Assuming that a team of junior lawyers is used, as a first review, to get rid of everything that is not obviously relevant, how long would it take to review all of the documents quickly? If each document takes just 60 seconds to look at and mark in the review platform as 'relevant' or 'non-relevant', it would take a team of ten lawyers 80 days (assuming 10-hour days) at a likely cost approaching £1m. And that is just for a first-pass email review.

The preference for keywords might be understandable, because internet search engines have proven the value of keywords as the means to quickly access the information we seek. Or have they? In fact, running a Google search on the internet is a radically different process compared to applying search terms against corporate data. Google uses sophisticated algorithms that rank and prioritize web pages, so you only normally see what Google thinks are the 'best' pages from what are often millions of pages responsive to the words you typed in. Most review platforms give you all the responsive pages without any ranking, and furthermore, abbreviations, misspellings, naming conventions and unknown references conspire to reduce the effectiveness of searches. The superficial similarity between Google and search terms is misleading, and offers a possible explanation for the over-reliance by lawyers on keyword searches.

Modern strategies for pinpointing the 'smoking gun' documents

Modern sampling and software-assisted tools can dramatically cut the time and cost spent in searching for potentially relevant documents.

Concept analysis

Software is available that uses statistical inference and ontology to group conceptually similar documents into different clusters, each one relating to a particular subject or theme. In this way, the review team can first target all the documents that concern the most interesting topics, rather than having to go sequentially through one custodian at a time.

Suspicious behaviour

Targeting 'suspicious' behaviour involves using metadata to pinpoint custodians who act unusually. For example, perhaps they:

- blind-copy external domains
- send zip files or encrypted content to outside parties
- rename documents and forward them under an innocuous name

- use proxy servers or services that disguise IP addresses
- use instant messaging or webmail to send documents
- use browsers or mail programs that are different to the corporate standard
- visit the domains of competitors, government agencies or regulators

Pattern analysis

People tend to communicate in patterns and according to relationships. Software is able to look at who people are emailing and highlight any unexpected patterns.

As an example, people within organizations most often email their immediate subordinates and their immediate supervisor. Often emails are copied one or two levels up, giving typically 'linear' patterns. It is rarer to get the most senior people directly emailing the most junior, or the most junior member of staff in one group emailing the most junior in another. Such unusual patterns lead to email exchanges that should be reviewed first. Modern software can indicate who knows who, and shows how the communities aggregate and evolve – as the figure below demonstrates.[253]

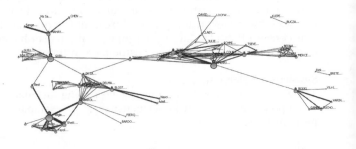

Further reading

Question 28.

Tillen, J.G. and Delman, S.M., A bribe by any other name, Forbes.com, 28 May 2010. Available from: http://onforb.es/mXtwbH (http://www.forbes.com/2010/05/28/bribery-slang-jargon-leadership-managing-compliance.html).

Pikko Software, information mapping and visualization (http://www.pikko-software.com).

The Electronic Disclosure Reference Model (EDRM)
The EDRM is a useful protocol for managing the data side of a compliance review. It contains best practice from how to manage and identify data, through the collection process, to its disclosure. In the figure demonstrating EDRM below, the lower shaded axis shows that the volume of data is reduced as the process continues, with only the data relevant to the matter in hand being identified and analysed.

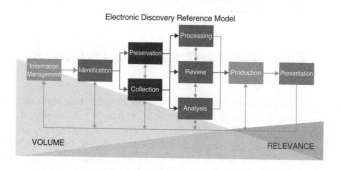

For more information, see http://www.edrm.net/.

Forensic Accounting and Financial Data Mining

Financial input is vital in any compliance review, because it's necessary to verify the answers given in interviews and confirm the hints picked up during document reviews.

Current estimates show that data volumes produced by companies are doubling every 12 to 18 months. At its peak levels of activity, Siemens was said to process up to 40 million transactions per day. That has challenges – but many advantages, because as more financial data is being captured, there is an enhanced ability to see trends and patterns, and spot outliers. To my mind, interviews and document reviews provide suspicion and innuendo, but forensic accounting actually shows how payments were recorded by the company in its accounts and can uncover red flags hidden deep in the accounting databases.

The forensic accountants concentrate on two main areas, discussed below.

Compliance testing: do controls work as designed?

A compliance test checks that a control has operated in accordance with its intended design. For example, if a control specified that all petty cash vouchers needed to be authorized by the financial controller, the compliance test would be to check a sample of petty cash vouchers to see if they were in fact correctly authorized.

Substantive testing of transactions

A substantive test is a check of the substance of transactions, ensuring they:

- have been properly authorized
- have been properly accounted for
- are for the company's benefit
- conform with the law and the company's compliance regime.

Much of the forensic accounting team's time will be spent on such a bottom-up review, trying to spot red flags and potential bribes in the detailed accounting data.

The first job of the forensic accountants is to obtain the right accounting data, clean it up and get it into a form that can be worked with and easily analysed. This can be done either by getting an extract of the relevant account codes directly from the accounting system or by getting the company's IT staff to go into the accounting database directly and obtain a data dump. From there, the data will be imported into an analysis program. Databases and sophisticated data analysis and manipulation tools are now used to process, analyse and query massive datasets more easily, and stratify, summarize, age, and look for gaps and duplicates in financial data. There are two essential steps: data analysis and data mining.

Data analysis
Data analysis, which involves taking a high-level view of pieces of financial data and searching for anomalies that suggest that it has somehow been manipulated or massaged. For example, I might take all payments that have been

allocated to the cost category 'freight charges'. At the push of a few buttons I would quickly:

- group and stratify the data, finding the totals, average and top and bottom entries, and pinpoint outliers
- age the data and see when the different costs were incurred, and to ensure all were current
- find duplicates and gaps
- perform statistical analysis to look at the distribution of numbers and pinpoint numbers more likely to have been made up.[254]

Data mining

Data mining enables an organization's transactions to be rapidly screened against predetermined high-risk situations:

- Forensic accountants are now able to programmatically work with 100% of a company's transactions to look for suspicious transactions. Gone are the days where teams of bright but inexperienced graduates sat in windowless rooms looking though ledgers and sampling only a fraction of the entire population. Forensic accountants are now experts in working with massive volumes of data, using database analytics to hunt out the high-risk transactions for further substantive testing.
- Query tools, scripts or macros can automate a set of data analysis procedures so that a forensic accountant can create a standard basic set of reports. Scripting also enables repeatable testing and is the precursor to continuous monitoring.

High-risk transactions

Rarely can we say that a transaction is definitely a bribe, but the forensic accounting process highlights transactions that warrant further attention: such as a payment with unusual characteristics that makes us ask 'Hang on – is this legitimate, or has someone tried to bypass our controls?'

The forensic accounting team will search the accounting system for the following types of high-risk transactions, and then review the supporting documentation and talk to those involved to ensure all was in order – and if not, what the implications were:

- multiple gifts to a single individual
- cheques made to 'cash'
- payments to suppliers made in cash
- transactions with entities on PEP lists or OFAC lists
- vendors where payee names or bank accounts have been changed
- payments to vendors not on the vendor master list
- payments made from out-of-country bank accounts or sent outside the country of operation
- payments just below authorization limits
- use of new lawyer/accountant/agent/consultants with no prior relationship
- invalid or suspicious journal entries to temporary or suspense accounts
- adjustments to inactive accounts
- missing descriptions or suspicious key words for payments, including 'services rendered', 'suspense', 'gift', 'facilitation', 'consulting', etc.

Reporting and Evaluation

Reports will ultimately be circulated to the audit committee or the board, but initial draft findings and recommendations should be reviewed by the CCO's 'triage committee' – however, this is made up. (In Appendix 7, which reproduces extracts of the Johnson & Johnson deferred prosecution agreement (DPA), you can read about the concept of a compliance oversight committee, termed the 'Sensitive Issue Triage Committee', whose responsibility is to review and respond to any FCPA issues that may arise during a review.)

Although the accountants and lawyers will obviously communicate the results of the reviews to the client, often by periodic meetings and presentations, all written material should generally be from the external lawyers to the company – and, as such, would be protected by privilege. The reports of the forensic accountants and other professionals should be addressed to the lawyers, to also try as much as possible to maintain confidentiality, although it is safer to always work on the basis that the report might end up being scrutinized by a court or regulator. Whether or not a payment constitutes a facilitation payment or a bribe is a legal matter for determination by a court, so accountants should never write 'The company has paid bribes to agents in ...'. I use the term 'red flag payments' to highlight transactions where I have concerns.

If there are major problems found during the review, such as a possible violation of the law, this needs bringing to the company's attention immediately – again through lawyers.

This is not a book on how to write an effective report, but I would remind you that it goes without saying that you should:

- avoid any mistakes
- use clear language
- be impartial – rely solely on the facts to document the circumstances, so avoid colouring the evidence and jumping to conclusions on important legal questions.

Remediation

After the compliance review for the location is complete there should be a detailed remediation plan, setting out the steps to be taken to sort out any problems identified. It should include the timeframe to accomplish the tasks (say 90 days), and there should be specific assignments of responsibility made to handle the designated tasks.

Finally, there should be a final report on the results of the implementation plan – hopefully confirming that all the recommended procedures have been implemented and are working properly!

Maintaining Proportionality

The amount of work and precise focus of a compliance review depends on the results of the risk analysis. While lower-risk regions and business units can get by with a less detailed and less intrusive exercise, a full compliance review – including document and email review – will typically be performed in companies that are known to have problems. (For example, where there has been a settled bribery action in the past, or perhaps a compliance monitor is in place.) In such a situation, there will be no escaping a full compliance review on every country in which there are operations, in advance or in conjunction with the monitor, and similarly, a full review will inevitably be required in response to a formal governmental investigation.

'You're joking – I'm not spending that much money!'

Compliance reviews are becoming an important source of business for anti-corruption lawyers and forensic accountants, and most practices in this field will happily spend hundreds of thousands to carry out a compliance review in far-flung locations. This is often simply too expensive for all except multinationals who are under investigation, and frankly who have little alternative.

For most companies the upside from such reviews is so intangible. If there is a regulator asking questions (or worse), then the money needs to be spent. But there may not be any problem at all with the compliance programme and the review can amount to a very expensive rubber stamp – is there a realistic alternative to a multi-million pound exercise?

Fortunately, there is. For companies of modest means, the important thing is not to strive for perfection, but to make sure that some sort of regular review takes place. A phased approach is often the best of both worlds: use external experts to plan and guide internal resources, who can then review findings and come in again to deal with anything difficult.

Routine compliance reviews on low-risk locations can work well with just one visit, as it is not usually necessary to do an email review (which requires people, and is therefore costly) on such locations. It is best to seek as much background information and financial data prior to the visit through a series of conference calls with the key managers. At least one visit is necessary, however. Interviews with the local staff need to take place and there is no substitute for face-to-face interviews. Review of some accounting records – not necessarily all the accounting records, but the potential to be able to do so – also needs to take place. Besides, flying in a team with the prior introduction to the local management team by the CEO, while scary to the local staff, does send a great message that anti-bribery is taken seriously. The trip is also a good opportunity to do some face-to-face training.

I am often asked whether internal audit or external auditors can do this work. Internal audit certainly can – if they have the time and the experience. I seldom see both of these coinciding, though. I am not a fan though of external auditors trying to do this work. For one, the audit team will not have the experience. But even if they bring in specialists from their company, if problems are found, there is always the question to be asked about why the auditors didn't find it. In extreme situations, there may well be a claim against the auditors, putting them in a difficult position with potentially insurmountable conflicts. Auditors also often have problems being objective: they want a smooth working relationship with their clients and they don't want to be fired, so they have an incentive not to ask awkward questions. Specialists brought in for a one-off assignment seldom feel so constrained.

Some Concluding Comments on the Practical Aspects of Overseas Compliance Reviews

- Ensure that your behaviour is always above reproach. Even though you are working on behalf of the company, sometimes you will meet resistance and people will be looking for any excuse to discredit you and your team, and send negative messages back to the CEO. So obtain business visas and ensure you are operating legally in the country, even if it is possible to enter the country on tourist visas without formality.
- Understand that depositions and formal interviews that might be used in foreign proceedings can be prohibited in some countries. Ensure that all communications seek to minimize the formality of interviews in lesser developed countries, and do not characterize them as depositions. Never accuse people of committing crimes.
- Explain that you are not interested in any personal things on their computers. This is likely to be a source of real concern, as most employees will have some personal emails, music and pictures on their computers. Explain carefully and sensitively before each custodian has anything imaged how only documents responsive to search terms will be looked at. Request and obtain formal consent, in writing, for any employees whose computers are imaged.

- Wear formal business dress – even in the tropics, where open-necked shirts etc. are the usual business attire for middle management. Senior management still invariably wears suits, and it is important to be seen as having equivalent status to the country manager.
- Although your in-country hosts have given you a comfortable office outside the main building, have a tour of the facilities and go out among the staff. Make sure that they take you everywhere and take some time to introduce yourselves to the employees. The staff will be aware that something is happening, so tell them who you are, where you will be located and why you are there (i.e. senior management has asked that you review part of their operations).
- It is invaluable for a local language speaker to be part of the team. However, I have never found language barriers to be insurmountable, since many international companies have English as the lingua franca across their offices, with expats in key positions and most internal forms and accounting documents being in English.
- Some practitioners advocate hiring in a local forensic accounting firm and local lawyers to assist with, or even do, the review in more challenging countries. I find that this is rarely the best or most cost-effective approach, and a skilled translator to bring in cultural and language assistance is all that is generally needed.

Chapter 7

Cautionary Tales – What Happens If You Get Caught?

Introduction

What are the largest penalties for bribery?

In a field as active as this, it is impossible to keep on top of a list of the largest settlements. What is certain is that the list below will be out of date by the time that you get to read this book (although Siemens is likely to be top for a while yet). The following list relates to fines, civil penalties and disgorgement of profit in worldwide settlements (not just under the FCPA) as at January 2012:

1. Siemens (Germany): $800m (US) + €596m (Germany) in 2008.
2. KBR/Halliburton (US): $579 (US) in 2009, $35m (Nigeria) in 2010, £7m (UK) in 2011.
3. BAE (UK): $400m (US) + £30m (UK) in 2010 (plus $79m export controls penalties).
4. Snamprogetti/ENI (Holland/Italy): $365m (US) plus $32.5m (Nigeria) in 2010.
5. Technip (France): $338m (US) in 2010.
6. JGC Corporation (Japan): $218m (US) in 2011 + $28.2m provision (Nigeria).
7. Daimler (Germany): $185m (US) in 2010.
8. Alcatel-Lucent (France): $137m (US) in 2010.
9. Magyar Telecom/Deutsche Telecom (Hungary/Germany): $95m (US) in 2011.
10. Panalpina (Switzerland): $81m (US) in 2010.

It will be noted that only one of the current top 10 involves a US company.

Numbers 2, 4, 5, and 6 all relate to the same Bonny Island scheme (page 438). The top 10 above is a corporate list; note that an individual, Jeffrey Tesler of the UK, agreed to an FCPA-related forfeiture of $149m in 2011 in relation to cash he still held in his role as agent in the scheme.

Also, as set out in Question 30, it is important to bear in mind that the true costs to the company are far larger than these numbers portray.

What then are the largest related actions?

Several of the companies above were prosecuted in relation to the same related scheme. It is instructive to look in further detail at these schemes – not from a legal perspective to analyse the law, but simply to look at 'the story' and see what the scheme entailed. I look here at:

- Siemens (a single group, but large enough in the size of its fine and pervasiveness of behaviour to warrant its own category)
- the Nigerian 'Bonny Island' scheme (the TSKJ consortium, comprising KBR, Technip, Snamprogetti and JGC)
- Panalpina and customs violations
- BAE Systems (again, large and interesting enough to warrant a category all of its own)
- the Oil-for-Food Programme
- the 'gun sting' – not on the top 10, but large in volume terms and a good story.

Siemens

Established in 1847, Siemens is the largest engineering group in Europe. Still headquartered in its native Germany, it is listed on the German, London and Swiss Exchanges, and has been listed on the New York Stock Exchange since March 2001 – the date that the US authorities charged behaviour from. The company is organized into 15 divisions in three main business sectors (industry, energy and healthcare), employing approximately 405,000 people in most countries of the world. It had reported global revenue of €73bn for the year ended September 2011.

The bribery scheme

According to court documents, from the mid-1990s Siemens had falsified its accounts and avoided internal controls to enable it to pay bribes to win contracts. This appears to have been authorized and even encouraged at the highest levels, and was reportedly ingrained in the culture of Siemens.

Specifically, from the time it became a US issuer in March 2001 until approximately 2007, Siemens made at least 4200 payments, totalling approximately $1.4bn, to bribe government officials in return for giving business to Siemens. In addition, the company made 1185 separate further payments totalling approximately $391m to third parties and agents to be used, at least in part, to pay bribes. The mechanism of paying the bribes was many and varied, and used internal 'cash desks' (where employees could obtain large amounts of cash, sometimes in suitcases), as well as bogus intermediaries and agents. Authorizations and approvals for payments were done on Post-it notes and later removed so as not to leave a permanent record or audit trail. Siemens used numerous 'slush funds', which were off-book bank accounts maintained at unconsolidated entities, and a system of business consultants and intermediaries to facilitate the corrupt payments.

The settlements

In November 2006, German police executed a series of search warrants on Siemens offices and the homes of senior executives. Siemens subsequently self-disclosed its bribery to the DOJ and SEC. In December 2008, Siemens AG, together with three of its subsidiaries, pleaded guilty as part of a settlement with the DOJ, SEC and the Munich Public Prosecutor's Office. Under the terms of the settlement, Siemens agreed to pay a combined $1.6bn in fines, penalties and disgorgement of profits, which was the largest monetary sanction ever imposed in an FCPA case. In the wake of the scandal more than 100 of the company's executives were replaced and six former executives, including the former CEO, reportedly agreed to pay a total of $27m in damages to the company. Criminal charges cannot yet be ruled out.

In July 2009, Siemens and the World Bank agreed to a settlement over bribery allegations in connection with an urban transport project in Russia that the World Bank had financed, and which was carried out by a Siemens subsidiary. The settlement included a commitment by Siemens to pay $100m over the next 15 years to support the Bank's anti-corruption work. It also agreed to forgo bidding on any of the Bank's projects for two years. The Siemens 2010 annual report contained some further details of cases around the world brought by local regulators and prosecutors that are still unresolved, including in Hungary, Austria and Russia.

Criminal breach of the FCPA books and records provisions

Although the combined penalties were the largest in anti-bribery history, the parent company Siemens AG only pleaded guilty to violations of the FCPA's internal controls and books and records provisions. In common with most of the largest settlements, there was no charge or acceptance of violating the FCPA's anti-bribery provisions, and to avoid any future debarment issues, no mention of bribery in the guilty plea by the parent company. Instead, Siemens' subsidiaries in Argentina, Bangladesh and Venezuela pleaded guilty to conspiring to violate the anti-bribery provisions.

This case was the first time that the DOJ had charged a company with a criminal (rather than merely civil) failure to maintain adequate internal controls. As explained on page 80, issuers must design and maintain a system of adequate accounting controls – but to be held criminally liable under this provision, a company must knowingly circumvent or knowingly fail to implement a system of internal accounting controls. According to the Information filed by the DOJ,

Siemens merely adopted a 'paper programme' limited to the distribution of anti-corruption circulars and the promulgation of FCPA policies. It failed to establish a 'tone at the top' that emphasized adherence to these policies, and failed to discipline employees who transgressed.

Further reading

For more information, see http://bit.ly/o7WhkU (https://www.traceinternational2.org/compendium/view.asp?id=124).

The Nigerian 'Bonny Island' Scheme (The TSKJ Consortium, Comprising KBR, Technip, Snamprogetti and JGC)

In 1994, a four-company consortium won contracts to design and build giant liquefied natural gas facilities on Bonny Island on the coast of Nigeria, in a project worth some $6bn. The contract was awarded by Nigeria LNG Limited, a joint venture company in which the state-owned Nigerian National Petroleum Corporation had the largest 49% share. Construction of the plant commenced in February 1996 and the first of seven LNG 'trains' commenced production in 1999. (As at 2011, the seventh is in its design phase).

The engineering consortium comprised four of the global leaders in oil services engineering:

- Halliburton, Inc., the US-based oil services giant and its subsidiary Kellogg, Brown & Root. KBR was spun off on its own in 2006. The UK arm of KBR played an important role in the consortium.

- ENI SpA of Italy, and its subsidiary Snamprogetti Netherlands BV.
- French-based Technip SA.
- JGC (formerly Japan Gasoline Co., Ltd), based in Japan.

The four companies were each 25% partners in the joint venture, which was known as TSKJ and operated through special-purpose companies based in Madeira. Former KBR chairman and chief executive Albert 'Jack' Stanley headed the consortium.

Early decisions taken by TSKJ included setting up what it termed a 'cultural committee' of TSKJ's senior sales managers to design and implement a scheme to bribe senior Nigerian officials. It did this by hiring two agents to pay bribes to the officials: Jeffrey Tesler, a London lawyer, and Marubeni, a Japanese trading company. Stanley met high-ranking Nigerian officials in Nigeria and London to discuss the designation of a representative with whom the joint venture should negotiate bribes to the foreign officials. Tesler appears to be the main go-between between TSKJ and the most senior levels in the Nigerian government, and the joint venture paid about $132m to his company located in Gibraltar through bank accounts in Switzerland and Monaco. At least three of the last four former presidents of Nigeria are reported to have received funds from the scheme. Another team, coordinated by Marubeni, was responsible for paying some $50m to lower-level Nigerian officials.

The settlements

Between 2009 and 2011, all four joint venture partners were investigated and settled with the DOJ and SEC, paying more than $1.5bn in penalties and disgorgement of profits.

In August 2008, Stanley settled with the DOJ and SEC, pleading guilty to conspiracy to violate the FCPA and to commit mail and wire fraud, knowingly falsifying books and records, and circumventing internal controls. His plea agreement contemplates a prison sentence of 84 months, but this can be reduced by the judge for cooperation with enforcement agencies. He was also ordered to pay $10.8m in restitution – the amount Stanley agreed that his former employer incurred as a monetary loss because of his conduct. As yet, he has not been sentenced.

Tesler fought extradition from the UK to the US to face trial, which was ultimately unsuccessful. He subsequently pleaded guilty to one count of conspiracy and one count of violation of the FCPA, and faces 10 years in prison when sentenced in February 2012. Nine other counts were dismissed under the plea deal. He also agreed to surrender £90m of TSKJ money, which had not yet been disbursed.

Further reading

ENI/Snamprogetti: http://bit.ly/phKGkU (https://www.traceinternational2.org/compendium/view.asp?id=192).

Halliburton/KBR: http://bit.ly/oUaf2Q (https://www.traceinternational2.org/compendium/view.asp?id=15).

JGC: http://bit.ly/nobeG7 (https://www.traceinternational2.org/compendium/view.asp?id=294).

Technip: http://bit.ly/qVnUuW (https://www.traceinternational2.org/compendium/view.asp?id=148).

Panalpina and Customs Violations

Panalpina is one of the world's largest freight forwarding and logistics services groups, specializing in intercontinental air and ocean freight services to the extractive industries. It also provides customers with importation, customs clearance and ground shipment services once the shipped goods reach their destination. Based in Switzerland, Panalpina operates through more than 500 international branches. Its shares are listed on the Swiss Stock Exchange. It is not a US issuer itself, but provides services to more than 40 customers that are.

Bribery and the freight forwarding process

Although the bribing of customs officials occurred in many jurisdictions, the settlements focus on Nigeria, where Panalpina had a substantial operation shipping items into the country on behalf of international oil and gas customers. It is no surprise that the customs and importation process in many countries is notoriously slow, bureaucratic and corrupt, and Nigeria is one of the worst of all. Prosecutors alleged that prior to 2007 corruption was rife within Panalpina, with its employees paying bribes on behalf of clients to have goods clear customs quicker, or for customs officials to overlook inadequate paperwork.

Panalpina was reimbursed by clients for these bribes through invoices that used false or misleading terms to characterize the payments. Panalpina used approximately 160 different terms internally and externally to falsely describe the bribes it paid in Nigeria relating to the customs process – often describing them as 'special fees', 'local processing' or 'interventions'. Unlike most other categories of official disbursements, no receipts were provided with Panalpina's invoices to the customer in respect of these disbursements.

The US settlement describes several types of bribery schemes undertaken by Panalpina, listed in the following.

Pancourier

Pancourier was Panalpina's express air freight service. Items shipped through the Pancourier service avoided the normal customs channels – through prior and corrupt agreement with Nigerian customs officials – by virtue of their distinctive packaging. Although there was no official Nigerian government receipt or paperwork for the goods that were imported, there was no delay either. Pancourier freight charges were generally based on weight (as opposed to value, which is the normal way that duty is calculated) and included a premium that comprised the bribe to Nigerian customs officials.

Temporary importation permits

According to the DOJ, the largest category of payments related to securing temporary importation permits (TIPs) on behalf of Panalpina's customers. The bribes ranged in value from $5000 to more than $75,000 per transaction.

TIPs are used in Nigeria and in several other countries where contractors need to import high-value equipment such as rigs and vessels into Nigerian water for short periods of time, to avoid full import duty becoming payable.

Companies, through a customs agent such as Panalpina, apply for a TIP, which is approved for an initial period of one year and can be extended through two six-month extensions. Vessels imported under a TIP cannot remain in Nigeria longer than the period allowed – when the TIP expires, the vessels need to be exported from Nigeria and, if appropriate, the customer can re-apply. Panalpina made improper payments to Nigerian government officials to assist some of its customers to circumvent TIP regulations. Specifically, TIPs were extended without the items having to be exported and then re-imported – a process that saved considerable time and money (in a process known as a 'paper move').

Special and other improper payments
When carrying out standard freight forwarding and shipping
services, Panalpina staff were generally responsible for ensuring that the clients' goods cleared customs. To avoid delays
where there was insufficient or missing documentation, or
simply the usual bureaucracy, Panalpina made cash payments
to local government employees to expedite customs clearance, do away with the required cargo inspections, avoid
fines, duty payments and tax payments, and circumvent legal
requirements.

The settlements

Panalpina became noticed by the US authorities back in 2007,
when Vetco International Ltd subsidiaries pleaded guilty to
violating the FCPA and were fined $26m. At that time Vetco
represented the largest criminal fine in an FCPA prosecution. In its plea documents, Vetco acknowledged making
improper payments to employees of the Nigerian Customs
Services 'through a major international freight forwarding
and customs clearance company'. That company was not
mentioned at the time by name, but was widely known to
be Panalpina. The Vetco investigation thus moved on to
Panalpina.

According to the DOJ, between 2002 and 2007 Panalpina paid
approximately $49m in bribes to foreign officials, including
$27m on behalf of 40 issuers and their subsidiaries. The
prosecutors contended that the majority of these customers
were aware, or should have been aware, that Panalpina
was making irregular payments to customs officials on
their behalf.

In December 2009, Panalpina announced that it had com-
menced settlement discussions with the DOJ. Not being a
US issuer, to be liable under the FCPA it was necessary for
Panalpina to take some action in furtherance of the scheme

within the US, and prosecutors refer to just one email and one conference call in which a bribe is discussed. Further, to give the SEC jurisdiction, it asserted that Panalpina acted as an agent for its customers who were US issuers, and it violated the FCPA by disguising the true nature of bribe payments in invoices submitted to its issuer customers that in turn enabled them to violate the FCPA. In 2008, Panalpina withdrew entirely from the logistics and freight forwarding market in the Nigerian domestic market, selling its local operations to a Nigerian group.

In November 2010, 13 separate settlements were announced by Panalpina's issuer customers, most of whom were major oil and gas companies. These enforcement actions principally focused on customs and related payments in Nigeria, but also including alleged improper conduct in Angola, Brazil, Russia, Kazakhstan, Venezuela, India, Mexico, Saudi Arabia, the Republic of Congo, Libya, Azerbaijan, Turkmenistan, Gabon and Equatorial Guinea. The combined DOJ–SEC settlement totals $236.5m and involved Panalpina itself, together with oil services companies Transocean Ltd, Tidewater Marine International, Inc., Pride International, Inc., GlobalSantaFe Corp. and Noble Corp. GlobalSantaFe merged with Transocean in 2007 to make the world's largest offshore drilling contractor. Tidewater is the world's largest offshore energy support-services company.

Settlements in Nigeria

Following the US settlements, three of the above companies have also settled with the Nigerian government over their dealings with Panalpina. Nigeria's anti-corruption agency, the Economic and Financial Crimes Commission, arrested executives in February 2011 in connection with the investigation – but in return for the settlements, the Nigerian government agreed not to bring any criminal charges or civil claims.

- Tidewater agreed to pay $6.3m
- Noble agreed to pay $2.5m
- Shell agreed to pay $10m.

Further reading

Panalpina: http://bit.ly/nhvdog (https://www
.traceinternational2.org/compendium/view.asp?id=213).

Pride: http://bit.ly/nhFPdP (https://www.traceinternational2
.org/compendium/view.asp?id=169).

Royal Dutch Shell: http://bit.ly/roymDU (https://www
.traceinternational2.org/compendium/view.asp?id=221).

Tidewater: http://bit.ly/riBj7J (https://www.traceinternational2
.org/compendium/view.asp?id=229).

Transocean/GlobalSantaFe: http://bit.ly/oXU68J (https://www
.traceinternational2.org/compendium/view.asp?id=230).

BAE Systems

BAE Systems plc is a defence, security and aerospace
company, and the world's largest military contractor. It was
formed in 1999 by the merger of Marconi Electronic Systems
and British Aerospace. Based in the UK, it is listed on the
London Stock Exchange and forms part of the FTSE 100.
In 2004 the SFO started an investigation into BAE's deals
in Chile, the Czech Republic, Hungary and Austria, Qatar,
Romania, Saudi Arabia, South Africa and Tanzania.

Saudi Arabia and Al-Yamamah

One of the cornerstones of the investigation concerned the
Al-Yamamah air defence programme, which involved the

supply, support and maintenance of Tornado aircraft to the Saudi military. The programme had been ongoing since 1985 and was described as 'the biggest sale ever of anything to anyone'. But to get that contract, the BBC reported that 'BAE Systems paid hundreds of millions of pounds to the ex-Saudi ambassador to the US, Prince Bandar bin Sultan ... with the full knowledge of the Ministry of Defence'.

Between 2004 and 2006 a team of SFO investigators carried out an investigation into the Al-Yamamah contracts. In 2006, when the SFO was about to obtain access to Swiss bank accounts, Saudi representatives hinted to the UK government that if the investigation was not stopped there would be no contract for the export of Typhoon aircraft and the previous close intelligence and diplomatic relationship between the UK and Saudi Arabia would end. This was concerning not just to BAE, but to the governments of both countries. After the personal intervention of the UK Prime Minister Tony Blair, the SFO announced that it was ending its investigation in December 2006. Blair said that if the SFO investigation into BAE had not been dropped, it would have led to 'the complete wreckage of a vital strategic relationship and the loss of thousands of British jobs'.

A judicial review instigated by pressure groups challenged the SFO's decision to cease its enquiry. Although the judges were critical of the SFO's decision in giving in to the threats made by Saudi officials (which might well have amounted to an attempt to pervert the course of justice had they been subject to UK law), the House of Lords in 2008 decided that SFO had acted lawfully in stopping the investigation when faced with a threat to national security.

The settlement

The SFO continued its investigation into BAE's other dealings while the US authorities continued to investigate Saudi Arabia as well. In February 2010, BAE announced that it had reached a settlement with the DOJ and the UK, and agreed to pay a combined penalty of $450m.

The US plea agreement dealt largely with Saudi Arabia and the court formalities were concluded quickly.

In the UK, BAE had agreed to pay £30m and plead guilty to failing to keep accurate accounting records in relation to payments made to an agent in Tanzania. The UK case related solely to Tanzania, whose government paid £28m to BAE in 2001 for a military air defence radar system. Having no air force and a GDP per head of just £465, most observers now agree it did not really need and could ill-afford it. To secure the contract, 'commissions' of $12.4m were paid by BAE to a marketing agent that were recorded in BAE's accounts as payments for the 'provision of technical services'.

The £30m penalty in the UK comprised a financial order to be determined by a Crown Court judge with the balance paid as an ex gratia payment for the benefit of the people of Tanzania. After a couple of long-awaited and fairly frantic days in the UK courts, the settlement was finally consummated in December 2010. Although the judge was most reluctant to go along with the agreement, he eventually fined BAE £500,000 (plus £225,000 in costs) for aiding, abetting, counselling or procuring an offence under Section 221(5) of the Companies Act 1985, by the officers of its subsidiary, British Aerospace Defence Systems Ltd, ('BAEDS') 'to keep accounting records which were insufficient to show and explain payments' made pursuant to contracts with certain companies owned by the Tanzanian agent. (The offence under S221, with some minor variations, is now at S387 of the Companies Act 2006; as the S221 offence can only be committed by directors or officers of the company, BAE could only be prosecuted for aiding and abetting the offence.)

Tellingly, the judge asked how the payments to agents should have appeared in BAE's accounts instead of 'technical services'. The SFO's barrister said that they should have been recorded instead as 'public relations and marketing services'. It was that simple 'offence' that ostensibly made up the entirety of the case, although the judge sensibly spotted that such a minor offence in no way deserved a penalty of £500,000, let alone £30m.

The judge was clearly unhappy about allowing BAE to escape with a plea that excluded a bribery offence, and refused to sentence on the basis of an accounting mis-description. He formulated the sentence instead on the basis that BAE had been concealing from auditors (and ultimately the public) the fact that they were making payments to offshore companies, with the intention that an agent should have free reign to make such payments to such people as he thought fit in order to secure the radar contract for the defendants, but that the defendants did not want to know the details.

Further reading

For more information, see http://bit.ly/qC7y7M (https://www.traceinternational2.org/compendium/view.asp?id=140).

The BAE files, *The Guardian*. Available from: http://bit.ly/nSJWdB (http://www.guardian.co.uk/world/bae).

The Oil-for-Food Programme

Originally conceived as a temporary programme to bring food and medicines to the Iraqi people, the Oil-for-Food Programme was established by the United Nations in 1995 following claims that ordinary citizens were suffering as a result of international economic sanctions imposed on Iraq following the first Gulf War. Under the programme, Iraq was again permitted to sell oil on the world market in exchange for food, medicine and other humanitarian products, but without allowing it to buy arms or otherwise boost its military capabilities.

The programme used an escrow system. Oil exported from Iraq was paid for by the recipient into an escrow account rather than to the Iraqi government. The money was then apportioned to pay for war reparations to Kuwait, and ongoing coalition and United Nations costs within Iraq. The remainder, the majority of the revenue, was available to the Iraqi government to purchase food and other regulated items. Transactions taking place under the programme had to be approved by the UN in a process that could take several months before a shipment was authorized. Under the programme, the Iraqi government sold $64bn of oil to 250 companies. In turn, 3600 companies sold $34bn of humanitarian goods to Iraq. The first shipments of oil under the programme came in March 1997.

The Iraqi government soon manipulated the scheme to receive kickbacks and commissions, and the UN failed to prevent this happening. The programme was just under three years old when the Iraqi regime began to openly demand illicit 'surcharges' from its oil customers. Oil sales increasingly took the form of contracts with front companies, backed financially and technically by several international trading companies willing to facilitate surcharge payments. Companies often disguised surcharge payments by funnelling them through offshore bank accounts or labelling them as legitimate oil-related expenses, such as 'loading fees'. Most surcharges were paid through deposits to designated bank accounts in Jordan and Lebanon or through cash payments made at Iraqi embassies abroad. Such illicit surcharges were paid by at least 139 companies. The diagram below shows the illicit income made by Iraq under the Oil-for-Food scheme.[255]

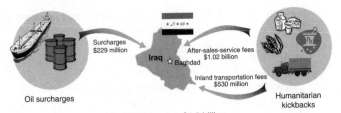

Oil surcharges

Surcharges $229 million

Iraq ☆ Baghdad

After-sales-service fees $1.02 billion

Inland transportation fees $530 million

Humanitarian kickbacks

Total illicit income: $1.8 billion

Furthermore, kickbacks to the Iraqi government were demanded from those selling goods. These were initially disguised as inflated transportation fees for moving goods to inland destinations after their arrival by sea, but in 2000, Iraq instituted a broader policy to impose an additional 10% kickback requirement on all humanitarian contractors as an 'after-sales-service' fee. After-sales-service fee provisions were incorporated into contracts to inflate prices and permit contractors to recover from the UN escrow account amounts they had paid secretly to Iraq in the form of kickbacks. More than 2000 companies were involved in these illicit payments.

In total, more than $1.8bn in illicit surcharges and kickbacks was diverted from the humanitarian purposes of the programme, involving some of the world's largest companies. Some of the companies have settled with US authorities; others are still under investigation, but it's uncertain now whether charges will ever be brought.

In common with other Oil-for-Food cases, the DOJ does not allege FCPA anti-bribery offences. This is because the kickbacks typically went directly to the Iraqi government and not to foreign officials. (Bribes made to foreign governments and not to specific foreign officials fall outside the scope of the FCPA.) Instead the DOJ uses other laws, such as the mail and wire fraud statutes, to prosecute the conduct; in the case of issuers, the SEC uses the FCPA books and records and internal controls provision.

Novo Nordisk: Oil-for-Food

Denmark-based Novo Nordisk is a biosciences company and a leader in manufacturing insulin, and hormone and associated therapies.

In 2009 it announced a settlement with the DOJ and SEC. The charges were in connection with improper payments totalling $2.7m made by its agents to the former Iraqi government between 2000 and 2003. The payments comprised kickbacks that had been made to obtain contracts worth €22m to provide medicines to Iraq.

The payments were made by inflating the true price of goods by 10% for the kickbacks paid to the Iraqi government. The kickbacks were called 'after-sales service fees' (ASSFs), which were included on the invoices submitted to the UN for approval. They were paid to bank accounts in Jordan and elsewhere controlled by the Iraqi government. Novo Nordisk recorded the kickbacks as 'commissions' in its accounts.

The DOJ charged Novo Nordisk with one count of conspiracy to commit wire fraud and to violate the books and records provisions of the FCPA. As a result the company entered into a DPA with the DOJ, agreeing to pay a $9m criminal fine. The SEC charged the company with violating the FCPA's books and records and internal controls provisions, resulting in a civil penalty of $3m, and disgorgement of $4.3m in profits plus $1.6m in prejudgement interest.

Further reading

For more information, see http://bit.ly/nvLGbA (https://www
.traceinternational2.org/compendium/view.asp?id=59).

Independent Inquiry Committee into the United Nations Oil-for-Food Programme, *Report on Programme Manipulation – Chapter One: Summary of Report*, 27 October 2005. Available from: http://bbc.in/pO2TLd (http://news.bbc.co.uk/1/shared/bsp/hi/pdfs/27_10_05_summary.pdf).

Oil-for-food scandal: key reports, BBC. Available from: http://bbc.in/qZv6sh (http://news.bbc.co.uk/1/hi/world/americas/4550859.stm).

The 'Gun Sting'

Although not involving some of the highest fines, this series of cases is important for being the largest single investigation and prosecution against individuals in the history of the DOJ's enforcement of the FCPA, and the undercover police tactics – such as telephone taps and video surveillance – that are now rarely seen in combating bribery. The so-called 'gun sting' (or 'shot show sting') was the culmination of a two-and-a-half-year investigation in which 22 executives of multiple armaments companies were indicted for supposedly agreeing to pay $3m in bribes to undercover FBI agents posing as Gabonese nationals. The defendants were a mix of corporates and individuals, from publicly traded Smith & Wesson to individual managers of small defence products companies.

It was alleged that the defendants engaged in a scheme to pay a 20% 'commission' to a sales agent who the defendants believed represented the Minister of Defence for Gabon. They believed that the agent would help them to win a portion of a $15m deal to outfit the country's presidential guard. The scheme was put together by FBI agents, but there was no actual involvement from any minister of defence. Instead, a former executive at defence company Armor Holdings assisted the FBI in posing as a representative of Gabon.

The indictments were unsealed in January 2010 after the arrests of all but one of the defendants in a well-managed sting operation at the annual Shooting, Hunting & Outdoor Trade Show held in Las Vegas. The show is for industry professionals and the trade press, and was clearly done to get maximum attention and send a message to the industry.

> 'The undercover techniques used in this case should cause all would-be FCPA fraudsters to pause and to ask: am I really paying off a foreign official or could this be a federal agent? ... Of course, if you even have to ask yourself this question in all likelihood you shouldn't be doing whatever it is that you are doing.'
>
> US Assistant Attorney General Lanny Breuer[256]

For trial, the 22 defendants were split into four groups. During the trial of the first batch, however, the jury really didn't like the way the government had put the case together: there was no real foreign official and federal agents were doing some play-acting, having being introduced into the group by an informant with a colourful past who had turned state's evidence. The judge declared a mistrial after the jury ultimately deadlocked. At the time of publication, the defendants are waiting to see if the DOJ will request a retrial.

Further reading

For more information, see http://bit.ly/n5A9aD (https://www.traceinternational2.org/compendium/view.asp?id=172).

DOJ, Twenty-two executives and employees of military and law enforcement products companies charged in foreign bribery scheme, press release, 19 January 2010: http://1.usa.gov/pc0ALd (http://www.justice.gov/opa/pr/2010/January/10-crm-048.html).

Chapter 8

What Are My Predictions for 2012 and Beyond?

*I*n this section, I set out some of my predictions for 2012 and beyond.

The US Authorities Will Use Other Legislation to Expand the Reach of the FCPA

The US regulators are increasingly finding new and imaginative ways to fill in any gaps that might be present in the FCPA, or prosecute bribery where the FCPA is in some way unavailable: perhaps where the individuals involved had insufficient nexus to the US, or because not all elements of the FCPA can be successfully proved.

In the Oil-for-Food cases, when payments were made directly to the Iraqi government rather than to a 'foreign official', the DOJ had to prosecute under the wire fraud statutes instead of the FCPA. But several other laws can form the basis for supplemental charges, including money laundering, wire fraud, the Travel Act, export control violations and false accounting.[257]

One fundamental difference between the Bribery Act and the FCPA is that the FCPA does not criminalize private sector bribery. The US authorities though have already used Money Laundering and the Travel Acts to prosecute this; I expect this to continue.

Money laundering

The Money Laundering Control Act 1986 consists of two sections: 18 USC Chapter 95 § 1956[258] prohibits individuals from engaging in a financial transaction with proceeds that were generated from certain specific crimes, known as 'specified unlawful activities', and § 1957[259] requires that an individual specifically intends, in making the transaction, to conceal the source, ownership or control of the funds.

Under these provisions, if criminally derived property that forms part of a bribery scheme has contact with the US, then it is likely also that a money laundering offence will have been committed.

Hans Bodmer: Money Laundering Charges to Target Pre-1998 Overseas Bribery[260]

Hans Bodmer is a Swiss lawyer who acted on behalf of an investment consortium that engaged in bribery of Azerbaijan officials as part of a scheme to profit from the privatization of Azeri state assets. (Frederick Bourke – see below – was a member of the consortium, along with Vicktor Kozeny.) A federal grand jury indicted Bodmer on one count of conspiracy to violate the FCPA and one count of conspiracy to launder money.

The court held that prior to the 1998 amendments to the FCPA, foreign nationals who served as agents of domestic concerns and who were not residents of the US could not be criminally liable under the FCPA because they were outside the US's jurisdiction. The court accordingly had to dismiss the FCPA counts against Bodmer, but he subsequently pleaded guilty to conspiracy to money laundering.

Bodmer testified against Frederick Bourke, an alleged co-conspirator who was ultimately convicted. He is currently on bail, awaiting sentencing. It is likely that if Vicktor Kozeny comes (or is extradited) to the US to face trial, Bodmer would be a key witness. Therefore the DOJ is waiting to see the extent of cooperation forthcoming from Bodmer.

The DOJ has also used money laundering laws to target the bribe takers. In 2009 the DOJ charged former directors of Haiti Teleco, who were public officials, with conspiracy to commit money laundering for their part in agreeing to be part of a bribery scheme.[261]

Kleptocracy Asset Recovery Initiative
In 2010, the DOJ unveiled its Kleptocracy Asset Recovery Initiative to target and recover the proceeds of foreign official corruption that have been laundered into or through the US.[262] The campaign relies on civil forfeiture law and, once fully implemented, the Initiative will allow the Department to recover assets on behalf of countries victimized by high-level corruption if it comes into the US. Assistant Attorney General Lanny Breuer said:

> 'We are going to bring cases against the assets of those around the world who have stolen from their citizenry and have taken money that obviously belongs to their country.'

One of the first targets of the group is reported to be the ousted Tunisian leader Zine El Abidine Ben Ali and his associates.[263]

Wire fraud

Wire fraud is any fraudulent activity that has involved electronic communications of any kind, at any phase of an illegal transaction. The government has used the Federal Wire Act to prosecute corruption.

The crime of wire fraud is codified at 18 USC § 1343 and requires a party to:[264]

> 'devise, or intend to devise, a scheme or artifice to defraud another person on the basis of a material representation with the intent to defraud through the use of interstate wire facilities (i.e. telecommunications of any kind).'

Schnitzer Steel Industries (SSI): Wire Fraud to Catch Private Sector Bribery[265]

SSI, Inc. is a US company that purchases and recycles scrap steel in the US and abroad.

It admitted to violating the FCPA and the wire fraud statute in connection with more than $1.8m in corrupt payments paid over a five-year period to officers and employees of nearly all of its customers in China and South Korea to induce them to purchase scrap metal. Some $204,000 was paid to managers of government-owned customers and $1.6m to managers of private customers.

Because of its cooperation, the US company was able to enter into a DPA with the DOJ, but its Korean subsidiary, SSI International Far East Ltd, had to plead guilty to violating the FCPA in respect of the bribes to foreign officials and wire fraud charges in respect of the bribes to private customers.

The company also settled an SEC action admitting that the bribes were falsely accounted for, being variously termed 'refund to customer', 'rebate to customer', 'quality claims', 'discounts', 'credits', 'freight savings', 'gratuities', 'congratulations money' or even 'condolence money'. SSI agreed a $7.7m civil penalty with the SEC on top of its DPA with the DOJ. SSI International Far East agreed to plead guilty to violating the anti-bribery and accounting provisions of the FCPA and pay a $7.5m penalty.

Travel Act

The Travel Act prohibits the use of communications and travel facilities to promote or facilitate the promotion or carrying on of 'unlawful activity'. This is specified broadly, to include bribery in violation of the federal and state laws of the US and so includes private commercial bribery.[266]

So if, for example, in promoting a private business transaction in a foreign country, a sales agent in the US offers by telephone and pays by wire transfer an amount to the foreign buyer to influence his decision, and such activity is a violation of the state law where the agent is doing business, the DOJ may prosecute under the Travel Act. The Travel Act means that all foreign private citizens can be effectively brought into the FCPA by application of the Travel Act.

Control Components Inc. ('CCI') – Travel Acts Catch Private Sector Bribery[267]

CCI is a US-based company that supplies valves for use in the power, oil and gas industry, and pulp and paper plants worldwide.

CCI admitted that, between 2003 and 2007, its employees made more than 150 corrupt payments, totalling almost $7m, to officials of state-owned and private companies in China, Korea, Malaysia, and the UAE, to influence them to award contracts to CCI or bias the technical specifications of tenders in CCI's favour.

Four executives of CCI were indicted for alleged violations of the FCPA's anti-bribery provision and the Travel Act. The Travel Act came into play as the DOJ alleged the CCI employees violated or conspired to violate California's state anti-bribery law which bans corrupt payments of more than $1000 between any two persons. CCI itself pleaded guilty to substantive FCPA anti-bribery charges and to conspiring to violate both the FCPA and the Travel Act and agreed to pay a criminal fine of $18.2m.

There will Continue to be Calls for the FCPA to be Modified

There are two main (and arguably related) aspects of the FCPA that cause continual concerns:

- Because cases invariably settle, few ever see a contested trial where the facts and the law have been subjected to critical judicial review. So with virtually no case law being made, the FCPA becomes not what judges decide it should be but what the DOJ and SEC decide it should be.
- The application of the 'respondeat superior' rule, which means automatic liability for companies whose employees commit crimes. Even if a company has an effective compliance programme and has done everything possible to prevent a violation of the FCPA, that does not function as an effective defence. An 'adequate procedures' or 'good faith' defence (as is seen with the Bribery Act) would function as an incentive for companies to put in place effective compliance programmes and allow them to defend themselves against anti-bribery charges by showing that they tried their best to prevent it.

At a hearing in November 2010 before the US Senate Judiciary Subcommittee on Crime and Drugs, entitled the 'Examining Enforcement of the Foreign Corrupt Practices Act', three FCPA experts (Mike Koehler, Assistant Professor of Business Law at Butler University and writer of 'The FCPA Professor' blog, Andrew Weissmann from Jenner & Block, and Michael Volkov from Mayer Brown) explained how the DOJ and SEC had 'pressed the limits of enforcement'. They presented proposed changes to the FCPA to bring:

- FCPA enforcement into line with Congressional intent
- a more balanced approach in providing incentives to companies to comply with the law

- greater certainty and fairness to statutory interpretation and enforcement.

The calls for modification of the FCPA will continue, and I think there is a good chance that some of these proposals are taken on board in the next few years.

Further reading

FCPA Professor, Examining enforcement of the FCPA, 1 December 2010. Available from: http://bit.ly/qGLkdO (http://fcpaprofessor.blogspot.com/2010/12/examining-enforcement-of-fcpa.html).

FCPA Professor, House hearing – overview and observations, 14 June 2011. Available from: http://bit.ly/nRNulf (http://fcpaprofessor.blogspot.com/2011/06/house-hearing-overview-and-observations.html).

Koehler, M., The facade of FCPA enforcement, *Georgetown Journal of International Law*, **41**(4), 2010. Available from: http://bit.ly/qVe5Tb (http://papers.ssrn.com/sol3/papers.cfm?abstract_id=1705517).

Koehler, M. Senate Judiciary Committee Subcommittee on Crime and Drugs Hearing 'Examining enforcement of the Foreign Corrupt Practices Act' – questions from Senator Specter for Professor Mike Koehler, 9 December 2010. Available from: http://bit.ly/rdp8Ty (http://papers.ssrn.com/sol3/Delivery.cfm/SSRN_ID1739163_code1191864.pdf?abstractid=1739163&mirid=1).

Senate Judiciary Committee Subcommittee on Crime and Drugs, Examining enforcement of the Foreign Corrupt Practices Act. Available from: http://1.usa.gov/q3KlDt (http://judiciary.senate.gov/hearings/hearing.cfm?id=e655f9e2809e5476862f735da164f9be).

Subcontractors Will Become the New Commercial Agents

Anti-bribery compliance now exists on two levels:

- Still at the starting post are the many companies that have not yet got even a basic anti-bribery compliance regime. They still don't think it can happen to them. They may still use a commercial agent who is the brother-in-law of the oil minister and pay them 15% of all contracts obtained, in dollars, wired to the account of an off-the-shelf company based in northern Cyprus. Frankly, these companies are going to get caught someday, because these payments are not that difficult to spot by seasoned forensic accountants who have been working in this area for a while. (The regulators might also spot the occasional one as well …)
- At the more advanced level are those companies who are alive to all the basic risks and ruses, and who have gone beyond the obvious. They do not use commercial agents as they once did and have carried out due diligence on the rest.

But what we have found recently is that some companies are using the occasional trade suppliers and subcontractors to make payments that they themselves do not want to make. These are legitimate service providers providing legitimate technical supplies and services, but with a few 'added extras':

- Suppliers can be used to establish slush funds, which are off the company's books and maintained by the subcontractor. The subcontractor would maintain the funds until instructed to spend the money (usually on a bribe or something else illicit). The most common scheme involves moving the funds out of a company under the guise of an invoice for fake purchases or services that were never provided by the subcontractor.
- Suppliers can be beneficially owned by foreign officials or other key influencers, and charge well above market rates

to provide the products or services. The foreign official creams off the excess profits as a 'quasi-bribe'. Subcontractors, labour suppliers, visa agents, business advisors and translation services are prime candidates for such front companies.

These sorts of bribery schemes are far more difficult to spot, and payments to trade suppliers and subcontractors are therefore increasingly seen as higher-risk. It is therefore more important than ever that vendors are pre-approved and undergo risk-based due diligence.

The US Government Will Continue to Prosecute Bribery Extremely Harshly

'I have made combating corruption, generally and in the United States, a top priority.'
US Attorney General to African leaders in Uganda, July 2010[268]

The level of FCPA enforcement is at an all-time high and is likely to remain there. Both the DOJ and the SEC have zealously enforced the FCPA over the last few years, and there was further growth in FCPA actions during 2010, with a total of $1bn being levied in penalties. The increase has likely come about because of several reasons:

• Increased self-disclosure in the expectation of receiving leniency from prosecutors.
• More resources in the DOJ and SEC. The DOJ increased in size by 50% in 2010 and was set to do the same in 2011; the FBI has announced an increase in its staff dedicated to FCPA enforcement; and the SEC has created its own specialized unit.
• Cooperation and assistance among the government investigators in different nations have been increasing.

- The Sarbanes–Oxley Act in the US requires executives to certify that their company's financial records are complete and accurate, and imposes harsh penalties for misstatements and non-disclosures. SOX compliance procedures assist in spotting bribes.
- The new Dodd–Frank Act in the US. *The Wall Street Journal* reported that, as a result of the new law, 'plaintiffs' lawyers eager to handle complaints on behalf of whistleblowers are getting the word out, issuing press releases and publishing articles about the new law, and in some instances running ads soliciting work'.[269]

In 2007, US oil services firm Baker Hughes paid $44m to settle DOJ and SEC actions, which at the time was the largest ever FCPA penalty. In 2010, six companies paid more than $50m in fines; fines of more than $100m are now routine.

The chart below shows how the number of enforcement actions every year by the SEC and DOJ has grown between 2004 and 2010. The enforcement activity shows no signs of abating.

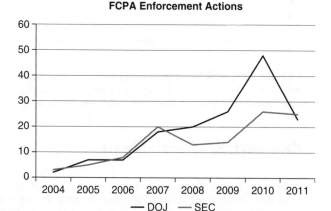

FCPA Enforcement Actions

Relating penalties to gain

Although it is a fairly blunt tool, a new metric measuring the size of FCPA penalties maintained by the website Main Justice suggests that FCPA penalties have shot up in the last three years. In 2010, companies paid an average of $2.14 in penalties per dollar gained from violating the FCPA. The dramatic rise in penalties appears to have started in 2009 (as shown in the figure below), when companies paid $1.97 in penalties per dollar gained, up from just $0.13 in 2008 and $0.11 per dollar gained in 2007.

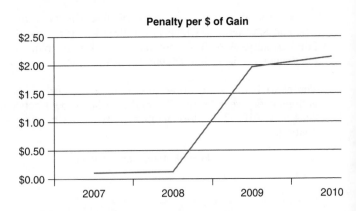

Penalty per $ of Gain

With the DOJ and SEC committing more resources to FCPA enforcement, and Dodd–Frank bounties now law, the number and size of FCPA cases will only continue to grow.

Prosecutions of individuals

'Let me be clear, prosecuting individuals is a cornerstone of our enforcement strategy because, as long as it remains a tactic, paying large monetary penalties cannot be viewed by the business community as merely "the cost of doing business". The risk of heading to prison for bribery is real, from the boardroom to the warehouse.'

US Attorney General Eric Holder[270]

In many respects, prosecuting companies is far easier than prosecuting individuals – they are more willing to settle, get highly paid professionals in to carry out detailed investigations and disclose the result to the prosecutors, and the fines are higher. The deterrent effect of putting executives in jail, however, is massive, and prosecutions have risen steadily in recent years. In 2004, the DOJ charged two individuals under the FCPA; in 2009 and 2010, it charged more than 50. Prosecuting senior company executives in their individual capacities is going to remain a priority of the DOJ.

As well as quantity, the DOJ is also going for quality, pressing for ever-longer prison sentences. In April 2010, Charles Jumet, a former executive of Ports Engineering Consultants Corporation, was sentenced to the longest prison sentence yet imposed under the FCPA: 87 months inside, with three years of supervised release to follow and a $15,000 fine. Jumet paid $212,400 to senior Panamanian officials to obtain contracts for his company and pleaded guilty to conspiring to violate the FCPA and to making a false statement to federal agents.[271]

The prosecutors don't just go after the top people, though: where they initially lack the evidence to proceed against the senior executives, they may file cases against more junior executives. Many of these plead guilty to reduced charges and more lenient sentences in return for providing evidence against their managers.

The DOJ is now pressing for extremely harsh sentences (it has indicated in some cases that it would look for life sentences), a sentiment not always shared by the courts. But, despite high sentences, it is very common for FCPA defendants to be sentenced to prison terms far shorter than that requested by the DOJ. Judge Scheindin stated at Frederick Bourke's sentencing that 'after years of supervising this case, it's still not entirely clear to me whether Mr Bourke is a victim or a crook or a little bit of both'.[272]

The SEC is also looking to pursue personal actions, including orders banning individuals from acting as officers of public companies.

Further reading

Cavico, F.J. and Mujtaba, B.G., Baksheesh or bribe: payments to government officials and the Foreign Corrupt Practices Act, *Journal of Business Studies Quarterly*, **2**(1), 83–105, 2010. Available from: http://bit.ly/nSidP4 (http://jbsq.org/wp-content/uploads/2010/12/JBSQ_5G.pdf).

Serious Bribery Cases Will Increasingly Require Admissions of Bribery

In the US, the DOJ took the lead role in many of the high-profile FCPA cases throughout the 1990s, which led to the accounting provisions of the Act being somewhat relegated to the background. The DOJ's perennial challenge, though, is that it has to prove to the criminal standard – beyond reasonable doubt – that a company has wilfully violated the FCPA. Compare this with the much lower 'balance of probabilities' test in a civil enforcement action that could be brought by the SEC. This heavy burden borne by the DOJ has led it over the years to explore the certain 'win' of settlement agreements and plea bargains.

On the other side of the coin, criminal indictment can have severe consequences on a company; for example, it is reported to have led to the complete collapse of the accounting and consulting firm Arthur Andersen. From the defendant's perspective also, then, there is an advantage to the certainty of a settlement – albeit at a high figure, but one far less than it might be following a contested trial. Settlements allow the company to get on with its business (albeit – usually – with compliance monitoring for two or three years).

In recent years the enforcement of the Act's accounting standards has become more important, especially when the DOJ might not be able to make out clear proof of criminal intent. With a books and records violation easier to establish, many FCPA investigations settle based wholly or largely on an admission of a breach of the accounting provisions.

Accounting violations

There does not have to be criminal intent to successfully prosecute a breach of the accounting provisions – the US prosecutors take the view that it is a strict liability offence. In other words, if an issuer does not have adequate controls, or if its books and records contain any false, incomplete or misleading entries, it can face civil penalties without having to demonstrate that it had any knowledge of the underlying bribes. Several recent examples highlight the trend:

- **Siemens:** The DOJ alleged that Siemens engaged in pattern of bribery 'unprecedented in scale and geographic reach' and that the 'corruption involved more than $1.4bn in bribes to government officials in Asia, Africa, Europe, the Middle East and the Americas'. The DOJ resolved the matter against Siemens without charging FCPA anti-bribery violations.[273]

- **BAE Systems plc:** The DOJ alleged that BAE 'provided substantial benefits', including through US payment mechanisms, to a highly influential Saudi public official. The DOJ resolved the matter against BAE without charging FCPA anti-bribery violations.[274]
- **Daimler AG:** The DOJ alleged that Daimler 'engaged in a long-standing practice of paying bribes' to foreign officials in at least 22 countries. The DOJ resolved the matter against Daimler without charging FCPA anti-bribery violations.[275]

UK judges point out the elephant in the room

In the UK, both the SFO and companies such as BAE Systems quickly realized that a civil confiscation order on the back of an admission of failing to keep proper books and records under Section 386 of the Companies Act 1989 (Section 221 of the Companies Act 1985) is a convenient way of settling bribery offences.

However, the UK courts are not impressed by charging bribery offences without mentioning 'bribery' at all. In the BAE case, Mr Justice Bean was very unhappy about allowing BAE to settle based on accounting transgressions only. He went into detail about the prosecution for incorrect accounting, asking why it was such a big deal unless corruption was involved:[276]

> 'If this wasn't money to be used for corrupt purposes, then why was 97 per cent of it paid through a British Virgin Islands company established by British Aerospace?'

Crucially, the judge also asked how the payments to the agent's companies should have appeared in BAE's accounts instead of 'technical services'. The SFO's barrister said that they should have been recorded instead as 'public relations and marketing services'. It was that simple offence that ostensibly made up the entirety of the case. The judge noted that there were no sentencing guidelines for accounting offences under the Companies Act, and questioned why the case had been brought at all if the payments had truly been for PR and marketing services and that the case hung on a simple mis-description in a set of accounts.

> 'Certainly the S.221 offence would have been suitable for being sentenced in the magistrates' court. I would myself have imposed a fine of at most £5000.'

The fact that a far larger penalty had been agreed led him to suspect that bribery was the elephant in the room – looming large, but never mentioned. In the event, he said he would not sentence on the basis of an accounting mis-description.

I expect UK settlements based on accounting irregularities to become much rarer. With the Bribery Act now properly in force, the majority of future actions will be brought under the new Act wherever possible, where a real bribery conviction and higher fine will be easier to secure.

Had it taken place under the Bribery Act 2010, a conviction for BAE would have looked more likely on the strict liability corporate offence under Section 7. (BAE would have had to try to satisfy the court that it had adequate procedures in place designed to prevent corruption. But if the SFO told the court that BAE had deliberately set up a structure involving a secret offshore corporate known only to the most senior executives in the company in order to pay large commissions to intermediaries to assist BAE to win business, without wishing to know how they did it, then my money would not be on the defence succeeding.)

Further reading

Questions 25–27.

International Prosecutors Will Work More Closely Together

International investigations are now the rule, rather than the exception. Although there used to be a degree of rivalry between prosecutors, there is now considerable cooperation that has arisen in conjunction with increased channels for mutual legal assistance. Working together not only makes prosecutions of international companies more likely, but also exposes companies to liability in other jurisdictions as prosecutions (and therefore settlements) increasingly become global and coordinated.

MLATs

For the purposes of investigating criminal cases, Mutual Legal Assistance in Criminal Matters Treaties (MLATs – usually pronounced 'em-lats') are agreements between countries that facilitate evidence and information-sharing in criminal investigations and proceedings. MLATs also allow criminal authorities to share requested information with regulatory agencies, such as the SEC or its foreign counterparts. They generally allow witnesses to be summoned, documents and other evidence to be produced, searches to be executed, and documents to be served.

MLATs can only be used between law enforcement authorities.

In addition to MLATs, authorities can obtain information through less formal, case-by-case arrangements between the regulatory bodies of different nations. The SEC often uses what are known as Memoranda of Understanding, which provide for the sharing of evidence and cooperation in compliance and enforcement cases.

International 'double jeopardy'

In many countries there is a long-standing legal principle that a defendant cannot be prosecuted twice for the same crime on the same set of facts, whether previously found guilty or innocent. This can also apply across international boundaries, meaning that in the UK a person or company cannot usually be tried for the same offence that they have just been found guilty of in the US.

In the BAE Systems case, for example, although the SFO's settlement with BAE is often described as a coordinated transatlantic deal, there had to be careful thought to avoid 'double jeopardy'. According to the SFO it was aiming to submit papers in mid-February to the Attorney General, requesting consent to prosecute for Eastern European bribery, when it was contacted by the DOJ just two weeks before this to indicate that a plea agreement was imminent in relation to Saudi Arabia and Eastern Europe. Because of double jeopardy, it is likely that the Eastern Europe aspect of the US agreement would have prevented prosecution in the UK for these offences.[277]

As such, there has to be some careful crafting of charges to prevent this. This is one reason why prosecutions for accounting offences sometimes take place in one jurisdiction, as this can give a sufficiently different factual matrix and charges of sufficiently dissimilar character to allow more than one country to take action over the same broad bribery scheme.

Article 4.3 of the OECD Anti-Bribery Convention requires parties to 'consult with a view to determining the most appropriate jurisdiction for prosecution'. With increased priority being given to enforcement of bribery offences, the questions of multi-jurisdictional enforcement and double jeopardy will increasingly come into play, and international prosecutions will have to become increasingly carried out according to these principles, and less by those of land-grabbing.

In October 2010, the US Court of Appeal in *US v. Jeong* held that the OECD Convention did not bar the US enforcement of the same bribery offence as other OECD countries. The case concerned a South Korean national who had been prosecuted by Korean authorities for bribery under Korea's equivalent of the FCPA, and whether the DOJ could also prosecute him in the US for bribery and wire fraud.[278]

Further reading

Crown Prosecution Service, International enquiries, obtaining evidence and information from abroad. Available from: http://bit.ly/vwCWxB (http://www.cps.gov.uk/legal/l_to_o/obtaining_evidence_and_information_from_abroad/index.html).

United Nations Model Treaty on Mutual Assistance in Criminal Matters: http://bit.ly/p0Jlgs (http://www.unodc.org/pdf/model_treaty_mutual_assistance_criminal_matters.pdf).

We Will Have Some Early Bribery Act Prosecutions

It is too early to predict how successfully the SFO will enforce the Bribery Act. But it is known that the SFO has a number of pending corporate bribery investigations that it will look to settle during 2012 to get a few early wins under its belt, and introduce the new Act as something to be taken seriously.

The old SFO investigation model was to start in the middle and seize all the documents in a blaze of publicity, then work out what to do. The SFO seem to have modified this slightly and borrowed some tricks from the DOJ. It now works far more smartly, and starts with the end in mind. And it is getting better at investigations.

One major question, though, is whether and how it will enforce the private sector bribery provisions. Another is how it will start to request disgorgement in bribery cases.

Real-Time Financial Analytics Will Flag and Delay Suspicious Transactions Before They are Processed

Can't we do the forensic accounting aspect of compliance reviews automatically? It's a question often asked of me by general counsels with budgetary constraints and overworked heads of internal audit. The real world – unfortunately – is not *quite* that straightforward. Not for reasons of lack of processing power or ability, but because most companies simply don't collect and collate data of sufficient quality to enable such a simple 'plug and play' solution.

Real-time data monitoring

However, some companies are starting to take a continuous approach to compliance reviews: rather than periodic reviews and sampling, they are trying to look at all of the data, all of the time. They use their IT systems and databases to highlight irregular high-risk transactions as they are processed to stop them being completed.

This has some significant positives:

- greater coverage of transactions and 100% testing
- ability to stop high-risk transactions pending further review and authorization
- lower review costs
- as employees and business partners get to know that the likelihood of them being able to hide something is diminished, illicit activity diminishes also.

Is it the magic bullet?

Continuous monitoring for bribery transactions can be a real benefit, but getting it right is not easy. The main problem is the quality and accessibility of good-quality data: systems need to capture the right information before testing can be done. Inaccessible data or insufficiently detailed information makes continuous monitoring almost impossible. Rather than 'garbage in, garbage out', it's more like 'nothing in, nothing meaningful out'.

Furthermore, these are not out-of-the box solutions. Each company's bribery risks and red flags are unique: therefore the solution requires lots of customization, and finding the right consultants with the right skills can be challenging.

Starting off slowly

The best way to incorporate continuous monitoring is to start slowly and use off-the-shelf software to monitor select high-risk areas, or run programs every night to pinpoint areas where more analysis is required. This can demonstrate that it works, is useful and can be expanded. A giant exercise to be implemented across the entire organization in one fell swoop is doomed to failure.

Your first steps need only be to implement a handful of properly deployed analytics:

- Define some simple yet key red flags that are most important to your anti-bribery compliance strategy. For example, you might want to know all orders and payments made to high-risk vendors, or all orders and payments made to government contractors.
- Identify the data you need to answer your questions, e.g. payment data, vendor lists, PEP list, OFAC list.
- Design queries/run analyses/email reports to the right people – then automate the process.
- Once this is working, build on the success.

Further reading

ACL, *Don't Get Bitten by the FCPA: Leveraging Audit Analytics for Compliance Testing*, 2010. Available from: http://bit.ly/oJCzlY (http://www.acl.com/pdfs/eBook_fcpa.pdf).

Follow-On Civil Claims Will Become More Prevalent

The FCPA does not create a private cause of action. This means that private individuals cannot commence proceedings against a company for damages based solely on an FCPA violation. Action can only be taken by the DOJ or SEC.

This does not mean, however, that other companies and individuals who feel they have suffered as a result of a company's bribery are left without a remedy – the last few years has seen an increase in shareholder derivative lawsuits and similar parallel civil litigation arising out of breaches of the FCPA. Indeed, settlement of bribery charges can create such uncertainty, cost and follow-on litigation, that rating agency Fitch has confirmed that violations of the FCPA can cause a downgrade of a company's credit rating.

There are several ways that third parties have used the FCPA as a springboard for follow-on litigation.

Shareholder loss actions

FCPA charges are often followed by shareholders contending that directors and officers breached their duty by taking part in behaviour that led the company to violate the FCPA, or by failing to prevent others from doing so.

A shareholders derivative lawsuit is now a frequent accompaniment to an FCPA enforcement proceedings. In the Willbros case, for example, the company's share price fell by 30% when an FCPA investigation was announced, which resulted in a $10.5m settlement of a securities-fraud lawsuit.[279] Similarly with Titan, not only was a proposed merger between Lockheed and Titan aborted in light of its FCPA investigation, but the company's market capitalization fell from $1.68bn to $934m, and the company was subsequently forced to pay $61.5m to settle related shareholder class actions.

Frequently shareholder claims will involve allegations of breach of fiduciary duty or fraud, but they are not easy to prove and many claims fall by the wayside. A shareholder action against Dow Chemical Co., for example, was dismissed because the court felt that while bribery might well have occurred, the claimants failed to prove that the board knew or had reason to suspect it. There is no respondeat superior rule in these actions and effective compliance programmes have provided a defence to shareholder loss claims. The court stated in the Dow case that 'plaintiffs cannot simultaneously argue that the Dow board "utterly failed" to meet its oversight duties yet had corporate governance procedures in place'.[280]

Directors should not, however, exaggerate the strength of their compliance procedures. Immucor agreed to pay $2.5m to settle claims that the company and certain directors and officers misled investors by downplaying the extent of the company's corrupt business practices, and overstated the strength of its internal controls. Even if disclosures are merely attached to an SEC filing or incorporated by reference, they may create liability to a company's shareholders.[281]

Actions by competitors

Companies that have lost business or bids to those who have allegedly offered bribes in order to secure business can take action to recover lost profits and costs that were wasted in the bidding process. Laws that have been used include:

- unfair competition laws
- antitrust actions
- Racketeer Influenced and Corrupt Organizations Act (RICO).

Bribery may give rise to a private cause of action under the RICO. (Under RICO, a person who is a member of an enterprise that has committed any two of 35 crimes within a 10-year period can be charged with racketeering. RICO permits a private individual harmed by the actions of such an enterprise to file a civil suit; if successful, the individual can collect triple damages.) Violation of the anti-bribery provisions of the FCPA is not a predicate act under RICO, although money laundering or violation of the Travel Act is.

Actions by foreign governments

In June 2008, the Iraqi government filed an action in the New York court against 91 companies and two individuals that allegedly paid kickbacks to the Saddam Hussein regime in connection with the UN Oil-for-Food Programme. The action alleges that the defendants committed fraud, breach of fiduciary duties and RICO violations, among other things. Several of the companies, including Chevron, Daimler, Akzo Nobel and Siemens, had already settled FCPA–related charges with the SEC and DOJ in connection with their involvement in the Oil-for-Food Programme. The complaint sought more than $10bn in damages and is ongoing.

A more recent development has been the emergence of civil litigation arising from alleged corrupt activities where no formal investigation preceded the lawsuit. For example, a state-owned company Aluminum Bahrain BSC filed a lawsuit against Alcoa, an Alcoa affiliate and two individuals, alleging that the defendants engaged in a 15-year bribery conspiracy involving a Bahraini government official. The company sought to recover damages based on alleged violations of fraud and RICO.[282]

Wrongful termination

In another recent trend, employees have alleged wrongful termination of employment for bringing bribery concerns to the attention of their managers, if whistleblowing has resulted in the employee being disadvantaged or dismissed.

The US courts have held that an employee allegedly dismissed because they either reported or refused to participate in conduct that includes predicate acts under RICO can bring a civil RICO suit if they can demonstrate their dismissal was part of a conspiracy to violate RICO.

Other actions

Also following on from the Oil-for-Food claims, a group of survivors and descendants of terrorist bombings in Israel have made claims against those companies alleged to have paid bribes to the Iraqi regime. The claims are on the basis that the companies knew, or should have realized, that the Iraqi regime was a supporter of Hamas and Palestinian terrorist organizations, and therefore some of the money paid in bribes was used to support terrorism. These claims are ongoing.

In the UK

Neither class actions nor derivative shareholder actions have historically existed in the UK; therefore, many of the above claims cannot get off the ground.

Parallel shareholder litigation was recently given a boost though by Part 11 (Sections 260–264) of the Companies Act 2006, which is now in force. This section now allows a UK shareholder to bring a derivative claim following an actual or proposed act or omission involving negligence, default, breach of duty or breach of trust by a director or former director. Although such an action will only succeed where the shareholders have obtained permission from the court and have established a prima facie case against the company, this is a significant development that may prompt UK shareholders to bring parallel litigation where corrupt activities are suspected.

Further reading

FCPA Professor, FCPA enforcement and credit ratings, 9 June 2010. Available from: http://bit.ly/qFfJoi (http://www.fcpaprofessor.com/fcpa-enforcement-and-credit-ratings).

Huggard, S.G. and Gardner, J.W., Another reason to fear the foreign corruption practices act – the private tag-along suit, *Bloomberg Law Reports*, 2009. Available from: http://bit.ly/nZLk4K (http://www.eapdlaw.com/files/News/06680be9-589a-4424-bc17-544143c2c103/Presentation/

NewsAttachment/c10a980a-47e5-404d-a68c-59413889e4a8/
another%20reason%20to%20fear%20the%20fcpa.pdf).

Tillen, J.G. and Torbett, L.H., Multiplying the risks: parallel civil litigation in FCPA investigations, *Bloomberg
Law Reports*, 2010. Available from: http://bit.ly/q79viC
(http://www.millerchevalier.com/portalresource/lookup/poid/
Z1tOl9NPl0LTYnMQZ56TfzcRVPMQiLsSwG3Em83!/
document.name=/miller_chevalier_tillen_torbett_article.pdf).

Chapter 9
Appendices

Appendix 1: The FCPA (extracts)
Anti-bribery provisions

TITLE 15 > CHAPTER 2B > § 78dd–2

Prohibited Foreign Trade Practices by Domestic Concerns

(a) Prohibition

It shall be unlawful for any domestic concern, other than an issuer which is subject to section 78dd–1 of this title, or for any officer, director, employee, or agent of such domestic concern or any stockholder thereof acting on behalf of such domestic concern, to make use of the mails or any means or instrumentality of interstate commerce corruptly in furtherance of an offer, payment, promise to pay, or authorization of the payment of any money, or offer, gift, promise to give, or authorization of the giving of anything of value to –

1. any foreign official for purposes of –
   A. i influencing any act or decision of such foreign official in his official capacity,
      ii inducing such foreign official to do or omit to do any act in violation of the lawful duty of such official, or
      iii securing any improper advantage; or
   B. inducing such foreign official to use his influence with a foreign government or instrumentality thereof to affect or influence any act or decision of such government or instrumentality,
      in order to assist such domestic concern in obtaining or retaining business for or with, or directing business to, any person;

2. any foreign political party or official thereof or any candidate for foreign political office for purposes of –
   - **A.** i influencing any act or decision of such party, official, or candidate in its or his official capacity,
     - ii inducing such party, official, or candidate to do or omit to do an act in violation of the lawful duty of such party, official, or candidate, or
     - iii securing any improper advantage; or
   - **B.** inducing such party, official, or candidate to use its or his influence with a foreign government or instrumentality thereof to affect or influence any act or decision of such government or instrumentality,

     in order to assist such domestic concern in obtaining or retaining business for or with, or directing business to, any person; or

3. any person, while knowing that all or a portion of such money or thing of value will be offered, given, or promised, directly or indirectly, to any foreign official, to any foreign political party or official thereof, or to any candidate for foreign political office, for purposes of –
   - **A.** i influencing any act or decision of such foreign official, political party, party official, or candidate in his or its official capacity,
     - ii inducing such foreign official, political party, party official, or candidate to do or omit to do any act in violation of the lawful duty of such foreign official, political party, party official, or candidate, or
     - iii securing any improper advantage; or
   - **B.** inducing such foreign official, political party, party official, or candidate to use his or its influence with a foreign government or instrumentality thereof to affect or influence any act or decision of such government or instrumentality, in order to assist such domestic concern in obtaining or retaining business for or with, or directing business to, any person.

(i) Alternative Jurisdiction

1. It shall also be unlawful for any United States person to corruptly do any act outside the United States in furtherance of an offer, payment, promise to pay, or authorization of the payment of any money, or offer, gift, promise to give, or authorization of the giving of anything of value to any of the persons or entities set forth in paragraphs (1), (2), and (3) of subsection (a), for the purposes set forth therein, irrespective of whether such United States person makes use of the mails or any means or instrumentality of interstate commerce in furtherance of such offer, gift, payment, promise, or authorization

2. As used in this subsection, a 'United States person' means a national of the United States (as defined in section 101 of the Immigration and Nationality Act (8 U.S.C. § 1101)) or any corporation, partnership, association, joint-stock company, business trust, unincorporated organization, or sole proprietorship organized under the laws of the United States or any State, territory, possession, or commonwealth of the United States, or any political subdivision thereof[.]

Accounting provisions

TITLE 15 > CHAPTER 2B > § 78m

Periodical and Other Reports

(b) Form of report; books, records, and internal accounting; directives

2. Every issuer which has a class of securities registered pursuant to section 78l of this title and every issuer which is

required to file reports pursuant to section 78o (d) of this title shall –

A. make and keep books, records, and accounts, which, in reasonable detail, accurately and fairly reflect the transactions and dispositions of the assets of the issuer;

B. devise and maintain a system of internal accounting controls sufficient to provide reasonable assurances that –

  i transactions are executed in accordance with management's general or specific authorization;

  ii transactions are recorded as necessary

(I) to permit preparation of financial statements in conformity with generally accepted accounting principles or any other criteria applicable to such statements, and

(II) to maintain accountability for assets[.]

Appendix 2: The Bribery Act (extracts)

Section 1. Offences of bribing another person

1. A person ('P') is guilty of an offence if either of the following cases applies.
2. Case 1 is where –
   a. P offers, promises or gives a financial or other advantage to another person, and
   b. P intends the advantage –
      i to induce a person to perform improperly a relevant function or activity,
      or
      ii to reward a person for the improper performance of such a function or activity.
3. Case 2 is where –
   a. P offers, promises or gives a financial or other advantage to another person, and
   b. P knows or believes that the acceptance of the advantage would itself constitute the improper performance of a relevant function or activity.
4. In case 1 it does not matter whether the person to whom the advantage is offered, promised or given is the same person as the person who is to perform, or has performed, the function or activity concerned.
5. In cases 1 and 2 it does not matter whether the advantage is offered, promised or given by P directly or through a third party.

Section 2. Offences relating to being bribed

1. A person ('R') is guilty of an offence if any of the following cases applies.

2. Case 3 is where R requests, agrees to receive or accepts a financial or other advantage intending that, in consequence, a relevant function or activity should be performed improperly (whether by R or another person).
3. Case 4 is where –
   a. R requests, agrees to receive or accepts a financial or other advantage, and
   b. the request, agreement or acceptance itself constitutes the improper performance by R of a relevant function or activity.
4. Case 5 is where R requests, agrees to receive or accepts a financial or other advantage as a reward for the improper performance (whether by R or another person) of a relevant function or activity.
5. Case 6 is where, in anticipation of or in consequence of R requesting, agreeing to receive or accepting a financial or other advantage, a relevant function or activity is performed improperly –
   a. by R, or
   b. by another person at R's request or with R's assent or acquiescence.

Section 7. Failure of commercial organisations to prevent bribery

1. A relevant commercial organisation ('C') is guilty of an offence under this section if a person ('A') associated with C bribes another person intending –
   a. to obtain or retain business for C, or
   b. to obtain or retain an advantage in the conduct of business for C.
2. But it is a defence for C to prove that C had in place adequate procedures designed to prevent persons associated with C from undertaking such conduct.

3. For the purposes of this section, A bribes another person if, and only if, A –
   a. is, or would be, guilty of an offence under section 1 or 6 (whether or not A has been prosecuted for such an offence), or
   b. would be guilty of such an offence if section 12(2)(c) and (4) were omitted.

Section 14. Offences under sections 1, 2 and 6 by bodies corporate etc.

1. This section applies if an offence under section 1, 2 or 6 is committed by a body corporate or a Scottish partnership.
2. If the offence is proved to have been committed with the consent or connivance of –
   a. a senior officer of the body corporate or Scottish partnership, or
   b. a person purporting to act in such a capacity, the senior officer or person (as well as the body corporate or partnership) is guilty of the offence and liable to be proceeded against and punished accordingly.
3. But subsection (2) does not apply, in the case of an offence which is committed under section 1, 2 or 6 by virtue of section 12(2) to (4), to a senior officer or person purporting to act in such a capacity unless the senior officer or person has a close connection with the United Kingdom (within the meaning given by section 12(4)).
4. In this section –
   'director', in relation to a body corporate whose affairs are managed by its members, means a member of the body corporate,
   'senior officer' means –

a. in relation to a body corporate, a director, manager, secretary or other similar officer of the body corporate, and
b. in relation to a Scottish partnership, a partner in the partnership.

Appendix 3: Section 386 of the Companies Act 1989: Accounting Provisions (extract)

The wording of the relevant section – Section 386 – is substantially the same in the both the 1985 Act and the 2006 Act.

Section 386 – Duty to keep accounting records

1. Every company must keep adequate accounting records.
2. Adequate accounting records means records that are sufficient –
   a. to show and explain the company's transactions,
   b. to disclose with reasonable accuracy, at any time, the financial position of the company at that time, and
   c. to enable the directors to ensure that any accounts required to be prepared comply with the requirements of this Act (and, where applicable, of Article 4 of the IAS Regulation).
3. Accounting records must, in particular, contain –
   a. entries from day to day of all sums of money received and expended by the company and the matters in respect of which the receipt and expenditure takes place, and
   b. a record of the assets and liabilities of the company.
4. If the company's business involves dealing in goods, the accounting records must contain –
   a. statements of stock held by the company at the end of each financial year of the company,
   b. all statements of stocktakings from which any statement of stock as is mentioned in paragraph (a) has been or is to be prepared, and
   c. except in the case of goods sold by way of ordinary retail trade, statements of all goods sold and purchased, showing

the goods and the buyers and sellers in sufficient detail to enable all these to be identified.

5. A parent company that has a subsidiary undertaking in relation to which the above requirements do not apply must take reasonable steps to secure that the undertaking keeps such accounting records as to enable the directors of the parent company to ensure that any accounts required to be prepared under this Part comply with the requirements of this Act (and, where applicable, of Article 4 of the IAS Regulation).

Appendix 4: The OECD (extracts)

Article 1. The Offence of Bribery of Foreign Public Officials

1. Each Party shall take such measures as may be necessary to establish that it is a criminal offence under its law for any person intentionally to offer, promise or give any undue pecuniary or other advantage, whether directly or through intermediaries, to a foreign public official, for that official or for a third party, in order that the official act or refrain from acting in relation to the performance of official duties, in order to obtain or retain business or other improper advantage in the conduct of international business.
2. Each Party shall take any measures necessary to establish that complicity in, including incitement, aiding and abetting, or authorisation of an act of bribery of a foreign public official shall be a criminal offence. Attempt and conspiracy to bribe a foreign public official shall be criminal offences to the same extent as attempt and conspiracy to bribe a public official of that Party.

Article 8 of the OECD Convention – 'accounting'

1. In order to combat bribery of foreign public officials effectively, each Party shall take such measures as may be necessary, within the framework of its laws and regulations regarding the maintenance of books and records, financial statement disclosures, and accounting and auditing standards, to prohibit the establishment of off-the-books accounts, the making of off-the-books or inadequately identified transactions, the

recording of non-existent expenditures, the entry of liabilities with incorrect identification of their object, as well as the use of false documents, by companies subject to those laws and regulations, for the purpose of bribing foreign public officials or of hiding such bribery.

Appendix 5: Which Countries have Ratified the OECD?

Country	Deposit of instrument of ratification/ acceptance	Entry into force of the Convention	Entry into force of implementing legislation
Argentina	08 Feb 01	09 Apr 01	10 Nov 99
Australia	18 Oct 99	17 Dec 99	17 Dec 99
Austria	20 May 99	19 Jul 99	01 Oct 98
Belgium	27 Jul 99	25 Sep 99	03 Apr 99
Brazil	24 Aug 00	23 Oct 00	11 Jun 02
Bulgaria	22 Dec 98	20 Feb 99	29 Jan 99
Canada	17 Dec 98	15 Feb 99	14 Feb 99
Chile	18 Apr 01	17 Jun 01	08 Oct 02
Czech Republic	21 Jan 00	21 Mar 00	09 Jun 99
Denmark	05 Sep 00	04 Nov 00	01 May 00
Estonia	23 Nov 04	22 Jan 05	01 Jul 04
Finland	10 Dec 98	15 Feb 99	01 Jan 99
France	31 Jul 00	29 Sep 00	29 Sep 00
Germany	10 Nov 98	15 Feb 99	15 Feb 99
Greece	05 Feb 99	06 Apr 99	01 Dec 98
Hungary	04 Dec 98	15 Feb 99	01 Mar 99
Iceland	17 Aug 98	15 Feb 99	30 Dec 98
Ireland	22 Sep 03	21 Nov 03	26 Nov 01
Israel	11 Mar 09	10 May 09	21 Jul 08
Italy	15 Dec 00	13 Feb 01	26 Oct 00
Japan	13 Oct 98	15 Feb 99	15 Feb 99
Luxembourg	21 Mar 01	20 May 01	11 Feb 01
Mexico	27 May 99	26 Jul 99	18 May 99
Netherlands	12 Jan 01	13 Mar 01	01 Feb 01
New Zealand	25 Jun 01	24 Aug 01	03 May 01
Norway	18 Dec 98	16 Feb 99	01 Jan 99
Poland	08 Sep 00	07 Nov 00	04 Feb 01

Country	Deposit of instrument of ratification/ acceptance	Entry into force of the Convention	Entry into force of implementing legislation
Portugal	23 Nov 00	22 Jan 01	09 Jun 01
Slovak Republic	24 Sep 99	23 Nov 99	01 Nov 99
Slovenia	06 Sep 01	05 Nov 01	23 Jan 99
South Africa	19 Jun 07	18 Aug 07	27 Apr 04
South Korea	04 Jan 99	05 Mar 99	15 Feb 99
Spain	04 Jan 00	04 Mar 00	02 Feb 00
Sweden	08 Jun 99	07 Aug 99	01 Jul 99
Switzerland	31 May 00	30 Jul 00	01 May 00
Turkey	26 Jul 00	24 Sep 00	11 Jan 03
United Kingdom	14 Dec 98	15 Feb 99	14 Feb 02
United States	08 Dec 98	15 Feb 99	10 Nov 98

Appendix 6: DOJ Opinion Procedure Releases

Release no.	Issue	Approved declined
80-01	**Charitable contributions:** US law firm donated $10,000 per year to pay for schooling of adopted children of elderly and honorary public official.	Approved.
80-02	**Employee in public office:** Employee of subsidiary asks to run for public office as part-time legislator in foreign country while maintaining outside employment.	Approved. Salary must be time-based.
80-03	**FCPA clauses:** US firm requested a review of its engagement contract with a lawyer in west Africa. The contract contained an FCPA clause.	FCPA clause is not enough to insulate company from liability. Due diligence and precautionary steps also required.

Release no.	Issue	Approved declined
80-04	**Foreign official on board of foreign partner:** Lockheed solicits approval to enter into a joint venture with a Saudi company for potential business with the Saudi government and Saudi Airlines. The chairman of the joint venture partner is a non-executive director of Saudi Airlines, but has no other government position and will refrain from voting on all Lockheed-related matters.	Approved.
81-01	**Reimbursement of expenses to business partner:** Bechtel requests approval for its contract with Philippine consultants. Contract allows reimbursement of entertaining, meals, gifts and travel expense consistent with local laws.	Approved. No reimbursement in cash or to third parties.

Release no.	Issue	Approved declined
81-02	**Promotional material to foreign officials:** Iowa Beef Packers wanted to send ten $250 sample products to officials of Soviet Ministry of Foreign Trade. Packages were provided to officials in their capacity as representatives of government agency, not for their own use, and the government is informed.	Approved.
82-01	**Conference and travel expenses:** The Missouri Department of Agriculture wanted to host ten delegates from the Mexican government and private sector to promote agricultural business in Missouri. Missouri pays for travel, meals, lodging and entertainment; private companies will supply samples and host dinners.	Approved.
82-02	**Finder's fee to foreign official:** Shoup & Co. had a contract with the Nigerian Electoral Commission and proposed to pay a 1% finder's fee to a Nigerian national, who is also employed by consulate in US performing clerical duties.	Approved. Fees paid in US and disclosed to Electoral Commission.

Release no.	Issue	Approved declined
82-03	**Travel and entertainment expenses:** Delaware Corporation wishes to sell equipment to Yugoslavia's military; in return it pays a percentage of the contract value to government-controlled trade, as required by Yugoslavian law.	Approved.
82-04	**Hiring foreign representative related to employee of foreign government:** Thompson & Green intends to pay a foreign executive used as an agent for the sale of a generator to a foreign country; the agent's brother is an employee of a foreign government.	Approved.
83-01	**Foreign agent appointed by president of Sudan:** A California firm seeks to do business with a Sudanese corporation that develops communications networks. The Sudanese corporation is member of group representing several countries, acting as an agent for the US firm in deals with those countries.	Approved, as no Sudanese official will benefit from the proposed relationship.

Release no.	Issue	Approved declined
83-02	**Travel and entertainment expenses:** A US firm has a joint enterprise with two foreign companies and has a long-term relationship with government-controlled foreign entity. The US firm wants an executive from the government-controlled entity to tour US facilities, with extra expenses to be paid by the US firm.	Approved.
83-03	**Travel and entertainment expenses:** The Missouri Department of Agriculture and CAPCO, Inc. want to pay reasonable expenses for Singapore government official to tour Missouri sites. CAPCO does not do business with Singapore; individual officers of the company may enter into supply, services or sales contracts with that government in future.	Approved.
84-01	**Hiring foreign representative related to head of state:** A US firm wants to hire a foreign marketing agent in a foreign country where principals of the agent are related to the head of state. The agent's principals personally manage a certain of head of state's private business affairs and investments.	Approved.

Release no.	Issue	Approved declined
84-02	**Small payment for regulatory approval:** A US firm wants to transfer assets of a foreign branch office to a foreign-owned firm, then invest in the new foreign company. The proposal requires foreign regulatory approval, and an agent of the foreign company requested to pay a small gratuity to a low-level foreign government employee to facilitate the transaction.	Approved. US firm retains the rights but is not obligated to sever its relationship with foreign company.
85-01	**Travel expenses for US site visit:** ARCO constructs a plant in France and wants to pay expenses for French officials to travel to the US to inspect similar plants in order to address their management and environmental concerns.	Approved.
85-03	**Hiring foreign agent:** A US firm wants to hire a foreign agent to help identify a proper agency and officials in a foreign country with whom the US company can negotiate a settlement of claim against the foreign country.	Approved.

Release no.	Issue	Approved declined
86-01	**Hiring foreign legislators as representatives:** US corporations want to hire members of the UK and Malaysian parliaments to represent the companies in business operations in their respective countries.	Approved.
87-01	**Commission/finder's fee:** Lantana wants to sell military patrol boats to Milverton, which resells the boats to the Nigerian government. Lantana will be paid in full before Milverton independently negotiates with the Nigerian government.	Approved. Commission would not be used to violate FCPA.
88-01	**Participation fees:** Mor-Flo intends to acquire property in Mexico to build a plant and participate in debt equity swaps with Mexican government to finance the project. The company pays non-refundable participation fees to a Mexican government agency and a US financial institution chosen by Mexico as the agent for the transaction.	Approved.

Release no.	Issue	Approved declined
92-01	**Training and travel expenses:** An oil firm wants to enter a joint venture with a ministry in Pakistan. Pakistani law requires companies to provide training to government personnel in technical and management disciplines related to the industry.	Approved.
93-01	**Salaries paid to foreign directors of foreign government-owned joint venture partner:** A US firm entered a joint venture to supply management services to a quasi-commercial entity wholly owned by the government of a former Eastern bloc country. Foreign directors will be paid $1000 per month to approximate their salaries from the foreign partner.	Approved.
93-02	**Commission to government-owned business:** A US firm seeks to enter a sales agreement with a foreign government-owned business to supply equipment to the country's military. The country's laws require military deals only through government-owned enterprise, and the supplier must be paid a percentage of all total contracts.	Approved. US firm will make no payments to the government-owned enterprise or to any foreign officials.

Release no.	Issue	Approved declined
94-01	**Consulting agreement:** A US firm entered into a consulting agreement with a foreign national. The consultant will be paid $20,000 over one year for assistance in obtaining consents, governmental approvals for accessing rights and submitting application to a local power authority to connect to the power grid.	Approved.
95-01	**Charitable donation:** A US energy firm plans to acquire and operate in south Asia, where there is no modern medical facility. If acquisition is completed, the firm plans to donate $10m through a US charity to a public LLC in the foreign country. A medical facility will be open to the public, including US company employees.	Approved. US energy firm requires audited financial reports from US charity, accurately detailing the disposition of the donated funds.
95-02	**Payments for services and offset credits:** Company A has offset obligations from contract with a foreign government. Offset agreements are negotiated with Offset Office. Company B is to receive millions of dollars for establishing a new company, majority-owned by foreigners, to generate and sell offsets. A will pay B for offsets.	Approved.

Release no.	Issue	Approved declined
96-01	**Training courses and travel expenses:** A non-profit firm offers to sponsor and provide funding for foreign government delegates to attend training courses regarding the dangers of environmental accidents in their region. The firm will pay $10–15,000 per year for travel, lodging and expenses to attend training.	Approved. All other expenses, including meals other than lunch, taxis, phone calls, etc., not covered by non-profit entity.
96-02	**Commission to government-owned broker:** A US defence firm wants to renew a marketing agreement with a foreign state-owned enterprise, which will serve as exclusive sales rep and be paid commission for sales.	Approved.
97-01	**Commission to representative in connection with sales to government-owned entity:** A US firm enters into a representative agreement with a privately owned company in a foreign country in connection with a bid to a foreign government-owned entity to sell and service high-tech equipment.	Approved. DOJ advised US firm to closely monitor performance of the representative under the agreement.
97-02	**Charitable donation:** A US utility firm in Asia, where primary level education is lacking, wants to donate $100,000 directly to a government entity responsible for the construction of a new school.	Approved. Provisions of FCPA do not appear to apply to this transaction.

Release no.	Issue	Approved declined
98-01	**Payment to foreign officials as part of required environmental cleanup:** A US industrial firm held liable by Nigeria for environmental cleanup and wants to hire a Nigerian cleanup contractor to resolve liability. The contractor was recommended by a Nigerian agency and $30,000 of $170,000 cleanup costs would be paid to Nigerian officials.	Declined. DOJ reconsider taking enforcement action with respect to the proposed transaction.
98-02	**Fees to representative in connection with sales to government-owned entity and settlement to terminate unlawful agreement:** A US firm submitted a bid to a foreign government-owned entity to sell and service a military training programme. The US firm enters into consulting agreements with a privately held representative in the foreign country.	Approved.

Release no.	Issue	Approved declined
00-01	**Severance payment to partner appointed to foreign government post:** A foreign partner of a US law firm is appointed to high-ranking position in a foreign government. The foreign partner will take leave of absence, but the firm proposes paying insurance while in office and paying a lump sum for client business, along with guarantee of return to the partnership when he leaves public office.	Approved.
01-01	**Acquisition of pre-FCPA contracts involving foreign officials:** A US firm seeks to enter a joint venture with a French company that contribute contracts procured before enactment of French bribery law. Contracts do not appear to violate any French laws.	Approved, but DOJ reserved the right to prosecute FCPA violations. Wanted to see an ability to get out of joint venture if there are violations.

Release no.	Issue	Approved declined
01-02	**Foreign official partner in joint venture:** US and foreign firms to form consortium to bid for business with a foreign government. The chairman and shareholder of the foreign company acts as advisor to foreign officials and is a senior public education official.	Approved.
01-03	**Continuing business with foreign dealer after investigation did not substantiate FCPA concerns:** A US firm (with assistance from a foreign dealer) submits a bid for sale of equipment to a foreign government. US employee heard that the dealer may have bribed foreign officials to approve the bid. A subsequent investigation resulted in no evidence.	Approved.
03-01	**Due diligence uncovers bribes:** A US issuer intends to purchase stock of US company A, which has foreign subsidiary. Due diligence discloses that officers of the foreign subsidiary paid bribes. The issuer and company A discloses to DOJ and SEC.	Approved in respect of payments made after the date of acquisition. Approval does not apply to individuals involved in making or authorizing the payments.

Release no.	Issue	Approved declined
04-01	**Conference and travel expenses:** A US law firm proposes to sponsor a comparative law seminar with a Chinese ministry, paying expenses for Chinese officials to travel to Beijing.	Approved.
04-02	**Due diligence for acquisition post-guilty plea:** US investors acquiring ABB upstream petro-chemical business. ABB previously pleaded guilty to FCPA violations.	Approved.
04-03	**Conference and travel expenses:** A US law firm proposes to sponsor a trip to the US for Chinese ministry officials to meet with US public sector officials and discuss US labour law.	Approved.
04-04	**Conference and travel expenses:** A US firm proposes to fund a 'study tour' by foreign officials who are members of a committee drafting a new law on mutual insurance.	Approved.
06-01	**Contribution for foreign anti-counterfeiting enforcement initiative:** A US firm seeks to contribute $25,000 to the Customs Department of a Finance Ministry in an African nation as part of pilot project to improve local enforcement of anti-counterfeiting laws. The money will be used to fund incentive awards to local customs officials to improve enforcement.	Approved.

Release no.	Issue	Approved declined
06-02	**Hiring foreign law firm to assist in applications before foreign agency:** A US issuer's subsidiary in foreign country seeks to retain a foreign law firm to assist in preparing foreign exchange applications and represent the company before a foreign government agency. The firm will pay 'substantial', though reasonable, commission at a flat rate.	Approved.
07-01	**Conference and travel expenses to promote business:** A US issuer proposes to pay expenses for a six-person delegation from an Asian country for a promotional tour of the US issuer's facilities, designed to bolster the issuer's 'business credibility'. The US issuer wants to establish business in the foreign country.	Approved.
07-02	**Conference and travel expenses to promote business:** A US insurance firm wants to pay expenses for six junior- to mid-level foreign officials for an educational/internship programme at the US company's headquarters.	Approved.

Release no.	Issue	Approved declined
07-03	**Expense for foreign court-appointed administrator:** A US resident involved in foreign court estate proceedings was directed by a foreign court to prepay the expenses of a court-appointed administrator. The requestor obtained a legal opinion that payment is lawful under the foreign country's written laws, and the payment will be made to the court clerk's office, not to the individual presiding judge.	Approved.
08-01	**Due diligence and paying premium for acquisition of foreign government-owned interests:** A US firm bid for a majority investment in a foreign government-owned company, which reflected a significant premium to acquire the majority stake. The US firm conducted extensive due diligence and required public disclosures to foreign government.	Approved. Reasonable due diligence required on seller of shares. FCPA risks and compliance with local laws and regulations, and will maintain documentation in US.

Release no.	Issue	Approved declined
08-02	**Due diligence and amnesty for pre- and post-acquisition FCPA violations:** The DOJ approves a framework for a US acquirer to seek amnesty for a target's FCPA violations where, as a result of foreign law restrictions on pre-acquisition due diligence, the acquiring company is unable to complete due diligence review until after acquisition is completed.	Approved.
08-03	**Paying promotional expenses to journalists in China:** TRACE International Group, specializing in anti-bribery training, compliance and due diligence, seeks approval to pay expenses for journalists employed by state-owned media outlets to attend a press conference to promote anti-corruption and a new anti-corruption initiative. The DOJ approves reasonable payments under promotional expenses affirmative defence.	Approved. With respect to the planned provision of stipends and payment of transportation and lodging costs described in this request.

Release no.	Issue	Approved declined
09-01	**Charitable donation to foreign government:** A medical device maker wants to introduce a product to a foreign government by donating samples to government health centres. The government will conduct a technical evaluation to earn a government endorsement to sell products eligible to participate in a government-subsidized medical device programme.	Approved.
10-01	**Hiring qualified foreign official as required by contract:** A US firm's contract with a foreign government agency to perform work in the foreign nation requires the US firm to hire and compensate certain foreign individuals. A US government agency is involved in the contract and directed the US firm to hire the individual. The individual will be paid $5000 per month for one year.	Approved.

Release no.	Issue	Approved declined
10-02	**Microfinance institution making grant as directed by foreign government:** A US non-profit institution has a subsidiary in a Eurasian country and wishes to transform into a more bank-like institution. The Eurasian country's government requires the subsidiary to make a grant of 33% of its capital to a local microfinance association. The Eurasian subsidiary conducted extensive due diligence and identified one local MFI that the due diligence did not identify information of potential corruption. The DOJ stated it appeared unlikely the payment will result in the corrupt giving of anything of value to foreign officials.	Approved.
10-03	**Retention of consultant who represents foreign government in other matters:** A US company plans to hire a consultant and the owner of a consultant with extensive contacts in the business community and government in a foreign nation to do business. The consultant is a registered agent of the foreign government pursuant to the Foreign Agents Registration Act. The consultant will be paid a signing bonus upon signing a contract and receive success fees if a contract is negotiated.	Approved. Opinion is limited to the question of whether the consultant would be a 'foreign official'. The DOJ states the consultant and owner would not qualify as foreign officials.

Release no.	Issue	Approved declined
11-01	**Travel costs for foreign officials:** A US company wants to pay for foreign governmental officials to visit its US operation. The foreign government selected the officials. The trip is for two days in economy class and involves no spouses. The US company will pay all the vendors, airlines, hotels, local transportation and food directly. There will be no per diems.	Approved. (Not a terribly challenging one, this.)

Further reading

Question 19.

DOJ, Review Procedure Releases 1980–1992. Available from: http://1.usa.gov/o0qaAE (http://www.justice.gov/criminal/fraud/fcpa/review/).

DOJ, Opinion Procedure Releases, 1993 to date. Available from: http://1.usa.gov/pbcphZ (http://www.justice.gov/criminal/fraud/fcpa/opinion/).

Appendix 7: Johnson & Johnson: Enhanced Compliance Undertakings

In addition to and building upon the commitments enumerated in Attachment C, Johnson & Johnson and its subsidiaries and operating companies (collectively, 'J&J') agree that they have or will undertake the following, at a minimum, for the duration of this Agreement:

General

1. J&J will:
   a. Appoint a senior corporate executive with significant experience with compliance with the FCPA, including its anti-bribery, books and records, and internal controls provisions, as well as other applicable anticorruption laws and regulations (hereinafter 'anticorruption laws and regulations') to serve as Chief Compliance Officer. The Chief Compliance Officer will have reporting obligations directly to the Audit Committee of the Board of Directors.
   b. Appoint heads of compliance within each business sector and corporate function. These compliance heads will have reporting obligations to the Chief Compliance Officer and the Audit Committee.
   c. Maintain a global compliance leadership team, including regional compliance leaders and business segment compliance leaders, with responsibility for overseeing its company-wide compliance program. That leadership team will have reporting obligations directly to the Chief Compliance Officer.
2. J&J shall institute gifts, hospitality, and travel policies and procedures in each jurisdiction that are appropriately designed to prevent violations of the anticorruption laws and regulations. At a minimum, these policies shall contain the following

restrictions regarding government officials, including but not limited to public health care providers, administrators, and regulators:

a. Gifts must be modest in value, appropriate under the circumstances, and given in accordance with anticorruption laws and regulations, including those of the government official's home country;

b. Hospitality shall be limited to reasonably priced meals, accommodations, and incidental expenses that are part of product education and training programs, professional training, and conferences or business meetings;

c. Travel shall be limited to product education and training programs, professional training, and conferences or business meetings; and

d. Gifts, hospitality, and travel shall not include expenses for anyone other than the official.

Complaints, Reports, and Compliance Issues

3. J&J shall maintain its mechanisms for making and handling reports and complaints related to potential violations of anticorruption laws and regulations, including referral for review and response to a standing committee that includes internal audit, legal, and compliance personnel, and will ensure that reasonable access is provided to an anonymous, toll-free hotline as well as to an anonymous electronic complaint form, where anonymous reporting is legally permissible.

4. J&J will ensure that its Sensitive Issue Triage Committee reviews and responds to FCPA and corruption issues promptly and consistently; this Triage Committee will include members from J&J's internal audit, legal, and compliance functions.

Risk Assessments and Audits

5. J&J will conduct risk assessments of markets where J&J has government customers and/or other anticorruption compliance

risks on a staggered, periodic basis. Such risk assessments shall occur at reasonable intervals and include a review of trends in interactions with government officials, including health care providers, to identify new risk areas. On the basis of those assessments, as needed, J&J will modify compliance implementation to minimize risks observed through the risk assessment process.

6. J&J will conduct periodic audits specific to the detection of violations of anticorruption laws and regulations ('FCPA Audits'). Specifically, J&J will identify no less than five operating companies that are high risk for corruption because of their sector and location 2 and will conduct FCPA Audits of those operating companies at least once every three years. High risk operating companies shall be identified based on J&J's risk assessment process in consultation with the Chief Compliance Officer, sector compliance leaders, corporate internal audit, and the Law Department, taking into account multiple risk factors including, but not limited to: a high degree of interaction with government officials; the existence of internal reports of potential corruption risk; a high corruption risk based on certain corruption indexes; and financial audit results. The list of high risk operating companies shall be reviewed annually and updated as necessary. FCPA Audits of other operating companies that pose corruption risk shall occur no less than once every five years.

   Each FCPA Audit shall include:

   a. On-site visits by an audit team comprised of qualified auditors who have received FCPA and anticorruption training;
   b. Where appropriate, participation in the on-site visits by personnel from the compliance and legal functions;
   c. Review of a statistically representative sample appropriately adjusted for the risks of the market, of contracts with and payments to individual health care providers;
   d. Creation of action plans resulting from issues identified during audits; these action plans will be shared with

appropriate senior management, including the Chief Compliance Officer, and will contain mandatory undertakings designed to enhance anticorruption compliance, repair process weaknesses, and deter violations; and

e. Where appropriate, feasible, and permissible under local law, review of the books and records of distributors which, in the view of the audit team, may present corruption risk.

Acquisitions

7. J&J will ensure that new business entities are only acquired after thorough FCPA and anticorruption due diligence by legal, accounting, and compliance personnel. Where such anticorruption due diligence is not practicable prior to acquisition of a new business for reasons beyond J&J's control, or due to any applicable law, rule, or regulation, J&J will conduct FCPA and anticorruption due diligence subsequent to the acquisition and report to the Department any corrupt payments, falsified books and records, or inadequate internal controls as required by Paragraph 11 of the Deferred Prosecution Agreement.

8. J&J will ensure that J&J's policies and procedures regarding the anticorruption laws and regulations apply as quickly as is practicable, but in any event no less than one year post-closing, to newly-acquired businesses, and will promptly:

a. Train directors, officers, employees, agents, consultants, representatives, distributors, joint venture partners, and relevant employees thereof, who present corruption risk to J&J, on the anticorruption laws and regulations and J&J's related policies and procedures; and

b. Conduct an FCPA-specific audit of all newly-acquired businesses within 18 months of acquisition.

Relationships with Third Parties

9. J&J will conduct due diligence reviews of sales intermediaries, including agents, consultants, representatives, distributors, and

joint venture partners. At a minimum, such due diligence shall include:

   a. A review of the qualifications and business reputation of the sales intermediaries;

   b. A rationale for the use of the sales intermediary; and

   c. A review of FCPA risk areas.

10. Such due diligence will be conducted by local businesses and reviewed by local healthcare compliance officers. New intermediaries that have not worked for the company prior to the date of this agreement, or where due diligence raises any red flags, shall be reviewed by a regional compliance officer with specific knowledge of and responsibility for anticorruption due diligence of sales intermediaries. Due diligence will be conducted prior to retention of any new agent, consultant, representative, distributor, or joint venture partner and for all such intermediaries will be updated no less than once every three years.

11. Where necessary and appropriate and where permitted by applicable law, J&J shall include standard provisions designed to prevent violations of the FCPA and other applicable anticorruption laws and regulations in agreements, contracts, grants, and renewals thereof with agents, distributors, and business partners, including:

   a. Anticorruption representations and undertakings relating to compliance with the anticorruption laws and regulations;

   b. Rights to conduct audits of the books and records of the agent, distributor, or business partner that are related to their business with J&J; and

   c. Rights to terminate the agent, distributor, or business partner as a result of any breach of anticorruption laws and regulations or representations and undertakings related to such anticorruption laws and regulations.

Training

12. J&J shall provide:
    a. Annual training on anticorruption laws and regulations to directors, officers, executives, and employees who could present corruption risk to J&J.
    b. Enhanced and in-depth FCPA training for all internal audit, financial, and legal personnel involved in FCPA audits, due diligence reviews, and acquisition of new businesses.
    c. Training as necessary based on risk profiles to relevant third parties acting on the company's behalf that may interact with government officials at least once every three years.
13. J&J shall implement a system of annual certifications from senior managers in each of J&J's corporate-level functions, divisions, and business units in each foreign country confirming that their local standard operating procedures adequately implement J&J's anticorruption policies and procedures, including training requirements, and that they are not aware of any FCPA or other corruption issues that have not already been reported to corporate compliance.

Further reading

'How Do I Set Up Proportionate Yet Effective Anti-bribery Compliance Procedures?', page 343.

Johnson & Johnson's fill DPA can be found at http://scr.bi/t216xQ http://www.scribd.com/doc/52727873/Johnson-Johnson-Deferred-Prosecution-Agreement).

References

1. http://1.usa.gov/pTogEG (http://www.justice.gov/criminal/fraud/fcpa/history/1977/senaterpt-95-114.pdf).
2. http://bit.ly/subxNF (https://www.traceinternational2.org/compendium/view.asp?id=33).
3. http://bit.ly/oyq0zu (http://www.public-standards.org.uk).
4. http://1.usa.gov/nL4exv (http://www.justice.gov/criminal/fraud/fcpa/docs/antibribe.pdf).
5. The first international convention to address the question of corruption: http://bit.ly/r3Ad6h (http://www.oas.org).
6. The European Union Convention on the Fight against Corruption involving Officials of the European Communities or Officials of Member States of the EU: http://bit.ly/osHeDR (http://europa.eu/legislation_summaries/fight_against_fraud/fight_against_corruption/l33027_en.htm).
7. Council of Europe Criminal Law Convention on Corruption: http://bit.ly/oyelj8 (http://conventions.coe.int/Treaty/EN/Treaties/Html/173.htm). Council of Europe Civil Law Convention on Corruption: http://bit.ly/ri3EcS (http://conventions.coe.int/treaty/en/treaties/html/174.htm).
8. http://bit.ly/mR2fnz (http://www.oecd.org/document/35/0,3746,en_34982156_35315367_35029667_1_1_1_1,00.html).
9. http://bit.ly/nPjfQx (http://europa.eu/legislation_summaries/fight_against_fraud/fight_against_corruption/l33308_en.htm).
10. http://bit.ly/ofcMB8 (http://www.africa-union.org/official_documents/Treaties_%20Conventions_%20Protocols/Convention%20on%20Combating%20Corruption.pdf).

11. http://bit.ly/nlhqtl (http://www.unodc.org/unodc/en/treaties/CAC/index.html).
12. http://bit.ly/qmccDE (http://www.g20.org/Documents 2010/11/seoulsummit_declaration.pdf).
13. http://bit.ly/rroKIT (http://www.legislation.gov.uk/ukpga/2001/24/contents).
14. http://bit.ly/p7mIwk (http://www.public-standards.org.uk/Library/OurWork/1stInquiry_Summary.pdf).
15. http://bit.ly/p0tStt (http://www.archive.official-documents.co.uk/document/cm47/4759/4759-00.htm).
16. http://bit.ly/oRlF1k (http://www.oecd.org/dataoecd/62/32/34599062.pdf).
17. http://bit.ly/qOcHdb (http://www.oecd.org/dataoecd/23/20/41515077.pdf).
18. http://bit.ly/vKQ8M9 (https://www.traceinternational2.org/compendium/view.asp?id=93).
19. See page 00.
20. http://bit.ly/n74Im6 (http://www.official-documents.gov.uk/document/cm75/7570/7570.pdf).
21. http://bbc.in/vhkuso (http://www.bbc.co.uk/news/uk-england-london-15310150).
22. Johnston, M. and Hao, Y., China's surge of corruption, *Journal of Democracy*, **6**(4) 80–94, 1995. Available from: http://bit.ly/pxS42s (http://www.unc.edu/~wangc/Michael%20Johnston%20and%20Yufan%20Hao%20-%20China's%20Surge%20of%20Corruption%20-%20Journal%20of%20Democracy%2064.htm).
23. http://bit.ly/nMDHkT (http://www.prsgroup.com/ICRG.aspx).
24. http://bit.ly/pCbVm5 (http://www.transparency.org/publications/publications/conventions/oecd_report_2011).
25. http://on.wsj.com/osG8Qp (http://online.wsj.com/public/resources/documents/111709breuerremarks.pdf).
26. http://1.usa.gov/plvHvh (http://www.sec.gov/news/press/2010/2010-214.htm).

27. http://bit.ly/qZWoBc (https://www.traceinternational2
.org/compendium/view.asp?id=202).
28. http://bit.ly/nFFpsI (https://sites.google.com/
a/olympismproject.org/olympism-project/).
29. http://bbc.in/psBpxX (http://news.bbc.co.uk/1/hi/world/
asia-pacific/271072.stm).
30. http://tgr.ph/pmkwtp (http://www.telegraph.co.uk/
finance/london-olympics-business/8641977/London-2012-
Olympics-The-Olympic-Stadium-made-in-Britain.html).
31. http://bit.ly/oh0eW1 (http://corporate.betfair.com/
about-us/key-facts.aspx).
32. http://bit.ly/r0sMtu (http://www.guardian.co.uk/
sport/2010/may/02/john-higgins-snooker-bribe-match-
fixing).
33. http://thetim.es/n9Kqqv (http://www.timesonline.co.uk/
tol/sport/racing/article3019158.ece).
34. http://bit.ly/r8xvNG (http://en.wikipedia.org/wiki/
2002_Olympic_Winter_Games_figure_skating_scandal).
35. http://bit.ly/qgC48E (http://sportsgambling.about.com/
od/nfl/a/wackyprops.htm).
36. http://tgr.ph/qUZRUS (http://www.telegraph.co.uk/
sport/football/teams/southampton/6130280/Matthew-
Le-Tissier-admits-being-part-of-attempted-betting-scam-
at-Southampton.html).
37. http://bit.ly/nQNdaT (http://www.guardian.co.uk/
sport/2011/may/20/pakistan-cricketers-spot-fixing-
hearing).
38. http://bit.ly/tFjucl (http://www.judiciary.gov.uk/
Resources/JCO/Documents/Judgments/butt-others-
sentencing-remarks-03112011.pdf).
39. http://bit.ly/pOX9hV (http://www.guardian.co.uk/football/
2010/nov/29/panorama-bbc-fifa-accused).
40. http://bbc.in/qzbsw9 (http://www.bbc.co.uk/news/
uk-11841783).
41. http://bit.ly/sVk76z (http://www.guardian.co.uk/sport/
2011/dec/08/lamine-diack-issa-hayatou-ioc).

42. http://tgr.ph/til2nU (http://www.telegraph.co.uk/sport/football/8181639/England-World-Cup-bid-how-did-we-get-it-so-wrong.html).
43. http://bit.ly/tGgbwB (http://mideastposts.com/2011/11/28/worrying-times-fifa-opens-door-to-investigation-of-qatar%E2%80%99s-world-cup-bid/).
44. http://bit.ly/nMwEuc (http://www.theage.com.au/rugby-league/league-news/melbourne-storm-stripped-of-premierships-for-salary-cap-breaches-20100422-td91.html).
45. http://thetim.es/q4nKfj (http://www.timesonline.co.uk/tol/sport/tennis/article3964492.ece).
46. http://bit.ly/pmFAeL (http://nbcsports.msnbc.com/id/20107781/).
47. http://bit.ly/nvUeLv (http://www.dailymail.co.uk/news/article-567361/New-betting-scandal-hits-tennis-45-matches-investigated-corruption.html).
48. http://bit.ly/r64ewx (http://www.fifa.com/aboutfifa/organisation/footballgovernance/codeethics.html).
49. http://1.usa.gov/p5pwjU (http://lobbyingdisclosure.house.gov/).
50. http://bit.ly/qm73x4 (http://influenceexplorer.com/).
51. http://bit.ly/q4wnMc (http://en.wikipedia.org/wiki/Jack_Abramoff).
52. http://1.usa.gov/rnCTq5 (http://fpc.state.gov/documents/organization/41338.pdf).
53. http://usat.ly/qMX4xG (http://www.usatoday.com/news/politicselections/nation/2003-10-15-cover-bundlers_x.htm).
54. http://bit.ly/oHycnN (http://www.law.cornell.edu/uscode/18/usc_sec_18_00000201--000-.html).
55. http://bit.ly/pgLOu2 (http://www.guardian.co.uk/politics/2010/mar/28/cash-for-promises-lobbying).
56. http://bit.ly/nfkIoS (http://www.newint.org/features/2011/01/01/corporate-lobbying-shame/).
57. http://thetim.es/qSVWuE (http://www.timesonline.co.uk/tol/news/uk/article7069795.ece).
58. http://bit.ly/ndUQnW (http://en.wikipedia.org/wiki/2009_Cash_for_Influence_Scandal).

59. http://bit.ly/omDmHH (http://ethicnet.uta.fi/united_kingdom/code_of_conduct).
60. http://bit.ly/pQUpSC (http://www.guardian.co.uk/info/guardian-editorial-code), updated August 2011.
61. http://1.usa.gov/orkegK (http://www.ftc.gov/os/closings/100420anntaylorclosingletter.pdf).
62. http://dthin.gs/oXcNGi (http://allthingsd.com/about/#walt-ethics).
63. The UK's self-regulatory system is the Code of Practice of the Press Complaints Commission, which also has rules prohibiting acting on sensitive information: http://bit.ly/pJ8e32 (http://www.pcc.org.uk/cop/practice.html).
64. http://bit.ly/nh3YEN (http://www.pcc.org.uk/news/index.html?article=MTc4NQ).
65. 47 USC § 317, 47 CFR § 73.4180 Payment disclosure: Payola, plugola, kickbacks (http://law.justia.com/cfr/title47/47-4.0.1.1.2.8.1.165.html).
66. http://bit.ly/qClaRa (http://www.ag.ny.gov/media_center/2005/jul/jul25a_05.html).
67. http://bit.ly/q8hm7w (http://www.commercialalert.org/fcc.pdf).
68. http://bbc.in/n7Y3kk (http://www.bbc.co.uk/news/uk-14120244).
69. http://scr.bi/uhwF3G (http://www.scribd.com/doc/62262162/HP-Pretexting-Scandal).
70. http://bbc.in/pyRJ1N (http://www.bbc.co.uk/news/uk-11204150).
71. http://bbc.in/qwlGYh (http://news.bbc.co.uk/1/hi/uk/3690886.stm).
72. Ratification status as of March 2009: http://bit.ly/nrX8Up (http://www.oecd.org/dataoecd/59/13/40272933.pdf).
73. http://bit.ly/o6lEr4 (http://www.oecd.org/document/24/0,3746,en_21571361_44315115_47983768_1_1_1_1,00.html).
74. http://bit.ly/sHc945 (https://www.traceinternational2.org/compendium/view.asp?id=4); SEC complaint: http://bit.ly/qzdzbn (http://162.138.185.33/litigation/complaints/2009/comp21156.pdf).

75. http://bit.ly/uZFKSJ (https://www.traceinternational2
.org/compendium/view.asp?id=159).

76. The accounting provisions state that no criminal liability
shall be imposed for failing to comply with the
provisions of 15 USC § 78m(b)(4). However, criminal
liability may be imposed where a person knowingly
circumvents or fails to implement a system of internal
controls, or knowingly falsifies any book, record or
account described above. 15 USC § 78m(b)(5).

77. Section 3(a)(37) of the Securities Exchange Act 1934.

78. http://bit.ly/tl1Fyw (https://www.traceinternational2
.org/compendium/view.asp?id=40).

79. DOJ Review Procedure Release 92-01: http://1.usa.gov/
pfRHwM (http://www.justice.gov/criminal/fraud/fcpa/
review/1992/r9201.pdf).

80. http://bit.ly/mRmCaq (http://www.oyez.org/justices/
potter_stewart/).

81. http://bit.ly/p6SmVA (http://www.transparency.org/
news_room/faq/corruption_faq).

82. Nye, J. S., Corruption and political development: a
cost-bene?t analysis, *American Political Science Review*,
LXI(2), 417–27, 1967.

83. Waterbury, J., Endemic and planned corruption in a
monarchical regime, *World Politics*, **XXV**(4), 533–5,
1973.

84. http://bit.ly/o3FyuC (http://www1.worldbank.org/
publicsector/anticorrupt/corruptn/cor02.htm).

85. http://bit.ly/qFPC5t (http://www.oecd.org/dataoecd/
31/55/36587302.pdf).

86. Alam, M.S., Anatomy of corruption: an approach to the
political economy of underdevelopment, *American
Journal of Economics and Sociology*, **48**(4), 441–56, 1989.

87. http://bit.ly/qXoG1g (http://www.kubatana.net/html/
archive/demgg/080731actsa.asp?sector=econ&year=2008
&range_start=241).

88. http://www.bis.gov.uk/files/file46888.pdf.

89. http://bit.ly/rmfAvN (http://www.blackslawdictionary
.com/Home/Default.aspx).

90. http://bit.ly/pjce5o (http://www.realizingrights.org/
    index.php?option=com_content&view=article&id=128
    &Itemid=134).
91. http://bit.ly/o05VMt (http://www.oecd.org/dataoecd/
    4/40/37575976.pdf).
92. Huntington, S., *Political Order in Changing Societies*, Yale
    University Press, 1968. Available from: http://bit.ly/
    nj6Cxj.
93. http://bit.ly/qgs7S2 (http://web.worldbank.org/WBSITE/
    EXTERNAL/NEWS/0,,contentMDK:20190187$~menuPK:
    34457~pagePK:34370~piPK:34424~theSitePK:4607,00
    .html).
94. http://bit.ly/rjDli3 (http://info.worldbank.org/etools/antic/
    docs/Business%20Case/TheBusinessCaseAgainst
    Currption.pdf).
95. http://bit.ly/npYVT1 (http://www.un.org/Docs/SG/
    Report97/97con.htm).
96. http://bit.ly/reLTzC (http://www.transparency.org/
    publications/gcr/gcr_2008).
97. http://bit.ly/mVhLfV (http://www.cgdev.org/doc/event%20
    docs/Ngozi%20Remarks.pdf).
98. http://bit.ly/ucbwD6 (http://www.gutenberg.org/ebooks/
    3178).
99. http://bit.ly/qiXJVO (http://onlyagame.typepad.com/
    only_a_game/2009/01/gifts-tips-bribes.html).
100. Noonan, J.T., Jr, *Bribes: The Intellectual History of a Moral
    Idea*, 1984. Available from: http://www.amazon.com/
    Bribes-Intellectual-History-Moral-Idea/dp/0520061543.
101. Mauss, M., *The Gift: The Form and Reason for Exchange
    in Archaic Societies*. Available from: http://bit.ly/nDUVK1
    (http://books.google.com/books?id=IyuwqqkFMzUC&
    printsec=frontcover&dq=gift+inauthor:mauss&hl=en&ei
    =OWIaToLXL87F8QPEz9ioDA&sa=X&oi=book_result&ct
    =result&resnum=1&ved=0CCkQ6AEwAA#v=onepage
    &q&f=false).
102. Klitgaard, R.E., Maclean-Abaroa, R. and Parris, H.L.,
    Corrupt Cities: A Practical Guide to Cure and Prevention,
    Oakland: ICS Press, 2000.

103. http://cnnmon.ie/mX3GNz (http://money.cnn.com/
magazines/fortune/fortune_archive/2003/02/03/336434/).

104. Fisman, R. and Miguel, E., How economics can defeat
corruption, *Foreign Policy*, September/October, 2008.
Available from: http://bit.ly/nWOo7Y.

105. Fisman, R. and Miguel, E., Cultures of corruption:
evidence from diplomatic parking tickets, NBER working
paper no. 12312, June 2006. Available from:
http://bit.ly/pIsNLI.

106. http://bit.ly/p7JfB6 (http://ipaidabribe.com/content/
corruption-formula-0).

107. http://1.usa.gov/r2a4S0 (http://www.justice.gov/opa/
pr/2011/January/11-crm-085.html).

108. http://bit.ly/pXRAew (http://www.sfo.gov.uk/media/
54848/criminal_justice_act_1987_140708_foi.pdf).

109. http://bit.ly/n2O7So (http://www.fsa.gov.uk/pages/
Library/Communication/PR/2011/056.shtml).

110. http://bit.ly/p4IJaY (https://www.traceinternational2
.org/compendium/view.asp?id=92).

111. As one of its four statutory objectives, the FSA has to
reduce the extent to which regulated persons and
unauthorized businesses can be 'used for a purpose
connected with financial crime': http://bit.ly/oArWhY.

112. http://bit.ly/pjgakz (http://www.fsa.gov.uk/pages/Library/
Communication/Speeches/2011/0622_tm.shtml).

113. http://tgr.ph/onVIDR (http://www.telegraph.co.uk/news/
election-2010/7629536/Osborne-to-replace-Serious-Fraud-
Office-with-super-agency.html).

114. http://bbc.in/qNzTim (http://www.bbc.co.uk/news/
13585972).

115. http://on.ft.com/qu0RlB (http://www.ft.com/cms/s/0/
112eb732-91c2-11e0-b4a3-00144feab49a.html#axzz1WYCIz
smY).

116. http://ti.me/nKgZEA (http://www.time.com/time/world/
article/0,8599,1870443,00.html).

117. http://bit.ly/vpRI90 (https://www.traceinternational2.org/
compendium/view.asp?id=115).

118. http://bit.ly/rllkdW (http://www.unafei.or.jp/english/pdf/ PDF_rms/no60/ch03.pdf).
119. http://bit.ly/rP8NOE (https://www.traceinternational2 .org/compendium/view.asp?id=166).
120. http://bit.ly/tVjqiG (https://www.traceinternational2 .org/compendium/view.asp?id=306).
121. http://bit.ly/rpKphU (http://www.bundesanwaltschaft.ch/ content/ba/en/home/die_oe1.html).
122. http://bit.ly/rNoVZf (https://www.traceinternational2.org/ compendium/view.asp?id=270).
123. http://bit.ly/peaiAx (http://www.eurojust.europa.eu/).
124. http://bit.ly/oLjf3b (http://www.larouchepac.com/node/ 2667).
125. http://bit.ly/r5Ib5d (http://english.peopledaily.com.cn/ 90001/90776/90785/7189742.html)
126. http://bit.ly/otVLdL (http://www.uschinacounsel.com/ files/Chinese%20Anti-Bribery%20Law%20pdf.pdf).
127. http://bit.ly/r5Ib5d (http://english.peopledaily.com.cn/ 90001/90776/90785/7189742.html).
128. http://bit.ly/tgol8j (https://www.traceinternational2.org/ compendium/view.asp?id=263).
129. http://bit.ly/qKQCa2 (http://thebriberyact.com/2011/ 05/30/from-may-1st-new-china-anti-corruption-laws-follow-long-arm-jurisdiction-trend/).
130. http://www.efccnigeria.org/.
131. http://www.icpc.gov.ng/.
132. http://bit.ly/q7EZYV (http://allafrica.com/stories/ 201011300681.html).
133. http://bit.ly/p8invM (http://www.guardian.co.uk/world/ 2010/dec/15/nigeria-dick-cheney-plea-halliburton).
134. http://bit.ly/oSZ4C1 (http://234next.com/csp/cms/sites/ Next/News/5619080-147/gunmen_kill_efccs_forensic_ team_leader.csp).
135. http://bit.ly/qWAq1G (http://web.worldbank.org/WBSITE/ EXTERNAL/WBI/EXTWBIGOVANTCOR/0,,menuPK:1740542 ~pagePK:64168427~piPK:64168435~theSitePK:1740530,00 .html).

136. http://bit.ly/twmVn6 (https://www.traceinternational2
     .org/compendium/view.asp?id=241).
137. http://bit.ly/njsVfy (http://www.transparency.org/news_
     room/latest_news/press_releases_nc/2011/2011_03_30_ti_
     uk_government_guidance_deplorable_and_will_weaken_
     bribery_act).
138. http://bit.ly/mQOXLi (http://www.sfo.gov.uk/press-room/
     latest-press-releases/press-releases-2008/former-solicitor-
     jailed-for-six-months-imprisonment-in-corruption-
     conspiracy.aspx).
139. http://bit.ly/swQQDy (https://www.traceinternational2
     .org/compendium/view.asp?id=98).
140. http://bit.ly/namxOK (http://www.guardian.co.uk/
     business/2011/jan/31/british-firms-face-bribery-blacklist).
141. http://bit.ly/mTNvyD (http://www.thisislondon.co.uk/
     standard/article-23913831-review-of-bribes-act-ordered-by-
     no-10.do).
142. http://tgr.ph/rqwFb9 (http://www.telegraph.co.uk/
     finance/yourbusiness/8118495/Bona-fide-corporate-
     freebies-must-survive-Bribery-Act.html).
143. http://tgr.ph/pnMkDN (http://www.telegraph.co.uk/news/
     newstopics/howaboutthat/8335868/20-Christmas-tip-is-an-
     illegal-bribe-says-council.html).
144. http://bit.ly/pGAc3D (http://www.globalwitness.org/
     library/government-bows-pressure-business-allow-
     bribery-through-back-door).
145. http://bit.ly/oJkqCC (http://www.transparency.org.uk/all-
     news-releases/167-government-guidance-deplorable-and-
     will-weaken-bribery-act).
146. http://bit.ly/rzJOcI (https://www.traceinternational2.org/
     compendium/view.asp?id=81).
147. USC §§ 78dd-1(a); 78dd-2(a).
148. http://bit.ly/uDnaVg (https://www.traceinternational2.org/
     compendium/view.asp?id=106).
149. http://bit.ly/uMp1Jv (https://www.traceinternational2.org/
     compendium/view.asp?id=157).
150. For example, see: http://bit.ly/qderQn (http://www.fsa
     .gov.uk/pubs/hb-releases/rel38/rel38auth.pdf).

151. http://bit.ly/qmTgO2 (http://www.sfo.gov.uk/about-us/
     our-views/director's-speeches/speeches-
     2011/salans–bribery-act-2010.aspx).
152. http://bit.ly/r8LAck (http://www.complianceweek.com/
     qa-with-the-sfos-vivian-robinson-on-the-impact-of-the-uk-
     bribery-act-on-us-companies/article/194657/).
153. http://bit.ly/nKknaN (https://www.traceinternational2
     .org/compendium/view.asp?id=136).
154. http://bloom.bg/nLbDwZ (http://www.bloomberg.com/
     apps/news?pid=newsarchive&sid=aXO.vHLdvbcM).
155. http://1.usa.gov/rmBmWK (http://www.sec.gov/litigation/
     litreleases/2010/lr21451.htm).
156. http://1.usa.gov/q1PoqI (http://www.usaid.gov/policy/
     ads/300/308maa.pdf).
157. http://1.usa.gov/nNQuBd (http://www.justice.gov/
     criminal/fraud/fcpa/opinion/2010/1003.pdf).
158. http://bit.ly/uqiKWh (https://www.traceinternational2
     .org/compendium/view.asp?id=76).
159. http://scr.bi/opcaOR (http://www.scribd.com/doc/
     54500817/Carson-Foreign-Official-Challenge-Reply-Brief).
160. http://bit.ly/r8LAck (http://www.complianceweek.com/
     qa-with-the-sfos-vivian-robinson-on-the-impact-of-the-uk-
     bribery-act-on-us-companies/article/194657/).
161. http://bit.ly/pAhJN7 (http://www.skadden.com/siteFiles/
     Files/Memorandum_and_Order.pdf).
162. http://bit.ly/vd4Ej2 (http://www.control-risks.com/
     OurThinking/CRsDocumentDownload/International%20
     business%20attitudes%20to%20corruption%20survey_
     2006.pdf).
163. http://bit.ly/onlk4B (http://www1.worldbank.org/
     publicsector/anticorrupt/Svensson%20Eight%20Questions
     %20About%20Corruption%20(JEP%20Vol%2019,%20No%
     203%202005).pdf).
164. http://bit.ly/qmTgO2 (http://www.sfo.gov.uk/about-us/
     our-views/director's-speeches/speeches-
     2011/salans–bribery-act-2010.aspx).
165. http://bit.ly/qWTFPi (http://www.oecd.org/dataoecd/
     7/35/35109576.pdf).

166. http://bit.ly/nSjwsS (http://www.sfo.gov.uk/fraud/fraud-in-your-organisation/involved-it's-in-your-interest-to-come-forward.aspx).

167. USC 2B § 78u–2, Civil Remedies In Administrative Proceedings: http://bit.ly/re1EEB (http://www.law.cornell.edu/uscode/usc_sec_15_00000078–u002-.html). These are periodically adjusted: http://1.usa.gov/oMUzG7 (http://www.sec.gov/rules/final/2009/33-9009.pdf).

168. USC § 3571, Sentence of Fine: http://bit.ly/q6cCku (http://www.law.cornell.edu/uscode/usc_sec_18_00003571––000-.html).

169. http://1.usa.gov/rbr3ZG (http://www.justice.gov/opa/pr/2010/April/10-crm-442.html).

170. http://1.usa.gov/oDYb5r (http://www.justice.gov/opa/documents/United_States_v_Booker_Fact_Sheet.pdf)

171. http://bit.ly/uMp1Jv (https://www.traceinternational2.org/compendium/view.asp?id=157).

172. http://bit.ly/uoYsW1 (https://www.traceinternational2.org/compendium/view.asp?id=80).

173. http://bit.ly/uqiKWh (https://www.traceinternational2.org/compendium/view.asp?id=76).

174. http://bit.ly/uDnaVg (https://www.traceinternational2.org/compendium/view.asp?id=106).

175. http://1.usa.gov/nCMW36 (http://www.sec.gov/news/press/2006-4.htm).

176. The Civil Asset Forfeiture Reform Act 2000 (CAFRA) expanded the list of civil forfeiture predicates to include each offence listed as a specified unlawful activity in the Money Laundering Control Act, 18 USC § 1956(c)(7). CAFRA further provided for criminal forfeiture for all offences for which civil forfeiture was authorized – see 28 USC § 2461(c).

177. http://bit.ly/tc9MnF (https://www.traceinternational2.org/compendium/view.asp?id=14).

178. The statutory maximum fine for a summary conviction is $5000 in England and Wales or Northern Ireland, and unlimited on indictment. The statutory maximum fine for

a summary conviction is £10,000 in Scotland and unlimited on indictment.

179. http://bit.ly/qYNw7t (http://www.bailii.org/ew/cases/EWHC/QB/2009/2307.html).

180. http://bit.ly/pT2Hdr (http://www.sfo.gov.uk/about-us/our-views/director's-speeches/speeches-2009/how-the-sfo-and-corporates-can-work-together.aspx).

181. http://bit.ly/nKhwT1 (http://codes.lp.findlaw.com/uscode/15/2B/78u).

182. http://scr.bi/nPCVEZ (http://www.scribd.com/doc/37367261/World-Bribery-and-Corruption-Compliance-Forum-Opening-Remarks-of-Professor-Mike-Koehler).

183. This can be estimated by looking at the historical likelihood of winning contracts on tenders uninfluenced by bribery.

184. The US Court of Appeal in *SEC v. First Jersey Securities* confirmed the disgorgement of $22.2m in unlawful gains, plus $52.6m in prejudgement interest: http://bit.ly/pE7Cxz (http://www.columbia.edu/~hcs14/FIRSTJERSEY.htm).

185. US v. Charles Conaway: http://on.wsj.com/rCTjIz (http://online.wsj.com/public/resources/documents/080309seckmart.pdf).

186. http://bit.ly/vKQ8M9 (https://www.traceinternational2.org/compendium/view.asp?id=93).

187. http://bit.ly/tlAbwy (https://www.traceinternational2.org/compendium/view.asp?id=91).

188. http://bit.ly/tZbxx3 (https://www.traceinternational2.org/compendium/view.asp?id=174).

189. BAE Systems. See page 445.

190. http://bit.ly/oUaf2Q (https://www.traceinternational2.org/compendium/view.asp?id=15).

191. Johnson & Johnson. See Page 256.

192. http://bit.ly/twmVn6 (https://www.traceinternational2.org/compendium/view.asp?id=241).

193. http://bit.ly/o1p3xq (http://www.thisismoney.co.uk/money/markets/article-1681815/SFO-may-make-500m-example-of-BAE.html).

194. http://bit.ly/raxUCf (http://www.judiciary.gov.uk/
     Resources/JCO/Documents/Judgments/sentencing-
     remarks-thomas-lj-innospec.pdf).
195. http://1.usa.gov/r2a4S0 (http://www.justice.gov/opa/
     pr/2011/January/11-crm-085.html).
196. http://bit.ly/raxUCf (http://www.judiciary.gov.uk/
     Resources/JCO/Documents/Judgments/sentencing-
     remarks-thomas-lj-innospec.pdf).
197. http://bit.ly/nwpAV5 (http://www.law.cornell.edu/uscode/
     18/usc_sec_18_00003771−−000-.html).
198. http://bit.ly/qvl4Vx (http://www.mediafire.com/?
     turaenl2l0ppdz6).
199. http://bit.ly/vLfZ4D (https://www.traceinternational2.org/
     compendium/view.asp?id=308).
200. http://bit.ly/mQwBxG (http://www1.worldbank.org/
     finance/star_site/).
201. http://1.usa.gov/pSPMPE (http://www.justice.gov/atr/
     public/press_releases/1992/211182.htm).
202. http://bit.ly/tFfRiX (https://www.traceinternational2.org/
     compendium/view.asp?id=301).
203. http://bloom.bg/tXrZer (http://www.bloomberg.com/
     news/2011-11-29/lindsey-manufacturing-judge-tentatively-
     dismisses-executives-bribery-case.html).
204. http://1.usa.gov/nxhYhT (http://www.sec.gov/news/press/
     2010/2010-6.htm).
205. http://1.usa.gov/o0c0ed (http://www.sec.gov/news/press/
     2010/2010-252.htm).
206. http://1.usa.gov/qjq9vL (http://www.sec.gov/news/press/
     2011/2011-112.htm).
207. http://bit.ly/tcySV8 (https://www.traceinternational2.org/
     compendium/view.asp?id=228).
208. http://bbc.in/poX4WM (http://news.bbc.co.uk/1/hi/
     8124838.stm).
209. http://bit.ly/ngAzjW (http://www.bailii.org/cgi-bin/
     markup.cgi?doc=/ew/cases/Misc/2010/7.html&query=
     innospec&method=boolean).
210. http://bit.ly/tZbxx3 (https://www.traceinternational2.org/
     compendium/view.asp?id=174).

211. Court of Appeal: http://bit.ly/n8sTf6 (http://www.bailii
.org/cgi-bin/markup.cgi?doc=/ew/cases/EWCA/Crim/
2010/1048.html&query=dougall&method=boolean). SFO
press release: http://bit.ly/o1x40q (http://www.sfo
.gov.uk/press-room/latest-press-releases/press-releases-
2010/british-executive-jailed-for-part-in-greek-healthcare-
corruption.aspx).
212. http://bit.ly/twmVn6 (https://www.traceinternational2
.org/compendium/view.asp?id=241). SFO press release:
http://bit.ly/oa2NW1 (http://www.sfo.gov.uk/press-
room/latest-press-releases/press-releases-2011/action-on-
macmillan-publishers-limited.aspx).
213. http://bit.ly/q89MeB (http://amchamvietnam.com/index
.php?id=3676).
214. http://bit.ly/pnQdcr (http://files.shareholder.com/
downloads/ZMH/1394449357x0xS950137-07-14977/
1136869/filing.pdf).
215. http://bit.ly/mYNbiS (http://www.siemens.com/press/en/
pressrelease/?press=/en/pressrelease/2008/corporate_
communication/axx20081220.htm).
216. http://bit.ly/vKQ8M9 (https://www.traceinternational2
.org/compendium/view.asp?id=93).
217. Referring to an infamous $52m contract awarded several
years ago to former Attorney General John Ashcroft, to
be a monitor for Zimmer, Inc. Ashcroft said he has a
team of 30 people working on the Zimmer project,
including lawyers, investigators, accountants and
business consultants.
218. http://bit.ly/vJBm7h (https://www.traceinternational2
.org/compendium/view.asp?id=16).
219. http://1.usa.gov/qPCuDj (http://sanders.senate.gov/
graphics/Defense_Fraud_Report1.pdf).
220. http://bit.ly/mXnlNZ (http://www.opencongress.org/bill/
111-h5366/text).
221. http://on.ft.com/p8WbDd (http://www.ft.com/cms/s/0/
f61bfd88-807d-11e0-adca-00144feabdc0.html#axzz1WYClz
smY).

222. The Bribery Act 2010 (Consequential Amendments) Order 2011 amends Regulation 23(1) of the Public Contracts Regulations 2006 to insert references under sections 1 and 6 of the Bribery Act. http://bit.ly/qbFz4v (http://www.legislation.gov.uk/uksi/2011/1441/made? view=plain).

223. http://bit.ly/opMgXK (http://www.debevoise.com/ newseventspubs/news/RepresentationDetail.aspx?exp_id =34c36f68-1fc1-439f-ba06-413436a3e417).

224. http://onforb.es/cQzp35 (http://www.forbes.com/global/ 2010/0607/companies-payoffs-washington-extortion-mendelsohn-bribery-racket_2.html).

225. http://on.wsj.com/qI0gr5 (http://online.wsj.com/article/ SB10001424052748703871904575215913745075480.html? KEYWORDS=avon).

226. http://bit.ly/olRSyx (http://corpuslegalis.com/us/code/ title18/suspension-of-limitations-to-permit-united-states-to-obtain-foreign-evidence).

227. 18 USC § 371, the conspiracy statute: http://bit.ly/rcYkJH (http://www.law.cornell.edu/uscode/18/usc_sec_18_ 00000371--000-.html).

228. Section 62 of the Policing and Crime Act 2009: http:// bit.ly/nqVhFQ (http://www.legislation.gov.uk/ukpga/ 2009/26/notes/division/4/8).

229. http://bit.ly/mPGZil (http://legaltimes.typepad.com/files/ lanny-a-breuer-compliance-week-speech-may-26-2010 .pdf).

230. http://bit.ly/syIRgU (https://www.traceinternational2.org/ compendium/view.asp?id=5).

231. http://bit.ly/uMp1Jv (https://www.traceinternational2.org/ compendium/view.asp?id=157).

232. A 50% discount for self-reporting is formalized in the case of US Office of Foreign Assets Control (OFAC) economic and trade sanctions: http://bit.ly/pq5gaE (http://www.mondaq.com/unitedstates/article.asp? articleid=129580).

233. http://bit.ly/onnajP (http://federalevidence.com/pdf/ Corp_Prosec/Former_DOJ_Lttr_9_5_06.pdf).

234. http://bit.ly/v7TOwQ (http://www.fcpablog.com/blog/ 2008/6/25/halliburton-expro-and-umbrellastream-star-in- opinion-procedu.html).

235. So-called 'seize and sift' powers under Section 50 of the Criminal Justice and Police Act 2001: http://bit.ly/nFUSH0 (http://www.legislation.gov.uk/ukpga/2001/16/contents).

236. An officer may allow the person supervised access to the document to copy it themselves, or copy it for them and provide the copy to them (Section 21(4)(6) of the Police and Criminal Evidence Act 1984).

237. Section 19(6) of the Police and Criminal Evidence Act 1984 for the Police and FSA; Section 2(9) of the Criminal Justice Act 1987 for the SFO. Legal professional privilege: http://bit.ly/n7DJe0 (http://www.sfo.gov.uk/ media/99280/legal%20professional%20privilege%20web% 201.pdf).

238. http://1.usa.gov/oHKcLO (http://www.sec.gov/news/ speech/2010/spch110310mls-whistleblowers.htm).

239. http://bit.ly/nDKThD (http://www.guardian.co.uk/money/ 2010/mar/22/tenfold-rise-whistleblower-cases-tribunal).

240. http://bit.ly/q8t52y (http://www.mainjustice.com/ justanticorruption/2011/04/11/johnson-johnson-saved-17- million-in-fcpa-settlement-by-informing-on-competitors/), subscription required.

241. http://1.usa.gov/qTKvZy (http://www.justice.gov/opa/pr/ 2011/April/11-crm-446.html).

242. http://bit.ly/pixF14 (http://en.wikipedia.org/wiki/Donald_ Cressey).

243. http://bit.ly/oB8017 (http://www.manhattan-institute .org/pdf/_atlantic_monthly-broken_windows.pdf).

244. http://bit.ly/o9HkJD (http://excen.gsu.edu/jccox/ Econ9940/cialdini-etal2006_social-influence.pdf).

245. http://onforb.es/q2iQid (http://www.forbes.com/2006/ 04/04/fraud-abroad-bribery-cx_hc_0405fraud.html).

246. http://bit.ly/qfriUo (http://www.justice.gov.uk/ consultations/docs/bribery-act-guidance-consultation1 .pdf).

247. http://1.usa.gov/ramPmX (http://www.justice.gov/
criminal/fraud/fcpa/opinion/2007/0701.pdf); http://1.usa
.gov/q26ZtM (http://www.justice.gov/criminal/fraud/
fcpa/opinion/2007/0702.pdf).

248. http://bit.ly/qXXAFw (https://www.traceinternational2
.org/compendium/view.asp?id=26).

249. http://bit.ly/pP2ovK (https://www.traceinternational2
.org/compendium/view.asp?id=65).

250. Panalpina. See page 440.

251. For example, the Protection of Trading Interests Act
1980 in the UK and Penal Law No. 80-538 in France. The
case law shows that these threats are real. Litigants face
sanctions in US courts if they object to discovery on the
basis of the French blocking statute. But a 2007 decision
by the French Cour de Cassation shows that the threat
of prosecution for violating the French blocking statute
is not an empty one, and can result in a custodial
sentence.

252. See, for example, Relativity: http://bit.ly/o4FSn4 (http://
kcura.com/relativity).

253. Pikko Software: http://bit.ly/q0Dz6L (http://www
.pikko-software.com/index-en.html).

254. Browne, M.W., Following Benford's law, or looking out
for no. 1, *The New York Times*, 4 August 1998. Available
from: http://bit.ly/pB19qV (http://www.rexswain.com/
benford.html).

255. http://bbc.in/pO2TLd (http://news.bbc.co.uk/1/shared/
bsp/hi/pdfs/27_10_05_summary.pdf).

256. http://on.wsj.com/owpKFf (http://blogs.wsj.com/law/
2010/01/19/fcpa-goin-prime-time-huge-bribery-sting-leads-
to-arrest-of-22/).

257. Oil-for-Food. See page 448.

258. http://bit.ly/oDxl35 (http://www.law.cornell.edu/uscode/
18/usc_sec_18_00001956--000-.html).

259. http://bit.ly/rmEriQ (http://www.law.cornell.edu/uscode/
18/usc_sec_18_00001957--000-.html).

260. http://bit.ly/n6qFOc (http://fcpa.shearman.com/
?s=matter&mode=form&id=138).

261. http://1.usa.gov/npG8tz (http://www.justice.gov/opa/pr/
2009/December/09-crm-1307.html).
262. http://1.usa.gov/noHWqh (http://www.justice.gov/
criminal/pr/speeches/2010/crm-speech-101019.html).
263. http://bit.ly/onaePd (http://www.alarabiya.net/articles/
2011/02/09/137010.html).
264. http://bit.ly/qSVILH (http://www.law.cornell.edu/uscode/
18/1343.html).
265. http://bit.ly/oeIOG9 (https://www.traceinternational2.org/
compendium/view.asp?id=1).
266. 18 USC § 1952, Interstate and Foreign Travel or
Transportation in Aid of Racketeering Enterprises:
http://bit.ly/sGPG3b (http://www.law.cornell.edu/
uscode/usc_sec_18_00001952--000-.html).
267. http://bit.ly/p6hd9K (https://www.traceinternational2.org/
compendium/view.asp?id=24).
268. http://1.usa.gov/rt8eYG (http://www.justice.gov/ag/
speeches/2010/ag-speech-100725.html).
269. http://on.wsj.com/pC1h6U (http://online.wsj.com/article/
SB10001424052702304879604575582603173894296.html).
270. http://1.usa.gov/nRWnaJ (http://www.justice.gov/ag/
speeches/2010/ag-speech-100531.html).
271. http://bit.ly/q9PiJ7 (https://www.traceinternational2.org/
compendium/view.asp?id=132).
272. http://bit.ly/qrNpYN (http://fcpaprofessor.blogspot.com/
2009/11/366-days.html).
273. Siemens. See page 435.
274. BAE Systems. See page 445.
275. http://bit.ly/qkrbfO (https://www.traceinternational2.org/
compendium/view.asp?id=168).
276. http://tgr.ph/nCJXzE (http://www.telegraph.co.uk/finance/
newsbysector/industry/defence/8215317/Judge-questions-
SFO-evidence-in-BAE-case.html).
277. http://bit.ly/tsPnlF (http://www.caat.org.uk/issues/bae/jr/
SFO_Grounds_2010-3-10.pdf).
278. http://bit.ly/pAmi3o (http://www.jenner.com/files/
tbl_s20Publications%5CRelatedDocumentsPDFs1252%

5C3332%5CFifth%20Circuit%20Holds%20That%20OECD%20Does%20Not%20Bar_110811.pdf).

279. http://bit.ly/rPn5hH (http://www.chron.com/business/article/Willbros-Group-settlement-approved-in-securities-1846350.php).

280. http://bit.ly/qEF9nj (http://www.law.du.edu/documents/corporate-governance/governance-cases/dow/Memorandum-Opinion-In-re-Dow-Chemical-Co-Civil-Action-No-4349-CC-Jan-11-2010.pdf).

281. http://bit.ly/pdNyx1 (http://www.willkie.com/files/tbl_s29Publications/FileUpload5686/2338/Securities_Class_Action.pdf).

282. http://bit.ly/vNkssP (http://www.law.com/jsp/law/LawArticleFriendly.jsp?id=1202533815252&slreturn=1).

Get the Text of the Statutes on Your Smartphone from the Following QR Codes

FCPA 1977

For more information, see http://1.usa.gov/p8ysqQ (http://www.justice.gov/criminal/fraud/fcpa/docs/ fcpa-english.pdf).

Bribery Act 2010

Bribery Act Guidance

OECD Convention

If you don't have a QR code reader on your smart-phone, then I-nigma is a good place to start the free download: http://bit.ly/pcZKFq (http://www.i-nigma.com/Downloadi-nigmaReader.html).

Do I Need to Read this Book (Again)?

- Do you have a written statement of commitment or ethics policy?
- Do you have a code of conduct for employees that prohibits bribery in any form?
- Is there a requirement for all employees to certify that they have read and complied with the code of conduct? (Records should be kept.)
- Have you had a company or team meeting within the last sic months at which bribery has been mentioned?
- Do you have a chief compliance officer, or similar senior manager, responsible for anti-bribery compliance?
- Do you conduct at least an annual risk assessment of fraud and corruption risks?
- Do you have a written anti-bribery compliance programme, including limits on gifts and hospitality and facilitation payments?
- Do you have a formal training programme for all employees that specifically addresses bribery?
- Do you carry out face-to-face bribery training for high-risk employees?
- Is there a requirement for all commercial agents and business partners to certify every year that they have read and complied with the code of conduct? (Records should be kept.)
- Do you have an effective payment approval matrix?
- Do you subscribe to one of the 'politically exposed person' (PEP) data services and use this data to research and vet who you do business with?

- Do you perform due diligence reviews and vetting on new business partners, including major suppliers, distributors and agents?
- Do you have automatic reporting of all entertaining of foreign officials to the compliance team?
- Do you carry out regular anti-bribery reviews?
- Do you have a whistleblower policy and effective channels for employees to report suspicious behaviour?
- Have you had any calls to the whistleblower helpline, and do you believe that employees have confidence in the whistleblower program?
- Do you have a crisis response programme for dawn raids or similar?
- Are sales staff appraised or remunerated on any ethical measures?
- Have you ever got rid of a member of staff for ethics violations?

If you have answered 'no' to two or more of the questions above, you need to revisit the adequacy of your anti-bribery compliance regime. Take another look at How Do I Set Up Proportionate Yet Effective Anti-Bribery Compliance Procedures? On page 343.

If you are not convinced of the need yet, take a look at 'Cautionary Tales – What Happens If You Get Caught?' on page 433.

Index